Writing the Body Politic

This book brings together key essays from the career of social theorist John O'Neill, including his uncollected later writings, focusing on embodiment to explore the different ways in which the body trope informs visions of familial, economic, personal, and communal life.

Beginning with an exploration of O'Neill's work on the construction of the biobody and the ways in which corporeality is sutured into social systems through regimes of power and familial socialisation, the book then moves to concentrate on O'Neill's career-long studies of the productive body and the ways in which the working body is caught in and resists disciplinary systems that seek to rationalise natural functions and control social relations. The third section considers O'Neill's concern with the ancient, early modern, and psychoanalytic sources of the post-modern libidinal body, and a final section on the civic body focuses specifically on the ways in which principles of reciprocity and generosity exceed the capitalist, individualist body of (neo)liberal political theory. The volume also includes an interview with O'Neill addressing many of the key themes of his work, a biographical note with an autobiographical postscript, a select bibliography of O'Neill's many publications, and an extensive introduction by the editors.

A challenging and innovative collection, *Writing the Body Politic: A John O'Neill Reader* will appeal to critical social theorists and sociologists with interests in the work of one of sociology's great critical readers of classical and contemporary texts.

Mark Featherstone is Senior Lecturer at Keele University, UK, and author of *Tocqueville's Virus: Utopia and Dystopia in Western Social and Political Thought* (2006) and *Planet Utopia: Utopia, Dystopia, Globalisation* (2017).

Thomas Kemple is Professor of Sociology at the University of British Columbia, Canada, and author of *Reading Marx Writing: Marx, Melodrama, and the 'Grundrisse'* (1995), *Intellectual Work and the Spirit of Capitalism: Weber's Calling* (2014), and *Simmel* (2018).

Classical and Contemporary Social Theory

Series Editor

Stjepan G. Mestrovic, Texas A&M University, USA

Classical and Contemporary Social Theory publishes rigorous scholarly work that re-discovers the relevance of social theory for contemporary times, demonstrating the enduring importance of theory for modern social issues. The series covers social theory in a broad sense, inviting contributions on both 'classical' and modern theory, thus encompassing sociology, without being confined to a single discipline. As such, work from across the social sciences is welcome, provided that volumes address the social context of particular issues, subjects, or figures and offer new understandings of social reality and the contribution of a theorist or school to our understanding of it.

The series considers significant new appraisals of established thinkers or schools, comparative works or contributions that discuss a particular social issue or phenomenon in relation to the work of specific theorists or theoretical approaches. Contributions are welcome that assess broad strands of thought within certain schools or across the work of a number of thinkers, but always with an eye toward contributing to contemporary understandings of social issues and contexts.

Titles in this series

The Unmasking Style in Social Theory
Peter Baehr

Writing the Body Politic
A John O'Neill Reader
Edited by Mark Featherstone and Thomas Kemple

Emotions through Literature
Fictional Narratives and the Management of the Self
Mariano Longo

For more information about this series, please visit: www.routledge.com/sociology/series/ASHSER1383

Writing the Body Politic

A John O'Neill Reader

**Edited by Mark Featherstone
and Thomas Kemple**

Routledge
Taylor & Francis Group

LONDON AND NEW YORK

First published 2020
by Routledge
2 Park Square, Milton Park, Abingdon, Oxon OX14 4RN

and by Routledge
52 Vanderbilt Avenue, New York, NY 10017

Routledge is an imprint of the Taylor & Francis Group, an informa business

British Library Cataloguing-in-Publication Data
A catalogue record for this book is available from the British Library

Library of Congress Cataloging-in-Publication Data
A catalog record has been requested for this book

ISBN: 978-1-138-63317-9 (hbk)
ISBN: 978-1-315-20782-7 (ebk)

Typeset in Times New Roman
by Deanta Global Publishing Services, Chennai, India

For our students

In memory of Gregory O'Neill (1967–2018)

Contents

Figures

Appendices

Acknowledgements

The original idea for an O'Neill reader emerged in 2003 in a discussion between one of the now editors, Mark Featherstone, and John himself. Mark proposed the book in order to try to collect together John's key texts which had been so influential in building his own career and understanding of sociology, social theory, and philosophy. This influence stretched back to late 1995 when Mark attended John's lectures on post-modernism and French theory at Staffordshire University and then became his PhD student in 1996, attending courses at York University in the late 1990s. The idea was revived when Mark met up with Tom Kemple at the European Sociology Association Meetings in Prague in the summer of 2015. Tom first met John in 1983 and completed his PhD under John's mentorship in the early 1990s. This book is thus a counter-gift of love and appreciation for our teacher's inspiration, influence, and generosity.

John's classes taught us the history of post-war Continental thought from Sartre and Merleau-Ponty to Foucault, Derrida, and Deleuze and Guattari, as well as the latest debates in Hegelian-Marxist critical theory and psychoanalysis (the so-called Monday night and Freud seminars). More importantly, they demonstrated what it means to be a teacher, a student, a reader, and a writer, that is, to take up the habitus of an intellectual. Unlike the majority of professors we had met at university, John embodied his work. Sitting in O'Neill's classes was a deeply affecting experience precisely because there was so little distance between the man and his texts. One could not help but be excited by John's approach to reading (nothing was off limits), writing (expression came before genre), and the delivery of teaching (open, informal, and mesmeric), but also his profound respect for tradition, work, and experience.

Being taught by John was a gift which involved becoming part of a family, supported by his wife Susan whose own generosity seems boundless, and a community of other students and academics who were equally inspired by his approach to his work. The book would not have happened without John, whose influence continues to shape our academic careers and who allowed us to consult his notebooks and library, and Susan, who has been endlessly supportive over the years and most recently in our efforts to compile the current collection. John's good friend and colleague Tom (H.T.) Wilson encouraged us at every step, often prompting us with his remarkable memory. We are also grateful to several of

John's other students, in particular Naomi Couto, Doug Arrowsmith, and Sun Feiyu, whose Afterword to his Chinese translation of *The Domestic Economy of the Soul* helped us with the biographical notes, translated for us by Yun Han Hap, and included in Appendix B. Tom's partner Stephen Guy-Bray and Mark's family, Siobhan Holohan and Paddy Featherstone, have known John and Susan from the beginning and have also contributed to the community of friends that has grown around John and his work over the years.

We must also thank the many colleagues and former students who spoke at and attended the O'Neill Festschrift at York in October 2013, especially Mauro Buccheri, Master of Founders College and organizer of the event, as well as Jay Goulding, Chris Jenks, Molly Mann, David McNally, Livy Visano, and Tom Wilson. The title of this event, 'Scholarship as a Re-source of Hope: John O'Neill's Body of Work Re-Joyced', captures the way John's writing and teaching suture his readers and his students into a scholarly tradition with a hopeful future founded upon the humble reason of the lived body in the world.

The following essays are reprinted with permission: Chapters 1, 5, and 6 (Routledge); Chapters 2, 3, and 10 (Northwestern University Press); Chapter 4 (SUNY Press); Chapters 8, 9, 12, and 14 (SAGE); Chapter 7 (Hampton Press); Chapter 11 (University of Oklahoma Press); Chapter 15 (Springer); Chapter 16 (Pontifical Academy of Social Sciences); and Appendix A (Simon Fraser University Institute for the Humanities). The interview in Appendix A was transcribed with the help of Jastej Luddu, and Misaqe (Mo) Ismailzai and Paul Woodhouse assisted us with the figures in Parts III and IV. The process of producing this book, including collecting, editing, and re-reading John's work, has been an enormous honour and pleasure which has enabled us to re-discover the subtle greatness of his readings of a range of thinkers from across the human sciences. In some way, this labour of love has allowed us to re-experience our world-making first contact with O'Neill, the teacher who inspired us through his own embodied praxis of reading and writing the body politic.

Editors' introduction

Writing and reading the body politic

Mark Featherstone and Thomas Kemple

With a distinguished research career spanning five decades punctuated by thirty books and hundreds of academic papers, John O'Neill is among the world's most creative, eloquent, and provocative social theorists. Beginning with his numerous translations of the French thinker Maurice Merleau-Ponty and his acclaimed breakout book from 1972, *Sociology as a Skin Trade*, O'Neill became well known for key essays on Marx's notion of estrangement, Simmel's theory of social order, the Weberian-Durkheimian concept of the disciplinary society, and Freud's ideas on selfhood. To be sure, he has always been more than a conventional commentator on classical social theory. From his studies of Merleau-Ponty, collected in *The Communicative Body* (1989), he developed an original thesis on the notion of corporeal knowledge and sought to locate this theory of embodiment in a consideration of familial relationships and social welfare. This work shows how human sociability predates our cognition of norms and values and relates instead to the tacit bond between mother and child, and more broadly between self and other. Insofar as he advances a critique of the concept of 'the (wo)man from nowhere' that characterises much of liberal social theory, O'Neill's phenomenological Marxism offers a powerful challenge to capital ideology and has provoked the rediscovery of the body by contemporary Anglo-American sociology. Against any scientistic vision of the necessity of discovering the objective truth of the social world, the notion that self, other, and world are entirely connected and interdependent is perhaps the key insight of O'Neill's 'wild sociology', as he puts it in *Making Sense Together* (1974), and explains why his thinking and writing remain so important to the discipline today.

O'Neill's concern with the relationship between body and writing is evident from his wide-ranging readings in the history of the human sciences in *Essaying Montaigne* (1982) and his studies of Giambattista Vico, Roland Barthes, Michel Foucault, and others in *Critical Conventions* (1992). His studies since the 1990s, such as *The Poverty of Postmodernism* (1995) and *The Domestic Economy of the Soul* (2011), have sought to interrogate the politics of textuality and its broader cultural and personal dynamics. In this later phase, O'Neill expands phenomenological sociology to undertake a political economy and cultural studies of the consumer body, television, empire, and friendship that show how post-modern society imagines social relations free from poverty, failure, and despair. Unlike other prominent cultural theorists, however, O'Neill never falls into the abyss of the post-modern image, nor does he lose sight of social impoverishment, political alienation, economic exploitation, personal fragmentation, and cultural stratification. In the face of the kaleidoscope of post-modern culture that has seduced so many, O'Neill remains a critical thinker, concerned with the relationship between social systems and the lived body. For this reason, essay collections such as *Plato's Cave* (1991/2002) and *Incorporating Cultural Theory* (2002) represent important interventions in the field of cultural theory that anchor the post-modern blizzard of signs in the world of the body.

Despite the importance of his studies in sociology, politics, philosophy, psychoanalysis, and literary and cultural studies, there is no single collection of O'Neill's later work that brings together his efforts to restate, revise, and complete his innovative theory of the body politic. *A John O'Neill Reader* remedies this situation by offering a selection of both previously collected and later uncollected writings around the key theme of embodiment, each exploring different ways in which the body trope informs conceptions of familial, economic, personal, and communal life. The 16 essays collected in this volume address distinct aspects of the model of the body politic that O'Neill first formulated in response to the counter-cultural movements of the 1960s and revisited throughout his career, culminating in the four-part schema he proposed in his masterpiece, *Five Bodies* (1985/2004), discussed below. The writings collected here thus trace his early focus on *the bio-body* and *the productive body* already formulated in his early writings and more fully elaborated in *For Marx Against Althusser* (1982). They also disclose the intellectual sources and larger political implications of his later concern with *the civic body* expressed in *Civic Capitalism* (2004), and *the libidinal body* expanded on in *The Domestic Economy of the Soul* (2011). The unity of O'Neill's thought lies in his sustained meditation on the history of attempts to think the good society constructed in sympathy with the lived reality of the body that has its own story. The essays collected here highlight O'Neill's unique talents as a writer, as well as his critical acumen as a reader of classical and contemporary texts, not excluding his own writings through constant reiterations and revisions. O'Neill's corpus can be understood in terms of what is perhaps the fundamental problem of social life today – the cybernetic problem of the (im)possibility of locating the lived body within biosocial, economic, personal, and political systems that are simultaneously modelled upon its needs, desires, hopes, and fears, but that so often forget their debt to corporeality in surrendering to the post-human horrors of technological and scientific rationality. (See Appendices A, B, and C for biographical and bibliographical details on O'Neill's career.)

O'Neill's 'other' sociology

Much of contemporary sociology's disciplinary imagination is defined by the philosophical tradition of Cartesian scientism, where sociologists observe their object of study from a distance, generating social facts free of the corrupting influence of subjective value. By contrast, reading O'Neill's corpus of work entails remembering and reconstructing an 'other' version of sociology, which exceeds this hegemonic history of Western thought by recalling and recovering the very flesh of our corporeality, the common ground of our essential, inescapable, embodied being in the world. From this perspective, reading and re-reading O'Neill today implies a conversation between this 'other' sociology and the wider discipline which his writings unsettle and displace in two inter-related ways. First, against the dominant mainstream project of establishing social facts and drawing strict disciplinary boundaries around objects that may be studied scientifically, O'Neill is committed to writing the social and expanding the source material of the subject matter and even the style of sociology itself. In contrast to the Durkheimian and Weberian projects of defining and interpreting social facts, O'Neill's sociology is polymorphous in addressing a sometimes bewildering array of topics and polymathic in drawing from a wide variety of literatures. Long before American sociologists rediscovered the lyrical strains of their own classics (Abbott, 2007), O'Neill's wild sociology could be viewed as perverse from a strictly disciplinary point of view that wants to contain transgressions into philosophy, psychoanalysis, anthropology, literature, and a range of other human sciences.

If the sheer span of O'Neill's inter-disciplinary repertoire may at times be challenging, intimidating, and disorienting, his methodological assumptions about the nature of the subject matter of sociology are also more open and democratic than his expansive erudition might first suggest. Hence, what also gives his writings their distinctiveness is, second, the ring of familiarity and even the comforting way in which he roots his sociology in the lived body and the experience of corporeality that everybody shares. Against any narrow conception of sociology that interprets and explains actions in terms of abstract categories that come from somewhere else, O'Neill never loses touch with the body that ensures our participation in the world with others. There is no privileged platform from which an alien observer can survey the social world as if from nowhere, but only ever embodied engagement in the world. O'Neill does not simply unsettle hegemonic sociology by incorporating an extraordinary range of inter-disciplinary sources. He also transgresses disciplinary boundaries and conventional methodological assumptions by deconstructing the Cartesian separations of mind and body, subject and object, and cause and effect. The *primacy of implication* which follows from our experience of the lived body in the world means that the sociologist is never an alien observer, but always a carnal, embodied thinker engaged with others.

Against the grain of a certain Nietzschean tradition of thought that emphasises the primordial individuality of experience, O'Neill adopts the Hegelian assumption that the embodied nature of our being in the world means that we share basic experiences in common. The primordial fact that we live through our bodies makes us capable of compassion and assumes that we share more in common with one another than not. Our similarities outweigh our differences because of our basic participation in the flesh of the world, and despite the power of systems that abstract from this reality and that have been naturalised over time through the divisions of class, race, gender, sexuality, age, and other social classifications. The objective of O'Neill's sociology is thus to understand how we make sense of our world on the basis of our embodied participation in events and systems that are themselves the result of the history of sense making. Since there is no privileged, outsider position and no disembodied observer, writing sociologically is always a partial and fundamentally political endeavour. And since each of us is born into historical systems that ensure relative differences in lived experience and perspective, sociology is *a life-science* founded upon our implication and participation in a changing world that is always in the process of dying and living, of growing, ageing, and being born. The sociologist writes from the perspective of one who understands the irreducible nature of partiality and remains humble about his or her limited vision and blindness, an insight that separates his or her thought from Cartesian doubts and ties him or her to Montaigne's scepticism and embrace of Socrates' philosophy of learned ignorance.

O'Neill's embodied perspectivism entails reading and writing the body politic in an effort to explore the ways we make sense through our experience of the body, and with reference to the history of the human sciences that have reflected upon this endless work of sense making. This expansive approach to the study of social life reflects on the 'abyssal depths' and 'infinite complexities' of a human social world that is founded upon the profound nature of embodied life. Insofar as the dominant disciplinary imagination seeks to address this complexity by carving up the world into bits and pieces (subject, object, cause, and effect), it expresses a nervous attempt to attain a total understanding of things with a view to exercising complete control over their essential unpredictability. Driven by this deep-seated anxiety about the unpredictability of the world, the academic notion of discipline as a bounded subject organised around a well-defined method of study merges with the carceral concept of discipline as the control and definition of behaviour and action. The history of classical utopia is the history of this attempt at disciplinary settlement in the face of unwieldy and bewildering events and the vulnerability and fragility of our embodiment. O'Neill's sociology may be seen as a response to the violence of this utopian conceit. Despite the enormous intellectual ambition of this life-long project, O'Neill embarks on a small sociology of intimacy and humility that speaks to anyone who has ever felt miserable, suffered, and tried to read out from their experiences into the wider universe of meaning.

O'Neill's sociology begins with human experience in the world before its reduction to abstract cognitive categories. The child learns about the world through its embodied experience and only really begins to understand things in the more restricted, anxious terms set out by its parents after gazing up into the inky blackness of the night sky and contemplating the possibility of the infinite with wonder and awe from the safe space of the good enough family. From this safe space, the child is secure in its smallness and in the knowledge that it is cared for within the family. Humbled before the infinite span of space, the young stargazer is able to dream of alien beings and gods who travel the cosmos, without the anxiety and dread that comes with the adult realisation of vulnerability and exposure to the elements. Against this sense of exposure and dread, which leads to retreat and enclosure in forms of discipline where thoughts become contained, O'Neill's work retains a deep sense of humility reflected in his focus on family life and an openness towards the infinite reflected in his Catholicism. Religious belief is an expression of the value of securing the meaning of the inherent good of human life and wonder before the social world that is the deep legacy of critical thought.

In short, O'Neill's sociology resists the anxiety of discipline (both academic and carceral) in its endless search for meaning. He is less interested in how particular isolated variables come together to produce particular effects than in how bodies live in the world, how particular experiences are understood and come to be understood historically, and how we understand our world on the basis of this history. Since there is no final state, no objective social fact that will supply all the answers, the challenge of O'Neill's sociology is to approach and to seek out the ground of the good life on the basis of what is common about our embodied experience. These are the perennial questions posed by Montaigne and before him Socrates in their humbling attempts to come to terms with their finitude in the face of the infinite. Neither ignored his ability to think by sinking into the world or propelling himself beyond it, reaching escape velocity and achieving a God's eye view on events. We remain bound to the earth, to family, and to the community of others who sustain life and civility. This is why we talk, make art, and engage in political debate. This is why we write.

O'Neill writes in order to make good sense of our embodied experience of social life in the name of making better sense for the sake of creating a more human world. His ethical project is concerned with creating communities of sense based upon common experience that might cement our understanding of the value of human life in civilised institutions designed to make life more liveable. It is on the basis of this concern with humanism and civilisation that we should understand O'Neill's opposition to capitalism, which transforms humans into so many objects, commodities, and machines, and thus his identification with Marxist politics and theory. Against this vision of estranged life, O'Neill's early work is founded upon a Marxist ontology where the essence of work is the externalisation of experience in the creation of meaning. When this is achieved cooperatively, we make the world in common and create a living space that makes us more human.

Although O'Neill prefers the phenomenology of the early Marx to the later scientism of Louis Althusser, his discovery of Merleau-Ponty in the early 1960s provided him with a way to deepen his theory of the social, productive, and political body (see Appendix A). While the focus on the Marx of the 1844 economic and philosophic manuscripts was the contrast between the worker body in the world and the estranged body of the proletarian labourer, Merleau-Ponty's work enabled O'Neill to flesh out his theory of the body that perceives, experiences, and expresses in relation to others whom it touches and is touched by in turn. The concept-metaphor of 'the skin trade' in his early work thus draws attention to the way capitalism is conducted through the commerce in bodies transformed into objects, commodities, and machines and converted into monetary value. The dialectical idea of the skin trade thus refers, first, to the ways we are connected on a primordial level through the very tissue of our bodies in the world, and second, to the capitalist violence that transforms the qualities of the body into quantitative value to be bought and sold on the market or conscripted into war.

Although O'Neill introduced his notion of the skin trade in the early 1970s, today it can help us understand the political struggle between humanist and technological, democratic and authoritarian, and socialist and capitalist approaches to social organisation. As he argues in *Plato's Cave* (1991/2002), for example, in the age of mass media we seem to become almost totally individualised and behave as if society no longer existed. In the age of Facebook, Twitter, and Instagram, the individual and the imagined body are now everything and everywhere. The very same social media platforms that enable the total individualisation of the self online also transform the individual into quantitative data in a vast techno-scientific system under the reign of a new regime of what can be called *algorithmic power*. The technologies that promise absolute individual freedom also produce subordination to power, as O'Neill shows in examining how the specular image of the self is also its alienation into objectivity. In other words, the total self of both broadcast and social media is already lost through its transformation into its own imaginary other.

While scientific approaches to sociology have no response to this bind, because their very scientism means that they cannot move beyond their own object ontology, O'Neill's phenomenological sociology offers an alternative perspective that privileges the immanence of experience, the body, and what Merleau-Ponty (1968) in his final work calls the flesh. From this point of view, the individual body is always created by and already implicated in the cosmic, social, and political body. The relationship between the individual and the other is premised on common experiences that take the form of expression and lead to the co-creation of social meaning. The movement of this process is never simply a sequence of isolated events, but rather entails the creation and communication of meaning in narrative and lyrical form. We are never more mistaken than when we imagine ourselves to be infinite, and thus to be human means to not be God but to remain rooted in the world. By placing the body at the centre of his social theory, O'Neill suggests that addressing many of the great problems of humanity – poverty, misery, inequality, cruelty – entails remembering our common experience in more or less the same body. This is O'Neill's compassion.

O'Neill's two *Bodies*

Books, like bodies, have lives of their own. The different editions of Montaigne's *Essays* (1580/1595), Vico's *New Science* (1725/1744), Marx's *Capital* (1867/1883), Freud's *Interpretation of Dreams* (1900/1930), and John O'Neill's *Five Bodies* (1985/2004) present readers with the challenge of following a writer compelled to respond to changing times and temperaments. O'Neill's two *Bodies* are literally an expression of two bodies teaching, reading, and writing across distinct historical moments and addressing different generations of students and readers. Like the essays in this collection, the two editions exemplify the difference (*différance*), fold (*pli*), or criss-crossing (*chiasm*) between the *physical body* and the *communicative body* (O'Neill 2004: 2–8). While the physical body is situated as an object among other objects, it is also experienced as a thinking thing and an acting subject. That is, the physical body is at the same time a communicative body, our socio-symbolic means of expression in the world as we become caught up in the embodied look of others, and incorporate the carnal knowledge of our looking-glass selves. The space between these two bodies is therefore marked by the cross-over or chiasm (X) of their intertwining (*entrelacs*) and thrownness (*Geworfenheit*) in the world. In the words of Merleau-Ponty: 'There is a body of the mind and a mind of the body and a chiasm between them' (1968: 21; O'Neill, 1989: 21).

These intricate relationships between the physical and communicative body, along with the institutions that sustain them and the discourses through which they are expressed, might be pictured in Leonardo Da Vinci's famous anatomical drawing of Vitruvian Man, the double time-lapsed body who graces the cover of the first edition of *Five Bodies* (Figure 0.1; O'Neill, 1985). With its overlaid square and circle and the surrounding notes on the measured relationship between architectural and embodied space, Leonardo's drawing suggests the ways in which bodies are doubled: virtual and real, self and other, physical and communicative (Suh, 2005: 52–54; see O'Neill's essay on Freud's analysis of the doubling of mother bodies in Leonardo's paintings in 2002: 47–64). In practice, of course,

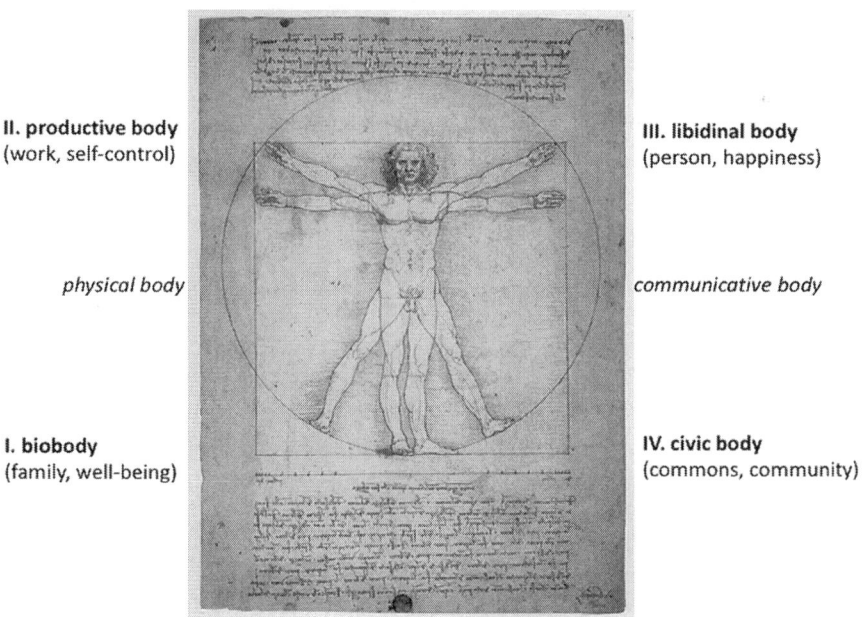

II. productive body
(work, self-control)

physical body

I. biobody
(family, well-being)

III. libidinal body
(person, happiness)

communicative body

IV. civic body
(commons, community)

Figure 0.1 The body politic (chiasm) (based on Leonardo Da Vinci's Vitruvian Man).

we have many bodies – cosmic and social, political and productive, consumer and medical, which are woven into the tissue and texture of lived experience and overlaid by knowledgeable and textual bodies engaged in a variety of everyday routines, including drawing and drafting, reading and writing. Simply put, we read and write books with our bodies in the course of a transaction or semiosis that O'Neill (in his commentary on Roland Barthes) calls *homotextuality* or *gynema* (O'Neill, 1992: 271). Just as O'Neill finds a fellow writer, friend, and family member through his successive readings and revised writings on Montaigne's *Essays* (1982/2001), so do we encounter O'Neill's literary body in the body of texts that make up the corpus of his books and essays.

O'Neill invites us to take up the task of rethinking the anthropomorphic shape of the world in the first instance on the grand scale of the cosmic body, which is itself *a biobody* that suffers the pains of illness and enjoys the benefits of health and well-being. The challenge that the biological sciences have posed to the body politic, especially in the period separating the two editions (Gilbert, 1995; O'Neill, 2004: xii), compel him to consider how the organic basis of experience is integrated within the orders of the *neural body* for which historically and culturally specific norms and legal regulations have established the classical hierarchy of mind over matter. The classic images of the cosmopolitan body, such as Leonardo's Vitruvian Man or Geoffrey Tory's L'Homme Scientifique ('Encylopedic Man', see O'Neill, 2004: 17), do not envision a solitary astral body circulating endlessly though time and drifting rootlessly in space. Even in our wildest states or loneliest moments, we can sense the complementarity and overlap between the larger order of a common world (*cosmos*) and those smaller microcosms that we make sense of as the stuff of story, myth, legend, and imagination. The frame of this primal order therefore grounds and precedes the generative capacities of the *productive body*, which strives for self-control against exploitation, and a measure of immunity or protection against the ravages of attack and the threat of death. In other words, the physical body is stretched across the levels of the biobody that suffers and dies and the productive body that works and consumes.

It is apparent, then, that the physical body is always and already a *communicative body*, where the classic problem of order and rebellion is played out at each of the 'levels' of the body politic. Against the organic analogies and cybernetic models of political rule that have dominated mainstream sociology since its inception, O'Neill develops his own original critical theory of the body politic by revising the Christian, medieval, and Renaissance imagery of 'the king's two bodies', the one subject to natural demise and the other living on in symbolic and institutional form beyond death. In fact, citizens and rulers alike engage in the '*embodied rationalities* of everyday living, family, survival, health, self-respect, love, and communion' (O'Neill, 2004: 46). In a sense, then, *the civic body*, which sustains the separation between public commons and private life as the 'phenotypical' mark distinguishing order and chaos, is situated beneath the desires of the *libidinal body*, which strives for love and happiness despite the 'genetic' divisions of sex and race. Today the civic ethos of capitalism is threatened less by its ascetic or industrial work ethic than by the spirit of hedonistic consumerism that panders to the desires of the libidinal bodies of both the labouring and leisure classes. In *Five Bodies*, O'Neill describes this civic economy as the gendered labour of reproduction and the generational work of care, organised around the two 'tiers' of exchange for subsistence, on the one hand, and the desire for identity, distinction, or prestige, on the other. Today, for example, we can observe how consumer bodies are squeezed between the ethical requirements of the civic body and the dream-work of the libidinal body, with its aspirations of love, freedom, and symbolic distinction. Generally speaking, every material economy is also a moral economy that remains open to the ecological cycles of political management and ethical self-correction.

Here we cannot recite O'Neill's most memorable stories from *Five Bodies* – about Dogon cosmology, ancient Hebrew dietary rules, medieval and Renaissance images of rulership, the rituals of fast-food communion, the semiotics of cars and cigarettes, and the gift economies of blood transfusions and organ transplants. His larger argument is that the cosmomorphism of the world's body and the sociomorphism of natural and human collectives are under threat form the mechanomorphism of the modern administrative state, the gynomorphism of consumer bodies, and the biomorphism of medical bodies. In other words, the survival and revival of our planetary existence rests on 'alliances and … exchanges [which], taken together, are what define the *anthropos* – a weaver of morphisms' (Latour, 1993: 137). O'Neill's account of the most recent of these metamorphoses is marked by what we might call the 'textual turn' in his thinking, which he frames in terms of *the historical shift from biotext to sociotext*: 'our power over nature – or our power over life – is a power over ourselves inscribed through the state and the economy, and through its laws and sciences (*sociotext*)' (O'Neill, 2004: 1).

For instance, he notes that today the medicalisation of the body and the therapeutic management of the mind and its moods follow the logic of technical/textual rationality. Genetic disorders such as heart disease, culturally created sicknesses like lung cancer, not to mention the socially generated pathologies of racism and sexism, may supposedly be treated or even cured through biotechnological interventions, prostheses, and pharmaceuticals. Similarly, the dream of rewriting the constitution of the body through 'edits' to its DNA code, or by gathering data on every imaginable technique of the body, also aims to rewrite the biotext as sociotext. With the rise of 'spare-part man', whose very organs and tissues are replaceable, the collective order of the cosmos that was once figured in the astral virtues of Leonardo's Vitruvian man can presumably be rewritten in the algorithms of a cyborg script. Humans may then become 'the creatures of the dominant ethos of *the market or the state as matrix*' (O'Neill, 2004: 83). This new frontier of biopower compels us to confront the origins and ends of life as (post)human (dis) orders, and to rethink our social and political worlds as the gifts we give to one another and reciprocate on behalf of our own civility and survival.

For our purposes, it helps to imagine O'Neill's broader scheme here by juxtaposing the iconic figure of Leonardo's Vitruvian Man with a lesser known drawing, Paul Klee's 'Leaning' (*Angelehnte*), presented opposite the title page of the first edition of *Five Bodies* and again on the cover of *Critical Conventions*

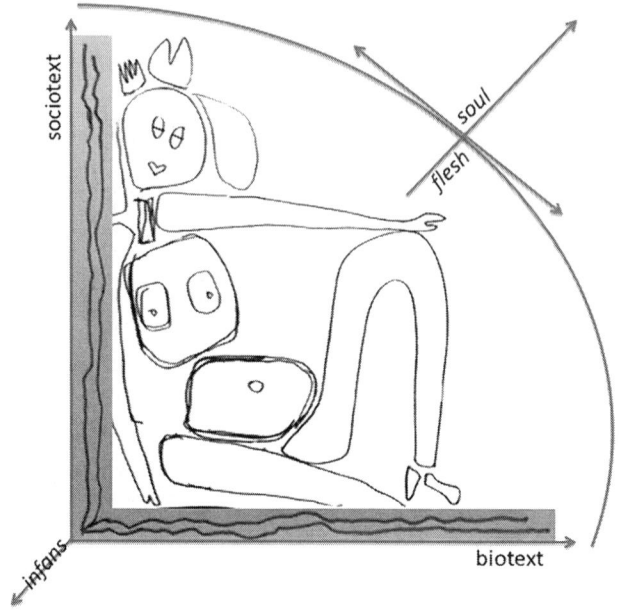

Figure 0.2 The body politic (matrix) (based on Paul Klee's 'Leaning'. Copyright 1985 ADAGP, Montreal).

(Figure 0.2; O'Neill, 1985: 3; 1992, cover image). Once again we note O'Neill's emphasis on the central significance of the corporal bond of mother and infant bodies as the space of inscription (*chora*), or what he calls the *matrix*. Against the historical tendency to write this bond through the biotechnologies of the state and the market, O'Neill's later works launch a two-fold defence of the welfare state (in *Civic Capitalism*) and of the intergenerational debts of our familied being (in *The Domestic Economy of the Soul*). The latter project entails a critical re-reading of Freud's use of evolutionary and energetic metaphors in analysing the interface of soma and psyche, or the entwining of flesh and soul. In O'Neill's view, Freud's achievement is to combine these perspectives in his conception of the folding and binding, or rather, leaning, opening, and propping (*Anlehnung*) of mute natural needs (*infans*) onto cultural drives (*Triebe*) through the articulate 'dream-work' of displacement and condensation. As he puts this point in 'Infant Theory', 'the daily transcriptions of the flesh provide us with the soul's reading' (O'Neill, 2002: 12). In short, Freud is not just a therapist of mental suffering but also a theorist of the sexual body as *sociotext* and an interpreter of its symptoms as *biotext*. In his 'autocritique' of *Five Bodies* in *Critical Conventions*, O'Neill explains how in Klee's drawing (itself perhaps a feminised redrafting of Michelangelo's 'Creation') and other iconic figures he 'reproduces and defends a history of the world's body under the concept of a radical anthropomorphism that shapes our economy, medicine, and nuclear politics' (O'Neill, 1992: 173).

According to scholarly convention, writers are expected to refrain from being readers of and commentators on their own work, and readers are presumed to become writers mainly through a mere role reversal, or at most as a residual pastime. Nevertheless, our everyday habits of reading and writing are intellectual and intergenerational pursuits, just as researching and teaching are embodied as well as intelligent encounters. The essays gathered in this reader illuminate O'Neill's own life-long engagement with predecessors who prefigure an alternative social theory, a kind of 'genealogy' for thinking otherwise than is conventional in the humanities and social sciences (Figure 0.3). As we suggest in our overview of the essays below, the heart of O'Neill's thought lies at the intersection of Marx's concern with the potential resurrection of the suffering productive body in the civic communal body (Chapters 7, 8, 15, and 16), on the one hand, and Freud's passion for examining the struggle of the libidinal body with the unruly biobody of family life (Chapters 4 and 12), on the other hand. Cutting across these personal and collective histories, O'Neill traces a deeper phenomenology of mind and body expressed in the works of Hegel (Chapter 14) and Merleau-Ponty (Chapters 2, 3, 4, and 11). Rounding out these studies of modern life are Foucault's insights into how the biobody and productive body have been conscripted by disciplinary institutions (Chapters 1 and 5), and Marcuse's efforts to show how the labouring body

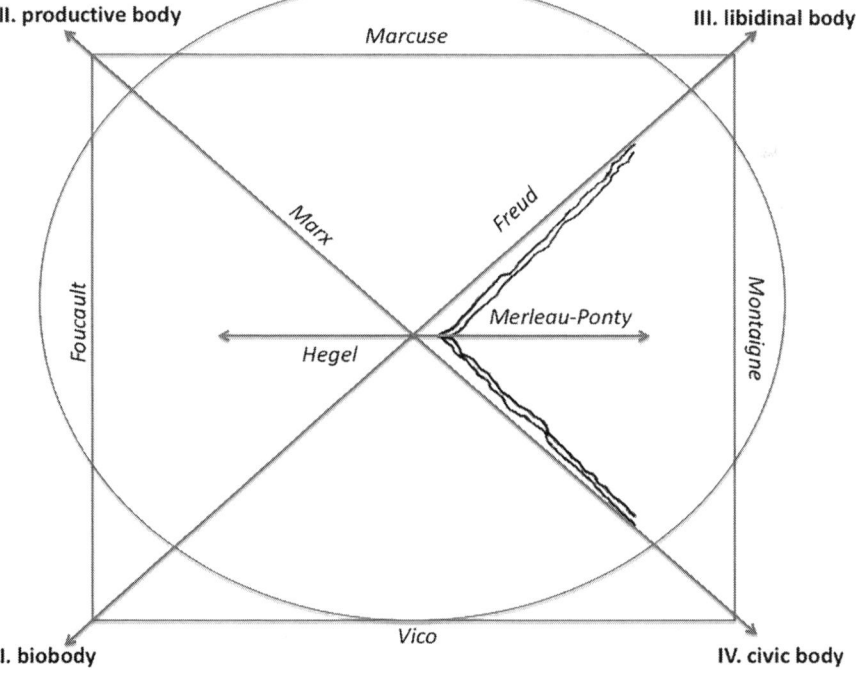

Figure 0.3 The body politic (genealogy).

of late capitalism is potentially revitalised through the revolution of love's body (Chapters 6 and 9). Not forgetting the contributions of the early modern writers, O'Neill recalls how Montaigne cultivated his writing self at the crossroads of his libidinal desires and his civic duties (Chapter 10), and how Vico conceived the biobody itself as a knowledgeable body of social order and civil institutions (Chapter 13). These essays teach us that if the university is not to become a mind-less training camp for consumerism and employment but also a forum for critical thinking, scholarship, and citizenship, then it must remain open to changes in the composition of classes and the reshuffling of statuses through the ordinary and divine routines of civic action and critical intelligence.

Reading/writing the body politic

In arranging the 16 essays in this reader according to the four levels of the body politic, we do not assume that O'Neill himself composed these pieces explic-itly with these themes in mind, or that he would necessarily classify his writings this way. Like the 16 essays distributed across the four parts of *Sociology as a Skin Trade*, each piece in the present collection points in multiple directions and exceeds the terms of its titles. Just as that earlier book began with a Conclusion and ended with an Introduction, so our remarks here can be read as an Afterword of sorts, with the appendixes serving as a kind of Foreword to the collection as a whole, if not as an invitation to a patient study of the whole of O'Neill's oeuvre. In any case, a few notes on how these essays fit within the overall project of *Writing the Body Politic* might help readers find connections and continuities that they might otherwise miss. (Our commentaries below can be read in tandem with the more focused summaries in the abstracts in the online version of this book):

Biobodies: the infant gaze after phenomenology, psychoanalysis, and medical science

The collection begins with O'Neill's exploration of the construction of the *bio-body* (Part I) and the ways in which corporeality is sutured into social systems through specular regimes of power and familial socialisation that locate the infant body in the world. As an artefact of modern science, the biobody can be distin-guished from the physical body that renders everybody both an object for others and a subject of our own experience. Following Nietzsche's critique of the human sciences and taking up the case of the medical sciences, the opening paper of the collection, 'Foucault's optics' (1995), captures the meaning of O'Neill's phe-nomenological and ethical project, which revolves around the need to re-found the human sciences as *life-sciences* by drawing on the experiential and intersub-jective world and not just the empirical and objective body. O'Neill explains that Foucault's great achievement was to show how modern medicine can be understood as a response to (1) the death of God, (2) the death of man, and (3) the post-human attempt to realise a God's eye view of existence (echoing Foucault's comic irony, the gendered and generic reference to 'man' is deliberate here).

The problem of the death of God is the problem of the loss of the infinite. In this situation man is thrown back upon himself, but devoid of deeper meaning his anxiety is such that he seeks to replace God with scientific truth, thus fleeing from himself into abstraction. On the one hand, this saves man from taking responsibility for himself, but on the other hand, he also loses touch with his body that experiences and provides the common ground for understanding what it means to be human. This is why, in O'Neill's view, the practice of writing is essential in modern society insofar as the writer recognises that there is no final truth underwritten by God, but only provisional truths based in meaning systems created by humans. The practice of writing is, therefore, based on the recognition of limitation and the finitude of the human body capable of taking leave of itself in thought, but that always remains essentially part of the metabolism of the natural world.

In the following three essays of this Part, 'The specular body' (1986/1989), 'Childhood and embodiment' (1973/1989), and 'Infant theory' (2002), O'Neill's concern with the phenomenology of the body is foregrounded in a critique of Lacanian psychoanalysis, which seeks to project self-identity beyond the biobody and into the virtual space of the image. O'Neill argues that Jacques Lacan's error – or rather, his productive 'misreading' of Freud – is to ignore the space of the communicative body that connects child to mother and establishes corporeality as the medium through which we engage with the world for the rest of our lives. Contrasting this process of estrangement, O'Neill turns to Merleau-Ponty's later writings to argue that the world of the lived body always comes before the abstract space of the known body, and to show that this insight might enable us to remember the essential sociability of humanity. That is to say, O'Neill finds the origins of human reciprocity in the original embrace between mother and child that includes the mother's loving gaze and the child's equally loving response brought about by the fact that they see themselves in her vision of them. Just as there is no originary individual, there is no self out on its own. Humans are always in the world, contained by a primordial intersubjectivity. Endless interactions and relations set the scene for our arrival into the world, socialise us into a life lived with others, and then enable us to create and recreate a common life that extends into a future beyond the life of any one individual. The primordial relation between mother and child comes before the abstraction of language, and thus before science which separates subject and objects, and forms the basic human text upon which we write out future social development. Here O'Neill explains that our relation to the world is established on the basis of our phenomenal body which perceives, experiences, and expresses its visceral knowledge in the form of biotexts that simultaneously reflect reality and articulate imaginative representations of our interactions. This is why O'Neill suggests that a kind of childhood philosophy or 'infant theory' is necessary to make sense of the history of the body politic as both a personal concern and a collective pursuit. In short, from the beginning, the 'deviation' (*clinamen*) of the biobody into the psychic and communicative body already entails the project of writing the body politic.

Productive bodies: alienation and discipline in the media age

O'Neill's concern with the biobody as both an object of scientific observation and the intersubjective ground of lived experience informs his career-long studies of the *productive body*. In the essays included in Part II, he explores the many ways in which the working body is caught up in disciplinary systems that seek to rationalise natural functions and control social relations which might otherwise be expressed creatively in mytho-poetic terms. It is this violence, which might be called 'objective' for the way that force is concealed or legitimised through a process of rationalisation, that O'Neill began to respond to with his critique of Marxist scientism in his doctoral dissertation at Stanford under the mentorship of Paul Baran and Paul Sweezy (see Appendix B). In effect, the elevation of the mind and the neglect of the body in capitalist work processes is the moral and theoretical concern of the young Marx in *The Economic and Philosophical Manuscripts of 1844*, where work is described as conscious praxis and the provision of meaning in the world that is otherwise unintelligible. In 'The disciplinary society' (1986/1995) O'Neill argues that Foucault's historical studies must therefore be expanded to include the whole complex of bureaucratic, carceral, therapeutic, and industrial controls over bodies and populations as they are constantly underwritten by the human sciences (including law, economics, education, and administration, not to mention sociology). To gain some analytical clarity and critical perspective on this dimension of capitalist history, in 'Orphic Marxism' (1995) O'Neill draws attention to Marx's implicit distinction between externalisation (*Entäusserung*) or objectification (*Vergegenständlichung*), on the one hand, and alienation (*Entfremdung*) or reification (*Verdinglichung*), on the other. Where the former is essential for the human making of history, the latter is destructive of the essence of what it means to be human by virtue of the way the process of estrangement cuts off working bodies from their ability to project themselves into the world. While this phenomenological description of the worker recalls the philosophies of Hegel, Heidegger, Merleau-Ponty, and the later Sartre, O'Neill is sensitive to the problems this model encounters in post-modern societies and consumer bodies.

Beyond these foundational essays in Marxist theory, we include two more rhetorically and polemically charged papers, '*Televideo ergo sum*' (1982/2002) and 'Empire versus empire' (2002). These essays are concerned with the intersection of the mediatised body that ceases to exist off-screen and the globalised, imperial mode of corporeality that represents both the intensification of consumer capitalism and a new mode of immanent resistance to power. Here O'Neill argues that, insofar as everything in the post-modern media society seems to be mobile, mobility has no return, and the great escape technologies of the age – the automobile, the television, and the computer – never really lead us anywhere. Against this model of endless flight, the past returns to us in the form of fantasies that we consume from a safe distance – in visions of history, work, family, countryside, and nature. This is what O'Neill means by the mediatisation of the cogito, where a post-modern Descartes declares: 'I appear on screen, therefore I am', thereby distorting Sartre's (2003) dialectic of being and nothingness in the emergence of a new media reality where the other of being is one's appearance or self-exposure on screen. In the 1980s the model for thinking about the mediatisation of the world in an age where we 'amuse ourselves to death' (Postman, 1987) and where 'the medium is the message' (McLuhan, 1964) was Ronald Reagan's America, whereas today's populist and liberal authoritarians understand that appearance is everything, and substance is literally nothing. In this regard, the info-tech revolution ends in what has been called algorithmic governmentality (Rouvroy and Berns, 2013), and O'Neill's analysis of the power of the American empire in the immediate post-9/11 world order remains as relevant today as it was then. His point is that the media floats political issues in the form of pseudo-politics and pseudo-critique while creating the need for conservative and neoliberal responses that restore order where difference itself is the problem and structural injustices and inequalities remain hidden. O'Neill's political critique of the image and spectacle thus extends to the cultish millenarianism of right and left alike. In the twenty-first century, of course, we have yet to witness the collapse of empire before the power of the multitude, only the effects of American imperial overreach, slowdown, and withdrawal towards a kind of paranoid isolationism in ways that confirm O'Neill's reading of stratified global power at the turn of the century.

Libidinal bodies: inscriptions of desire in the utopian imagination

O'Neill's concern with the poverty and excesses of post-modernism in the late 1990s and early 2000s is taken up in a more focused way in Part III of the collection, which explores the *libidinal body* and the flows of desire that situate the self within the wider human environment. The essays 'Marcuse's maternal ethic' (2002) and 'Structure, flow, and balance in Montaigne's essay "Of Idleness"' (2001) pivot on O'Neill's reconsideration of the problem of how the thinking and desiring being is always part of a natural cosmology of procreation and waste, love and monstrosity. As he argues in his lyrical books on Montaigne (1982/2001) and Freud (2011), it is impossible to escape the state of indebtedness expressed in our personal and corporeal existence embedded in familial history and sociocultural interdependence. The memory of a certain 'maternal ethic' (or 'Madonna Complex') that does not psychologise feminine emotion and imagination therefore turns on a political conception of utopia in which regression might actually be progressive by virtue of its potential for rescuing the imagination from the unconscious. Against Freud's patriarchal reading of the Promethean myth, and even Herbert Marcuse's radical feminist interpretation of Orphic phantasy, O'Neill recovers J.J. Bachofen's thesis of mother right, in which utopian and cosmic impulses emerge from a kind of polymorphous sexuality before their transformation (sublimation) into figures of abjection. In certain key respects, this vision is shared by Montaigne (as well as his philosophical hero, Socrates), whose ideas on the structure, flow, and balance of the desiring self draw upon a maternal imaginary and a symbolic order that embrace embodied finitude rather than submit to abject corporeality.

In many respects O'Neill's ethical position in these papers is not entirely different from the one advanced by the post-modern left that has taken its lead from Marcuse or Foucault, as well as Gilles Deleuze and Félix Guattari, in returning to the unconscious body in order to find some way to resist power. The key difference is that O'Neill offers a more differentiated analysis and stratified vision of opposition to capitalism and scientism, often with reference to a range of scales and social institutions that these critics would probably find restrictive. His sociologically more realist approach focuses on durable alternatives and malleable institutions for creating secure spaces for further renewal in the future. In 'Mecum meditari' (1992) and 'Psychoanalysis and sociology' (2001), the tension between these utopian and sociological strains of thinking and writing is what propels O'Neill's critique of the duelling scientific legacies of Cartesian philosophy and Freudian psychoanalysis. Where Descartes builds an entire worldview on his mediations about self-doubt and divine fiat, Freud presents an anti-social vision of civilisation, where cultural creation is often a poor substitute for the natural expenditure of libidinal energies in sexual and racial violence that we cannot escape. We are never free from our past, any more than we can liberate ourselves from our bodies, but we are never burdened by these realities to the point where no future opens up the possibility of creating some alternative society or expressing another self. Despite O'Neill's eclectic and dispersed approach to phenomenology, psychoanalysis, Marxism, feminism, post-modern, and early modern social thought, these essays converge in his desire to write a political theory in which the self is neither repressed by nor released from the civilising process, but seeks out some measure of equitable order and even personal happiness.

Civic bodies: reciprocity and generosity against the capitalist rule of exchange

A more positive and expansive theory of social justice is the focus of the essays included in Part IV of the collection, where O'Neill explores the formation of the *civic body* and specifically the ways in which principles of reciprocity and generosity exceed the capitalist, individualist body of (neo)liberal political theory. 'Vico's arborescence' (2009) and 'Oh, my others, there is no other!' (2001) disclose the intellectual sources of his novel ideas concerning the socialisation of knowledge and literacy as well as his distinctive political theology of intergenerational indebtedness. Vico's image of the tree of knowledge offers an alternative to both the modern positivist assumption of the unity of the sciences and the post-modern relativism of affect and cognition. The latter is expressed in the anti-Oedipal rhizomatic theory of Gilles Deleuze and Félix Guattari, which largely ignores the civic and world-building project of historical difference and repetition. In a similar way, O'Neill develops his critique of Jacques Derrida's reading of G.W.F. Hegel and Marcel Mauss concerning otherness and friendship and its implicit acceptance of the contemporary politics of identity and difference. Although he does not discuss Derrida's work in depth on this occasion as he does elsewhere (O'Neill, 1992, 2002), it is clear that O'Neill critically engages with his philosophy, and in particular *The Politics of Friendship* (1997), which refers to Montaigne's take on Aristotle's statement, 'O friends, there are no friends', in order to oppose the politics of difference and alienation. Insofar as the left is no longer able to speak about structure or see beyond difference, O'Neill's point is that economy is rendered invisible, with the effect that difference effectively collapses into indifference. Under global capitalism difference makes no difference, and everybody is equally expendable in the economic state of nature that is entirely democratic and objective about its approach to making a profit. Against this situation, O'Neill suggests that the left needs to rediscover a politics based upon our commonality in difference (a politics of the 'we'), which he finds articulated in Hegel's philosophy of recognition and which he calls 'other-wiseness'.

The final two essays of the collection '*Ecce homo*' (2010) and 'The circle and the line' (presented at the Vatican in 2006), capture the essence of O'Neill's moral position in articulating his own version of a political or *civic theology*. In contrast to Hannah Arendt and Giorgio Agamben, as well as the liberal political theory of John Rawls, O'Neill critiques an intellectual and cultural politics that celebrates difference by taking up the point of view of a Christian politics of welfare, love, and civic recognition. His larger argument, developed in *The Missing Child in Liberal Theory* (1994) and *Civic Capitalism* (2004), is that the welfare state has become a symbol of potential totalitarianism for liberals and neoliberals (not to mention the neoconservative new right), with the result that one can no longer talk about structural inequalities and institutional solutions. Instead, the left has turned towards a politics of individualism and self-realisation that easily bleeds into the ideological positions taken up by the new right on self-responsibility and economic freedom. Alliances between global capitalism and the politics of difference based upon a consumer model and ideology of self-realisation have recently come under severe pressure. In a state of seemingly endless economic crisis, global capitalism has intensified the enforcement of discipline and austerity against an ethics of individualism and its critique of racial and gender violence. Considered in this light, O'Neill's politics of recognition and unity remain relevant to the present conjuncture in suggesting a way to transcend the current culture wars in the name of a broad-based leftist opposition to capitalism.

The neoliberal focus on the entrepreneur of the self, on the possessed and possessive individual that is so prevalent today, leaves no room for social sacrifices and civic gifts that appear so hopelessly inefficient or an-economic. Why would anybody give to others? Why would anybody take care of children when what matters is taking advantage now? Why would anybody worry about elders when they are no longer productive or profitable? O'Neill's answer is that giving, welfare, civic virtue, and care for the most vulnerable are the core principles of any civilisation committed to abandoning the barbaric ethics of individual greed. He tells us that children are the treasure of the world, but that we have forgotten their true value in our scramble to commodify everything. The end of childhood thus represents the victory of the ageing of the world, the end of civilised society and its return to the brutal (Hobbesian) state of nature, as expressed in the image of the line of the starving stretching off into the future. The contrasting image of the circle of the round world full of love captures a civic future, the womb of the world that starts in the love between mother and child and grows out of this experience into a social body sustained through institutions ruled by human principles. We live in a universe where the death of God has created a space of uncertainty and instability, and where no transcendental father will tell us how to live. There are no final answers, no objective truths, only writing and making sense together in a world that both is and is not our own making. This is why we must keep our feet on the ground and listen to our bodies, because understanding experience is the key to creating a truly human future. This is O'Neill's key lesson – the core message he seeks to communicate in writing the body politic.

References

Abbott, A. (2007). 'Against Narrative: A Preface to Lyrical Sociology'. *Sociological Theory* 25(1): 67–99.

Derrida, J. (1997). *The Politics of Friendship*. London: Verso.

Gilbert, S. F. (1995). 'Resurrecting the Body: Has Postmodernism had Any Effect on Biology?' *Science in Context* 8(4): 563–577.

Latour, B. (1993). *We Have Never Been Modern*. Trans. Catherine Porter. Cambridge: Harvard University Press.

McLuhan, M. (1964). *Understanding Media: The Extensions of Man*. New York: McGraw Hill.

Merleau-Ponty, M. (1968). *The Visible and the Invisible*. Evanston, IL: Northwestern University Press.

O'Neill, J. (1972). *Sociology as a Skin Trade: Essays Towards a Reflexive Sociology*. London: Heinemann.

O'Neill, J. (1974). *Making Sense Together: An Introduction to Wild Sociology*. London: Heinemann.

O'Neill, J. (1982). *For Marx Against Althusser, and Other Essays*. Washington, DC: Center for Advanced Research in Phenomenology and University Press of America.

O'Neill, J. (1985). *Five Bodies: The Human Shape of Modern Society*. Ithaca, NY: Cornell University Press.

O'Neill, J. (1989). *The Communicative Body*. Evanston: Northwestern University Press.

O'Neill, J. (1992). *Critical Conventions: Interpretation in the Literary Arts and Sciences*. Norman, OK: University of Oklahoma Press.

O'Neill, J. (2002). *Incorporating Cultural Theory: Maternity at the Millennium*. Albany, NY: SUNY Press.

O'Neill, J. (2004). *Five Bodies: Re-figuring Relationships*. Los Angeles and London: SAGE Publications.

Postman, N. (1987). *Amusing Ourselves to Death: Public Discourse in the Age of Show Business*. London: Penguin.

Rouvroy, A. and Berns, T. (2013). 'Algorithmic Governmentality and Prospects of Emancipation: Disparteness as a Precondition for Individuation through Relationships?' *Réseaux* 1(177): 163–196.

Sartre, J-P. (2003). *Being and Nothingness: An Essay on Phenomenological Ontology*. London: Routledge.

Suh, H. Ann (ed.) (2005). *Leonardo's Notebooks: Writing and Art of the Great Master*. New York: Black Dog and Levanthal Publishers, Inc.

Part 1
The biobody

1 Foucault's optics*

The (in)vision of mortality and modernity

At the high point of modernity, God and man are called upon to die in favour of each other. Or, as Michel Foucault tells it, our vision of ourselves now derives from an 'autopsical' finitude grounded in the clinical optic that has opened the dark interior of the human body to the light of mankind's own practices of pleasure and suffering. With the effacement of the divine landscape of infinite time-space, mankind has begun to inhabit the earth and the body for the first time and to essay a history of good and evil that is likewise to be inscribed for the first time on a human scale. Thus, 'mankind' set aside any comparative transcendental measure in favour of its own embrace, the fold (*le pli*) within which we must see and think and speak for ourselves (Deleuze, 1986; Merleau-Ponty, 1968: 103).

Whereas so much commentary has focused upon Foucault's genealogical and archaeological studies, I propose to explore Foucault's poetics of the visual regime of modernity and morality that have constituted modern man in a moment of history that may be about to efface itself. Since I consider this next moment of modernity not to be very well understood in current celebrations of post-modernity (O'Neill, 1989, 1990), I shall try to set it out with particular attention to the pathos and poetry given to it in Foucault's work.

What I think is most noticeable in Foucault's text is an effect of writing, an extraordinary poetry, grafted upon the genealogies of life and death, of reason and madness, of order and transgression. Within the new institutions of human finitude and their rational discourses, there persists a capacity for lyrical, oneiric flights and for fantastic epiphanies which reveal the bright darkness as well as the sombre enlightenment of human existence. In Foucault's thought rationality is re-visioned; its pursuits are limited and materialised. The life of 'finite man' opens up from the standpoint of death. This is the starting point both of modern science and of modern literature. And this brings about a fusion of philosophy and literature because the philosopher without total knowledge must become a writer. Here the prototype is Montaigne, the essayist of anti-foundational knowledge, himself an exemplar of the

* Text of this essay taken from *Visual Culture* (1995). Edited by Chris Jenks. London: Routledge. Pages 190–201. Reprinted with permission.

new finitude which is opened up like the New World by death and not by immortality. The sovereignty of death hollows out a void in the present from which we speak and write. Before death, which both proceeds and follows it, language turns back upon itself and prolongs the story which tells of everything that can befall us until we can no longer speak or write. In Foucault words are kept on the surface; they avoid sinking to any depth, or rising towards any transcendental perspective; they flit between the shadows left by the death of the subject. With the loss of this solidary presence every other thing necessarily slides. From where, then, can anything be said or seen? The question itself is refused. There are discourses. They hold for a time; they break and are reorganised. Their authority derives from their style which privileges catachresis (the misuse of words). The very flow of Foucault's text confounds reviewers who see in it the faults but not the virtues of Bataillean expenditure (*de-pens*). Logorrhea appears to be the consequence of transgressing logocentrism. Nevertheless, Foucault's discourse is marked by its own style, i.e., a mode of uncovering the absence at the heart of being and language, together with artifices whereby we conceal this void with anthropomorphic fictions. Style coexists with repression and grammar, i.e., desire and power masked in the will to truth. The latter functions to rule out the arbitrariness in every rule with respect to the free play in both the signifiers and, we should say, the signifieds.

The emergence of the modern individual is inseparable from 'hir' (that is, his and/or her) effacement. Like a Segal sculpture, the individual is woven from a fabric of anonymous and invisible forces which project 'hir' along their surface. In such images of modernity, materiality overrides transcendence with the awkward insistence of a kind of singularity that we have still to accept. The individual will never appear in full light. 'She' has lost for ever the aura of even a borrowed divinity. Neither angel nor beast, hir footprints mark the sands of time that just as easily erase hir trace on the shore of the earth. In the empty place abandoned by the gods, humans must erect their own shaky institutions, as the mark and laughter that momentarily recollect the diaspora of their kind:

> Strangely enough, man – the study of whom is supposed by the naive to be the oldest investigation since Socrates – *is probably no more than a kind of rift in the order of things*, or, in any case, a configuration whose outlines are determined by the new position he has so recently taken up in the field of knowledge. Whence all the chimeras of the new humanisms, all the facile solutions of an 'anthropology' understood as a universal reflection on man, half-empirical, half-philosophical. It is comforting, however, and a source of profound relief to think that *man is only a recent invention*, a figure not two centuries old, a new wrinkle in our knowledge, and *he will disappear again as soon as that knowledge has discovered a new form*.
>
> (Foucault, 1973: xxv; my emphasis)

The death of 'man' completes the death of God. (In view of contemporary concerns about non-sexist terminology, it should be understood that all references to 'man' are intended in the archaeological sense defined here, as well as being subject to Foucault's philosophical laugh. See Foucault, 1973: 385.) With the last gasp of transcendentalising humanism, there opens up human finitude within which we interrogate the 'unthought' (*Ungedacht*) of our thought, the silence of our language, the social determinisms in our freedom and the morbidity which spreads through our life:

> For can I, in fact, say that I am this language that I speak, into which my thought insinuates itself to the point of finding in it the system of all its own possibilities, yet which exists only in the weight of sedimentations my thought will never be capable of actualizing altogether? Can I say that I am this labor I perform with my hands, yet which eludes me not only when I have finished it, but even before I have begun it? Can I say I am this life I sense deep within me, but which envelops me both in the irresistible time that grows side by side with it and poses me for a moment on its crest, and in the imminent time that prescribes my death? I can say, equally well, that I am and that I am not all this; the *cogito* does not lead to an affirmation of being, but it does lead to a whole series of questions concerned with being: What must I be, I who think and who am my thought, in order to be what I do not think, in order for my thought to be what I am not? What is this being, then, that shimmers and, as it were, glitters in the opening of the *cogito*, yet is not sovereignly given in it or by it?
>
> (Foucault, 1973: 324-5)

Thus modern man will have an empirical affinity for the languages of the body. He will be driven to excavate the body's dreams, its pathologies and its death, to enter the body's spaces, to explore the abyss beneath its illness and to open up discourses 'involving fidelity and unconditional subservience to the coloured content of experience – to say what one sees; but also a use involving the foundation and constitution of experience – *showing by saying what one sees*' (Foucault, 1975: 196). The emergence of modern medical discourse and its anatomo-clinical method required that death and disease be removed from the metaphysics of evil and decay to be treated as material processes in the living bodies of mortal individuals. It was only by treating himself as morbid and as insane that modern man could create the two human sciences – medicine and psychology – that have individualised him by inscribing health and illness in a collective series and an homogeneous space. The reversal of human finitude with respect to the classical concept of universality occurred through the internalisation of the series of life and death. Clinical medicine is that positive science at the heart of the anthropological sciences which assigns a supreme value to individual life through its struggle with death. The latter struggle, however, is no longer based upon a romantic myth, to be found, for example, in Hegel's master and slave dialectic. Rather, our struggle to the death opens up an incarnate history armed with its own science inscribed upon our very flesh and tissue and in a language for which the positive phenomenology of the body is also predestined:

And, generally speaking, the experience of individuality in modern culture is bound up with that of *death*: from Hölderlin's Empedocles to Nietzsche's Zarathustra, and on to Freudian man, an obstinate relation to death prescribes to the universal its singular fall, and lends to each individual the power of being heard forever; the individual owes to death a meaning that does not cease with him. The division that it traces and the finitude whose mark it imposes link, paradoxically, the universality of language and the precarious, irreplaceable form of the individual. The sense-perceptible, which cannot be exhausted by description, and which so many centuries have wished to dissipate, finds at last in death the law of its discourse, it is death that fixes the stone that we can touch, the return of time, the fine, innocent earth beneath the grass of words.

(Foucault, 1975: 197)

The Preface to *The Birth of the Clinic* opens with the announcement that Foucault's book is about space, language, death and the medical gaze. We are immediately plunged into the body, into its intestines, into its brain, that is to say, into the dark interior of life brought to light through an optical shift whose articulation is absolutely tied to Foucault's combination of poetics and discourse analysis. Thus in the mid-eighteenth century Pomme's treatments of hysteria operated in terms of a conception of the membraneous tissue in the nervous system as a 'dry parchment' that could be steamed away, an operation that could be repeated on the intestines, the oesophagus and the trachea by means of hot baths taken for ten or twelve hours a day over ten months. A century later, Bayle's observations of an anatomical lesion of the brain remark upon 'false membranes', often transparent and of variegated colours over their surface which itself varies in depth from the thinness of a spider's web to the albuminous skin of an egg. The discourses of Pomme and Bayle are separated by a shift in the ratio of the visible and invisible interior of the body where light is thrown only in death, i.e., only through the *autopsy* which opened up a space where bodies and eyes could meet. The semantic shift between the two descriptions of the membraneous tissues did not involve a shift from a subjective to an objective medical discourse. Indeed, the discursive shift is barely perceptible unless we can ask a retrospective question concerning the articulation of words and things in order to discern the points at which their identity is broken, where their separation was amplified and then abandoned for a new plenitude of things and words:

In order to determine the moment at which the mutation in discourse took place, we must look beyond its thematic content or its logical modalities to the region where 'things' and 'words' have not yet been separated, and where – at the most fundamental level of language – seeing and saying are still one.... We must place ourselves, and remain once and for all, at the level of the fundamental *spatialization* and *verbalization* of the pathological, where the loquacious gaze with which the doctor observes the poisonous heart of things is borne and communes with itself.

(Foucault, 1975: xi–xii)

The rise of medical empiricism is not a matter of the construction of quantitative studies such as Meckel's proposal to correlate brain disorders with changes in the weight and volume of affected parts. Rather, it is due to the artisanal skill of the brain-breaker that the *medical gaze* owes its perception of the membraneous tissues, colours and texture of the brain. But the truths that come to light in this way differ entirely from those revealed under the *heliotropism* of earlier science. The latter grounded all perception in the prior light of ideality through which all appearances were rendered adequate to their essence. *The new empiricism sees in the darkness of things*; it introduces visibility into the invisible interiors of the body for whose description it must again apprentice words to things:

> At the end of the eighteenth century…seeing consists in leaving to experi-
> ence its greatest corporeal opacity; the solidity, the obscurity, the density
> of things closed in upon themselves, have powers of truth that they owe not
> to light, but to the slowness of the gaze that passes over them, around them,
> and gradually into them, bringing them nothing more than its own light. The
> residence of truth in the dark center of things is linked, paradoxically, to this
> sovereign power of *the empirical gaze* that turns their darkness into light.
>
> (Foucault, 1975: xiii)

It is the opening into the interior of the body, with the submission of its gaze to the irreducible qualities of the body's depths, that made possible a true science of the individual inscribed at the objective site of the surgery, or the hospital bed and clinic. Here a new perception of tissue, pathology and morbidity, based upon the subordination of disorders to the non-verbal, corporeal conditions of medical discourse, created for the first time a science of the individual under the sign of death. Thus the medical probe learned to locate in the living body what it had found in the corpse, recovering what it saw in 'the white brightness of death'. Visibility acquired its sovereignty only through death in which the body's truth was brought into a light from which in life it is always concealed. Immortality receded and life was extended as the host of death, revealing itself in the language of colours, consistency, texture and sound, as in Laënnec's description of a cirrhosis of the liver:

> The liver, reduced to a third of its volume, was, as it were, hidden in the region
> that it occupies; its external surface, slightly mamillated and emptied, was a
> yellowish grey in colour; when cut, it seemed to be made up entirely of a mass
> of small seeds, round or oval in shape, varying in size from a millet seed to
> a hemp seed. These seeds, which can easily be separated, left almost no gap
> between them in which one might be able to make out some remaining part of
> the real tissue of the liver; they were fawn or reddish-yellow in colour, verg-
> ing in parts on the greenish; their fairly moist, opaque tissue was slack, rather
> than soft, to the touch, and when one squeezed the grains between one's fin-
> gers only a small part was crushed, the rest feeling like a piece of soft leather.
>
> (Laënnec, 1819: 368;
> see Foucault, 1975: 169–70)

Here language and death conspire to express the individual case with a fidelity that had always escaped earlier medical perception based on Aristotelian metaphysics. Previously, death had appeared only in the guise of philosophy and art, i.e., as an obsession, even a certain eroticism of death. In the Renaissance, death danced upon all social differences, pronouncing an empty equality of individuals before its *memento mori*. Yet we can see in Montaigne's *Essays* a perception of the true singularity of the individual who lives with death in life towards death (O'Neill, 1982). This anticipation of the individualisation of death is fulfilled in the techniques of the clinic:

> The privilege of the consumptive: in earlier times, one contracted leprosy against a background of great waves of collective punishment; in the nineteenth century, a man, in becoming tubercular, in the fever that hastens things and betrays them, fulfils his incommunicable secret. That is why the chest diseases are exactly the same nature as diseases of love: they are the Passion, a Life to which death gives a face that cannot be exchanged. Death left its old tragic heaven and became the lyrical cave of man; his invisible truth, his visible secret.
>
> (Foucault, 1975: 171–72)

The diseases that inhabit the body, its lesions, fevers, allergies and viruses require that we revise the body's spaces, volumes, contents, and surfaces, imposing upon the living organism a geometry and history that has not always been fundamental. Thus the diagnostic discourse upon disease had to learn to shift from a medicine of species, in which the form of the disease could be abstracted from its contingent history in the individual body, to serial medicine, in which the historical progress of an individual disease is measured within a population whose collective history is known for certain because it is underwritten, so to speak, by the practice of *autopsy*:

> Through the introduction of probabilistic thought, medicine entirely renewed the *perceptual values* of its domain: the space in which the doctor's attention had to operate became an unlimited space, made up of isolatable events whose form of solidarity was of the order of the series. The simple dialectic of the pathological species and the sick individual, an enclosed space and an uncertain time, was, in principle, dislocated. Medicine no longer tried to see the essential truth beneath the sensible individuality; it was faced by the task of perceiving, and to infinity, the events of an open domain. This was the *clinic*.
>
> (Foucault, 1975: 97–98; my emphasis)

Thus the healthy body is a clinical body: it is known precisely because it is mortal and its death is the site of medical knowledge that can be employed in the promise of individual treatment. Similarly, the medicine of epidemics, of scrofula, smallpox, dysentery and the plague, of whooping cough, the measles and scarlet fever, had to shift attention to the course of an illness between bodies, requiring a combination of medical and police control in the provision of information, supervision and constraint. The *body politic* and the *medical gaze* were aligned in the *therapeutic state* and its discourses upon crime, disease, population (O'Neill, 1986). Public health and political economy became informed by a generalised medical gaze:

> The years preceding and immediately following the Revolution saw the birth of two great myths with opposing themes and polarities: *the myth of a nationalized medical profession*, organized like a clergy, and invested, at the level of man's bodily health, with powers similar to those exercised by the clergy over men's souls; and *the myth of a total disappearance of disease* in an untroubled, dispassionate society restored to its original state of health. But we must not be misled by the manifest contradiction of the two themes: each of these oneiric figures expresses, as if on black and white, the same picture of medical experience.
>
> (Foucault, 1975: 31–32)

The shift in medical discourse that separated pre- and post-eighteenth-century medicine occurred with the displacement of the concept of health and its classificatory procedures by the concept of morbidity or the distinction between normal and pathological processes grounded in anatomo-clinical knowledge. This shift was established with the 'defamilisation' of disease and the removal of its treatment to the hospital under the authority of the state and science. However, this transition was not a smooth one. As Foucault observes, the generalised freedom of the medical gaze was slower to enter the hospital than it might have been because it rested upon an Enlightenment vision without the requisite technology of the medical gaze which the clinic would later offer. Here the change involved the re-embodiment of the medical gaze, a reorganisation of the medical eye, ear and touch through the technique of auscultation – the art of listening once again to bodies, an art that is tactful, not straining to hear esoteric languages, an art that is direct and to the point. Through the stethoscope, the interior body opened to a new *triangulation of medical perception*:

> Thus armed, the medical gaze embraces more than is said by the word 'gaze' alone. It contains within a single structure different sensorial fields. The sight/touch/hearing trinity defines a perceptual configuration in which the inaccessible illness is tracked down by markers, gauged in depth, drawn to the surface, and projected virtually on the dispersed organs of the corpse. The 'glance' has become a complete organization with a view to a spatial assignation of the invisible. Each sense organ receives a partial instrumental function. And the eye certainly does not have the most important function; what can sight cover other than 'the tissue of the skin and the beginning of the membranes'? Through touch we can locate visceral tumors, scirrhous masses, swelling of the ovary, and dilations of the heart;

while with the ear we can perceive 'the crepitation of fragments of bone, the rumbling of aneurism, the more or less clear sounds of the thorax and the abdomen when sounded'. *The medical gaze is now endowed with a plurisensorial structure.* A gaze that touches, hears, and, moreover, not by essence or necessity, sees.

(Foucault, 1975: 164; my emphasis)

Modern medicine announces itself with the abandonment of the nosological model of disease: life is regarded as the permanent host of diseases travelling through communicable tissues, feeding on them, until their course is run, as life moves towards a death that has always marked it. Once the medical gaze comes to view life from its endpoint in death, as it does by means of the techniques of autopsy, then the dark interiors of the body become the true source of medical enlightenment:

Life, disease and death now form a technical and conceptual trinity.... Death is the great analyst that shows the connections by unfolding them, and bursts upon the wonders of genesis in the rigor of decomposition: and the word *decomposition* must be allowed to stagger under the weight of its meaning. Analysis, the philosophy of elements and their laws, meets its death in what it had vainly sought in mathematics, chemistry, and even language; it is on this great example that the medical gaze will now rest. It is no longer that of a living eye, but the gaze of an eye that has seen death – a great white eye that unties the knot of life.

(Foucault, 2002: 144)

Foucault's archaeology of the clinic does its digging in that strange light with which medicine has illuminated the interior of the body. It is a light, and not a darkness, that is cast by death. It is the same light that opens up language to a new fidelity in the relation between the visible and the discursive orders of experience. Henceforth, humanity no longer sighs for the revelation of Death; it no longer waits for the redemption of the body's suffering through the broken body of Christ and His glorious resurrection. Once the human corpse is opened to the medical gaze, Christ's tomb is emptied for ever and men begin to live with a new trinity. Truth manifests itself in the discursive space of the corpse, refiguring language and death in the acceptance of man's finitude and his fundamental bond with life and death released from the metaphysics of evil and suffering. Whether or not man can ever rediscover a higher life, or an abundant economy, or a translucent language, one thing is certain. It is that 'man' has acquired a *body* that is neither animal nor angel – whose discursive elaboration is the glory and the hope of the modern age:

But to man's experience a *body* has been given, a body which is his body – a fragment of ambiguous space, whose peculiar and irreducible spatiality is nevertheless articulated upon things; to this same experience, *desire* is given as a primordial appetite on the basis of which all things assume a value, and relative value; to this same experience, a *language* is given in the thread of which all the discourses of all times, all successions and all simultaneities may be given. This is to say that each of these positive forms in which man can learn that he is finite is given to him only against the background of his own *finitude*...

(Foucault, 1973: 314)

The human body is the ground of all repetition; every positive difference of health, labour and language thrives against the background of the same death that inhabits each of us and of the same desire and the same expression that exceeds every one of our usages that we nevertheless seek to appropriate for ourselves. The inextricable tie between the transcendental and the empirical, between the *cogito* and the unthought, between the retreat and the return of origins – that is, analytic of man's finitude, rests upon the body we are and its sciences (O'Neill, 1989). This limit of embodiment has, of course, always been part of human experience. Illness, poverty and passion have always served to give man a sense that infinity lies beyond him. In the Classical age, man's limits could be expressed within the framework of a metaphysics of infinity which provided the impulse for an increase of knowledge, life and wealth. It was only when the analytic of finitude shifted the productivity of life, labour and language into the interiorised values of a finite being whose history and institutions ground themselves in the body that the modern age of man truly began and that Renaissance humanism and Classical rationalism receded:

> modernity begins when the human being begins to exist within his organism, inside the shell of his head, inside the armature of his limbs, and in the whole structure of his physiology; when he begins to exist at the center of a labor by whose principles he is governed and whose product eludes him; when he lodges his thought in the folds of a language so much older than himself that he cannot master its significations, even though they have been called back to life by the insistence of his words.
>
> (Foucault, 1973: 318)

Henceforth knowledge is tied to a conception of man whose *nature* and *history* is the condition of all knowledge such that truth can no longer anticipate its own operation but must be discerned by an embodied perception exemplified in the clinical gaze. The latter optic opens up the field of empirical facts at the same time that it is the historical form of the possibility of man's appearance to himself in grounded descriptions. The humility – groundedness, mortality, earth – of the post-Cartesian *Cogito* is the best achievement of Husserlian phenomenology and it constitutes the necessary link between phenomenology and the positive human sciences exemplified in Foucault's own genealogical studies. Henceforth, man labours in the shadow of his Other, that is, of every form of his being that is not irradiated by a perfectly translucent language; in the shadows of the unconscious, of the inert, of the alienated labour of mind and body. It is this contestation that constitutes an *ethics of modernity*. But in this instance what is involved is the inescapable morality of knowledge that controls everything that separates man from himself but without any external measure of man's identity other than what his historical struggles open up in the sedimentations of life, language and labour, pushing man's origins ever further behind him and only gradually and painfully opening him up to his own emergence. This ethical struggle is motivated by the attempt to align the chronology of things with human time, or rather to subordinate the time of things to the time of man's humanity, to his desire to become human which has shone over the world like a star whose bright life is not lived for ever but between two deaths.

We can no longer posit any continuity between the two discourses of the classical and modern ages. The copula of being and language in the modern age derives from a discursive will to constitute orders of language and power that oscillate between origins and end, or between foundations and history. Because of the rift between language and being, a pressure arises to cross the gap with an anthropology which would again renew the project of a general critique of reason. But such an anthropological project comes too late. The double death of God and Man announced by Nietzsche means that we can only think of man as anthropologically extinct. Only then are we aroused from the 'anthropological sleep' which we have considered our most vigilant state:

> Thus, the last man is at the same time older and yet younger than the death of God; since he has killed God, it is he himself who must answer for his own finitude, but since it is in the death of God that he speaks, thinks, and exists, his murder itself is doomed to die; new gods, the same gods, are already swelling the future Ocean; man will disappear.
>
> (Foucault, 1973: 385)

What dies when man announces the death of God is the end of infinity as that to which man approximates or rather as a thought of himself that is supervenient to his own forces. Henceforth, man conceives of himself as a force within a field of forces composed by language, labour and life-processes in which he achieves subject-status only on the basis of object-status in the specific sciences that constitute his self-knowledge. Man's loss of a divine hinge, so to speak, does not leave him to free-fall in a vortex of forces of which perhaps the most dangerous are his own instincts for domination and evil. Or such is our finite faith. Man is a precarious form as long as he is dependent upon the divine infinitude. But once death, desire and meaning are appropriated in man's own corporeal history as co-extensive historicisations of man's being (*Menschsein*), then it is possible that we shall assume responsibility for the refiguration of our humanity. Meantime, Foucault's commentaries turn in a discursive space punctuated by the black holes in his own extraordinary poetics whose vision still invites further exploration.

References

Deleuze, Gilles (1986). *Annexe: sur la mort de l'homme*. Foucault. Paris: Éditions de Minuit.

Foucault, Michel (1973). *The Order of Things: An Archaeology of the Human Sciences*. A. M. Sherdan Smith (trans.). New York: Vintage Books.

Foucault, Michel (1975). *The Birth of the Clinic: The Archaeology of Medical Perception*. A. M. Sherdan Smith (trans.). New York: Vintage Books.

Foucault, Michel (2002). *The Birth of the Clinic: The Archaeology of Medical Perception*. A. M. Sherdan Smith (trans.) New York: Routledge.

Laënnec, René T. H. (1819). *Traité de l'auscultation médiate*, Vol. I. Paris: Brosson & Chaudé.

Merleau-Ponty, Maurice (1968). *The Visible and the Invisible: Followed by Working Notes*. Claude Lefort (ed.). Alphonso Lingis (trans.). Evanston, IL: Northwestern University Press.

O'Neill, John (1982). 'On living and dying as we do'. In: *Essaying Montaigne: A Study of the Renaissance Institution of Writing and Reading*. London: Routledge.

O'Neill, John (1986a). 'Sociological nemesis: Parsons and Foucault on the therapeutic disciplines'. In: *Sociological Theory in Transition*. Stephen P. Turner (ed.). Boston, MA: Allen & Unwin, pp. 21–36.

O'Neill, John (1986b). *The Communicative Body: Studies in Communication, Philosophy, Politics and Sociology*. Evanston, IL: Northwestern University Press.

O'Neill, John (1989). 'Religion and postmodernism: The Durkheimian bond in Bell and Jameson—With an allegory of the body politic'. In: *Postmodernism/Jameson/Critique*. Douglas Kellner (ed.). Washington, DC: Maisonneuve Press, pp. 139–161.

O'Neill, John (1990). 'Postmodernism and (Post) Marxism'. In: *Postmodernism, Philosophy, and the Arts*. Hugh J. Silverman (ed.). New York: Routledge, pp. 69–82.

2   The specular body*

Merleau-Ponty and Lacan on infant self and other

It would appear to be an ordinary academic task to compare the views of Lacan and Merleau-Ponty on the mirror image. Both writers are intrinsically interesting; their views are original and worth the difficulties one might experience in trying to understand them. Having said this, however, it is necessary to caution against the hope that one can introduce anything like a common terminology to rule the exercise of comparison and evaluation. Nothing of the sort exists for studies in child psychology, psychoanalysis, or phenomenology. We are, therefore, obliged to 'misread' (Bloom, 1973) our authors as responsibly as we can. There seems to be no general usage in the literature for the concept of body image or of the uses of the mirror image. Seymour Fisher (1970) and Fisher and Cleveland (1968) virtually ignore phenomenological and psychoanalytical usage in their vast series of quantitative psychological studies. Fisher, Gorman, (1969) and Shontz (1969) make reference to Schilder (1950), as does Merleau-Ponty (1962). But neither Merleau-Ponty nor Lacan finds any important place in the literature. The phenomenological and psychoanalytical interpretation of the body image and the mirror stage, although itself not ignorant of experimental literature, seems to fall outside contemporary experimental psychology. Lacan's *stade du miroir* involves a revised psychoanalytical reading of psychological and biological data concerning the infant period from six to eighteen months (Lacan, 1970). Of course, at the time Freud was hardly available to French readers, and so we must realize that to a large extent we are dealing with Lacan's retrospective revisionism. But in view of the multiple discourses involved, and the casual practices of cross-reference, nothing is to be gained from trying to coordinate concepts and theory. This is, to be sure, a venerable academic exercise (Laplanche and Pontalis, 1973), but it misses the life of science. In practice, each theorist is likely to try to win over everyone to his distinctive discourse rather than try to subordinate himself to a lingua franca. Beyond that, the normal scientists will generally stay behind their chosen leader, defending, patching, and repairing his usage.

---

* Text of this essay taken from *The Communicative Body: Studies in Communicative Philosophy, Politics and Sociology* (1989). Evanston: Northwestern University Press. Pages 58–73. Reprinted with permission.

1.

Merleau-Ponty's (1964a, 1964b) treatment of the mirror image consists of an extensive commentary on the work of Wallon (1949). In the course of his critical evaluation of Wallon, he draws upon Lacan's views. The question we have to decide is whether the Lacanian view of the body image at the mirror stage is really as compatible with Merleau-Ponty's phenomenology of the infant's corporeal schema as he himself takes it to be. In short, as Dillon (1978) has observed, we need to be careful with the 'visual bias' in the specular image, and we shall have to see whether in fact it faults Merleau-Ponty's better understanding of the mother-infant bond. A similar caution has been raised by Henri Ey, who considers the infant's intersubjective experience of embodiment prior to the visual moment of self-knowledge at the mirror:

> On one level what has so often been repeated to us is true, that the self and the 'body image' become confused with one another. Though this is certainly not true for the self which has unfolded in its history, it is true for the 'I' appearing in its prehistory. This body among other objects is mine. It is in effect the proto-experience of the subject in its own space. It is as a spatial modality of a spatial property that the self perceives itself as an object in its first self-consciousness. This is the reason for the importance of the 'mirror stage'. It would doubtlessly be naive to pretend that in order for the self to become conscious for itself it would be enough for it to 'see itself' or to perceive itself in the reflected image of its body. This is true precisely because the self cannot see itself unless it knows itself. We should instead understand the necessity of the reflection of the self upon itself as the absolute of a fundamental structure: that of the relationship of the self to others. To see oneself appear 'as other' which is the self, the mirror image of which sends back its image to myself, is the objectification of the self, or as is often said, as its 'alienation'. The self appears as a person opposite oneself, in the eclipsing of the subject, in its 'fading' (Lacan's term), and, as it were, in its disappearance. The self is grounded in and through this negation of its absolute.
>
> (Ey, 1966: 27)

According to Lacan, the acquisition of subjectivity is achieved only at the level of language, or in the symbolic order. This stage is reached on the basis of two prior moments: (1) *the mirror phase* and (2) through the relationships experienced as *the castration complex*. The first stage of 'I' constitution occurs in the infant's confrontation with his mirror image, or with the experience of a unified body image that is both present and absent. In its wholeness, however, the unified body image projects for the infant an ideal of integrity that his own bodily experience of taste, smell, and motor relations toward things has yet to achieve. To this imaginary wholeness the infant adopts a narcissistic attitude, caught up in the split between self-presence and self-absence.

Lacan treats the infant's grasp of his total body form in the mirror image as an event that is entirely premature and as the prefiguration, so to speak, of an alienated destination:

> The *mirror stage* is a drama whose internal thrust is precipitated from insufficiency to anticipation and which manufactures for the subject, caught up in the lure of spatial identification, the succession of fantasies that extends from a fragmented body-image to a form of its totality that I shall call orthopaedic and, lastly, to the assumption of an armour of an alienating identity, which will mark with its rigid structure the subject's entire mental development. Thus, to break out of the circle of the *Innenwelt* into the *Umwelt* generates the inexhaustible quadrature of the ego's verification.
>
> (Lacan, 1966: 97)

Thus the mirror image, as Lacan interprets it, constitutes a prospective-retrospective complex of identity and separation that prefigures all later separations, from weaning to castration. The ego is constituted in imaginary servitude for which the love of others is always an intrusion upon the madness of the self project. It is beyond the scope of this argument to trace Lacan's account of the oedipal triangulation of the infant's desire for his mother as the primordial real object and his father as an imaginary ideal self. Thus in-the-name-of-the-father the mother weans her infant on to desire, that is, the discovery of absence, or lack ruled by law. A point of controversy is whether we consider the infant to be a 'body in bits and pieces' (*corps morcelé*) prior to the mirror stage. On this interpretation, the event of the mirror image offers to the broken body an ideal of integration and harmony, an ideal self, *Idealich*. I shall argue instead that the mother's face is the original reflecting mirror of what in the eyes of her infant she sees as the bond that, because it is not yet ready for separation, is unquestioned (Winnicott, 1967). The 'Madonna' thereby constitutes a presence that can become an absence, a plenitude that can be symbolized in the separation and embrace of the other in the endless negativity or play (*jeu*) of discourse.

2.

It must be remembered that the *Phenomenology of Perception* argues that both the body and the mind are structures of experience in their own right. In particular, then, the mind, so far from making sense of the body, itself trades upon a preconceptual carnal knowledge of worldly relations within which self, things, and others are articulated in a mode of 'reciprocity', for which 'intelligence' is only another name. The body is our fundamental yet contingent (that is, mortal and pathological) relation to the world that funds symbolic consciousness, habit, and reflexivity (Zaner, 1964, 1981). Man's senses and intelligence are ways of being in the world rather than outside it, however much of this is suggested by idealist and empiricist accounts. According to Merleau-Ponty, all individuality and every specific sociality presuppose an *anonymous intersubjectivity* that is the ground of our figural relations with things and persons in-and-as-our-world. This lived-world is ours through the lived-body; it rests on a perceptual faith that is prior to conceptual articulation. It is our primordial presence to a human milieu that inaugurates all other specific relations, experiences, and temporal expressions of our being-in-the-world. This lived-world is prior to the known-world and is coevally populated with others who as kindred bodies share the same lived-world as I do. This is our perceptual faith and not at all a contingent achievement of reasoned argument, despite the conceits of the Cartesian ego or of the Kantian imperative.

The articulation of the infant's world likewise presupposes this funding of anonymous intersubjectivity. We shall otherwise misconstrue the infant's developmental stages as a continuous fall from intersubjectivity, or else as a yearning for a future incorporation as fantastic as its first loss. Before a mirror, the infant believes both that he is in the mirror and that he sees himself therein from where he stands. Thus he has not yet constructed a mirror image distinct from himself; he dwells in an *interworld* in which he has not yet articulated either his own 'egological' perspective or yet a sociological orientation toward the other in his propriety. Yet it is only from this ground of anonymous intersubjectivity – not yet ego, not yet alter – that he can experience the generics of a bodily and personal self in a world similarly incorporated. At the same time, this primordial intersubjectivity grounds all later perception, desire, identity, and alterity in the faith that the individual can be valorized for himself by another who in turn shares similar expectation of mutual recognition.

The structure of identity, according to Merleau-Ponty, is a *psychophysical* posture that arises within the field of intersubjectivity, within the familial field, disposing the infant toward self-knowledge and social understanding. The structure of comportment that will generate identity and sociality is not a field of drives and instincts. It is rather a mode of experiencing biopsychic and sociopsychic relations charged with individualizing and 'familizing' significance, that is, with situationally specific desires, loves, hates, and fears projected by the infant upon the social body. Thus the infant body and psyche are reciprocal modes of existence and not at all instrumental functions whose integration or hierarchization would require a further function. Each is given in the primordial intersubjectivity of anonymous being, of the life one has before the life one thinks, feels, and lives with specific others.

Merleau-Ponty is concerned to modify the cognitivist approach to the mirror image and the infant's approach to space, self, and other relations. From this standpoint, and given the basic assumption of psychology that the psyche is accessible only to its owner, the problem of intersubjective experience involves the following quadrature:

> The problem of the experience of others poses itself, as it were, in a system of four terms: (1) myself, my 'psyche'; (2) the image I have of my body by means of the sense of touch or of cenesthesia, which, to be brief, we shall call the 'introceptive image' of my own body; (3) the body of the other as seen by me, which we shall call the 'visual body'; and (4) a fourth (hypothetical) term

which I must reconstitute and guess at the 'psyche' of the other, the other's feeling of his own existence, to the extent that I can imagine or suppose it across the appearances of the other through his visual body.

(Merleau-Ponty, 1964: 115)

The cognitive troubles of this approach are evident. The 'monodological' psyche, once assumed, is embroiled in an exhausting guessing game with regard to the relation between inside and outside experiences of the other projected on the basis of his own trust in his own correlations of inside-outside experience. But in practice the infant short-circuits this game of correspondences with a global body overlap, as when the infant responds to a smiling face with his own smile. Here no judgment is involved, no point-to-point correspondence, since the infant cannot see his own face, except in the eyes of his mother. What he 'sees' there is not a reflection so much as a gesture that provokes a gesture 'within' or from him. This means, however, that the infant's body is not solidary with its own sensations. Its sensations are rather gestures that flow from a 'postural' or '*corporeal schema*', the ability to respond to the situated conduct of others with the very conduct elicited in situ and as the embodied sense of interaction.

The infant's corporeal consciousness is at first fragmentary and fixated on parts of the body (feet, mouth, and hands), in himself, and in others. As yet, the infant self is latent and submerged in an overlap with the maternal body: *une vie à deux*. The necessary separation of the infant and maternal bodies may be conceived from the very start as a precipitation of self and not-self in every motor and sensory behaviour, involving social mediations and possibly a critical moment such as the mirror stage. The latter, in turn, may be seen as critical to a series of later maturational crises, in particular those of weaning and castration. In every case, there is surely a neurophysiological infrastructure, and Merleau-Ponty refers to the function of myelinization in connecting the 'introceptive' and 'extroceptive' body functions.

After a very close reading of Wallon's account of the specular image, Merleau-Ponty concludes that the problem it poses from the cognitive bias of the adult – namely, how to reduce the mirror image to a mere reflection – should be distinguished from the child's acquisition of a self-image that remains of interest throughout his life. In other words, the mirror image is transvalued into a corporeal conduct in which reality and appearance are occasioned distinctions. Thus the specular image functions to raise the visual body into a sociopsychological space in which the infant continues to explore self and other relations. In psychoanalytic terms, the specular image is the basis for a superego. Sociologically, the looking-glass self is the basis for life among others. (Cooley, 1964; Goffman, 1967; Mead, 1967; O'Neill, 1973) The mirror image, then, prefigures the jubilation of the child's narcissistic self as well as the sorrows and pain of life among others to whom the infant has access only through the lack recognized in him by others. As Merleau-Ponty expresses it in a gloss on Lacan:

From this moment on, the child is also drawn from his immediate reality: the specular image has a de-realizing function in the sense that it turns the child away from what he effectively is, in order to orient him toward what he sees and imagines himself to be. Finally, this alienation of the immediate me, its 'confiscation' for the benefit of the me that is visible in the mirror already outlines what will be the 'confiscation' of the subject by the others who look at him.

(Merleau-Ponty, 2007: 166)

3.

The process of identification involves a double structuration of identifying something or someone and identifying one's self in the same course of interaction. Thus *identification* may be said to include a double process of *introjection*, bringing another into the self, and *projection*, bringing the self into another. The mother-infant relation is the primordial relation of identification in this double sense. It is, however, a genetic relation from conception, to embryo, to infant and later child years, if not throughout one's life. It is perhaps best to speak of a relation of *projective pre-identification* in recalling the infant's most early experience of the mother's womb, face, voice, and hands, and of introjective pre-identification in the feeding experience at the breast. This, too, is the stage at which the infant's musculature and coordination are relatively undeveloped and he is submerged in visceral and emotional experiences of the human world. It should not be overlooked that with respect to the issue of the emergence of ego identification as the necessary boundary implied by the mechanisms of projection and introjection, Freud appears to have had in mind a body-ego, a cutaneous surface upon which the subject can explore insides and outsides, part and whole, pleasure and pain. Thus, according to Laplanche, Freud derived the ego from a double source:

> On the one hand, the ego is the surface of the psychical apparatus, gradually differentiated in and from that apparatus, a specialized organ continuous with it; on the other hand, it is the projection of metaphor of the body's surface, a metaphor in which the various perceptual systems have a role to play.
>
> (Laplanche, 1976: 82)

With each passing month, the infant's motor and perceptual comportment achieves increasing articulation and thereby engages a claim upon identity and character whose linguistic and socially organized achievement at this stage is closely bound to the pronominal and oedipal systems. In other words, the infant embarks upon an anthropomorphosis that involves mutually articulated levels of structuration that are:

1. motor-perceptual
2. psychosocial
3. linguistic-conceptual

However, the phenomenological interpretation of these levels is radically different from what we find in textbook psychology and psychoanalysis. At the motor-
perceptual level, we are not dealing with mechanical drives, pushes, and pulls, nor
with instincts. Rather, we are in the presence of a physical *posture* that is capable
of empathizing immediately and nonverbally with the other's postural attitude,
as though each were a physical sketch of the other. Thus mutual co-orientation is
struck intuitively in-and-as the setting of any further articulation of co-presence.
It involves a pre-knowledge that is prior to explicitly imitative behaviour that is a
later phase of infant intersubjectivity. Even in the latter case, what is involved is
a psycho-muscular response, rather like that of a conductor whose bodily movements reproduce the orchestra's efforts without imitating them. Literal imitation
of persons constitutes a hostile social gesture, a potential degradation rather than
communion. At this level, introjection involves a mutual coordination of bodies,
a postural agreement that under-writes being-together, upon which talk, thought,
and other conducts can be articulated. Understood in this way, introjection is the
other side of a projective comportment in which we bring our own posture within
another's pastural schema in order to articulate further communion (Goodwin,
1981). Taken together, these introjective and projective postures cast us in a psycho-muscular, or motor-perceptual, field of the corporeal presence of ourselves
to others and of the self to itself. Thus, there can be nothing inert or inexpressive
about the lived-body, not even in sleep. The existence of another human being is
reciprocal with my own existence.

It is this norm of reciprocity that is further articulated at the psychosocial and
linguistic-conceptual levels of anthropogenesis. Here language and the oedipal myth are the primordial sociolinguistic structurations of identity. The postural identification we have described lies at the basis of later child and adult
dramaturgical identification with other human senses, emotions, and events into
which he can be drawn 'conaturally', as it were. Here, again, the neutral observer
standpoint of the sciences trades upon a postural involvement that is preconceptual but nevertheless funds all participant and quasi-neutral observation. Thus we
relive human dramas, identify with their personages, not because we know the
lines but because corporeally we are the text in which life's lines are inscribed
from earliest infancy.[1] In this sense, we live our lives through others before ourselves and only with difficulty, as Montaigne observes, do we learn to preserve
for ourselves a 'backstage'.

4.

Dillon has argued that Merleau-Ponty mistimes the correlation of self and other
recognition at the mirror stage. The infant cannot handle the recognition that he
is an object for others at the same time as he struggles with the recognition of
himself as an object for himself. This is because he has not yet freed himself
from syncretic sociability. But to do so, Dillon argues, requires much more than
a visual experience. This is because the phenomenal body is a synesthetic whole

of affective and conative behaviour sensitive to the rejecting, weaning, and punishing behaviour of others. It is from these experiences rather than the mirror image as such that the infant learns self and other relations as *alienative* modes of being-in-the-world.

It is not easy to decide this argument on purely textual grounds. I think, therefore, that it may be pertinent to introduce further data upon the infant-mother relationship in order to contextualize the experiences attributed to the specular image. Thus Winnicott has argued for an intermediate developmental stage between the infant's inability and increasing ability to distinguish 'not-me' objects. This occurs in the first few months as the infant moves from fist-to-mouth exploration onto some favoured object, blanket, or teddy bear. He calls the shift from oral eroticism to object relations and the attendant babbling 'transitional phenomena'. Although the teddy bear or favourite blanket is clearly a partial object (the mother's breast), it is just as important that it is not the breast. Hence the symbolic value of the transitional object demonstrates that the infant is already exploring similarity and difference, and so moving from magical control to reality testing (Stack Sullivan, 1953: 100). The mother's cooperation in this transition is absolutely vital. In Winnicott's terms, the 'good-enough' mother must lead her baby into abandoning the magical omnipotence with which she at first conspired. Precisely because she has sustained the infant's early illusion, she can then successfully 'disillusion' the infant in the transition to reality testing. In other words, weaning can only be successful if the question it eventually resolves is not posed from the very start: that is, what is the thing in the outside world that might match my inside world?

> The transitional object and the transitional phenomena start each human being off with what will always be important for them, i.e., a neutral area of experience which will not be challenged. *Of the transitional object it can be said that it is a matter of agreement between us and the baby that we will never ask the question: 'Did you conceive of this or was it presented to you from without?' The important point is that no decision on this point is to be expected. The question is not to be formulated.*
>
> (Winnicott, 1971: 12)

It is this provision that enables the infant to deal with the loss of omnipotence. Through the transitional object the infant creates an objective environment. The good-enough mother at first allows the infant to experience a sense of being, that is, the lack of any need to question the boundary between the breast and the infant. Thereafter, the drive satisfactions within the infant and the mother's independence, alternative commitments, and need to be elsewhere involve the infant in coming to terms with the boundary between inside and outside worlds and the exploration of object relations and uses. This is achieved in what Winnicott calls a 'potential space', the place where we come to live and play:

> I refer to the hypothetical area that exists (but cannot exist) between the baby and the object (mother or part of mother) during the phase of the

repudiation of the object as not-me, that is, at the end of being merged in with the object. From a state of being merged in with the mother the baby is at a stage of separating out the mother from the self, and the mother is lowering the degree of her adaptation to the baby's needs (both because of her own recovery from a high degree of identification with her baby and because of her perception of the baby's new need, the need for her to be a separate phenomenon).

(Winnicott, 1971: 107)

Bettelheim (1967) also stresses the infant's experiences at the breast as the basic source of trust in self and other persons. In the mutual give-and-take between infant and mother each educates the other in the articulation of the fundamental human bond. The mutuality of the infant and nursing mother sets the stage for all later intersubjective relations. It establishes the 'potential space' in which the infant creatively explores the transition to the world of not-me, of things and others, the world in which the infant self separated from its mother will learn what it can do on its own.

As I see it, prior to the games of *Fort! Da!* (Freud, 1974) and the great oedipal drama, the mother and infant bodies work between them to construct a potential space in which the events of identity and separation can be further articulated within the domains of language and the family. This space is celebrated in every Madonna and Child. It is recreated in the faces of every mother and infant mirroring each other, and by each of us in a lifelong personal reflection. The infant becomes more human, we might say, when it begins to be able to provoke desire rather than be subject to it. But this means that the infant begins to master the alternation of presence and absence in the light of his relations to his immediate family in which he first experiences the self and not-self. That is to say, as we have seen, that the mother-infant couple is the ground for the foregrounding-backgrounding of presence and absence vocalized in the infant's game of *Fort! Da!* Freud's observations can, I think, be repeated in the game of peek-a-boo. The infant's delight in hiding increases with every confession of the father that he can't find those toes sticking out from behind the curtains or that he can't hear the shrieks of laughter when he fails to see the little thing hidden before his eyes. The pleasure of peek-a-boo reaches a crescendo when the infant begins to fear that he may have hidden himself too well and be lost! At this point, the infant finds himself for his daddy: I'm here, daddy, I'm here! One can think of other infant experiences with the mediation of object and person relationships. For example, the same circuit of desire and recognition is involved in the infant's first steps toward the parent, trusting to be caught in a fall, or trusting to be caught when tossed by the parent, who thereby restores the risked body. By the very same token, by his body, the infant has learned to integrate his fear of disintegration in the social relations that continuously proffer sustenance and separation. I am suggesting, then, that we ought to think of the *stade du miroir* as a series of experiences that articulate the self-other circuit before language and before oedipal society. This is compatible with Lacan's own usage:

The jubilant assumption of his specular image by the child at his *infans stage*, still sunk in his motor incapacity and nursing dependence, would seem to exhibit in an exemplary situation the symbolic matrix in which the I is precipitated in a primordial form, before it is objectified in the dialectic of identification with the other, and before language restores to it, in the universal, its function as a subject.

(Lacan, 1970: 2)

5.

I think it is important for a phenomenological analysis not to fall into a narrow psychosexual schematization of the body image. We need to consider the body image as a synthesis of physiological and psychological organization heavily mediated by family relations. In its early months the infant's bodily experiences of food, hunger, warmth, cold, pleasure, pain, and gravitational swings are beyond his control. Simultaneously, he has to explore this world, to solicit support in it and continuous reassurance of love and care. His whole body communicates with the mother, who is the most immediate source and register of his experiments with her and his probes into the outer world. At the same time, the infant explores his mother's body as well as his own and must also acquire a sense of the consistency, size, weight, and texture of all of the bodies that make up his environment. Security and gratification alternate with fear and displeasure in the course of these bodily probes. Adult attitudes will be vital in the mediation of the infant's bodily inquiry, heightening and reassuring its positive experiences, rescuing and removing from painful encounters. Of course, the parent may also be an ambivalent participant, discouraging and disappointing the infantile inquiry. All this registers in the infant's posture and movements associated with the face, mouth, eyes, fingers, toes, and body arching. Thus the infant's search for security is not to be equated with passivity. On the contrary, security underwrites the infant's mobility, grasping, rhythm, gurgling, and play. These in turn will underwrite his efforts to achieve upright posture, to walk, and to climb, despite falls. The infant who begins with a strong attachment to his mother, seeking, grasping, and clinging, will simultaneously explore the distance between himself and his mother, continuously widening the circle of her watchful care until he can enter and leave it without fear. Considered in this fashion, then, there is a constant interplay among the infant's achievement of psychosomatic integration, security, and social separation.

For these reasons, Schilder argues that the infant fears for its whole body, for its insides, its orifices, and its outsides, and not just for its sexual organs. Thus in the psychoanalytic literature the notion of the castration complex has been widened to include any separation experience, such as birth and weaning (the child's experience of divorce?). Schilder's view, however, is that the integrity of the body image remains central to infant development:

It is perfectly true that there is something in common in all infringements on the integrity of the body, but the body is more than just an annex to the sex parts. It has a definite value in itself, and it is arbitrary to view the integrity of the body merely as an aspect to the integrity of the sex parts....I prefer to speak about the wish for the integrity of the body and the fear of being dismembered.

(Schilder, 1950: 80)

Empirical studies of the infant's response to the mirror image report a variety of self-conscious behaviour from embarrassment to coyness, delight, and suspicion. It appears then, that the mirror stage should be regarded as a continuous and multilevel experience, rather than as a climactic moment. Thus we might distinguish in the mirror experience the (1) beginning of awareness of oneself, (2) awareness of oneself as distinct from others, (3) awareness of oneself as seen by others, (4) affective self-consciousness allied to shame and social embarrassment (Kramer Amsterdam and Levitt, 1980). These experiences are related to kinesthetic and sensory feelings in the infant body during its first year of life. In the second year, the infant-self-conscious seems to acquire a representation level that permits it (1) to treat its own body as an object, (2) to struggle toward upright posture and locomotion, and (3) to direct its attention toward its own genitals. Thus the infant body, its orifices and erogeneous zones, becomes the focus of self-consciousness and its social counterpart in shame and embarrassment.

Infantile narcissism, therefore, cannot be restricted to the passive mirror image; the infant's delight there merely foreshadows his later joy in walking and climbing, even with its pitfalls. Thus Erikson (1963) has developed a theory of pre-genital body zones and stages infested with infantile libido that enhances the oral, anal, and limb movements. Each of these zones at a specific stage is the site of a changing pattern of mutual regulation between the infant and mother. Erikson first identifies an oral-respiratory-sensory stage in which the incorporative mode is dominant, including spitting up and nuzzling. This is not a passive stage. Rather, the infant, in learning to get someone to meet his needs, learns also to become a giver. In the next stage, with the appearance of teeth, the infant can bite on, off, and through things, as well as take, grasp, and hold on to things. At this stage, the infant's sense of trust and mistrust is tested; he may have teething problems, and weaning is imminent. The potential troubles of intake and release, therefore, are heightened around the anal zone inasmuch as the familial concern with retention and elimination is highly focused, at least in Western society. Finally (or as far as we shall go here), once the infant can sit squarely and achieve some locomotion, he is even more able to test his relations to things and others and thereby to himself. At each level, stress can be relieved or relived through regression to thumb sucking, crying, tantrums, and teddy bears.

From Melanie Klein (1932) we also learn that the processes of introjection and projection involve a continuous exchange of unconscious fantasies that enrich the infant's inner world and improve his relations with the external world. A specific mechanism engaged in this exchange is the process of 'splitting' whereby the dependent infant separates the good aspects of its mother from the bad or damaging aspects of its dependency upon her presence, breast, milk, smile. The bad aspects, absence, withholding, irritability, are then managed through projective identification. They are located in another person with whom the infant then identifies in order to protect the good mother from himself. What is fundamental in these processes is that they are set in the flesh, so to speak, of the mother-infant body. Their goodness and badness, their successes and failures are then translated into traces at each higher level of biopsychological self-awareness and relationship. The vital role of the mother's body is that its presence to the infant be 'good enough', as Winnicott says, not to raise prematurely the question of separation from the mother. Thereafter, she may initiate the infant into its own search for separation, without thereby prolonging the trauma of birth.

I also think we should set aside the notion of passivity of the infant in its relation to the mother as part of the retrospective myth of plenitude. Even in the womb the embryo is active and the activity increases until the crescendo of birth. Thereafter, of course, the infant responds to auditory and tactile stimuli, as well as to taste and smell. Visual stimuli increase, and the infant's body becomes at once the source of interior sensations and a perceptual object, at least partially, as a finger or toe. At this stage, then, sensation and perception are relativized, as we subjectivize experience and the external world. If anything, the value of the infant's milieu will be determined by its bodily sensations rather than perceptions of external reality, and its contact with the latter will also be mediated by those larger human bodies that solicit, interpret, and requite the infant's wants. At this stage, infant libido remains with the body but will develop beyond this primitive narcissistic level as the oral, anal, and genital levels of experience are organized and, so to speak, familized. Thus the libidinal body is psychologically and sociologically organized to shift pre-oedipal infantile sexuality into a secondary narcissism founded upon a family mediated ego ideal.

The infant's response to others as potentially helpful or harmful is *quasi-postural*. By the same token, it is not a constructed or conceptual attitude. It is a corporeal response to a lived social situation. Moreover, the infant is responsive to this social milieu more directly than to his physical milieu (Guillaume, 1969: 152–53; Elkin, 1972). Indeed, he seeks access to the latter through his social world long before he learns to interact directly with his physical world. In this 'parasitic' stage, psychological reality pervades the infant's body so that it seems to resonate pure pleasure and pain in its successes and failures with others and their mediation of the things he seeks. Indeed, the infant appears to be a natural social psychologist, moving the adult world around him, delighting and disappointing it according to the infant's register of smiles and cries. It is to free themselves from this helpless tyrant that parents begin to impute motive, reason, cause, and insight to the infant in their exchanges with him. In this way, they are able to draw the infant into a contract from which they can responsibly withdraw. Thus the pre-physical and pre-social world of the infant is gradually articulated into the two domains of the world of objects and the world of persons. The hinge, so to speak, of this double articulation of the physical and social world is the infant's own *body*.

The infant does not have a social world by means of a detour through his own world, although this may be true of the child once he has acquired language as part of the competent articulation of his relations to others and his own inter-ests. To the infant the social world is, so to speak, *physiognomic*. His own cor-poreal world resonates the sounds, smells, smiles, caresses, warmth, coldness, and hurts with which he is surrounded. But the infant does not project upon his mediators the responses evoked in himself before the spectacle he enjoys or dislikes. The infant's egocentrism at this stage is a bodily circuit rather than an intellectual circuit of reflexivity or *Verstehen*. Yet the expressivity of the infant's postural response, the way it seeks to prolong or to reject an approach, already conscripts the other as a witness, an accomplice, or a nuisance in the infant's world. Before language, the infant's body seems already to be a *text of pleasure and pain* (Barthes, 1975; O'Neill, 1983) with which its parents are obsessed, reading in every sound, in each stir, smile, or tear, their own fates. Thus each new generation of parents willingly enthrals itself to the royal panto-mime of its children.

Note

1 For a subtle analysis of the body boundary as a communicative texture between self-dis-closure (*Selbstdarstellung*) and self-centeredness (*Weltbeziehung durch Innerlichkeit*), see Bakan (1976). Bakan argues, however, that since self-disclosure is linguistically mediated it is both thought-centred and feeling-centred. Moreover, since feeling-cen-tred experience is shaped in the infant's early family environment, its communicative mode may never quite mesh with its later public communication and may need to be repressed or else released in special ritual techniques such as poetry, religion, and psychoanalysis. It is the task of critical social theory to bring together our two bod-ies, respecting in public discourse what cannot be said in the feeling, embodied self (O'Neill, 1983).

References

Bakan, Millie (1976). 'Alienation and the Interpretive Framework'. In: *The Crisis of Culture: Steps to Reform the Phenomenological Investigation of Man*, ed. Anna-Teresa Tymieniecka. Dordrecht: D. Reidel Publishing Co.

Barthes, Roland (1975). *The Pleasure of the Text*, trans. Richard Miller. New York: Hill and Wang.

Bettelheim, Bruno (1967). *The Empty Fortress: Infantile Autism and the Birth of the Self*. New York: Free Press.

Bloom, Harold (1973). *The Anxiety of Influence: A Theory of Poetry*. New York: Oxford University Press.

Cooley, Charles (1964). *Human Nature and the Social Order*. New York: Schocken Books.

Dillon, Martin C. (1978). 'Merleau-Ponty and the Psychogenesis of the Self'. *Journal of Phenomenological Psychology* 9: 84–98.

Elkin, Henry (1972). 'Towards a Developmental Phenomenology: Transcendental-Ego and Body-Ego'. In: *The Late Husserl and the Idea of Phenomenology: Idealism-Realism, Historicity and Nature*, ed. Anna-Teresa Tymienecka and Lawrence Haworth. Dordrecht: D. Reidel, pp. 258–66.

Erikson, Erik H. (1963). *Childhood and Society*. New York: W.W. Norton and Company.

Ey, Henri (1966). *L'Inconscient*. Paris: Desclee de Brouwer.

Fisher, Seymour (1970). *Body Experience in Fantasy and Behavior*. New York: Appleton-Century-Crofts.

Fisher, Seymour and Cleveland, S. E. (1968). *Body Image and Personality*. New York: Dover Press.

Freud, Sigmund (1974). 'Beyond the Pleasure Principle'. In: *The Standard Edition of the Complete Psychological Work of Sigmund Freud*, Vol. 18, ed. and trans. James Strachey. London: Hogarth Press.

Goffman, Erving (1967). *Interaction Ritual: Essays on Face-to-Face Behavior*. New York: Doubleday Anchor Books.

Goodwin, Charles (1981). *Conversational Organization: Interaction between Speakers and Hearers*. New York: Academic Press.

Gorman, Warren (1969). *Body Image and the Image of the Brain*. St. Louis: Warren H. Green.

Guillaume, Paul (1969). *Imitation in Children*. Chicago and London: University of Chicago Press.

Klein, Melanie (1932). 'Early Stages of the Oedipus Conflict and of Super-Ego Formation'. In: *The Psycho-Analysis of Children*. London: Hogarth Press, pp. 123–48.

Kramer Amsterdam, Beulah and Levitt, Moritt (1980). 'Consciousness of Self: and Painful Self-Consciousness'. In: *The Psychoanalytic Study of the Child*, Vol. 35. New Haven: Yale University Press, pp. 67–83.

Lacan, Jacques (1966). *Ecrits*. Paris: Editions du Seuil.

Lacan, Jacques (1970). 'The Mirror Stage as Formative of the Function of the I'. In: *Ecrits: A Selection*, trans. Alan Sheridan. New York: W.W. Norton and Company, pp. 1–7.

Laplanche, Jean (1976). *Life and Death in Psychoanalysis*, Jeffrey Mehlman (trans.). Baltimore and London: Johns Hopkins University Press.

Laplanche, J. and Pontalis, J. B. (1973). *The Language of Psycho-Analysis*. New York: W.W. Norton and Company.

Mead, George H. (1967). *Mind, Self, and Society*, ed. Charles W. Morris. Chicago and London: University of Chicago Press.

Merleau-Ponty, Maurice (1962). *Phenomenology of Perception*. London: Routledge and Kegan Paul.

Merleau-Ponty, Maurice (1964). 'Resumé des ses cours etabli par des étudiants et approuvé par lui-même'. *Bulletin de Psychologie* 18: 3–6.

Merleau-Ponty, Maurice (2007). 'The Child's Relations with Others'. In: *The Merleau-Ponty Reader*, trans. William Cobb, ed. Tedd Toadvine and Leonard Lawlor. Evanston, IL: Northwestern University Press, pp. 143–83.

O'Neill, John (1973). 'On Simmel's "Sociological Apriorities"'. In: *Phenomenological Sociology: Issues and Applications*, ed. George Psathas. New York: John Wiley and Sons, pp. 91–106.

O'Neill, John (1983). 'Homotextuality: Barthes on Barthes, Fragments (RB), with a Footnote'. In: *Hermeneutics: Questions and Prospects*, ed. Gary Shapiro and Alan Sica. Amherst: University of Massachusetts Press.

O'Neill, J. (1989) *The Communicative Body: Studies in Communicative Philosophy, Politics, and Sociology*. Evanston, IL: Northwestern University Press.

Schilder, Paul (1950). *The Image and Appearance of the Human Body*. New York: International Universities Press.

Shontz, Franklin C. (1969). *Perceptual and Cognitive Aspects of Body Appearance*. New York and London: Academic Press.

Stack Sullivan, Harry (1953). *The Interpersonal Theory of Psychiatry*, ed. Helen Swick Perry and Mary Ladd Gawel. New York: W.W. Norton and Company.

Wallon, Henri (1949). *Les origines du caractère chez l'enfant*. Paris: Presses universitaires de France.

Winnicott, D. W. (1967). 'Mirror-Role of Mother and Family in Child Development'. In: *The Predicament of the Family: A Psycho-Analytical Symposium*, ed. Peter Lomas. London: Hogarth Press, pp. 26–33.

Winnicott, D. W. (1971). *Playing and Reality*. New York: Basic Books.

Zaner, Richard M. (1964). *The Problem of Embodiment: Some Contributions to a Phenomenology of the Body*. The Hague: Martinus Nijhoff.

Zaner, Richard M. (1981). *The Context of Self: A Phenomenological Inquiry Using Medicine as a Clue*. Athens: Ohio University Press.

3   Childhood and embodiment*

Any theory of child socialisation is implicitly a theory of the construction of social reality, if not of a particular historical social order (Clausen, 1968). In this chapter I propose to give an account of the phenomenological approach to the basic presuppositions of child socialisation. I shall restrict my account to the writings of Maurice Merleau-Ponty, who, although widely known as a philosopher and political theorist, remains to be known for the lectures on child psychology that he gave for many years at the Sorbonne (Merleau-Ponty, 1964a, 1964b, 1973). For reasons of economy it is not possible to follow the whole of Merleau-Ponty's interpretation and critical evaluation of the literature concerning the physiological, intellectual, moral, and cultural development of the child with which he familiarised himself, not to mention his close reading of psychoanalytical and American anthropological research. Much of the literature is in any case now all too familiar to workers in child psychology, although Merleau-Ponty's close reading and phenomenological critique of Piaget's work might be given special mention because of its continuing interest (Merleau-Ponty, 1964a, 112–15, 176–85, 199, 204–10, 216; Zaner, 1966)[1].

Merleau-Ponty's analysis of the child's relation to others, his family, and the world around him may serve as introduction to the whole of Merleau-Ponty's phenomenology of perception, expression, and the sociohistorical world of human institutions (see O'Neill, 1989: chapters 5, 6, and 9). At all events, the topic and its phenomenological horizons are inseparable and can only be managed in a short space by focusing upon the very fundamental presuppositions of the phenomenon of the child's orientation to the world and others around him through the mediations of the body, language, perception, and reflection. The phenomenological concern with these basic structures of child development involves an implicit concern with the way in which they may be prejudged by the assumptions of unreflexive research.

* Text of this essay taken from *The Communicative Body: Studies in Communicative Philosophy, Politics and Sociology* (1989). Evanston: Northwestern University Press. Pages 46–57. Reprinted with permission.

The starting point in any study of child psychology and socialisation must be the child's relation to the adult world, its social relations, and its linguistic, perceptual, and logical categories. By insisting on this point, Merleau-Ponty dismisses any notion of a psychology of the child, the sick person, the man, the woman, or the primitive as an enclosed nature. Indeed, there is a *complementary feature* of the child-adult relationship, namely, the reverse adult-child relationship. This obliges us in the methodology of child studies to design research procedures that are sensitive to the two-way and even asymmetric relation between the child's orientation to the adult world and the adult world's interests in fostering, enforcing, and moralising upon its own interests and hopes in the child world. We cannot here look down the path toward the 'politics of experience' that this first methodological observation opens up (Laing, 1968). It must suffice to remark that it points to a cultural dilemma that is generic to human relations and thus makes it impossible to conceive of child psychology and psychoanalysis outside specific cultural frameworks.

Another general conclusion that we may elicit from the interactional nature of the object of child studies refers to a phenomenon that is common for the object of all social studies. The natural scientist for most purposes is concerned only with the observer's experience, however mediated by his instruments, of the object under study. Even if we take into account the problems of interference referred to by the Heisenberg uncertainty principle, the problem here is merely that the scientist must allow for changes in the behaviour of experimental objects due to the interference effects of his own methods of study. But although this problem produces a greater similarity between the natural and social sciences than was imagined earlier, it leaves unchanged an essential difference between them: namely, where the object of science is a human relationship or set of human relationships, a custom, or an institution, the 'ordering' of the relationship is not merely a scientific construct. It is first of all a pre-theoretical construct that is the unarticulated 'common sense' knowledge of others as 'relatives' who experience dependable needs and wants expressed through the 'relevances' of the human body, time, and place.

The burden of Merleau-Ponty's methodological critique of research methods in studies of child perception, language, and morals is that they proceed without the benefit of any reflection upon the way their methods already prejudge the nature of the phenomena they are intended to elicit. In the first place we must rid ourselves of a 'dogmatic rationalism' that consists in studying the child's world from above and thereby construing the child's efforts as prelogical or magical behaviour that must be sloughed off as a condition of entry into the objective, realist world of adults. Such a prejudice overlooks the way in which child and adult behaviour are solidary, with anticipations from the side of the child and regressions on the side of the adult that make their conduct no more separable than health and sickness. Indeed, the real task of a genuine psychology must be to discover the basis of communication between children and adults, between the unconscious and consciousness, between the sick and the sane.

'We must conceive the child neither as an absolute "other" nor just "the same" as ourselves, but as polymorphous' (Merleau-Ponty, 1964a: 8). This remark may serve as a guiding principle in following Merleau-Ponty's subtle interweaving of the processes of structure and development in the child's relation to others. The notion of *development* is, of course, central to the psychology of the child; it is, however, a complex notion since it implies neither an absolute continuity between childhood and adulthood nor any complete discontinuity without phases or transitions. It is here that we need to avoid the twin reductions of the phenomena of development that Merleau-Ponty labels 'mechanist' and 'idealist' exemplified, respectively, by the learning theory approach originated by Pavlov and the cognitive approach of Piaget. Here we are on explicitly philosophical ground because the continuity between childhood and adult life raises the question of how it is in principle that individual and intersubjective life are possible.

Mechanist, reflex, or learning theory accounts of child development involve us in the difficulty that their causal explanations fail to cover the phenomena of adult initiative, creativity, and responsibility. Reflex theory reduces conduct to a structure of conditioned reflexes built into increasingly complex patterns whose principle of organisation is always conceived as an environmental stimulus to which the responses of adaptation occur without internal elaboration. Reflex theory attempts to explain conduct in terms of physiological process without norms or intentionality. But even at its own level reflex theory is not sure of its foundations (Goldstein, 1963: chapter 5; Taylor, 1964: 270). Once one attempts to make the notions of stimulus, receptor, and reflex more precise, reflex theory becomes riddled with question-begging hypotheses about mechanisms of inhibition and control, acquired drives, and the like. The case of 'experimental neurosis' in one of Pavlov's dogs involved in repeated experiments reveals that the consequences of the restriction of a biologically meaningful environment in order to induce conditioned reflexes results in pathological behaviour (Merleau-Ponty, 1963: 25). By the same token, the acquisition of human habits is not a strictly determined reflex but the acquisition of a capability for inventing solutions to situations that are only *abstractly* similar and never identical with the original 'learning situation'. What is involved in the formation of human habits is the acquisition of a 'categorical attitude' (Goldstein and Gelb, 1955; Gurwitsch, 1966a) or a power of 'symbolic expression' (Head, 1926) and it is only in pathological conduct that atomistic and associationist explanations appear plausible.

While rejecting naturalistic reductions of child development, Merleau-Ponty is equally critical of idealist or cognitive accounts of the phenomena of perception, intelligence, and sensory-motor behaviour. The basic fault in cognitive approaches to the child's relation to the world and others is that they sacrifice the immediate, *visceral knowledge* of self, others, and the world that we possess without ever having apprenticed ourselves to the 'rules' of perception, language, and movement. This preconceptual knowledge is neither subjective nor objective and requires a conception of *symbolic form* that rests upon neither a realist nor an idealist epistemology but instead seeks what is complementary in them.

Because the philosophical presuppositions of psychology are implicitly dualistic, consciousness is usually described as the transparent possession of an object of thought, in distinction from perceptual and motor acts, which are described as a series of events external to each other. Thought and behaviour are juxtaposed or else set in a speculative hierarchy. Against these alternatives, Merleau-Ponty proposes to classify behaviour according to a continuum whose upper and lower limits are defined by the submergence of the structure of behaviour in content, at the lowest level, that is, 'synenetic forms', and, at the highest level, the emergence of structure as the proper theme of activity, that is, 'symbolic forms'.

The conceptualisation of behaviour requires the category of Form in order to differentiate the structures of quantity, order, and value or signification as the dominant characteristics, respectively, of matter, life, and mind and at the same time to relativise the participation of these structures in a hierarchy of forms of behaviour. Form is itself not an element in the world but a limit toward which bio-physical and psychobiological structures tend. In a given environment each organism exhibits a preferred mode of behaviour that is not the simple aim or function of its milieu and its internal organisation but is structured by its general attitude to the world. In other words, the analysis of form is not a matter of the composition of real structures but the perception of wholes. Human behaviour, which is essentially symbolic behaviour, unfolds through structures or gestures that are not in objective space and time, like physical objects, nor in a purely internal dimension of consciousness unsituated with respect to historical time and place.

Merleau-Ponty calls the objects of perception 'phenomena' in order to characterise their openness to perceptual consciousness to which they are not given a priori but as 'open, inexhaustible systems which we recognise through a certain style of development'. The matrix of all human activity is the *phenomenal body* that is the schema of our world, or the source of a vertical or human space in which we project our feelings, moods, and values. Because the human body is a 'community of senses' and not a bundle of contingently related impression, it functions as the universal setting or schema for all possible styles or typical structures of the world. These, however, are not given to us with the invariable formula of a *facius totius universi* but through the temporal synthesis of horizons implicit in intentionality. 'For us the perceptual synthesis is a temporal synthesis, and subjectivity, at the level of perception, is nothing but temporality, and that is what enables us to leave to the subject of perception his opacity and historicity' (Merleau-Ponty, 1965: 239). The cognitive approaches to child development overlook the *tacit* subjectivity that does not constitute its world a priori nor entirely a posteriori but develops through a 'living cohesion' in which the embodied self experiences itself while belonging to this world and others, clinging to them for its content.

Thus in his analysis of the child's perception of causal relations Merleau-Ponty (1964a: 185–87) argues that it is not a matter of a simple ordering of external data but of an 'informing' (*Gestaltung*) of the child's experience of external events through an operation that is properly neither a logical nor a predicative activity. Similarly, in the case of the child's imagination (Merleau-Ponty, 1964a: 194–98), it proves impossible to give any objective sense of the notion of image even as photograph, mimicry, or picture, apart from an 'affective projection'. Imagination is therefore not a purely intellectual operation but is better understood as an operation beneath the cognitive relation of subject and object. The 'imaginary' and the 'real' are *two forms of conduct* that are not antithetical but rest upon a common ambiguity that occasionally allows the imaginary to substitute for the real. The child lives in the hybrid world of the real and the imaginary that the adult keeps apart for most purposes or is otherwise careful of any transgression wherein he catches his own conscience. Again, in the analysis of the child's drawing (Merleau-Ponty, 1964a: 130–34, 187–94) it is also improper to treat the child's efforts as abortive attempts to develop 'adult', or rather perspectival, drawing, which is itself a historical development in art dominated by the laws of classical geometric perspective. The child's drawing is not a simple imitation of what he sees any more than of what he does not see through lack of detailed 'attention'. The child's drawings are expressive of his relations to the things and people in this world. They develop and change along with his experience with the objects, animals, puppets, and persons around him, including his own experience of his body, its inside and outside (Fisher and Cleveland, 1968; Myers, 1967; Zaner, 1965). 'The child's drawing is *contact* with the visible world and with others. This tactile relation with the world and with man appears long before the looking attitude, the posture of indifferent contemplation between the spectator and the spectacle which is realised in adult drawing' (Merleau-Ponty, 1964a: 133).

It is above all in the child's acquisition of language that we observe the complex interrelation of cognition and affectivity that can only be made thematic in later phases of development by presupposing the massive inarticulable background of the world into which we import our categories, distinctions, and relations. Language and intelligence presuppose one another without priority, and their development rests rather upon the ability of the child to assimilate his linguistic environment as an open system of expression and conduct, comparable to his acquisition of all his other habits. Again, for reasons of economy we cannot deal with the broad range of the phenomenology of language (Merleau-Ponty, 1972). Instead, we must focus attention upon Merleau-Ponty's interpretation of the social contexts of the acquisition of language (Merleau-Ponty, 1964a).

> It is a commonplace that the child's acquisition of language is also correlated with his relation to his mother. Children who have been suddenly and forcibly separated from their mothers always show signs of a linguistic regression. At bottom, it is not only the word 'mama' that is the child's first; it is the entire language which is, so to speak, maternal.
>
> The acquisition of language might be a phenomenon of the same kind as the relation to the mother. Just as the maternal relation is (as the psychoanalysts say) a relation of *identification*, in which the subject projects on his mother what he himself experiences and assimilates the attitudes of his mother, so one could say that the acquisition of language is itself a

phenomenon of identification. To learn to speak is to learn to play a series of *roles*, to assume a series of conducts or linguistic gestures.

(Merleau-Ponty, 1964b: 109)

This hypothesis on the development of language in relation to the child's familial roles is illustrated in terms of analysis of the expression of child jealousy (Merleau-Ponty, 1964b: 109, referring to Rostand, 1950). Upon the birth of a new baby the younger of two children displays jealousy, behavioural regression (carrying himself as though he were the baby), and language regression. There, phenomena represent an initial response to the threatened structure of the child's temporal and social world of the 'latest born' child. The emotional response of jealousy expresses the child's attachment to a hitherto eternal present. A little later the child begins to identify with his older brother, adopting the latter's earlier attitudes toward himself as the 'youngest'. The chance circumstance of the visit of another child bigger than his older brother relativises once and for all the 'absolute eldest' and the child's jealousy recedes. At the same time as these 'sociometric' experiences are acquired the child's linguistic experience of temporal structure also expands.

> He considered the present to be absolute. Now, on the contrary, one can say that from the moment when he consents to be no longer the latest born, to become in relation to the new baby what his elder brother had until then been in relation to him, he replaces the attitude of 'my place has been taken' with another whose schema might be somewhat like this: 'I *have been* the youngest, but I am the youngest no longer, and I *will become* the biggest.' One sees that there is a solidarity between the acquisition of this temporal structure, which gives a meaning to the corresponding linguistic instruments, and the situation of jealousy that is overcome.

(Merleau-Ponty, 1964b: 110)

The child's resolution of his jealousy permits us to make some general remarks upon the relation of the cognitive and affective elements in the child's conception of the world and others around him that will then permit us to deal finally with the fundamental problem of the possibility of social relations of any kind (O'Neill, 1972a). In overcoming his jealousy we might, as Piaget would say, speak of the child's having solved the egocentric problem by learning to decentre himself and to relativise his notions by thinking in terms of reciprocity. But these are clearly not purely intellectual operations; rather, what is called *intelligence* here really designates the mode of intersubjectivity achieved by the child. The intellectual and linguistic elaboration of our experience of the world always rests upon the 'deep structures' of our affective experience of the interpersonal world against which we elaborate only later our modes of inductive and deductive thinking.

The perception of other people and the intersubjective world are problematic only for adults. The child lives in a world which he unhesitatingly believes accessible to all around him. He has no awareness of himself or of others as private subjectivities, nor does he suspect that all of us, himself included, are limited to one certain point of view of the world. That is why he subjects neither his thoughts, in which he believes as they present themselves, without attempting to link them to each other, nor our words, to any sort of criticism. He has no knowledge of points of view. For him men are empty heads turned towards one single, self-evident world where everything takes place, even dreams, which are, he thinks, in his room, and even thinking, since it is not distinct from words. Others are for him so many gazes which inspect things, and have an almost material existence, so much so that the child wonders how these gazes avoid being broken as they meet. At about twelve years old, says Piaget, the child achieves the *cogito* and reaches the truths of rationalism. At this stage, it is held, he discovers himself both as a point of view on the world and also as called upon to transcend that point of view, and to construct an objectivity at the level of judgement. Piaget brings the child to a mature outlook as if the thoughts of the adult were self-sufficient and disposed of all contradictions. But, in reality, it must be the case that the child's outlook is in some way vindicated against the adult's and against Piaget, and that the unsophisticated thinking of our earliest years remains as an indispensable acquisition underlying that of maturity, if there is to be for the adult one single intersubjective world. My awareness of constructing an objective truth would never provide me with anything more than an objective truth for me, and my greatest attempt at impartiality would never enable me to prevail over my subjectivity (as Descartes so well expresses it by the hypothesis of the malignant demon), if I had not, underlying my judgements, the primordial certainty of being in contact with being itself, if, before any voluntary *adoption of a position* I were not already situated in an intersubjective world, and if science too were not upheld by this basic *doxa*. With the *cogito* begins that struggle between consciousnesses, each of which, as Hegel says, seeks the death of the other. For the struggle ever to begin, and for each consciousness to be capable of suspecting the alien presences which it negates, all must necessarily have some common ground and be mindful of their peaceful co-existence in the world of childhood.

(Merleau-Ponty, 1965: 355. My stress is on the first line)

Classical psychology, however, renders the intersubjective world that is the presupposition of all socialisation entirely problematic. This arises from the assumption that the psyche is *what is given to only one person*, intrinsically mine and radically inaccessible to others who are similarly possessed of their own experiences. The same assumption is also made with regard to the body, namely, that it is as *individual* as the psyche and knowable by me only through the mass of sensations it gives me. So conceived, the problem of the experience of others presents itself as a system with four terms: (1) myself, my 'psyche'; (2) the image I have of my body by means of the sense of touch or cenesthesia, that is, the 'introceptive image' of my own body; (3) the body of the other as seen by me, that is, that 'visual body'; (4) the hypothetical 'psyche' of the other, his feeling of his own existence that I must reconstitute by means of (3) the 'visual body' (Merleau-Ponty, 1964b: 115).

The difficulties intrinsic to the operation of this schema are apparent from what it assumes in the analysis of the child's response to the other's smile (Tillman, 1967). The child responds very early to facial expressions and, of course, verbal expressions of dos and don'ts without being able either to compare his 'motor smile' with the 'visible smile' of the other or to correlate just what it is that he is doing that meets with approval or disapproval. Rather than engage in point for point comparisons, the child can only respond to global situations and attitudes, in other words, to his surroundings, as motivation or conduct. This means that we must reject the individualist and solipsistic conceptions intrinsic to the dual worlds of the mind and body as conceived in classical psychology and its philo-sophical tradition (Merleau-Ponty, 1964: chapters 1 and 2; 1964c). We can no longer conceive of the psyche as a series of enclosed 'states of consciousness' inaccessible to anyone but myself. Consciousness is turned toward the world; it is a mode of conduct toward things and persons (Gurwitsch, 1966b) that in turn reveal themselves to me through their style and manner of dealing with the world. By the same token we must revise our conception of the body as an agglomeration of senses that are mine and that are only to be guessed at in the case of others. My awareness of body is the activity of a postural or corporeal schema that is the lived experience of a cenesthesia or play between my various senses and the senses of others visible in their comportment.

> Thus in today's psychology we have one system with two terms (my behav-iour and the other's behaviour) which functions as a whole. To the extent that I can elaborate and extend my *corporeal schema*, to the extent that I acquire a better organised experience of my own body, to that very extent will my con-sciousness of my own body cease being a chaos in which I am submerged and lend itself to a transfer to others. And since at the same time the other who is to be perceived is himself not a 'psyche' closed in on himself but rather a *conduct*, a system of behaviour that aims at the world, he offers himself to my motor intentions and to that 'intentional transgression' (Husserl) by which I animate and pervade him. Husserl said that the perception of others is like a 'phenomenon of coupling' (*accouplement*). The term is anything but a metaphor. In perceiving the other, my body and his are coupled, resulting in a sort of action which pairs them (*action á deux*). This conduct which I am able only to see, I live somehow from a distance. I make it mine; I recover (*reprendre*) it or comprehend it. Reciprocally I know that the gestures I make myself can be the objects of another's intention. It is this transfer of intentions to my own, my alienation of the other and his alienation of me, that makes possible the perception of others.
>
> (Merleau-Ponty, 1964b: 118)

Here we can only point to the complementarity between the role of the corporeal schema and the work of social actors in elaborating the field of impressions and visual data inadvertently and deliberately presented to him as the motives and expectations of social interaction or the typification of personal and institutional conduct, as analysed by Mead, Goffman, and Schutz (also see Cicourel, 1970 on the affective bases of reciprocity). Likewise, without any further comment upon the relation between transcendental phenomenology and mundane intersubjectivity (Schutz, 1966, 1967a, 1967b), we must now conclude with an analysis of the formation of the child's corporeal schema in the early stages of socialisation.

The problem is to account for how it is that we become aware of the distinction between our own body and the other's body while acquiring the ability to transfer our intentions to the facial and linguistic expressions of the other as the prima facie basis of their further elaboration and making our own gestures similarly available to the other's intentions and expectations (Goffman, 1967). We may distinguish three principal stages in this process, at each point commenting upon the conceptual revisions that are implicit in their structure and development during the first three years of the child's life.

The first phase is that of *precommunication* in which the child does not experience himself as a single individual set over against all others. The first *me* is still a latent or vertical possibility within our experience of an anonymous or collective existence. What is sometimes called egocentrism at this stage refers not to an experience of self-other contrast but precisely to the experience of a *me* that dwells as easily in others as in itself and is in fact no more aware of itself than it is of others. For this reason, however, the child's *me* can be extremely demanding and volatile. But the phenomena of the child's appearing to be wilfully different from situation to situation, playing several roles with himself, and even attributing his experiences to others ('transitivism') mislead us into attributing them to the child's egocentrism. But these phenomena are actually symptomatic of the as yet unacquired structure of his own perspective as an *I* and that of others in which every *you* is also an *I* and neither he nor they are an undifferentiated *me* without limits of time and space. The full development of this structure of experience has as its 'correlate' the development of linguistic competence with the system of pronouns that in turn elaborates an interpersonal order through this very perspective.

The second phase that we distinguish intervenes in the development of the first phase from precommunication to the acquisition of personal perspective and its implicit competence with orderly social life gained by the child's second year or so. This is the stage of the child's awareness of his own body (*corps propre*) and the specular image ('*image spéculaire*') (Merleau-Ponty, 1964a: 134–36, 300–02; Cooley, 1964: 182–85, 196–99; Mead, 1967: 173–78, 192–200). At this stage the development of consciousness toward what is called intelligence proceeds by means of an expanded awareness of the child's own body through the acquisition of its specular image that in turn involves a general mode of conduct beyond the episodic event of seeing his body image in a mirror. Moreover, the mastery of this specular image is more difficult for the child to achieve than the distinction between his father, say, and his father's image in the mirror – even though he still allows the image a quasi-reality similar to that we feel in the presence of portraits, however much we 'know better'. But in the case of his own specular image the child can make no visual comparison to establish the difference between the experience of his body seen in the mirror and his body of which he can only see the hands, feet, or other parts but that is otherwise a totality of which he has only a lived experience. Yet the child has now to understand that although he is his own body and not its image in the mirror, his own body is nevertheless visible to others like its mirror image.

Since Merleau-Ponty is not concerned to make an absolute distinction among the three phases of early child development, we may mention the overlap between the second and third phase here, that is, the 'crisis at three years'. This phase is marked by the child's refusal to allow his body and thoughts to fall under any perspective or interpretation than his own. He wants his own way and this he works out by stubbornly requiring the resistance of others to his own negativity. Through everything the child refuses – his parents, their words, and their food – there arises the structure of oedipal relations in which again the child's world and his conception of social reality are reducible neither to cognitive nor to solely affective factors.

The interpretation of the development of the specular image again involves taking a position on the reduction of cognitive and affective behaviour. Merleau-Ponty rejects the view that the specular image involves a cognitive process in which the relation between reality and image, the body here and its image or shadow over there, is established once and for all. The specular image involves a new form of conduct, a shift from the lived body to the visible body, the object of social attention, projection, and mimesis. The body is now a form of conduct, of an identification with others that is never quite stabilised but is the basis of the child's joys and sorrows, his jealousies and tender loyalties that are the experiences of growing up among others: the possibility of a super ego.

> Thus one sees that the phenomenon of the specular image is given by psychoanalysts the importance it really has in the life of the child. It is the acquisition not only of a new content but of a new function as well: the narcissistic function. Narcissus was the mythical being who, after looking at his image in the mirror of water, was drawn as if by vertigo to re-join his own image in the mirror of water. At the same time that the image of oneself makes possible the knowledge of oneself, it makes possible a sort of alienation. I am no longer what I felt myself, immediately, to be; I am that image of myself that is offered by the mirror. To use Dr. Lacan's terms, I am 'captured, caught up' by my spatial image. Thereupon I leave the reality of my lived *me* in order to refer myself constantly to the ideal, fictitious, or imaginary *me*, of which the specular image is the first outline. In this sense I am torn from myself, and the image in the mirror prepares me for another still more serious alienation, which will be alienation by others. For others have only an exterior image of me, which is analogous to the one seen in the mirror. Consequently others will tear me away from my immediate inwardness much more surely than

will the mirror. 'The specular image is the symbolic matrix', says Lacan, 'where the I springs up in primordial form before objectifying itself in the dialectic of identification with the other.'

(Merleau-Ponty, 1964b: 136–37; Lacan, 1949)

The acquisition of the specular image introduces the child into the drama of social life, the struggle with the other, ruled by desire and recognition, even to death. It lies outside the scope of this essay to pursue these themes in terms of the conjuncture between Hegelian phenomenology and Lacanian psychoanalysis[2]. But this is certainly a direction in which we might pursue the dialectic between personal and public life that we repeat in the spectacle of the *body politic* and the struggle between the 'organisation' of authority and the delinquencies of love's body (Brown, 1966; O'Neill, 1972b).

Notes

1 Here I think there is an obvious link between Merleau-Ponty's phenomenological psychology and the work of Lacan in psychoanalysis and Levi-Strauss in anthropology.
2 Lacan remarks that in treating the struggle between master and slave in which each seeks to be recognized without in turn recognizing the other as a symbol of the history of the world Hegel 'has furnished once and for all the true function of aggression in human ontology, to the point almost of prophesying the iron law of our age' (Lacan, 1966: 121; Ricoeur, 1965; O'Neill, 1969; Kojève, 1969).

References

Brown, Norman O. (1966). *Love's Body*. New York: Vintage Books.

Cirourel, Aaron V. (1970). 'Basic and Normative Rules in the Negotiation of Status and Role'. In: *Recent Sociology No. 2: Patterns of Communicative Behaviour*. Hans Peter Dreitzel (ed.). New York: Macmillan, pp. 4–45.

Clausen, John A. (ed.) (1968). *Socialization and Society*. Boston: Little, Brown and Company.

Cooley, Charles Horton (1964). *Human Nature and the Social Order*. New York: Schocken Books, 1964.

Fisher, Seymour and Cleveland, Sidney E. (1968). *Body Image and Personality*. New York: Dover Publications.

Goffman, Erving (1967). *Interaction Ritual: Essays on Face-to-Face Behavior*. New York: Doubleday and Co.

Goldstein, Kurt (1963). *Human Nature in the Light of Psychology*. New York: Schocken Books.

Goldstein, Kurt and Gelb, Adhemar (1955). 'Analysis of a Case of Figural Blindness'. In: *A Source Book of Gestalt Psychology*. W. D. Ellis (ed.). London: Routledge and Kegan Paul, pp. 315–25.

Gurwitsch, Aron (1966a). 'Gelb-Goldstein's Concept of "Concrete" and "Categorial" Attitude and the Phenomenology of Ideation'. In: *Studies in Phenomenology and Psychology*. Evanston, IL: Northwestern University Press, pp. 359–84.

Gurwitsch, Aron (1966b). 'A Non-egological Conception of Consciousness'. In: *Studies in Phenomenology and Psychology*. Evanston, IL: Northwestern University Press, pp. 287–300.

Head, Henry (1926). *Aphasia and Kindred Disorders of Speech*. New York: Macmillan.

Kojève, Alexandre (1969). *Introduction to the Reading of Hegel*. Allen Bloom (ed.). James H. Nichols, Jr. (trans.). New York: Basic Books.

Lacan, Jacques (1949). 'Le Stade du miroir comme formateur du fonction du je'. *Revue Française de Psychanalyse* 13(4): 449–55.

Lacan, Jacques (1966). *Ecrits*. Paris: Éditions du Seuil.

Laing, R. D. (1968). *The Politics of Experience*. New York: Ballantine Books, 1968.

Mead, George Herbert (1967). *Mind, Self and Society*. Charles W. Morris (ed.). Chicago and London: University of Chicago Press.

Merleau-Ponty, Maurice (1963). *The Structure of Behaviour*. A. L. Fisher (trans.). Boston: Beacon Press.

Merleau-Ponty, Maurice (1964a). 'Group d'Études de Psychologie de l'Université de Paris, Resumé des Cours de Merleau-Ponty'. *Bulletin de Psychologie* 236(xviii): 109–336.

Merleau-Ponty, Maurice (1964b). 'The Child's Relations with Others'. In: *The Primacy of Perception, and Other Essays*. William Cobb (trans.). James M. Edie (ed.). Evanston, IL: Northwestern University Press, pp. 96–155.

Merleau-Ponty, Maurice (1964c). 'Phenomenology and the Sciences of Man'. In: *The Primacy of Perception, and Other Essays*. William Cobb (trans.). James M. Edie (ed.). Evanston, IL: Northwestern University Press, pp. 43–95.

Merleau-Ponty, Maurice (1965). *Phenomenology of Perception*. Colin Smith (trans.). London: Routledge and Kegan Paul.

Merleau-Ponty, Maurice (1972). *The Prose of the World*. Claude Lefort (ed.). John O'Neill (trans.). Evanston, IL: Northwestern University Press.

Merleau-Ponty, Maurice (1973). *Consciousness and the Acquisition of Language*. Hugh J. Silverman (trans.). Evanston, IL: Northwestern University Press.

Myers, Gerald E. (1967). 'Self and Body Image'. In: *Phenomenology in America: Studies in the Philosophy of Experience*. James M. Edie (ed). Chicago: Quadrangle Books, pp. 147–60.

O'Neill, John (1969). 'History as Human History in Hegel and Marx'. In: *Studies on Marx and Hegel*. Hyppolite, Jean (ed.). John O'Neill (trans.). New York: Basic Books.

O'Neill, John (1972a). 'How Is Society Possible?' In: *Sociology as a Skin Trade: Essays Towards a Reflexive Sociology*. London: Heinemann Educational Books.

O'Neill, John (1972b). 'On Body-Politics'. In: *Recent Sociology No. 4: Family, Marriage and the Struggle of the Sexes*. Hans Peter Dreitzel (ed.). New York: Macmillan.

O'Neill, John (1989). *The Communicative Body: Studies in Communicative Philosophy, Politics, and Sociology*. Evanston, IL: Northwestern University Press.

Ricoeur, Paul (1965). *De l'Interprétation: Essai sur Freud*. Paris: Editions du Seuil.

Rostand, François (1950). 'Grammaire et Affectivité'. *Revue Française de Psychanalyse* 14(April–June): 299–310.

Schutz, Alfred (1966). 'The Problem of Transcendental Intersubjectivity in Husserl'. In: *Collected Papers III: Studies in Phenomenological Philosophy*. I. Schutz (ed.). The Hague: Martinus Nijhoff, pp. 51–91.

Schutz, Alfred (1967a). 'Scheler's Theory of Intersubjectivity and the General Thesis of the Alter Ego'. In: *Collected Papers I: The Problem of Social Reality*. Maurice Natanson (ed.). The Hague: Martinus Nijhoff, pp. 150–79.

Schutz, Alfred (1967b). 'Sartre's Theory of the Alter Ego'. In: *Collected Papers I: The Problem of Social Reality*. Maurice Natanson (ed.). The Hague: Martinus Nijhoff, pp. 180–203.

Taylor, Charles (1964). *The Explanation of Behavior*. New York: Humanities Press.

Tillman, Frank A. (1967). 'On Perceiving Persons'. In: *Phenomenology in America: Studies in the Philosophy of Experience*. James M. Edie (ed.) Chicago: Quadrangle Books, pp. 161–72.

Zaner, Richard M. (1965). 'Merleau-Ponty's Theory of the Body-Proper as Être-au-monde'. *Journal of Existentialism* 6(21): 31–39.

Zaner, Richard M. (1966). 'Piaget and Merleau-Ponty: A Study in Convergence'. *Review of Existential Psychology and Psychiatry* 6(1): 7–23.

4   Infant theory*

I want to rephrase the problem of social order as the problem of the symbolic relation between part and whole. It is then an inquiry that is already solved by the 'infant theorist.' This is so because we are bodies whose communicative competence is doubly articulated in a field of psycho-physical and linguistic expression. As Vico showed in *New Science* (1744), the human body constitutes the very figure of synecdoche (*pars pro toto*) that enables us to articulate a single model of wholeness and integration operative at each level of individual, social, and cosmic life (O'Neill, 1983a). While claiming that this first communicative body religiously funds all human institutions, I recognize that it is also subject to a history of discursive reformulation by the natural and social sciences in the context of the secondary institutions and economy in which they in turn function (O'Neill, 1985).

My approach to the issues surrounding the corporeal practice of synecdoche derives from the insights of Freud, as read by Lacan (1977: 1–17) and Merleau-Ponty's phenomenological revision of Lacan's theory of the mirror stage (O'Neill, 1986a), or as I might put it now, *the stage of synecdochic crisis*. I am starting here because I assume that the question of our primary participation in the world orients all later inquiry into the nature of our patterning and participation in the structures of meaning that reproduce the sense, value, and intelligibility of our relationships and institutions (O'Neill, 1989). Consequently, my analysis begins with the relationship between the mother and the infant body as an institution (*matrix*) that articulates the part/whole relationships of the body and speech. The speaking body, whose first figure of speech is generated by the body's own synecdochism, is therefore the first human body (Paul, 1977). And this I consider the proper ground of Freud's theory of infant sexuality. However, I make this argument by revising the apparently similar claim by Lacan, whose conception of our first body as a body-in-pieces (*corps morcelé*) I consider an inadequate ground of our essentially synecdochical world.

The empirical basis in child studies for the theory of the mirror phase is not in question. Lacan's empirical sources have been multiplied in Anglo-American

* Text of the essay taken from *Incorporating Cultural Theory: Maternity at the Millennium* (2002). Albany, NY: SUNY Press. Pages 5–17. Reprinted with permission.

infant research. Nevertheless, we may consider the mirror theory as a fundamental mythology of Lacanianism inasmuch as it responds to the original question of human division, i.e., not only the question of sexual difference but also of our internal 'splitting', and ultimately of mankind's separation from the divinity, that is, from love. In the Biblical story, these events are described as a single story of the loss of paradise and the pains of earthly existence. In the *Symposium*, the story is told in terms of our loss of androgyny, of a third force which might amplify our heterosexuality if ever the two could be rejoined in fourfold love.

Prior to the mirror stage, experience is shaped by the conjuncture of the infant's biological immaturity and an archaic image of the fragmented body (*corps morcelé*). 'Before' incorporation with the mother body, the infant has already identified with its fantasies of bodily fragmentation and mutilation, attached to the mouth, eye, ear, anus, genitals. Thus body, language, and sexuality are overlaid in the primary pleasure points of the infant body, which then furnishes reference points (*points de capiton*) for the secondary pleasure focused in the specular body which can be further overlaid with the cultural myths that sustain the narcissistic self's attachment to an adult identity whose infant origins it forgets. The speaking subject is unaware of its source of desire, whose objects are split off from transparent meaning. Its objects of desire precede the specular image and are introjected somewhere between the internal and external world, between ego and subject. The fusion with the mother body at the mirror stage is therefore never complete, since it is undermined by a flow of fragmentary images. In any case, the image of integrity remains outside in an other that offers us the lure of identity, so to speak, of 'our' perpetual alienation.

Narcissistic passion is exhibited in the desire for interaction with others who will confirm the value of the self which does not know that it seeks recognition nor the object of its desire. The other functions as a screen for the projection of narcissistic identity which remains unfulfilled in the play of the other and of language. Thus the 'I' never quite understands itself in language and culture because it is underwritten by the narcissistic 'me' which is in turn ruled by a specular logic of external and alienated recognition through

1. the gaze *(le regard)*
2. scripture *(l'écriture)*

The gaze or voice in the pre-mirror stage returns in dreams from which the I-subject captures only its slides and elisions. Yet to some extent it thereby objectifies its 'me' and can restructure it, i.e., 'where there was me there shall I place itself.' The function of the superego is conceived by Lacan as a structural mechanism through which the identificatory 'me' is repressed as an ego ideal in favour of the social 'I'. The Lacanian superego is a metaphor for individuation, i.e., for the 'me' reflected in others. In other words, in the shift from maternal to paternal identification, the 'me' takes on a cultural body whose mark is the double circumcision of language and heterosexuality that launches the infant into the system of exchange and difference we call society.

How synecdoche (*pars pro toto, totum pro partibus*) functions as a specifically phenomenological method has been nicely formulated by Medina (1985) in criticism of the Heideggerian and Lacanian usage of part-whole methodology. Thus synecdoche may be reformulated in terms of the following rules of interpretation:

1. Human consciousness constitutes itself in whole and parts.
2. Existential totalization and division must always be seen in the history and context of the social interaction of human individuals.
3. Human interaction is communicative rather than existential but is framed by the existential boundaries of love (*Eros*) and strife (*Thanatos*).
4. The intelligibility of unconscious objects and unfinished subjects derives from part/whole syntheses that are temporarily and contextually revisable (redeemable) so that all totalizing syntheses are deprived of causality in the last (or first) instance.

Lacan treats the infant's grasp of its total body form in the mirror image as an event that is entirely premature and as the prefiguration, so to speak, of an alienated destination. The mirror image constitutes a prospective/retrospective complex of identity and separation that prefigures all later separations, from weaning to castration. The ego is constituted in imagery of mastery and servitude where the love of others is always an intrusion upon the madness of the self project. The infant body is forever separated from the image of wholeness that it pursues in itself, in the mother body, in language, and in politics. Like Lacan himself, the child is condemned to life in ex-communication:

> The *mirror stage* is a drama whose internal thrust is precipitated from the insufficiency to anticipation – and which manufactures for the subject, caught up in the lure of spatial identification, the succession of phantasies that extends from a fragmentary body-image to a form of its totality that I shall call orthopaedic – and, lastly, to the assumption of an armour of an alienating identity, which will mark with its rigid structure the subject's entire mental development. Thus, to break out of the circle of the *Innenwelt* into the *Umwelt* generates the inexhaustible quadrature of the ego's verification.
>
> (Lacan, 1977: 4)

According to Lacan, the acquisition of intersubjectivity is achieved only at the level of language, or in the symbolic order. This stage is reached on the basis of two prior moments: (i) *the mirror phase* and (ii) through the relationships experienced as *the castration complex*. The first stage of 'I' constitution occurs in the infant's confrontation with its mirror image, or with the experience of a whole-body image that is both present and absent. In its wholeness, however, the body image projects for the infant an ideal of integrity that its own bodily experience of taste, smell, and motor relations has still to achieve. To this imaginary wholeness the infant adopts a narcissistic attitude, caught up in the split between self-presence and self-absence:

> The jubilant assumption of his specular image by the child at his *infans stage*, still sunk in his motor incapacity and nursing dependence, would seem to exhibit in an exemplary situation the symbolic matrix in which the I is precipitated in a primordial form, before it is objectified in the dialectic of identification with the other, and before language restores to it, in the universal, its function as a subject.
>
> (Lacan, 1977: 7)

Although such a world view is inimical to Merleau-Ponty's convictions, he nevertheless pays considerable attention to Lacan's early lectures on the mirror stage. However, I believe that Merleau-Ponty's phenomenology of embodiment and intersubjectivity is incompatible with and, in fact, offers a corrective to Lacan's concept of the fragmented body, forever alienated from its image of wholeness (O'Neill, 1970). In short, the visual moment at the mirror stage cannot produce effective self-recognition prior to the anonymously intersubjective constitution of the self in relation to others with whom it is kindred. According to Merleau-Ponty (1962: 215) all individuality and every specific sociality presupposes an *anonymous intersubjectivity* that is the ground of our figural relations with things and persons in-and-as-our-world. This lived-world is ours through the lived-body and it rests on a perceptual faith that is prior to conceptual articulation. It is our primordial presence to a human milieu that inaugurates all other specific relations, such as synecdoche, metaphor, and metonymy, that expresses our being-in-the-world. This lived-world is prior to the known-world and is coevally populated with others who as kindred bodies share the same lived-world as I do. This is our perceptual faith and not at all a contingent achievement of reasoned and rhetorical argument. The articulation of the infant's body likewise presupposes this funding of anonymous intersubjectivity overlooked by Lacan, who construes the infant's history as a continuous fall from intersubjectivity, forever yearning for a future incorporation as fantastic as its first loss.

Merleau-Ponty's interpretation of infant development is rather different from Lacan's alienated perspective. Before a mirror, the infant believes both that s/he is in the mirror and that s/he sees herself therein from where s/he stands. Thus s/he has not yet constructed a mirror image distinct from herself; s/he dwells in an *interworld* in which s/he has not yet articulated either her own ego-logical perspective nor yet a sociological orientation towards the other in her propriety. Yet it is only from this ground of anonymous intersubjectivity – not-yet ego, not-yet alter – that s/he can experience the generics of a bodily and personal self in a world similarly incorporated. At the same time, this primordial intersubjectivity grounds all later perception, desire, identity, and alterity in the faith that the individual can be valorized for 'herself' by an other who in turn shares a similar expectation of mutual recognition. This is not to deny that the later history of the infant body is shaped by separation from the mother body and its displacement within the family body (see O'Neill, 2002: chapter 4). Thus the specular image and the 'grammar' of the pronominal system represent two complementary behavioural modalities of the self-seen-in-other relations (O'Neill, 1982). The specular and linguistic body work together to raise the visual body into a socio-psychological space in which the infant can develop her psychic and social life on the way to childhood. The mirror image, then, not only prefigures the child's jubilation at her narcissistic self but also her entry into the duties of life among others who exercise upon her the constraints of kinship, family, and society (Wagner, 1986). The mirror stage, as Merleau-Ponty interprets it, adds a dimension of integration to the body schema so that the infant can 'regress' but never entirely separate herself from her own kind:

> The infant discovers a whole dimension of experience in the mirror image. He can contemplate himself and observe himself. The infant makes himself a visible self – a super ego that ceases to be identical with his desires. The infant is pulled out of his immediate reality. His attention is confiscated by the *me* whose first symbol he discovers in the mirror image: the de-realizing function of the mirror. This game already accomplishes, before social integration, the transformation of the 'I'…It produces an alienation of the immediate me to the benefit of the specular me.
>
> (Merleau-Ponty, 1964: 302)

I wish to argue that the human body is the point of articulation for all thought and language precisely because the infant body is not an alienated fragment of being whose destiny is to be haunted by an imaginary wholeness. If Lacan were right, then we are born into a synecdochical crisis of psychic division and social separation which love can never heal and which the law can hardly contain. We would be exiled from the potentially ideal speech community because our very language is fractured and can only repeat our split being (O'Neill, 1983b). Even the language of psychoanalysis could not repair our divided being, despite its efforts to expropriate the history and dialectic of recognition espoused in Christianity and Marxism. I propose, therefore, to reconsider Freud's discovery of the theory of infant sexuality in order to show how Lacan's conception of the fragmented body ignores the originary semiotics generated across the mother-infant body (the *matrix*). The latter constitutes a communicative surface – or *flesh* – upon which the figures of metaphor, metonymy, and synecdoche are inscribed as operations that shift the infant body into language and meaning and thereby underwrite its acquisition of psychic life in which it is attuned to the society of others of its kind. In short, I am arguing, against Lacan's vision of alienation and fragmentation, that Freud's theory of sexuality consists in the discovery of the body that becomes ill when its destiny for society is foreclosed. I consider, then, that Freud discovered the dynamics of the synecdochical body – the body destined to see itself as part of a whole which in turn it sees in its parts. This is the civilizable body – the body of health and illness are therefore modalities of this corporeal synecdoche.

The problem of the search for meaning in the embodied inquiry that is aroused in the *matrix* (the mother/infant body) obliges us to reconsider Freud's theory of the vicissitudes of the instincts (Freud, 1955 [1915]) to determine the deviation (*clinamen*) through which the *biological body*, so to speak, opens to the *psychical body*. Here we may be guided by Paul Ricoeur's observations:

> Freud is in line with those thinkers for whom man is desire before being speech; man is speech because the first semantics of desire is distortion and he never completely overcomes this initial distortion. If this is so, then Freud's doctrine would be animated from beginning to end by a conflict between the 'mythology of desire' and the 'science of the physical apparatus' – a 'science' in which he always, but in vain, tried to contain the 'mythology,' and which, ever since the 'Project,' was exceeded by its own contents.
>
> (Ricoeur, 1970: 313)

I am going to argue that there is an 'originary surface,' which I shall call the *flesh*, where the primitive language of the body is transcribed into the first language of the mind. Moreover, we want to stress that the circuit between the biological and the psychical body intertwines with the circuit between the mother and infant body. Thus the first language or 'mother tongue' (*la langue maternelle*) arises in the overlap of the *flesh* and the *matrix*. Even in his 'Project for a Scientific Psychology' (1895), Freud seems to have been aware that the 'physical apparatus' could not be closed off in what Paul Ricoeur calls 'an energetic without hermeneutics.' I think the real psychoanalytic discovery is that of the 'surface' of *flesh* upon which the symbolic processes (*semiotics*) are inscribed and where, so to speak, our hermeneutical life has its proper origin. It is here, too, that Freud's theory of sexuality and its clinical evidence are to be located, so that finally there is a radically hermeneutical turn in psychoanalysis away from the early theories of neurophysiology. In Ricoeur's words:

> Psychoanalysis never confronts one with bare forces, but always with forces in search of meaning. This link between force and meaning makes instinct a psychical reality, or, more exactly, the limit concept at the frontier between the organic and the psychical. The link between hermeneutics and economics may be stretched as far as possible – and the theory of affects marks the extreme of that distension in the Freudian meta-psychology; still the link cannot be broken, for otherwise the economics would cease to belong to psychoanalysis.
>
> (Ricoeur, 1970: 151)

In his 'Three Essays on the Theory of Sexuality' (1905) and various summary reformulations, Freud argues that whereas hunger is the model of *desire*, as we should say, of the *flesh* – it is sexuality that is the model of every desire. To argue this, as Jean Laplanche (1976) shows, Freud had literally to prop up (*étayer*, *anlehnen*) his theory of sexuality against the theory of life. In other words, Freud leaned upon biology to underwrite psychoanalysis. Here Freud's metapsychology repeats at its own level a disciplinary *anaclisis* which is motivated by his attempt to analyse the fundamental mother-infant dependency. To find in the beginning of life the origins of sexuality as life's own *clinamen* or deviation, Freud leans psychoanalysis upon the biology of the sexual drives – with a difference that results in the theory of the generalized sexuality of the infant:

> The first organ to emerge as an erotogenic zone and to make libidinal demands on the mind is, from the birth onwards, the mouth. To begin with, all psychical activity is concentrated on providing satisfaction for the needs of that zone. Primarily, of course, this satisfaction serves the purpose of self-preservation by means of nourishment; but physiology should not be confused with psychology. The baby's obstinate persistence in sucking gives evidence at an early age of a need for satisfaction which, though it originates from and is instigated by the taking of nourishment, nevertheless strives to obtain pleasure independently of nourishment and for that reason may and should be termed sexual.
>
> (Freud, 1949: 10–11)

As I see it, we can accept the theory of sexual *clinamen*, provided we see that is the *body of flesh* whose identity is 'organized' as the site and sequence of erogenous zones, mouth, tongue, anus, urethra, genitals, according to Freud's libidinal theory. It is the flesh which is already communicative from the embryo's first signs of uterine life (Hooker, 1943). The articulation or figuration of the flesh is the receptacle *(chora)* of all inscription, trace, and textuality (Kristeva, 1980a: 133–134). The flesh is the receptacle of lived presence and absence as well as of lived temporality of its own mobility or desire. In this sense, the flesh is not a passive tablet of experience, of dreams, or of pleasure and pain. Rather, the flesh prefigures every figuration, trace, and gesture, through a continuous difference which is the mark or sign of life itself. This token of life is pre-symbolic. That is to say, it is the very ground of the possibility of symbolism, of the distinction between presence and absence, whole and part, figure and ground. The flesh is the originary *difference*, the in-between of presence and absence, part and whole, satisfaction and desire. It continues to be this difference from the first sign of life until the last sign of death, and in all of its rhythms of desire, lack, abjection, incorporation, and satisfaction, the flesh repeats or represents itself as its own icon. The flesh is the proper transcript of its own vicissitudes, of its instincts, pleasure, desire, sexuality, love, pain, and suffering. It is this transcript that every living being records for itself and which it must continuously decipher in reading its own experience, instincts, dreams, likes and dislikes. The daily transcriptions of the flesh provide us with the soul's reading.

I am adopting Freud's suggestion that the *psychical* ego be regarded as both the surface of the *bodily* ego and its projection in order to stress the continuity of the body organ and the psychical apparatus of the ego. The psychoanalytic conception of the ego is otherwise reduced to a species of faulty psychology abstracted from the essential Freudian discovery of the precipitation of part objects in the constitution of the whole subject. In other words, the primary processes remain open on the body to the level of consciousness as its 'other scene.' Thus it can be argued that the basic clinamen in the instincts toward the drives, hence from death to life, occurs in two phases:

1. *metaphorization of the aim*, which shifts intake of milk in response to hunger (*saugen*) to the fantasmic incorporation of the mother breast in pleasure sucking (*lutschen*);
2. *metonymization of the object*, which substitutes milk for what is next to it, namely, the breast, so that the infant rediscovers not the lost object but its metonym (Laplanche, 1976: 137).

In 'Project for a Scientific Psychology' (1955 [1895]), Freud considered that it is in this second phase that perception and judgment are differentiated, to be taken later in language. At the breast, the infant is already engaged in separating the wishful cathexis of memory and a perceptual cathexis similar to it, while learning to deal with a constant perceptual component, on the one hand, and a variable perceptual component on the other, i.e., between *thing* and *predicate*. Freud again takes up this process at the stage of the feeding infant:

> Let us suppose, for instance, that the mnemonic image wished for (by a child) is the image of the mother's breast and a front view of its nipple, and that the first perception is a side view of the same object, without the nipple. In the child's memory there is an experience, made by chance in the course of sucking, that with a particular head-movement the front image turns into the side image. This side image which is not seen leads to the (image of the) head-movement; an experiment shows that this counter-part must be carried out; and the perception of the front view is achieved.
>
> There is not much judgement about this yet; but it is an example of the possibility of arriving, by a reproduction of cathexes, at an action which is already one of the accidental offshoots of the specific action.
>
> (Freud, 1955 [1895]: 328–29)

Equally interesting are Freud's observations in the 'Project' regarding the first phase of the metaphorization of sucking into sensual sucking that constitutes the *inter-corporeal basis of cognition*. Here the mother's body is the first object of theoretical interest, the first source of satisfaction. Thus the infant has to learn within the overlap (matrix) of her mother's body and her own body to recognize movements arising from the mother body as a constant structure of the thing, and sensations or motor image arising from within her own body. Due to the helplessness of the early infant body, her ability to fulfil specific actions in the external world requires the mother's mediation. This is called for in the infant's cry, which as an internal discharge requires the secondary function of *communication*. This allows the mother to begin the work of imputing moral motives to the infant as the basis for her later socialization (Tischler, 1957). There, too, Freud locates the origin of speech:

> Speech innervation is originally a path of discharge…operating like a safety valve, for regulating oscillations…It is a portion of the path to *internal change*, which represents the only discharge till the *specific action* has been found….This path acquires a secondary function from the fact that it draws the attention of the helpful person (usually the wished for object itself) to the child's longing and distressful state; and thereafter it serves for *communication* and is thus drawn into the specific action.
>
> (Freud, 1955 [1895]: 366)

At this stage, also, the early processes of cognition and communication link up in the perception of (a) objects that make the infant cry, and (b) crying that characterizes an object. Thus cognition involves a linking up of unconscious memories and objects of perceptual attention, including some which arouse a sound image, and later objects that will be associated with intentional sounds. 'Not much is now needed,' says Freud, 'in order to invent speech.' Indeed, there is considerable evidence to show that the infant oral stage affects the formation of the so-called soft consonants and vowels (L, M, I) with effects of sweetness and plenitude associated with sucking (Fonàgy, 1970, 1971).

The infant flesh is destined from the beginning to embody the very inquiry that constitutes a living being. The exploration of its own internal and external boundaries and testing of all experience/information that enters/exits its orifices and skin surfaces entirely absorbs the infant in its own carnal knowledge. The *flesh*, then, is neither a biological nor a psychical ground from the start. It becomes both in the mother-infant feeding relation, as the instinct to survive which is then diverted into a 'pleasure sucking' (Halveson, 1938) whose object is neither milk nor the breast but its own autoeroticism:

> Thus the first object of the oral component of the sexual instinct is the mother's breast which satisfies the infant's need for nutrition. In the act of sucking for its own sake the erotic component, also gratified in sucking for nutrition, makes itself independent, gives up the object in an external person, and replaces it by a part of the child's own person. The oral impulse becomes auto-erotic, as the anal and other erotogenic impulses are from the beginning. Further development has, to put it as concisely as possible, two aims: first, to renounce auto-eroticism, to give up again the object found in the child's own body in exchange again for an external one; and secondly, to combine the various objects of the separate impulses and replace them by one single one. This naturally can only be done if the single object is again itself complete, with a body like that of the subject; nor can it be accomplished without some part of the auto-erotic impulse excitations being abandoned as useless.
>
> (Freud, 1960: 338)

From its earliest days, the infant body entertains the possibility of becoming the partial body, or the 'body bit' (*corps morcelé*), of its mother or of its (incipient) self. 'Partial objects include breast, penis, and numerous other elements related to bodily life (excrement, child, etc.), all of which have in common the fundamental characteristic of being, in fact or in fantasy, *detached* or *detachable*' (Laplanche, 1976: 13). To some extent, this is given in the infant's somatic experience of her body with organs whose drives are represented in her mental life as though they had a source outside/inside herself which she has as yet to integrate in a whole-body image. Thus the hunger drive attaches the sucking infant to the mother's breast for her milk. But soon the infant internalizes her need for milk by diverting it towards the very pleasure of sucking, thereby psycho-sexualizing a biological drive or instinct, and replacing the partial mother body with her own partial mother body with its own partial body (tongue, thumb). 'We call this action "pleasure sucking" (German: *lutschen*, signifying the enjoyment of sucking for its own sake – as with a rubber "comforter"); and as when it does this the infant again falls asleep with a blissful expression we see that the action of sucking is sufficient in itself to give it satisfaction' (Freud, 1960: 322).

In the shift from *saugen* to *lutschen* the infant experiences, well before Lacan's mirror stage, essentially the same internal precipitation of the forms of the other by shifting from the mother-breast to his own tongue and thumb. Freud himself speaks of the derivation of the ego from the body's sensations arising from its exploration of its cutaneous surface, that is from the flesh as an inside/outside source of sensations that are the basis for the differentiation of perception and judgment in respect of the (un)pleasure principle and the reality principle:

> Freud thus indicates clearly two meshing observations of the ego from the 'surface': on the one hand, the ego is the surface of the physical apparatus, a specialized organ continuous with it; on the other hand, it is the projection or metaphor of the body's surface, a metaphor in which the various perceptual systems have a role to play.
>
> (Laplanche, 1976: 82)

Furthermore, the significance of this surface of flesh between the body and the ego is that the pre-libidinal ego is *not* from the very start in conflict with the primary process of sexuality, though this conflict may be 'organized' at higher or later levels of ego development. Rather, the infant's perception of the mother body is wholly absorbed with her expressive face, smile, and voice, which is, of course, a total body response communicated in the way she holds and handles the infant body and its expressive responses. Here, again, there is a surface of exchange in the communicative flesh recognized immediately in the mother/infant body. The infant's stage of autoeroticism, then, does not precede his attachment to the mother-breast. Rather, it represents the rediscovery of this lost object in his own body, from which he will have again to be detached in favour of a whole body whose image is for-himself-and-for-others. The mirror phase and the castration and Oedipus complexes are the circuits of the domestic body (O'Neill, 1985). If the circuit of pleasure could be closed at the biological level, then the infant would never acquire symbolic behaviour. Without the maternal mediation of the infant's bodily needs, and the radical contingency of satisfaction and dissatisfaction, the symbolization of desire would never arise, and the infant would never acquire speech. Freudian desire always speaks to the other before itself. Its demands are, so to speak, upon recognition and are rhetorical rather than physical. The semantics of desire, then, are necessarily domestic, for good and evil. Here, again, the consequences are clearly expressed in Ricoeur's comment:

> The intersubjective structure of desires is the profound truth of the Freudian libido theory; even in the period of the 'Project' and Chapter 7 of the *Traumdeutung*, Freud never described instincts outside of an intersubjective context; if desire were not located within an inter-human situation, there would be no such things as repression, censorship, or wish-fulfilment through fantasies; that the other and others are primarily bearers of prohibitions is simply another way of saying that desire encounters another desire – an opposed desire. The whole dialectic of roles within the second topography expresses the internalization of a relation of opposition, constitutive of human desire; the fundamental meaning of the Oedipus complex is that human desire is a history, that this history involves refusal and hurt, that desire becomes inflicted upon it by an opposing desire.
>
> (Ricoeur, 1970: 387)

I have analyzed an infant history with the purpose of showing that all later histories of alienation presuppose a first history of integration. Without such a ground, or synecdoche, we are condemned to a history without any intelligible origin or end. Our minds could then embrace only a metaphysics of absence from which our bodies would sicken. Some might say this is the price of human independence and it is redeemed in its great artistic, philosophical, and scientific assertions. I do not mean to deny the history and metaphysics of alienation as part of the human adventure since I think it is inseparable from Western consciousness and its social institutions (O'Neill, 1996). There can be no doubt that we have weaned ourselves from divine and maternal dependence. Our science of childhood is an obvious testament to the history of individualism (O'Neill, 1995). By the same token, our history is riddled with problems of separation, division, and alienation. We then turn to that other history of ours in which we are whole, bonded, and together (see O'Neill, 2002: chapters 2 and 3). In short, we then insist upon that great synecdoche in which the world and its parts are one, each in the other, before the living whole separated into mortal parts and we began to live and make our contracts between Eros and Thanatos, giving way to one another.

References

Fonàgy, Ivan (1970). 'Les bases pulsionnelles de la phonation'. *Revue française de psychanalyse* 34(1): 101–136.

Freud, Sigmund (1949). *An Outline of Psycho-analysis*. James Strachey (trans.). New York and London: W. W. Norton.

Freud, Sigmund (1955). 'Project for a Scientific Psychology' [1895]. *The Standard Edition of the Complete Psychological Works, vol. 1*. James Strachey (ed., trans.). London: Hogarth Press.

Freud, Sigmund (1955 [1905]). 'Three Essays on the Theory of Sexuality'. *Standard Edition, vol. 7*, pp. 125–243. James Strachey (ed., trans.). London: Hogarth Press, and Harmondsworth, Middlesex, England: Penguin Freud Library, vol. 7, pp. 33–170.

Freud, Sigmund (1955 [1915]). 'Instincts and Their Vicissitudes'. *Standard Edition, vol. 14*. James Strachey (ed., trans.). London: Hogarth Press.

Freud, Sigmund (1960). 'Development of the Libido and Sexual Organisation'. *A General Introduction to Psychoanalysis*. Joan Rivière (trans.). New York: Washington Square Press.

Halveson, H. M. (1938). 'Infant Sucking and Tensional Behaviour'. *The Journal of Genetic Psychology* 53: 365–430.

Hooker, Davenport (1943). 'Reflex Activities in the Human Fetus'. In: *Child Behaviour and Development*. Roger G. Barker, Jacob S. Kounin, and Herbert S. Wright (eds.). New York and London: McGraw-Hill, pp. 120–92.

Kristeva, Julia (1980). 'The Novel as Polylogue'. In: *Desire in Language: A Semiotic Approach in Literature and Art*. Leone S. Roudiez (ed.). Thomas Gora, Alice Jardine, Leone S. Roudiez (trans). New York: Columbia University Press, pp. 159–209.

Lacan, Jacques (1977). 'The Mirror Stage as Formative of the Function of the I'. In: *Écrits: A selection*. Alan Sheridan (trans.). New York: W. W. Norton, pp. 1–7.

Laplanche, Jean (1976). *Life and Death in Psychoanalysis*. Jeffrey Mehlman (trans.). Baltimore, MD: Johns Hopkins University Press.

Medina, Angel (1985). 'Heidegger, Lacan and the Boundaries of Existence: Whole and Partial Subjects in Psychoanalysis'. *Man and World* 18: 389–403.

Merleau-Ponty, Maurice (1962). *Phenomenology of Perception*. Colin Smith (trans.). London: Routledge and Kegan Paul.

Merleau-Ponty, Maurice (1964). 'Group d'Études de Psychologie de l'Université de Paris, Resumé des Cours de Merleau-Ponty'. *Bulletin de Psychologie* 236 (xviii): 109–336.

O'Neill, John (1970). *Perception, Expression and History: The Social Phenomenology of Maurice Merleau-Ponty*. Evanston, IL: Northwestern University Press.

O'Neill, John (1982). 'Embodiment and Child Development'. In: *The Sociology of Childhood: Essential Readings*. Chris Jenks (ed.). London: Batsford Academic and Educational, pp. 76–86.

O'Neill, John (1983a). 'Vico on the Natural Workings of the Mind'. In: *Phenomenology and the Human Sciences*. Denver, CO: Philosophical Topics, pp. 117–25.

O'Neill, John (1983b). 'Power and the Splitting (*Spaltung*) of Language'. *New Literary History* 14: 695–710.

O'Neill, John (1985). *Five Bodies: The Human Shape of Modern Society*. Ithaca, NY: Cornell University Press.

O'Neill, John (1986). 'The Specular Body: Merleau-Ponty and Lacan on Infant Self and Other'. *Synthèse* 66: 201–217.

O'Neill, John (1989). *The Communicative Body: Studies in Continental Philosophy, Politics and Sociology*. Evanston, IL: Northwestern University Press.

O'Neill, John (1995). *The Poverty of Postmodernism*. London: Routledge.

O'Neill, John (ed., intro.) (1996). *Hegel's Dialectic of Desire and Recognition: Texts and Commentary*. Albany, NY: State University of New York Press.

O'Neill, John (2002). *Incorporating Cultural Theory: Maternity at the Millenium*. Albany, NY: State University of New York Press.

Paul, Robert A. (1977). 'The First Speech Events: Genesis as the Nursery for Consciousness'. *Psychocultural Review* 1: 179–184.

Ricoeur, Paul (1970). *Freud and Philosophy: An Essay on Interpretation*. Daniel Savage (trans.). New Haven and London: Yale University Press.

Tischler, Hans (1957). 'Schreien, Lacheln, und Erstes Sprechen in der Entwicklung des Sauglings'. *Zeitschrift fur Psychologie* 160 (3–4): 210–263.

Wagner, Roy (1986). *Symbols that stand for themselves*. Chicago: University of Chicago Press.

Part 2
The productive body

5 The disciplinary society*
From Weber to Foucault

Here I want to show through an historical rather than analytic sketch how the formidable works of Weber and Foucault may be considered in terms of their convergence upon a single question, namely, *what are the techniques by which humankind has subjected itself to the rational discipline of the applied human sciences* (law, medicine, economics, education, and administration)? Clearly, it is not possible to pursue this question in the same historical and comparative detail to be found in either the Weberian corpus or in Foucault's recent archaeological studies. Rather, it will be argued that certain developments in Foucault's studies of the disciplinary society (1979a; 1979b) may complement Weber's formal analysis of the modern bureaucratic state and economy – despite Foucault's different conception of social rationality. Thus, the formal analytic and historical features of Weber's account of the bureaucratic state and economy may be related to Foucault's analysis of the discursive production of the human sciences of government, economics and social policy and to the concomitant regimentation of *docile bodies* under the disciplines of the prison, the workhouse, and the factory. Despite Foucault's critical stance on the Marxist theory of state power, we cannot overlook Marx's attention (as well as that of more recent social historians) to the rise of factory discipline since this is an essential presupposition in the theory of discipline and power espoused both by Foucault and Weber. An historical sketch of the struggle over the work process, labour discipline, Taylorism and the bureaucratization of controls backed ultimately by the State which also guarantees rights to work, health and education, is necessary to understand how labour is rendered docile in the disciplinary culture of the therapeutic state (Miller and Neussus, 1979; Hirsch, 1979).

State power, bureaucracy and biopolitics

It is not far-fetched to consider Weber an archaeologist of the power man exerts over himself, and thus to see him as a precursor of Foucault's conception of the disciplinary society. In each case, history is not ransacked for its rational essence, even

* Text of the essay taken from *The Poverty of Postmodernism* (1995). London: Routledge. Pages 43–63. Reprinted with permission.

though it is only understood as a process of increasing rationalization. Nor is history seen as the story of individual freedom, even though western political history is only intelligible as its invention. What intervenes is the logic of the institutions that bring together rationality, individualism and freedom in the large-scale disciplinary enterprises of capitalism, bureaucracy and the modern therapeutic state. Modern society makes itself rich, knowledgeable and powerful but at the expense of substantive reason and freedom. Yet neither Weber nor Foucault are much beguiled by the socialist diagnosis of these trends. Of course neither thinker is entirely intelligible apart from Marx's analytic concerns. But both are closer to Nietzsche than to Marx in their grasp of the radical finitude of human rationality (Foucault, 1970). In this, Weber and Foucault part company with Marx's ultimately romantic rationalism and its sad echoes in the halls of socialist state bureaucracy. Both of them are resolutely separated from any transcendental rationality, although Weber seems at times to have yearned for the desert winds of charisma to blow through the disciplinary society. But Foucault, distinguishing himself from Weber, shows no such equivocation.

> One isn't assessing things in terms of an absolute against which they could be evaluated as constituting more or less perfect forms of rationality, but rather examining how forms of rationality inscribe themselves in practices or systems of practices, and what role they play within them. Because it's true that 'practices' don't exist without a certain regime of rationality. But rather than measuring this regime against a value-of-reason, I would prefer to analyse it according to two axes: on the one hand, that of codification/prescription (how it forms an ensemble of rules, procedures, means to an end, etc.) and on the other, that of true or false formulation (how it determines a domain of objects about which it is possible to articulate true or false positions).
>
> (Foucault, 1981: 8)

The only possibility of any reversal in the discursive production of the disciplinary sciences and their technologies of administrative control, as Foucault sees it, is that archaeological studies of the knowledge/power complex will simultaneously unearth the subjugated knowledge of those groups (not simply identifiable with the proletariat) who have been condemned to historical and political silence (under socialism no less than capitalism). If Weber, on the other hand, saw no relief from his vision of the *bureaucratic production of the state, economy and society*, it is because he regarded science in general, and the social sciences in particular, as 'factions' in the production of the rationalization process they simultaneously discover as a topic and deploy as a resource for their own disciplinary organization (Wilson, 1976; 1977). Thus Weber carried out his own vocation as a 'specialist', limited by his reflections upon a politics and history unable to transcend positive finitude. Weber's commitment to his discipline did not represent a mode of self-alienation or of political bad conscience, so much as the responsible ethic of an individual who had seen the limits of our faith in science as an objective belief. The alternative is a leap into the barbarism of reflection and a Utopian invocation of the cycle of history to deliver new men on the back of the old man.

Weber's distillate of the formal features of bureaucratic organization and discipline (1947; 1967) is intended to assist in the study of hospitals, armies, schools, churches, business and political organizations, as well as of the institutions for the production of scientific knowledge of nature and society. Legal order, bureaucracy, compulsory jurisdiction over a territory and monopolization of the legitimate use of force are the essential characteristics of the modern state. This complex of factors emerged only gradually in Europe and is only fully present where legitimacy is located in the body of bureaucratic rules that determine the exercise of political authority. It should be noted that Weber's concept of the legitimacy of the modern legal state is purely formal: laws are legitimate if procedurally correct and any correct procedure is legal. Of course, Weber did not ignore the actual value-contexts of political legitimacy (Schluchter, 1981). He saw the historical drift moving from natural law to legal positivism but could not see that the events of the twentieth century would lead to attempts to reinstate natural law in an effort to bridle state barbarism. Foucault's studies of the rise of the modern state apparatus do not alter Weber's conception of the legitimation process but they are much more graphic. This is meant quite literally. Although Weber sees the documentary growth of the legal and bureaucratic administrative process, he does not judge its effects upon the *body politic*. By contrast, like Marx, Foucault never loses sight of the body as the ultimate text upon which the power of the state and the economy is inscribed. By the same token, Foucault is able to go beyond Weber's legal-rational concept of legitimacy to capture the medicalization of power and the therapeutic mode of the legitimation function in the modern state:

> In concrete terms, starting in the seventeenth century, this power over life evolved in two basic forms; these forms were not antithetical however; they constituted rather two poles of development, linked together by a whole intermediary cluster of relations. One of these poles – the first to be formed, it seems – centred on the body as a machine; its disciplining, the optimization of its capabilities, the extortion of its forces, the parallel increase of its usefulness and its docility, its integration into systems of efficient and economic controls, all this was ensured by the procedures of power that characterized the *disciplines*: an *anatomo-politics of the body*. The second, formed somewhat later, focused on the species body, the body as the basis of the biological processes: propagation and longevity, with all the conditions that can cause these to vary. Their supervision was effected through an entire series of interventions and *regulatory controls: a bio-politics of the population*.
>
> (Foucault, 1980: 139)

Weber's discussion of bureaucracy is largely framed in terms of the legal and rational accounting requirements of political and economic organization which in turn give to legal domination its administrative rationality and adequacy. The formal-analytic features of the Weberian concept of bureaucracy are to be found as constitutive practices in the operation of the army, church, university, hospital and political party – not to mention the very organization of the relevant discovering social sciences. Although Foucault (1975; 1979a) does not study the bureaucratic process in the Weberian mode, his studies of the prison, hospital and school go beyond Weber in grounding the legal-rational accounting process in techniques for the administration of corporeal, attitudinal and behavioural discipline. Foucault thereby complements Weber's formal-rational concept of bureaucracy and legal domination with a *physiology of bureaucracy and power* which is the definitive feature of the disciplinary society. It is for this reason that, despite the difficulties in his style, Foucault deserves the attention of social scientists. There is a tendency in Weber's account of bureaucracy to identify it with a ruling class, dominating the economy and the bourgeois democratic state. There are a number of overlapping issues here regarding the demarcation of the economy and the polity, of classes and élites, but especially of the distinction between the *state apparatus* and *state power*. Bureaucracy is the dominant mode of operation of the state apparatus, as it tends to be in the economy. But it is neither a class in itself nor is it the state power. Rather, bureaucracy might be treated as a strategy for the reproduction of the state's relation to the economy, and for the reproduction of socio-economic relations between individuals in the state. Thus we have to review, however briefly, the history of the separation of labour from the ownership of the means of production. In other words, we have to see how the bourgeois state assigns to the juridical individual his/her legal rights whereby he or she freely contracts into systems of exploitation and discipline (patriarchal, paternalist and bureaucratic) which the state defends even when it corrects its abuses. The ideological function of the state and legal process is to constitute individual agency at the juridical level precisely in order to reproduce the social division of labour and its bureaucratic rationalization independent of 'individuals' and their particularistic attributes (Poulantzas, 1973). The sociological codification of this effect is to be found in the Weberian and Parsonian (1951) analysis of the rational-legal accounting process and its pattern variable schematization of required conduct from adequately motivated, i.e., disciplined individuals concerned solely with role-specific functions.

What the ideological isolation of the independent juridical subject achieves is the *inversion* of the economic dependency of the subject who freely contracts into a system of labour dominated by the market. Or rather, precisely because the issue of independence is removed from the level of economy to the level of the polity, the economy can subject itself to the 'independent' discipline of external laws of the market before which capitalists are as unfree as labourers. These features are preserved when we replace the 'market' with 'bureaucracy' as a gloss upon the isolation of the state and socioeconomic processes of capitalist production. By the same token, the bourgeois state limits itself to the integration of the isolated effects of the underlying class system of production and labour discipline but without seeking to radically alter it beyond the defence of individualized rights and duties. But this argument needs to be considered in an historical perspective in order to recapture (however briefly) the movement from which Weber,

Marx and Foucault drew their theoretical insights into the stratagems of power that shape the disciplinary society.

The rise of industrial discipline

It may be worthwhile to consider the middle ground between Weber and Foucault by taking even a brief look at the history of *industrial discipline*. This will enable us to weigh the difference between Weber's formal-analytic approach to the rationalization of social and political control and Foucault's approach via the discursive strategies and physiology of *disciplinary power* which were devised in the context of the shift to the factory and its gradual bureaucratization of the work process. By the same token, this will put in perspective Foucault's (1980) critique of the Marxist theory of power by reminding us that industrial and bureaucratic discipline arise from the historical struggle between capital and labour over control of the technical means and social organization of production (Braverman, 1974; Burawoy, 1984; Pollard, 1963; Reid, 1976; Thompson, 1967). This is necessary since, while Foucault scores nicely against certain Marxist conceptions of state power, his own views are in danger of leaving us the victims of power that is everywhere and nowhere.

Although, as we know from Laslett (1965) and Wall (see Wall, Robin and Laslett, eds., 1983), it is no longer possible to indulge the myth of the family as a natural economy, it is generally agreed that in the mid-eighteenth century the family-based putting-out and domestic system of manufacture came under pressure as the industrial revolution got under way. In the specific case of the cotton industry, the family system had to adjust to a new pace, increasingly independent of the agricultural seasons (Smelser, 1959; Edwards and Lloyd-Jones, 1973; Anderson, 1976). The pull in this direction showed itself in productive bottlenecks, imbalances between spinning and weaving, and the master's increasing dissatisfaction with the independence, self-pacing and casual character of the workers engaged in the putting-out system (Reid, 1976). The putting-out system compared unfavourably (Landes, 1969) with the factory system of control and discipline and with the Methodist values which serviced the interests of continuous production (Burrell 1984). Thus workers were plagued with charges of idleness, dishonesty, drunkenness and immorality in the courts and the press. The factory masters responded in opposing ways to this perception of wayward labour, namely, with the imposition of harsh and cruel conditions, as a general rule, and with proposals for 'model communities', to transform the old rule. In either case, worker discipline was the main ingredient aimed at improving the moral habits of the labouring poor, to make them orderly, punctual, responsible and temperate:

> In all these ways – by the division of labour; the supervision of labour; fines; bells and clocks; money incentives; preachings and schoolings; the suppression of fairs and sports – new labour habits were formed, and a new time discipline was imposed.
>
> (Thompson, 1967: 90)

Further stress fell upon the domestic system and the family economy with the differential impact of technological changes in spinning and weaving. The spinning jenny and the water-frame moved spinning into the factory and, by simplifying the labour, at first displaced men with women and children. This, of course, seriously challenged the moral economy of the family, although a modified apprenticeship and family hiring survived in the factory for quite a while. Thus, as Smelser observes:

> the water-frame factory of the late eighteenth century moved only 'part way' toward the ideal conditions of economic rationality. Workers were segregated from their means of production, but the remnants of job appropriation by workers remained in the form of a modified apprenticeship system and family hiring. Discipline proved a major problem to the early capitalists, but its enforcement had not differentiated entirely from the more diffuse family ties of the pre-factory social structure.
>
> (Smelser, 1959: 107)

With the introduction of mule-spinning and steam power, the factory system and its discipline became more pronounced. The separation of the workers from the ownership of the means of production increased capital's control over labour. By the same token, workers lost control over their own pace (Thompson, 1967) and became increasingly subject to entrepreneurial discipline. The changes we have observed on the spinning side of the cotton industry could not continue without building pressure for similar changes, differentiation and realignments in the weaving trades. As spinning began to outstrip the weavers, pressure grew to separate weaving from its basis in the domestic putting-out system, moving it into hand-loom factories and eventually power-loom factories. The big difference here is that power-loom weaving, as opposed to mule-spinning, displaced males with women and children. Workers in the cotton industry responded to the changes in their family economy with machine breaking, strikes and riots. They struggled to come to terms with piece rates, child labour and the ten-hour day, always trying to preserve their skilled status (Penn 1982). The hand-loom weavers turned to pleas for relief, violence, political agitation and were attracted to the Utopian movements of Cobbett, Owen, and the Chartists. The Acts of 1833 and 1844 combined to reduce child labour and thereby to separate the adult and child working day, putting pressure once again on the family and state agencies to be concerned with child education and family welfare. Thus the workers turned to the organization of unions, friendly societies and savings banks as means of adjusting to circumstances that could no longer be handled by the old poor law relief system.

We cannot pursue these histories. Moreover, the complexity of the issues surrounding the evolution of the working class (Form, 1981, 1983) and its paths towards reformism or revolution (Burawoy, 1984) remains unresolved even by a host of empirical studies. Here it is enough to remark that in most instances worker discipline, even where it involves self-discipline, is always a ruling concern – food riots and strikes being taken as evidence of the naturally undisciplined nature of workers outside of administrative controls, while the workers struggle to maintain their skills and concomitant social status. The fact remains that industrial discipline has never wholly conquered the working classes. Workers have hung on to many pre-industrial values, they have learned to sabotage, slow down, quit and take off (Palmer, 1975; Stark, 1980; Littler, 1982). Thus labour discipline continues to challenge management and government to this day. It is therefore necessary to avoid a naïve economism when thinking of the capitalist control of the means of production. Such control may be more or less efficient when viewed from a strictly technical standpoint and there may even be some competitive push in this direction. But capitalism is a social system concerned to reproduce itself. In other words, any form of social control over the means of production must reproduce the class system of capitalism – and this rule must apply to bureaucracy no less than to technocracy: 'all means for the development of production transform themselves into means of domination and exploitation of the producers' (Marx, 1906: 709). Thus capitalists had also to bring themselves into line with the requirements of industrial rationalization (Pollard 1963). It is one thing to be Protestant in outlook and quite another to be so in narrow practice. For this reason, capitalists as entrepreneurs resisted feeding themselves into Taylorism as much as their workers, preferring, as Littler (1978; 1982) points out, to subcontract worker discipline and management. It fell to the engineers to devise for them the book-keeping and cost-accountancy functions that increased control over expenses, stocks, overheads, productivity and profitability (Hill, 1981). The engineers and middle managers, then, made themselves the servants of capital in this respect. Its prospective control of the work process, craft knowledge and labour solidarity further extended the appeal of scientific management and professional engineers (Rodgers, 1979). Here it is vital to see that what was at stake was capitalist hegemony over the primary work process and not some abstract attachment to scientific efficiency. Taylorism was morally alien to the values and dignity of independent labour. Taylor's conception of the labouring man as lazy, bestial and intemperate, working only under the threat of discipline and strict supervision was hostile to self-paced labour. However, Taylorism was gradually adjusted to accommodate unionism, collective bargaining and various paternalistic and welfare concessions to labour, and owners came to terms with working-class struggles against premium systems, piecework, and loss of control of pace and decision in the smallest of tasks. Indeed, the union movement itself incorporated features of scientific management, particularly during World War II. Whenever management fails to negotiate between labour and capital, labour returns to its historical struggle and capital will call upon the police and, if necessary, the army to maintain law and order. It is, however, in the interest of both the state and capital to reserve legal force for exceptional use. This can be achieved so long as the disciplinary society, to which we now turn, can be relied upon to operate with quasi-natural effect, i.e., removed from historical and political consciousness. How this can be uncritically assumed will be seen in some closing remarks upon the liberal conception of bureaucracy (Crozier, 1964) and power.

The prison and the factory

The labour history we have briefly sketched needs to be relocated in the original framework of classical political economy and its concerns with 'policing' an impoverished, unhealthy, rebellious and criminal population created by the new industrial economy. The autonomy of modern economics was achieved at the expense of abstracting its concerns from the original disciplinary science of government and morals that occupied classical political economy. Thus it is necessary, in the light of Foucault's studies, to review how industrial discipline arose in relation to prison discipline in the production of a docile labour force suited to the needs of early industrial capitalism. It is then possible to see how the bureaucratic discipline of late capitalism presupposes this early history of bodily discipline which, so to speak, funds society's more superficial attitudinal controls. The formal (contractual) freedom of labour expresses its separation from the ownership of the means of production.

The decline of feudalism, the enclosure movements and the confiscation of monastic property at first released large numbers of former peasants into vagabondage and criminality. Fifteenth- and sixteenth-century legislation was faced with the task of separating 'the impotent poor' from the anomalous 'able bodied poor'. The former were authorized to beg; the latter were lucky to find their way into the workhouse and forced labour, a slight-step away from prison. In part, the segregation of forced labourers functioned to regulate the supply of free labour; but, in a broader way, it set the model for the discipline and surveillance of former peasants and artisans while they resisted their new freedom. Early capitalists needed not only to depress wages as far as possible; they also needed wage-labour disciplined to accept long hours and harsh conditions of work. They had also to destroy the popular culture and habits of pre-industrial labour, yet to avoid entirely destabilizing the social order (Ignatieff, 1978:183–4). Thus Calvinism was nicely instrumental as a substitute for Catholic attitudes to charity, holidays and the like. It might be said that if Protestantism removed religious authority from the community, it restored it inside the factory. In fact, Protestantism reinvigorated patriarchy both in the family (Stone 1979:103–5) and in the workhouse which it ran on family lines, as it would later the hospital and prison:

> If prison is a model of society – and here one is still concerned with metaphor – it will not take many years for the Protestant and above all the Calvinist view of society to create a model of the prison of the future in the shape of the workhouse.
>
> (Melossi and Pavarini, 1981: 28–9)

In England, despite the challenge to law and order and the ineffectiveness of its terrible punishments, the propertied classes were not in a hurry to embrace rationalist and utilitarian penal reforms. Such reluctance may well have been inspired by a better sense of the workings of law and authority that enabled the eighteenth-century bourgeoisie to exercise its hegemony without either a large army or a police force. Between them patronage and pardon seem to have increased respect for the law in its mercy and through the very arbitrariness that might strike equally at rich and poor gave rise to a general sense of justice. A curious balance was attempted between the law as an instrument of class privilege and the panoply of its impartiality (Hay, 1975).

However, it was inevitable that the increasing demand for labour at lower wages would destroy the Elizabethan Poor Laws, replacing charity with forced labour in the workhouse. But the confusion between the workhouse and the house of correction continued – they were often parts of the same building. When labour became increasingly plentiful, unemployed and driven to crime and rebellion, the houses of correction became even more punitive, while labour in the houses of correction was limited to grinding and useless tasks so that no one would enter them voluntarily. The overall effect was to teach free labour the discipline of the factory both outside and inside the factory, in prisons and workhouses. Thus the employed and the unemployed learned their respective disciplines. Thereafter, we might say that in the bourgeois social order the prison, the factory, and the school, like the army, are places where the system can project its conception of the disciplinary society in the reformed criminal, the good worker, student, loyal soldier, and committed citizen. In every case, it is a question of reproducing among the propertyless a sense of commitment to the property system in which they have nothing to sell but their labour and loyalty. The articulation of the disciplinary society in the factory, prison, army, schools and hospitals represented a response to social and moral problems arising from industrial change and conflict:

> The new science called political economy arises out of the registering of the new network of constant and multiple relations between population, territory and wealth; and this corresponds to the formation of a type of intervention characteristic of government, namely intervention in the field of economy and population. In other words, the transition from an art of government to a political science, from a regime dominated by structure of sovereignty to one ruled by techniques of government occurs in the 18th century around the theme of population and consequently centres on the birth of political economy....We must consequently see things not in terms of the substitution for a society of sovereignty by a disciplinary society and the subsequent replacement of a disciplinary society by a governmental one; in reality we have a triangle; sovereignty-discipline-government, which has as its primary target the population and its essential mechanism apparatuses of security.
>
> (Foucault, 1979b: 18–19)

However repressive these disciplinary strategies may look to us, in their own day they were part of the reformist, humane and enlightened discourse that responded to the needs of the times and were often inspired by a pedagogic intention to transform individuals into able-bodied citizens. The broad issue here is a complex, shifting relationship between industrialization, law, criminality and the labourers in the town and countryside (Tobias, 1967). Thus it is not always easy to decide whether such responses as food riots, poaching, machine breaking, reform movements and trade unionism were popular politics or mob crimes. From the standpoint of the propertied classes, such activities were more likely to be criminalized than politicized, so to speak, since the propertied class had trouble in imagining the kind of political order that might be built upon a propertyless mass. From the standpoint of the peasants and urban labourers faced with immiseration, certain criminal activities were often desperate strategies of maintenance, however colourful they may have made London life. Although the law was used to enact severe and terrible punishments for crimes against rural and urban property, it nevertheless seems to have been employed also to teach lessons of mercy and a universal sense of order. In other words, the bourgeois state tempered the force of law with the ideology of respect for the Law. To the extent that this was achieved, the labouring class also won from the bourgeoisie extensions in the rule of law, freedom of speech and assembly, as well as the right to strike and to organize in the work place. The law, therefore, is not simply the oppressive agency for the bourgeois state. Inasmuch as capitalism must be concerned with its own social reproduction, it will be driven to motivate moral consent as well as sheer physical compliance. Thus the class struggle will propel the law to universalize its prescriptions in the search for solutions on a higher level of control.

In the eighteenth century, the role of the state was at first minimal in the sense that it served to sweep away the feudal order and to institute the necessary discipline of the new industrial labour force. Later, it began to adjust the conditions of labour, passing the factory legislation that to some extent restricted capital while accommodating labour. At this stage, the state's task in softening domination with education is shared by humanitarian, paternal and religious welfare in helping the poor, sick, criminal and ignorant. Foucault (1979a) argues that the disciplinary institutions were conceived to open up a field for the practices of evaluating, recording and observing large populations in order to administer them through the therapeutic institutions of health, education and penalty. This is the original matrix of the human and social sciences, rather than any abstractive generalization such as Comte's Law of the Three Stages. Instead, we might speak of the social sciences as *strategies of power* designed to minimize the cost of power, to maximize its coverage and to link 'economic' power with the educational, military, industrial, penal and medical institutions within which the docility and utility of populations can be maximized. In a disciplinary society power works by a sort of capillary action, drawing itself up from individual conduits. Thus, in a certain sense, the operation of power is individualized in order to achieve its maximum concentration:

> In a disciplinary regime...individualization is 'descending': as power becomes more anonymous and more functional, those on whom it is exercised tend to be more strongly individualized; it is exercised by surveillance rather than ceremonies, by observation rather than commemorative accounts, by comparative measures that have the 'norm' as reference rather than genealogies giving ancestors as points of reference, by 'gaps' rather than deeds....

All the sciences, analyses, or practices employing the root 'psycho-' have their origin in this historical reversal of the procedures of individualization. The moment that saw the transition from historico-ritual mechanisms for the formation of individuality to the scientific-disciplinary mechanism, when the normal took over from the ancestral, and measurement from status, thus substituting for the individuality of the memorable man that of the calculable man, that moment when the sciences of man became possible is the moment when a new technology of power and a new political anatomy of the body were implemented.

(Foucault, 1979a: 193)

Behind the state: bureaucracy and the disciplinary society

When Weber considers the historical roots of bureaucratic discipline, as well as of the factory, he traces them directly to the model of military discipline. 'The discipline of the army gives birth to all discipline' (Weber, 1967: 261). This emphasizes the uniformity of obedience and command in an impersonal office. Emotions, status, devotion and charisma are subordinated to a rational calculus of success or profitability from the objective standpoint of the organization. At the same time, Weber concedes that there is no direct link between military discipline and various economic institutions such as the Pharaonic workshops, slave plantations and the factory. He remarks upon the intensification of rational discipline achieved through the American systems of 'scientific management'. But his observations on these topics are not developed and his interest is absorbed by the most general features of formal bureaucratic administration. Thus it may be argued that, while Weber (1950) saw the direct line from monastic discipline through Luther and Calvin to bureaucracy and scientific management, he did not pay sufficient attention to the circuits of the factory, workhouse and prison in the creation of industrial discipline and social control. Discipline in the factory, prison and school involves much more specific strategies of corporeal discipline than is captured by the generalized attitude of Protestant asceticism. In this respect, Weberianism implies a too cognitivist version of capitalist, state and bureaucratic controls. Moreover, it leaves the impression that in late capitalism the state only employs brute force, of a police or military nature, in the last instance. Thus the history we have reviewed makes it possible to see how the Weberian approach can result in Crozier's (1964) portrayal of enlightened bureaucracy produced by taking for granted the *disciplinary society* (family, schools, hospitals and prisons) that underwrites discipline in the workplace and allows the State to reserve its violence on behalf of the property system:

Modern organizations, in contrast to their predecessors, use a much more liberal set of pressures. They deal with people who, through their education, have already internalized a number of basic conformities and a general ability to conform easily to an organization's way....Most important of all, human behaviour is now better understood and therefore more predictable. Because of this, a modern organization does not need the same amount of conformity to get as good results as did earlier organizations. The modern organization can tolerate more deviance, restrict its requirements to a more specialized field, and demand only temporary commitments. For all these reasons, it can and does rely more on indirect and intellectual means to obtain conformity: communication structure and work flow, the technical setting of jobs, economic incentives, and also, perhaps, rational calculus of a higher sort. The punitive aspect of the conformity achievement process has declined. Direct coercion is still in reserve as a last resort, but it is very rarely used, and people apparently no longer have to see it operate often to retain it in their calculations.

(Crozier, 1964: 184–5)

Crozier's view of workers' compliance will seem plausible only to the extent that it can presume upon the *natural discipline*, so to speak, of the work place and of the wage system. But this, as we have seen, is always the arena of a struggle with formally free labour to accept its substantive lack of freedom due to the persistent efforts of capitalism to separate labour from control of the work process. Thus the rights of labour to freely contract for wages guaranteed before the law is reproduced in the system of punishment calculated in retribution for crimes against property, against property in persons and ultimately against the crime of propertylessness (Melossi and Pavarini, 1981). The legal contract is therefore the sacred fiction of the bourgeois social and political order since it simultaneously reproduces formal freedom and equality with substantive inequality and oppression. The discipline of the factory and the wage system, however much it is bureaucratized, remains the ultimate source of labour's docility. Indeed, it is the work place discipline that funds the apparent organizational effectiveness of state and bureaucratic controls. In fact, these controls also require for their effectiveness that the greater part of the bureaucratic structure be itself subject to the very discipline its middle management employees imagine they are supervising with respect to labour. What is called bureaucratic control must be seen to involve a continuous struggle over:

(a) the *technical control* over the work process, and
(b) *disciplinary and punitive control* over the social relations of production

Whereas in early capitalism paternalist power derived from the personal relationships between the owner and his labourers, technical and bureaucratic control grow out of the formal structure of the firm. The difference is that technical control is embedded in the production process and, as such, may be employed to *naturalize* bureaucratic controls which are embedded in the social organization or power structure of the firm. In practice, paternalistic, technical and bureaucratic discipline will be found to coexist and, while they may be regarded as stages of industrial discipline (Perrot, 1979), they have arisen in a pragmatic way as responses to owner/worker struggles for control. Although it is preferable from the standpoint of management to address control issues in terms of a Weberian vocabulary of rational accounting, efficiency and universalistic-achievement requirements – in fact to naturalize the social relations of production to technical relations of production – the reality is that it is relations of power and ideology that are at stake. Where labour freely contracts to meet the wage discipline, it thereby subordinates itself to the conditions of mental and bodily control (Sohn-Rethel, 1978) arising from its separation from the ownership of the means, pacing and purpose of production in a substantively rational social enterprise. In detail, this means that workers submit to the direction of their tasks, their nature, method, pace and quality of work (Edwards, 1979; Thompson, 1961). They thereby simultaneously submit themselves to a system of worker evaluation, punishment and reward. It is, of course, in the interests of bureaucratic management to make worker discipline, punishments and rewards, appear to flow from naturally established organizational rules and procedures. Analytically, there occurs a kind of progression in industrial discipline moving from paternalistic controls to assembly line, machine paced routines and, finally, to bureaucratically imposed discipline. What is involved is a shift from heteronomous paternalist controls to autonomous, internalized discipline, and identification with corporate goals and values. To achieve this, worker evaluation is concerned less with physical productivity than with workers' attitudes to the corporation. In a certain sense, the modern corporation seeks to refamilize the workers while cutting them off from their own class culture. Since such a disciplinary achievement takes time, corporations seek to minimize labour turn-over and to maximize loyalty, ever solicitous of worker attitudes:

> What distinguishes bureaucratic control from other control systems is that it contains incentives aimed at evoking the behaviour necessary to make bureaucratic control succeed. It is this *indirect path* to the intensification of work, through the mechanism of rewarding behaviour relevant to the control system, rather than simply to the work itself, that imposes the new behaviour requirements on workers.
>
> (Edwards, 1979: 148–9)

These considerations suggest further political studies of the internalization of discipline in the enucleated family, in schools, sports and much of modern entertainment. The family has long ceased to be the natural scene of work discipline, while still charged with the production of able-bodied citizens. It has fallen to the schools, social and medical agencies, and the media – inasmuch as the message is still the ordinary society – to provide the secondary socialization which Crozier takes for granted in shifting the disciplinary burden from modern bureaucracy onto an 'educated' citizenry. In short, we need to re-examine the division between public and private conduct in terms of historically variable strategies of discipline – even in so-called leisure – which subserve the social and political imperative of a disciplined labour force and its current levels of manual, mental and emotional 'education'. Such a tactic would treat social discipline as a socio-political strategy whose organizational features are historically and institutionally variable. Moreover, it would avoid any retrospective myth of an undisciplined state of nature generated from a Freudian or a Hobbesian perspective. At the same time, it would not reduce political discipline to a work place activity, nor indulge prospective fantasies of an undisciplined society ruled by play and the absence of the state. By the same token, the approach recommended here might give social scientists direction in the empirical study of the embodiment of power as it is achieved in the lives of individuals, families and educational institutions.

Conclusion

Weber's formal theory of bureaucracy needs to be complemented by the history of factory discipline, the latter overlapping with prison discipline and eventually overlaid with bureaucratic discipline. Thus we return to Weber via Foucault and Marx. The benefit of this approach is that it makes it clear how Weber's concept of state and bureaucratic discipline alternates between (i) obedience based upon the observation of rules of technical efficiency, and (ii) obedience required as a governmental end in itself, or what Gouldner (1954: 216–17) calls 'punishment centered' bureaucracy. In reality, the sphere of the technical expert is subordinate to that of the true bureaucrat whose administration derives from a presumption of power. For this reason, the disciplinary tasks of punitive bureaucracy are directed to the industrial control of minds and bodies, of attitudes and behaviour. Here the studies of Foucault and the social historians we have cited broaden the Weberian concept of administrative power into the embodied strategies of industrial power. Bureaucrats cannot make the Prussian assumption that their goals are beyond criticism and resistance (Gouldner, 1976). Industrial bureaucracies are less privileged than government bureaucracies in this respect. For this reason, the two bureaucracies of state and economy share an interest in depoliticizing the perception of their power and ideology by subordinating them to the neutral image of disciplined technology and expertise. With this strategy, the two bureaucracies seek to manufacture public docility and in this way have citizens support the state which in turn supports them with a modicum of legal force exercised against their occasional disobedience.

References

Anderson, M. (1976). 'Sociological History and the Working Class Family: Smelser Revisited'. *Social History* 3: 317–34.

Braverman, H. (1974). *Labour and Monopoly Capital, The Degradation of Work in the Twentieth Century*. New York: Monthly Review Press.

Burawoy, M. (1984). 'Karl Marx and the Satanic Mills: Factory Politics Under Early Capitalism in England, the United States and Russia'. *The American Journal of Sociology* 90 (2): 247–82.

Burrell, G. (1984). 'Sexual Organizational Analysis'. *Organizational Studies* 5 (2): 97–118.

Crozier, M. (1964). *The Bureaucratic Phenomenon*. Chicago: The University of Chicago Press.

Edwards, M. and Lloyd-Jones, R. (1973). 'N. J. Smelser and the Cotton Factory Family: A Re-assessment'. In: *Textile History and Economic History*. N. B. Harte and K. G. Ponting (eds.). Manchester: Manchester University Press, pp. 304–19.

Edwards, R. (1979). *Contested Terrain: The Transformation of the Workplace in the Twentieth Century*, New York: Basic Books.

Form, W. (1981). 'Resolving Ideological Issues on the Division of Labour'. In: *Theory and Research in Sociology*. H. M. Blalock, Jr. (ed.). New York: The Free Press, pp. 140–61.

Form, W. (1983). 'Sociological Research and the American Working Class'. *The Sociological Quarterly* 24 (Spring): 163–84.

Foucault, M. (1970). *The Order of Things: An Archaeology of the Human Sciences*. A. M. Sheridan Smith (trans.). New York: Vintage Books.

Foucault, M. (1975). *The Birth of the Clinic: An Archaeology of Medical Perception*. A. M. Sheridan Smith (trans.). New York: Vintage Books.

Foucault, M. (1979a). *Discipline and Punish: The Birth of the Prison*. A. M. Sheridan Smith (trans.). New York: Vintage Books.

Foucault, M. (1979b). 'Governmentality', *Ideology and Consciousness (I and C), Governing the Present* 6: 5–21.

Foucault, M. (1980). *The History of Sexuality Volume I: An Introduction*. R. Hurley (trans.). New York: Vintage Books.

Foucault, M. (1981). 'Questions of Method', *Ideology and Consciousness (I and C), Power and Desire: Diagrams of the Social* 8: 3–14.

Gouldner, A. W. (1954). *Patterns of Industrial Democracy*. Glencoe, IL: The Free Press.

Gouldner, A. W. (1976). *The Dialectic of Ideology and Technology: The Origins, Grammar and Future of Ideology*. New York: The Seabury Press.

Hay, D. (1975). 'Property, Authority and the Criminal Law'. In: *Albion's Fatal Tree, Crime and Society in Eighteenth Century England*. D. Hay, P. Linebaugh, J. G. Rule, E. P. Thompson, C. Winslow (eds). London: Allen Lane.

Hill, S. (1981). *Competition and Control at Work: The New Industrial Sociology*. Cambridge: The MIT Press.

Hirsch, J. (1979). 'The State Apparatus and Social Reproduction: Elements of a Theory of the Bourgeois State'. In: J. Holloway and S. Picciotto (eds.). *State and Capital: A Marxist Debate*. Austin: University of Texas Press, pp. 57–107.

Ignatieff, M. (1978). *A Just Measure of Pain: The Penitentiary in the Industrial Revolution 1750–1850*. New York: Pantheon Books.

Landes, D.S. (1969). *The Unbound Prometheus: Technological Change and Industrial Development in Western Europe from 1750 to the Present*. Cambridge: Cambridge University Press.

Laslett, P. (1965). *The World We Have Lost—Further Explored*. London: Methuen and Co. Ltd.

Littler, C. R. (1978). 'Understanding Taylorism'. *British Journal of Sociology* 29 (2): 185–202.

Littler, C. R. (1982). 'Deskilling and Changing Structures of Control'. In: *The Degradation of Work? Skill, Deskilling and the Labour Process*. S.Wood (ed.). London: Hutchinson, pp. 122–45.

Marx, K. (1906). *Capital: A Critique of Political Economy*. Chicago: Charles H. Kerr and Company.

Melossi, D. and Pavarini, M. (1981). *The Prison and the Factory*. New York: Macmillan.

Miller, W. and Neussus, C. (1979). '"The Welfare State Illusion" and the Contradiction Between Wage Labour and Capital'. In: *State and Capital: A Marxist Debate*. J. Holloway and S. Picciotto (eds.). Austin: University of Texas Press, pp. 32–9.

O'Neill, J. (1995). '*The Poverty of Postmodernism*'. London: Routledge.

Palmer, B. (1975). 'Class, Conception and Conflict: The Thrust for Efficiency, Managerial Views of Labor and the Working Class Rebellion, 1903–22'. *The Review of Radical Political Economics* 7 (2): 31–49.

Parsons, T. (1951). *The Social System*. New York: The Free Press of Glencoe.

Penn, R. (1982). 'Skilled Manual Workers in the Labour Process, 1856–1964'. In: *The Degradation of Work? Skills, Deskilling and the Labour Process*. S.Wood (ed.). London: Hutchinson, pp. 90–108.

Perrot, M. (1979). 'The Three Ages of Industrial Discipline in Nineteenth Century France'. In: J.Merriman (ed.). *Consciousness and Class Experience in Nineteenth Century Europe*. New York: Holmes and Meier, pp. 149–68.

Pollard, S. (1963). 'Factory Discipline in the Industrial Revolution'. *The Economic History Review* XVI (2): 254–71.

Poulantzas, N. (1973). *Political Power and Social Classes*. London: NLB.

Reid, D.A. (1976). 'The Decline of Saint Monday 1766–1876'. *Past and Present* 71: 76–101.

Rodgers, D. T. (1979). *The Work Ethic in Industrial America* 1850–1920. Chicago and London: The University of Chicago Press.

Schluchter, W. (1981). *The Rise of Western Rationalism: Max Weber's Developmental History*. G. Roth (trans.) Berkeley: University of California Press.

Smelser, N. J. (1959). *Social Change in the Industrial Revolution: An Application of Theory to the British Cotton Industry*. Chicago: The University of Chicago Press.

Sohn-Rethel, A. (1978) *Intellectual and Manual Labour: A Critique of Epistemology*. London: Macmillan.

Stark, D. (1980). 'Class Struggle and the Transformation of the Labour Process: A Relational Approach'. *Theory and Society* 9: 89–130.

Stone, L. (1979). *The Family, Sex and Marriage in England* 1500–1800. New York: Harper & Row.

Thompson, E. P. (1967). 'Time, Work, Discipline, and Industrial Capitalism'. *Past and Present* 38: 56–97.

Thompson, V. A. (1961). *Modern Organization*. New York: Alfred A. Knopf.

Tobias, J.J. (1967) *Crime and Industrial Society in the 19th Century*. New York: Schocken Books.

Wall, R., Robin, J. and Laslett, P. (eds.) (1983). *Family Forms in Historic Europe*. Cambridge: Cambridge University Press.

Weber, M. (1947). *The Theory of Social and Economic Organization*. A. M.Henderson and T.Parsons (trans). New York: Oxford University Press.

Weber, M. (1950). *General Economic History*. F.H.Knight (trans.). Glencoe, IL: The Free Press.

Weber, M. (1967). *From Max Weber: Essays in Sociology*. H. H. Gerth and G. Wright Mills (trans). New York: Oxford University Press.

Wilson, H. T. (1976). 'Reading Max Weber: The Limits of Sociology'. *Sociology* 10: 297–315.

Wilson, H. T. (1977). *The American Ideology, Science, Technology and Organization as Modes of Rationality in Advanced Industrial Societies*. London: Routledge & Kegan Paul.

6 Orphic Marxism*

I now want to give the preceding introduction to the historical rationality of human institutions – which I think must be opposed to contemporary post-rationalist and minoritarian doctrines – a positive reformulation in Marxist humanism (O'Neill, 1995). This exercise benefits from the critique of alienation in both socialist and capitalist societies since Marxism has itself practised scientism and a crude Prometheanism. My reformulation of Marxist humanism gives emphasis to its civility over its industrialism.

Since I have at several points rejected the postmodern fragmentation of cultural myth and narrative, I propose to put the opposite case in terms of the mytho-poetics of an Orphic mythology of the self-civilizing functions of the human body. Whereas in postmodernism the body is reduced to the sensory register of fleeting simulacra of desire without end, I believe it can be argued that the human body is also the figure of a great civilizing narrative that cannot be separated from the equally humanizing figure of work. In short, I shall develop from Vico and Marx an Orphic Marxism which I believe to be the necessary complement to the largely Promethean mythology that has underwritten Marxism, for better or worse. In this way, we may oppose the easy postmodern rejection of 'historism', i.e., the notion that history can be subject to a technical practice (although it sometimes celebrates this very error) on the ground that it loses sight of the more difficult concept of 'historicism', namely, that we never achieve an absolute distance between our history and our modes of historical understanding. This must be recognized not because history shapes us through forces larger than ourselves, whether institutional or unconscious, but because even our ability to formulate these modifications in our understanding never places us out of ourselves. Certainly, men and women make their own history, but they do so in the same way that they make music or art, i.e., with a religious sense that they exceed us and are therefore inexhaustible gifts to the whole of humankind:

> The human mind is naturally inclined by the senses to see itself externally in the body, and only with great difficulty does it come to understand itself by

* Text of the essay taken from *The Poverty of Postmodernism* (1995). London: Routledge. Pages 94–107. Reprinted with permission.

means of reflection. This axiom gives us the universal principle of etymology
in all languages: words are carried over from bodies and from the properties
of bodies to signify the contributions of the mind and spirit.

(Vico, 1948: paras 236–37)

Vico and Marx are two great naturalists. They are, by the same token, two great
humanists. Today, such a claim would seem paradoxical inasmuch as nothing
threatens humanism so much as the naturalist method of the human and social sciences in their embrace of a universal scientism. Yet Vico and Marx rejected both
materialism and idealism because of their inadequate conception of humankind's
embodied mind and sensuous history.

Alienation, as Marx understood it, is neither a spiritual condition nor the lament
of the soul imprisoned in the body. The human mind would not be more efficacious
if its operation were unmediated by language, sensory perception and corporate, i.e.,
incarnate and collective life. Wherever the mind constructs its own heavenly palace,
the body lives in a neighbourly hovel. But neither is alienation the lament of the natural body, uninhibited by thought and the confinements of collective life, labour and
language. Rather, Marx, like Vico before him, argued that human beings are thinking bodies whose nature is entirely second nature. Human nature is the historical
and civil achievement of ways of thought, perception, language and labour through
which we mediate our own humanity. Understood in this way, alienation is a necessary moment in the history of our lived being. To refuse alienation is to suspend
our living, to imagine ourselves as wholly spiritual beings, as divinities, or full-time
philosophers. Yet to embrace alienation is not to embrace animality, nor to content
ourselves with the world as a pasture in which we graze as innocently as sheep or
with as little foresight as the birds. Alienation does not adorn us; the civil beauty of
our kind is at once far less and greater than the beauty of the lilies of the field.

As early as the 'Economic and Philosophical Manuscripts' of 1844, Marx had
developed an unswervingly Viconian conception of the historical nature of human
nature:

> But man is not only a natural being, he is a human natural being. This means
> that he is a being that exists for himself, thus a species-being that must con-
> firm and exercise himself as such in his being and knowledge. Thus human
> objects are not natural objects as they immediately present themselves nor is
> human sense, in its purely objective existence, human sensitivity and human
> objectivity. Neither nature in its objective aspect nor in its subjective aspect
> is immediately adequate to the human being. And as everything natural must
> have an origin, so man too has his process of origin, history, which can,
> however, be known by him and thus is a conscious process of origin that
> transcends itself. History is the true natural history of man.
>
> (Marx, 1971: 169)

It follows from such passages that Marx rejected equally the idealist and materialist conceptions of subjectivity and objectivity. The human world is neither an

idea nor an organism, neither a given nor a projection. The human world is at every level of sensation, perception, thought and action a *social praxis* in which our inner and outer worlds are mutually articulated. The human eye is civilized by what it sees in the field of art as is the human ear by the music to which it listens. In each case, human physiology is inserted into a hermeneutical field whose own historical articulation includes the relatively autonomous praxes of optics, acoustics, art and music. In this way, vision and art are entirely relativized by one another, and the same can be said of the rest of the human senses and their correlative institutions and histories. Thus the body has a history because human history has a body:

> Only through the objectively unfolded richness of man's essential being is the richness of subjective human sensibility (a musical ear, an eye for beauty of form – in short, senses capable of human gratification, senses affirming themselves as essential powers of man) either cultivated or brought into being. For not only the five senses but also the so-called mental senses – the practical senses (will, love, etc.) – in a word, human sense – the human nature of the senses – comes to be by virtue of its object, by virtue of humanized nature. *The forming of the five senses is a labour of the entire history of the world down to the present.*
>
> (Marx, 1964a: 141)

If Marx separates himself from the Hegelian vision of spiritual alienation – and we shall argue against that view – it is on the ground that epistemological alienation, or the irreducible excess of the spirit beyond its fall into matter, is merely an idealist lament incapable of redeeming the history it has constructed out of its own self-alienation. In keeping with this argument, Hegel deprives history of its body and thereby reduces the spirit to an unhappy history of unmediated self-reflection. In turn, Hegel's disembodied history can only imitate life by absorbing its history into the abstract laws of logic, while continuing to grasp at reality through the mirror of dialectics. Consequently, Hegel's sublimation of the historical movement of alienation arises from his substitution of a mistaken separation of mind from matter – which can only occur on the level of philosophy – with the immoral separation of human beings from their humanity – which can only occur on the level of political economy:

> What is supposed to be the essence of alienation that needs to be transcended is not that man's being objectifies itself in an inhuman manner in opposition to itself, but that it objectifies itself in distinction from and in opposition to, abstract thought.
>
> (Marx, 1964a: 162)

But against this critique of Hegel, which Marx himself fostered, there is another reading of Hegel which Marxism has more recently espoused in order to revise its own potential for positivism and bureaucratized alienation. Here the convergence between Marxism and phenomenology is necessary, despite Althusser's strenuous attempts to separate them on behalf of scientific Marxism. It is often remarked that Hegel spiritualized action where Marx materialized it. Marx himself believed this to be the substance of his critique of Hegel. But I think there is some evidence for the argument that Hegel and Marx are engaged in a similar critique of alienation as estrangement from action as expression; and thus there is a continuity between Hegel's *Phenomenology of Mind* and Marx's *Economic and Philosophic Manuscripts*.

In his remarks on physiognomy Hegel argues that the externalization of consciousness is not contingently related to its purpose but is essential to consciousness as embodied being. Thus the human hand and human speech are essential organs of conscious expression and it is by means of them that we establish a common world of artefacts and meanings. It is through the body that we give to our immediate surroundings 'a general human shape and form, or at least the general character of a climate, of a portion of the world', just as we find regions of the world characterized by different customs and culture. It is through the expressive organs of the hand and speech that we realize a unity of purpose and object which conveys our presence in the world and to others. The human body is thus the expressive instrument of spirit and not its simple objective alienation; it is the instrument whereby there can be culture and history which in turn shape human sensibility, thought, and perception.

> For if the organs in general proved to be incapable of being taken as expression of the inner for the reason that in them the action is present as a process, while the action as a deed or (finished) act is merely external, and inner and outer in this way fall apart and are or can be alien to one another, the organ must, in view of the peculiarity now considered, be again taken as also a middle term for both.
>
> (Hegel, 1910: 343)

Thus self-consciousness is not estranged by its natural being, for the human body is an expressive organ through which meaning is embodied in speech and the work of human hands which together articulate the nature of humankind:

> That the hand, however, must exhibit and reveal the inherent nature of individuality as regards its fate, is easily seen from the fact that after the organ of speech it is the hand most of all by which a man actualizes and manifests himself. It is the animated artificer of his fortune; we may say of the hand it is what a man does, for in it as the effective organ of his fulfilment he is there present as the animating soul; and since he is ultimately and originally his own fate, the hand will thus express this innate inherent nature.
>
> (Hegel, 1910: 343)

The ultimate goal of self-consciousness is to recover the unity of the self and the world which it discovers abstractly in the unity of the mind and its objects.

The recovery of the world is mediated by desire which reveals the world as my praxis. But this is still only abstractly a world until my interests are recognized by the other. The dialectic of recognition appears as a life and death struggle because of desire which binds consciousness to the world of things and simultaneously reveals its transcendence as the negation of things and the Other. But the categories of subject and object, negation, self, other and recognition are not a priori categories of experience. They arise in the course of the self-interpretation by consciousness of its modes of lived experience which involve consciousness in a dialectic between intentionality and an irreducible ontological difference which generates the world and the recognition of the Other. For if consciousness did not encounter the resistance of things and others, it could only know things perceptually and others by analogy and it would have no organic or social life. But this means that consciousness can never be satisfied in a desire for objects and the Other. For in this it would only consume itself whereas it needs a common world in which things and others reflect consciousness back upon itself: 'Self-consciousness, which is absolutely *for itself*, and characterizes its object directly as negative, or as primarily desire, will really, therefore, find through experience this object's independence' (Hegel, 1910: 221). Desire, then, is not the actuality of self-consciousness but only its potentiality for actualizing itself in a common world and intersubjectivity. Hence the struggle to the death which originates in desire is exteriorized in the relation to objects established between the Master and the Slave which preserves their independence in the form of a living dependency: 'In this experience self-consciousness becomes aware that life is as essential to it as pure self-consciousness' (Hegel, 1910: 234).

With respect (fear) for life that is born from the struggle to the death there is initiated a further dialectic in which the Slave's apprenticeship to things makes possible the practical observation of the laws of their operation. Though he works for another, the Slave learns to work with objects whose independence now submits to his production though not to his consumption. By the same token the Master's independence of things mediated by the Slave becomes his dependence upon the Slave's cultivation:

> Labour, on the other hand, is desire restrained and checked, evanescence delayed and postponed; in other words, labour shapes and fashions the thing. The negative relation to the object passes into the form of the object, into something that is permanent and remains; because it is just for the labourer that the object has independence.
>
> (Hegel, 1910: 238)

Thus from the recognition of the value of life and the fear of death, expressed in submission to things for the sake of life, the experience of domination and servitude opens up the cycle of culture as the objective mediation of self-expression and the world. It is through work that the world is revealed as conscious *praxis*, as a field of individual interests which are in turn opened to the interests of others and hence to a common measure of good and evil. As a field of practical intentions the world is the element of consciousness, its 'original nature' which the activity of consciousness moulds to its purposes. Hegel is quite explicit that there is no room for the experience of estrangement in the act whereby the self externalizes itself in the world of objects. It is the very nature of consciousness to act to externalize itself in the deed, or work.

Marx's own theory of alienation is, of course, idealist in its critique of any theory of cultural objects, such as rent, or of social relations, such as poverty, where these phenomena are treated as quasi-natural objects in a world external to their social and historically produced effect. His theory is equally materialist in the sense that it involves the history and social production of ideas and values in its critique of idealist ideologies of the determination of the human world. In short, Marx insisted that the human mind is historical and social because it is an embodied mind and that the human body is similarly social and historical because it is intelligent. People are thinking bodies whose humanity is their own historical achievement. Human nature is neither given nor a singular possession, although this may appear to be the case within certain theo-philosophical ideologies and in fact be the case within a socio-economic system dominated by private property:

> Private property is only the sensuous expression of the fact that man is both objective to himself and even more becomes a hostile and inhuman object to himself, that the expression of his life entails its externalization, its realization becomes the loss of its reality, an alien reality. Similarly the positive supersession of private property, that is, the sensuous appropriation by and for man of human essence and human life, of objective man and his works, should not be conceived of only as direct and exclusive enjoyment, as possession and having. Man appropriates his universal being in a universal manner, as a whole man. Each of his human relationships to the world – seeing, hearing, smelling, tasting, thinking, contemplating, feeling, willing, acting, loving – in short all the organs of his individuality, just as the organs whose form is a directly communal one, are in their objective action, or their relation to the object, the appropriation of this object. The appropriation of human reality, their relationship to the object, is the confirmation of human reality. It is therefore as manifold as the determinations and activities of human nature. It is human effectiveness and suffering, for suffering, understood in the human sense, is an enjoyment of the self for man.
>
> (Marx, 1971: 151)

We may now summarize the basic propositions in Marx's humanist theory of alienation. Before we do so, however, a terminological distinction is required with respect to the usage of the term 'alienation' since, unless we are aware of its double reference, we unwittingly reduce the theory of alienation to an idealist dimension. Thus the humanist theory of alienation which we are developing has nothing to do with a lament over mind's embodiment or that the exercise of every human faculty involves world shaping activity that is reciprocally anthropomorphizing. Thinking bodies necessarily express themselves in a 'world'. We call this the movement of externalization (*Entäusserung*) to the necessary worldly expression of incarnate minds. Only entirely angelic beings could lament alienation as externalization since even God seems to have emptied himself into the created world. Having said as much, both God and man find themselves in a world they have made but which nevertheless is not entirely responsive to their designs for it. We must set aside God's patience with this state of affairs. In man's case we speak of alienation or estrangement (*Entfremdung*) in respect of man's freely creative self-image failing to be reflected and amplified in the social institutions through which our kind preserves its own humanity. Therefore, while it is essential to humankind that its incorporation is realized in a historically and socially produced world of institutions, it is a contingent but corrigible fact that the anthropomorphizing design of those constitutions is distorted by the socio-economic system of private property. This corrigible history of estrangement is in turn the matter for an analytic social science to which Marx gave his own name.

We conclude, then, that Marx's humanist theory of alienation is, first of all, a philosophy of anthropomorphosis that, like Vico's *New Science*, is discovered as both nature and norm, or as *quasi-nature* and absolute *norm* of all human history. But this means that Marxism is simultaneously the discovery of a history within history that humanizes our condition. However, we cannot overlook the need to restate the categorical claim in Marx's humanist theory of alienation as one that applies equally to the history of socialist and communist societies. In this regard, we consider the weakness of Marxist social science to derive from its fundamental tenet that, whereas the system of private property is the source of human estrangement, the common ownership of the means of productions would constitute the end of human alienation. Rather, socialist societies seem to have engendered their own specific modes of alienation deriving from the hegemony of state capital, single Party politics, the suppression of civil liberties including the practice of physical and mental torture, as well as socialist colonialism and nuclearism. Much of this history of alienation exceeds Marx's vision. It now falls to contemporary socialist discussion to rethink the nature of political power and its modes of alienation as universal effects of collective life whose corrigibility is the test of any humane society.

Ultimately what is at issue in Marx's theory of alienation is not so much its claims as a social science but its conception of humanism. Everyone can recall the exhilaration of Marx's claim that all previous history is the pre-history of our kind hitherto unable to develop its humanity until it has delivered 'species-man', the universal essence of humanity, a model of sensuous and intelligent integrity whose capacities are playfully exemplified in socialist society:

> The ancient conception, in which man always appears (in however narrowly national, religious or political a definition) as the aim of production, seems very much more exalted than the modern world, in which production is the aim of man and wealth the aim of production. In fact, however, when the narrow bourgeois form has been peeled away, what is wealth, if not the universality of needs, capacities, enjoyments, productive powers, etc. of

individuals, produced in universal exchange? What, if not the full development of human control over the forces of nature – those of his own nature
as well as those of so-called 'nature'? What, if not the absolute elaboration
of his creative dispositions, without any preconditions other than anteced-
ent historical evolution which makes the totality of this evolution – i.e., the
evolution of all human powers as such, unmeasured by any previous established yardstick – an end in itself? What is this, if not a situation where man
does not produce himself in any determined form, but produces his totality?
Where he does not seek to remain something formed by the past, but is in the
absolute movement of becoming? In bourgeois political economy – and in
the epoch of production to which it corresponds – this complete elaboration
of what lies within man, appears as the total alienation, and the destruction
of all fixed, one-sided purposes as the sacrifice of the end in itself to a wholly
external compulsion.

(Marx, 1964b: 84)

In short, the *radical anthropomorphization* of the fundamental concepts of theology, philosophy, and political economy must stand as the central dogma of
Marxist humanism. However, this anthropomorphic dogma is more than a renaissance trope of creative hierarchy in view of what we may call its *deconstructive
power*. By the latter, we refer to the analytic power of Marx's tireless critique of
every binary usage which separates our kind from its humanity by compound-
ing the separations of mind and body, male and female, owner and non-owner,
individual and society. In short, every discursive production of our self-estrange-
ment is seized upon in Marx's emancipatory prose – in passage after passage
from which anyone of us can recall the exhilaration of our first vision of socialist man and of human reason cleared of thought fetishes. The 'thing-ification'
(*Verdinglichung*) of social practices and relationships to which men and women
subordinate themselves is deconstructed in Marx's complete rejection of the
metaphysics of absence. Man's absence from man is circulated throughout the
commodity system and its property relations, in the state, and in all the ideological discourses of philosophy, the arts and social sciences that expand upon the
absence of integral discourse for human conduct and community:

We have seen that the whole problem of the transition from thought to reality, hence from language to life, exists only in philosophical illusion, i.e., it
is justified only for philosophical consciousness, which cannot possibly be
clear about the nature and origin of its apparent separation from life. This
great problem, insofar as it at all entered the minds of our ideologists, was
bound, of course, to result finally in one of these knights errant setting out in
search of a word which, as a *word*, formed the transition in question, which,
as a word, ceases to be simply a word, and which, as a word, in a mysterious
superlinguistic manner, points from within the language to the actual object it
denotes; which, in short, plays among words the same role as the Redeeming

God-Man plays among people in Christian fantasy...thus the triumphant entry into 'corporeal' life.

(Marx and Engels, 1976: 449)

Marx's critique of classical political economy is a tireless deconstruction of its capital-logical discourse. It unmasks the hegemony of capital over labour through which the life-force of labouring individuals is expropriated and assigned to the driving force of capital shaping its materials of nature in and around humankind. (O'Neill, 1982) By the same token, the expropriative logic of capital fearfully engenders its own deconstruction in the proletariat whose social conditions and historical intelligence opens up the possibility of revolution, i.e., the expropriation of the expropriators. Thus capitalism can never achieve the closure that marked feudalism since it cannot foreclose the discourse of humanism once it is appropriated by the proletariat and amplified in the deconstructive analytic of Marxism. In *The German Ideology* Marx and Engels decisively undermine any notion of ideas and social objects or process which assigns to them a singular, external, and quasi-natural constitution. All conceptual languages are articulated within the longer 'material intercourse of men, the language of real life' (Marx and Engels, 1959: 247) which is the practical ground of collective life and history whose effects of externality are abstracted into the ideologies of a quasi-natural or ideal society. The movement of human history is grounded in the double reproduction of human needs as culturally and biologically open circuits that continuously redefine one another. Hence, 'the "history of humanity" must always be studied and treated in relation to the history of industry and exchange'. (Marx and Engels, 1959: 247) However, it is the social production of humane life which Marx treats as the basic framework of all modes of intellectual and manual production. It is this anthropomorphic principle which provides the basic humanist norm of every other economy of effort through which it is articulated. In fact, it constitutes the highest form of the pragmatics of language and the historical development of '*universal* intercourse', i.e., an intergenerational goal of the world-historical development of humankind which is no less a critical standard for the success of communist society.

Modern social science knowledge has reduced its independence as a form of theoretical life to a rule of methodology founded upon the auspices of technical rationality. This results in a disenchanted objectivism or rationalization of the interest and values which guide technological domination as a form or 'conduct of life', to use Max Weber's phrase. However, Weber's formal rationality, so far from resting upon 'value-free' auspices, is in fact an historical constellation whose pre-condition is the separation of the orders of knowledge, work, and politics. In the period of the bourgeois ascendency, the value-free conception of rationality furnishes a critical concept of the development of human potential locked in the feudal world of 'traditional' values. Weber makes a fatality of technical rationality, thereby identifying its historical role with political domination as such (Marcuse, 1968), whereas Marx's critique of class political economy showed the critical limits of economic rationality. Social science knowledge needs to be grounded in a limited but authentic reflexivity through which it recognizes its ties to individual values and community interests, notwithstanding its attempts to avoid bias and ideology.

Of course, Marx's notion of an essence of humanity (*Gattungswesen*) seems to continue the tradition of rationalist metaphysics rather than to deconstruct it and to contribute to scientific Marxism. But in fact the species-being of humanity is a thoroughly critical concept of a difference essential to a humanist socialism. It emphasizes that:

1. the human senses are historical;
2. human reason is practical;
3. human beings are thinking bodies inseparable from collective life;
4. human nature is the social product of a historically humanized nature;
5. the human development of human beings is the *telos* of socialist society and of socialist humanism;
6. since the history of humanity is a contingent achievement, its ratio of success depends upon a continuous struggle to deconstruct and resist all modes of discourse and praxis that separate humankind from the future of humankind;
7. discourse upon the human development of human beings (*Das Menschwerden des Menschen*) provides the practical norm of all social, economic, political, and communicative institutions.

The discourse of Marxist-humanism is predicated upon the suspension of every binarism that derives from the unquestioned separation (estrangement) of humanity and humane existence. It therefore rejects the dualist tradition of Western metaphysics through which humankind dispossesses itself of its proper essence in favour of every other sort of spiritual and worldly possession. But, as Marx observes, the new language of humanity is hard to understand by individuals who have yet to unlearn the grammar of possessive individualism and who cannot distinguish between *being and having* – whose god is still money and not humankind:

> The only intelligible language that we speak to one another consists in our objects in their relationship to one another. We would not understand a human speech and it would remain ineffective; on the one hand it would be seen and felt as an entreaty or a prayer and thus as a humiliation and therefore used with shame and a feeling of abasement, while on the other side it would be judged brazen and insane and as such rejected. Our mutual alienation from the human essence is so great that the direct language of this essence seems to us to be an affront to human dignity and in contrast the alienated language of the values of things seems to be the language that justifies a self-reliant and self-conscious human dignity.
>
> (Marx, 1971: 201)

It still cannot be said that Marxism has learned to speak its own language. Indeed, nothing privileges it in this respect – certainly not its claims to make a science of human history. Every reading of history stands to be judged by history. This is not the conclusion of an historical determinism, as it might seem, but is rather a statement of the problematic of the philosophy of history. It calls for an account of the relation between knowledge and action in which we must avoid both the scientism and simplistic realism and the nihilism of subjective relativism, which equally destroy the hermeneutic of reason in history. Marxist rationalism is more than an epistemology because it is concerned with the human meaning of knowledge, and is therefore always critical with respect to the uses of science. At the same time Marxism does not reduce knowledge to a class practice because this would barbarize its humanist aims. We must avoid altogether the idea that history is governed either by scientific laws or by an occult logic that makes human events rational, whatever the appearances. But this means we need a proper conception of human knowledge and the historical space in which it unfolds. Hegel and Marx between them have taught us that the human spirit does not exist outside of history, any more than history itself can unfold except as the externalization (*Entäusserung*) of human subjectivity. Idealism and materialism are false alternatives. They fail to describe the constitution of historical space as a praxis determined by the affinity of choices (*Wahlverwandtschaft*) human beings make in their economic, political, and religious lives.

References

Hegel, G.W.F. (1910). *Phenomenology of Mind*. J. B. Baillie (trans.). London: Allen and Unwin.

Marcuse, Herbert (1968). 'Industrialization and Capitalism in Max Weber. In: *Negations: Essays on Cultural Theory*. Boston: Beacon Press.

Marx, Karl (1964a). *The Economic and Philosophic Manuscripts of 1844*. M. Milligan (trans). D. J. Struik (trans.). New York: International Publishers.

Marx, Karl (1964b). *Pre-capitalist Economic Formations*. E. Hobsbawn (ed.). London: Lawrence and Wishart.

Marx, Karl (1971). *Early Texts*. D. McLellan (trans.). Oxford: Basil Blackwell.

Marx, Karl and Engels, Friedrich (1959). *Basic Writings on Politics and Philosophy*. L. S. Feuer (ed.). New York: Doubleday and Company.

Marx, Karl and Engels, Friedrich (1976). 'The German Ideology'. In: *Collected Works*, Vol. 5. London: Lawrence and Wishart.

O'Neill, John (1982) 'Marxism and Mythology'. In: *For Marx Against Althusser, and Other Essays*. Washington, DC: University Press of America, pp. 43–58.

O'Neill, John (1995). 'The Phenomenological Concept of Modern Knowledge and the Utopian Method of Marxist Economics'. In: *The Poverty of Postmodernism*. London: Routledge, pp. 64–93.

Vico, Giambattista (1948). *The New Science of Giambattista Vico* (3rd edition). T. Goddard Bergin and M.H. Fisch (trans.). Ithaca: Cornell University Press.

7 *Televideo ergo sum**

Some hypotheses on the specular functions of the media

In addition to the arguments advanced on communication and the legitimation problem (O'Neill, 2002), I propose to extend that discussion with the aid of some propositions drawn from critical theory, psychoanalysis, and semiotics, to show how we are to interpret the political economic and social integration of the media. I shall argue that the media simultaneously 'dehistoricize' and 'defamilize' production and consumption for the masses, while they re-float the professional and political legitimation of these processes. Thus *the prime specular function of the media is to close the ideological circuit between the visible and the invisible society.*

The dream of things

The lord of creation is drowning in his own act. We are swamped by things. We own much but find that we do not possess ourselves. A curious solution to the problem of scarcity – abundance as freedom nevertheless fails us. Go back to the beginning. Man is the measure of all things. In the days when the body was simple, things were simple. The body as a state of nature the naturally scenic truth of things not to exceed its needs. Somehow the body lost its senses. It became excessive. Wants took off from needs. The body became a Pandora's box with global dimensions, mythic at first, and by the same token or coinage, turned television – the box that is always on. Eye of the world, tireless machinery of the visible and the invisible.

Is there no exit from the dream that television dreams for us? Our answers are likely to be more ready the less we explore the functions of television's dream-work. Why should we sever ourselves from the warm and generous light of television? After all, television is at our service. It disgorges nothing but what we want and it does so without the seasonal moodiness of mother earth. Its corporate dispensaries are more paternal than our own fathers; its concerns on our behalf are endless. If it thereby succeeds in infantilizing us, hiding from us the realities of its

* Text of the essay taken from *Plato's Cave: Television and its Discontents* (2001). Cresskill: Hampton Press. Pages 169–84. Reprinted with permission.

political economy, it does so only to serve us. If it deceives us with what we see, it does so only to delight us. There is nothing malign or evil in this. No conspiracy.

If this seems fantastic, it is because we are fantastic, not because television manufactures our dreams without us. To believe that television invades our minds is to oppose the old rational myth of the sovereign consumer in a world of objects enumerable like the animals on Noah's Ark. It is to forget that the media are the extensions of our bodies, the means of our multiplication, whereby the body escapes the prison of the mind and desire conquers reality. If we are not liberated in the expansion of desire, any more than we are made knowledgeable by the expansion of information, it is because the essential activity of televised passivity is consumption, the hypnotic possession of powers that freed themselves only in imagination. If we lose our public will in all this, it is because television univer-salizes our most intimate desires, collecting us in the kingdom of cleanliness and self-rewarding justice, entered only by those who are television's children:

> The art of consuming is as much an act of the imagination (fictitious) as a real act ('reality' itself being divided into compulsions and adaptations), and therefore metaphorical (joy in every mouthful, in every perusal of the object) and metonymical (all of consumption and all the joy of consum-ing in every object and every action). This in itself would not matter if consumption were not accepted as something reliable, sound, and devoid of deception and mirage, but there are no natural frontiers separating imaginary consumption or the consumption of make-believe (the subject of publicity) and real consumption; or one might say that there exists a fluid frontier that is always being overstepped and that can only be fixed in theory. Consumer-goods are not only glorified by sign and 'good' in so far as they are signified; consumption is primarily related to these signs and not to the goods themselves.
>
> (Lefebvre, 1971: 90–91)

Television is our body, our vision, our mind, our sanity, our appetite, our will to live as we do. Television is our mother's body, endlessly materializing our appetite for security, nostalgia, and happiness. Television is our father's body, in heaven and on earth, patient and strong, loyal and free. Television is our brother's body, subversive and superfluous, the joker in the pack. Television is old bod-ies, black bodies, broken bodies, bodies resurrected, imprisoned, and burned. Television is Christ's body sacrificed in the same way every day everywhere in the world with the same benign indifference to the local sufferings, ignorance, injuries, and fears that it takes upon itself *per omnia saecula saeculorum*. It is to this god that we offer our detergents, our deodorants, our dog food, toothpastes, and beer that He take upon Himself our murders, rapes, deceptions, and insanity – *agnus dei televisionis*. Thus our metabolism turns symbolism in an unending Mass celebrating the bonds of everyday life before millions of families gathered at the altar of television. To realize this, things have ceased to be objects of use; rather, they exceed their uses in order to float as symbols of the desire-to-desire whereby ordinary men divinize themselves; thus the modern soul drifts on things, trusting to them, like a man sold to his own hi-fidelity system.

Things no longer serve us. We are all the sorcerer's apprentice. Knowledge no longer serves us. Class, like the encyclopaedia, is likewise an outworn container burst by the proliferation of things as signs, images of ourselves that no longer centre upon ourselves. Things continue to mutate, expand, self-destruct; there is nothing outside of this wild economy of signs flashing between signs. Of course, there are catalogues, texts that strain to reclassify things in terms of size, price, function, seeking thereby to tie them back to the referentials of the everyday world. Things, after all, must be generated according to the natural places of use-value – a demand that science no less than commonsense continues to make upon them. Yet phenomenologically we remain as ignorant of the technical constituents of things as we do of their nutritional contents. Let the machines talk to themselves of their inner lives, so long as they leave us their digital signs to play with. We are the absent landlords of technology, eating our way through the cornflakes to win more gadgets or to become a body burning in the distant sun of fly-away happiness.

Thus our categorical schemes do not hold; there is no centre to the modern political economy of things and their way of grafting upon everyday life. The engineer and the consumer sovereign are distant ends of an economy whose uses run to the irrealization of the real in the necessity of the unnecessary. In a carnival of the impossible, the engineer and the consumer divide between them the sense and nonsense of political economy. Each continues to think of his activity in terms of function and need, while recognizing that these are held hostage in an extravagant world that outruns its internal poverty and even forsakes its own sanity. The *pseudo-differentiation* of things is entirely dependent upon television and advertising to transform it into pseudo-choices. *Pseudo-differentiation* materializes abundance and choice. It thereby makes the consumer necessary to its act, seeks to advise and persuade its sovereign to make rational decisions in the very world it has made irrational (Schrank, 1977). Moreover, the same split is achieved as an ecological setting. The things that surround us are catalogued, shelved, inventoried, enumerated, and every effort made to restore them to their place if lost or stolen. Things are timed, weighed, and priced to ring the bell of modern accountability. Such things are adored, watched reverently in the windows of the economy, and even visited by tourists in the birthplace of their production. Such things celebrate themselves, animating our lives and our homes as a continuous avalanche of novelty, happiness, and utility.

Television fulfils itself in the show and tell of political economy (Goldsen, 1977). *The commodity fetish is a talking, seeing, feeling god inviting us into the liturgy of consumption to dispel the sorrows of production.* Nobody wants to work in an ice-cream factory. But everyone loves the ice cream shop as the dispensary of frivolous choice and pleasure, the natural setting of industrial freedom and the Americanization of happiness. Therefore things have their own life, their colours, shapes, surfaces, materials, and ambiance. And they do so because their life is our life. Because this is so, things necessarily sing themselves to us in the daily celebration of the life we have in common. The loveliest of these things used to be the automobile, our home away from home, suspended, floating, new, shiny, sexy, and safe. This work-horse sings of itself as a centaur, a space invader, conquering everything from the forest to the beach. Everyone wants to float in an automobile, but no one wants to see the sorrows of the assembly line or the traffic jam. Thus if public transport is eclipsed by the automobile, it is not because it is less efficient, but precisely because it is merely an efficient mode of transportation, a concession to the body that is hard on dreams. By contrast, the automobile is also the perfect expression of the body that dreams, the narcissistic and phallicized will-to-power that bends to no one but the pedestrian and the police-man who oppose to it the primal body in a civilizing risk of murder. Today, the computer is the ultimate escape machine.

Commodities, like men, praise themselves. In either case, the praise is most loud when men and things are dead. Once our ancestors no longer compete with us, we remember their presence. In a world of garbage, such worship would seem to escape things; or it would, were it not the case that things are able to intercede in the world of men. Thus we collect things we call antiques or originals, as memorials of their origins and collective life which they exempt from use and decay, setting them apart in their homes and museums like church relics. The town collects the countryside, and industrialized societies collect nature societies, arresting their history if necessary, in order to preserve a mirror of the civilized past. Such collections are produced by force and murder, to be enjoyed in peace and happiness at home or in decadent displays of tourism abroad.

The phenomenology of everyday life is largely a spectacle of things. However, this spectacle is not opened up to any transcendental viewer. In other words, we do not watch television in order to see things but rather we watch things in order to watch television or the Net. This is the heart of our passivity. For the more we watch ourselves, the less we see of ourselves. That is the price of our free admission to the theatre of things. By the same token, we are obliged to take our own place in the parade of things. Here we work out a marvellous symbiosis between necessity and choice. Things personalize themselves; they separate by price, quality, colour, and ambiance in order to allow us to insert our most intimate self into them while at the same time assuring us of a common fate. In this way, things enable us to make a choice on their behalf that has already been made for us. If there is any inconsistency in this, it is the necessary sacrifice of logic to myth, since we wish to honour the twin gods of consumption and production. To do so, we sacrifice the sovereign consumer and the rational engineer to the self-improvement of things that improve ourselves.

In the fashion show and the auto show man's two bodies are celebrated today for their embrace of the appearances that will degrade them tomorrow. But the god of fashion is never so honoured as by those who risk being out-of-fashion by being-in-fashion. For the existential risk, whatever Sartre may have thought, lies between Being and Appearance, not between Being and Nothingness. It is this difference that we monitor in ourselves through our television: *televideo ergo sum.*

Thus before/for us daily consumption assumes its dual aspect and its basic ambiguity. Taken as a whole, quotidian and non-quotidian, it is material (sensorial, something to be taken, used, consumed, experienced) and theoretical (or ideological-images, symbols, signifiers, language and meta-language being consumed); it is complete (tending towards a system of consumption based on the rationalized organization of everyday life) and incomplete (the system is forever unfinished, disproved, threatened, unclosed, and opening on to nothingness); it is satisfaction (of needs, this one or that one, the need for this or for that, therefore sooner or later it is saturation) and frustration (only air was consumed, so the desire re-emerges); it is constructive (choice of objects, ordering, filing, contrived freedom) and destructive (it vanishes in the center of things, slides down the slopes of piled up objects accumulated without love and for no purpose). The so-called society of consumption is both a society of affluence and a society of want, of squandering and of asceticism (of intellectuality, exactitude, coldness). The ambiguities proliferate, each term reflecting its opposite (its precise opposite, its contradiction, its mirror-image); signifying it and being signified by it, they stand surety for and substitute each other while each one reflects all the others. It is a pseudo-system, a system of non-systems, cohesion of incoherence. The breaking point may be approached but never quite attained: that is the limit.

(Lefebvre, 1971: 142)

Today we are born and die on television and computer screens. We mourn, starve, rave, and pray on television. Even the Pope has discovered that the world's roads need no longer lead to Rome so long as he can make the news. Thus television reaches ever greater heights of efficacy. For now theologians need to muse whether the Papal Blessing reaches those who watch it as well as those who kneel in His presence. And even Freud might wonder whether live assassinations reconfirm his fantasy of the historical murder upon which all civilization is founded. When Presidents, Queens, and Popes run this risk before world television, who is to say where reality and appearance begin or end? Perhaps the only test is whether these events are punctuated with commercials. If television is bad for anyone, it seems to go worst for Marx, unable to defend himself against even Frank Sinatra. If the leaders of old Europe could be dragged into Reagan's chorus line for Let Poland Be Poland, one can argue that was to defend their own domestic use of propaganda rather than from any faith in television as *realpolitik*. Yet viewed from another angle, this *festival of public opinion* represents an extension of air power that has always fascinated politicians in their war for minds. Thus the Presidency of Ronald Reagan was not embarrassing because he was an actor. It was embarrassing because his executives had still not yet discovered how to make politics show business. Their successes and failures in this direction are, however, tied to the same processes at work in the economy. Today, the economy has internalized the media and by the same process is subject to media (re)presentation.

The specular function of things

To proceed with my argument I need, first of all, to say something about the notion of *specularization* as I employ it, and then to connect it with the *theory of ideology and commodity fetishism*. What makes television the connecting link here is understandable only if we first situate media technology within the semiotization of all modern technology (Shapiro, 1970). We can no longer think of technology as a neutral instrument of mediation between man and nature. Modern technology is increasingly assimilated to the reciprocal adaptations of man, nature, and society which occur in a horizontal field of information or communication. Within this field, objects, values, and experiences of every kind function as interchangeable elements of a semantic field in which reality, persons, events, and things are reduced to the possession of style.

What is now needed in media studies is a *structural theory of fetishism* – analogous to the psychoanalytic theory of the structure of perversion – functioning on the same level as Marx's structural theory of the commodity process (Baudrillard, 1972; Debord, 1967; Goldman, 1992). This involves recovering the original sense of the practice of making fetishes. Originally the fetish is an artefact made to imitate something else through the signs and marks inscribed upon it. The fascination is with the power of the signs to manipulate forces beyond the fetish. Thus what we mean by *commodity-fetishism* is not any desire for objects or experiences as such but the *desire of desire*, that is, desire of the structural codes through which desire of any sort is mediated. Commercial desire is not stimulated by the novelty of objects and experiences, or by the need to fill expanding leisure time. Desire derives from the continuous expansion of the system of commodity-signs towards which the consumer is directed by means of the media which furnish up-to-date readings, or *messages assembled within-and-as the settings of everyday life*. It is here that *models, styles*, and *collections* (see any large store's catalogue) function as structures of desire, as absolute moments in a stream of commodities.

Moreover, commodity fetishism must deal with the body politic, that is to say, with family health, working life, and personal happiness, since these must be refloated as the basic referentials/representations of the social structure (class, race, gender, ethnicity) through which the specularization of the commodity system functions. We can then realize how the media are obliged to beautify and transfigure the body and its everyday settings in order to *re-write the gap between reality and desire* within a self-sufficient system of symbols invulnerable to individual failure or class limits (O'Neill, 1978). It is this self-reflecting specularity of the commodity system that constitutes its fetishistic power to engage us in its charm, fun, and fantasy.

Television is perfectly suited to the specular work of breaking down the tension between public and private life, work and consumption, vicariousness and authenticity. All public and personal relations are now mediated through the communicative pattern of objects and experiences transfigured in the lights, sounds, colours, and scenarios of media technology. By projecting the passive viewer into the spectacle of his or her own everyday life as an environment from which all signs of the structure of social and political domination are *erased*, television hides the system.

The specular function of things – their symbolic proliferation, unbounded by space and time, their instant and imaginary availability – is to *make modern political economy impossible to understand*. It is to hide society as a circus or carnival of things. Above all, it ties things to the life of consumers, subordinating the world of production to the service of desire (Aronowitz, 1973). If there is a real world that sets any parameters upon the economy of desire, it arises only in the contingencies of domestic and international violence. Hence television regularly interrupts its celebration of things with the news of things that are recalcitrant to commercial celebration – such as war, murder, and the weather. In such portrayals of anarchy and scarcity, it reconfirms the homogeneity of its own comfortable world. It also achieves a *pseudocritical stance*, modifying its own integration of desire and the unconscious imagination which ordinarily functions to pacify criticism. Thoughtfulness is absorbed into the documentary and dialogue is enshrined in the talking portraits of the ABC News. The result is a perfect combination of docility and aggression – familiar staples of television. This combination is so potent that only Walter Cronkite and Barbara Walters could give it a family face. Thus television, like the Kremlin, has its succession problems: Nothing must destabilize the continuity of the image of stability in which America is anchored. Indeed, this formula appears so potent that Canada had to transform its national news centre into a spaceship transmitting world events through the gentle body of Knowlton Nash who in turn handed over the infighting to his avenging daughters Barbara Frum and Mary Lou Finlay. Since Knowlton was to Barbara as Barbara was to Mary, one could have predicted that Mary would disappear from The Journal, as the current affairs segment was called, in order to restore the heterosexual balance of truth and history in our nation. (In fact, this came to pass.)

World News reporting, if anything, might seem to confirm for us McLuhan's thesis that through the medium of television we all inhabit a global village. In my view, McLuhan's concept of the global village merely grasps superficial features of the new body politic without being able to relate them to any analytic framework of the ties between the modern administrative state and the political economy whose specular processes are serviced by the media. It is, nevertheless, hazardous to try to generalize upon the basic political functions of the media. The media employ a variety of audio-visual technologies, ranging from satellite television to newspapers, magazines, scientific journals, catalogues and handbills, each of which can play a specific role in raising or depressing the level of public awareness. Thus the specular functions of the media are at first sight extremely varied and not easily brought to order. Yet, as I have argued elsewhere (O'Neill, 2002), it may be useful to think of the media as functioning to *specularize the legitimation processes of state administered capitalism*. The latter necessitate the use of television in the production of the following spectacles:

1. On the *state level* the media communicate state or national issues, the 'national' news, and the national parliamentary or congressional proceedings;
2. On the *market level* the media continue to portray the market system as though it were the basic legitimating agency of bourgeois values, and encourage the pursuit of consumerism and leisure;

3. The function of the media at both the state level and the market level is to manage the necessary separation between expert and technical administration processes, on the one hand, and public participation, on the other;
4. This is achieved through the media-fix of turning the political and economic processes into spectacles, while at the same time raising the level of *civil privatism and depoliticizing the public realm* (Habermas, 1975);
5. To the extent that the media can be used to manage the legitimation problem at the market level, i.e., as *sociological propaganda*, then the state use of the media for political mobilization is reduced, and appears as a democratic instrument of information: *the right to know;*
6. In turn, the media generally assume an apparently benign function in filling the leisure time of a highly privatized mass democracy. By and large, the communicative process of *popular education* consists of the mobilization of persons into a structure of self-coercion and domination exercised against nature (*education for work*), against human nature (*education for living*), and against the collective potential for freedom and expression (*political education*).

It is important to see that the specular function of television lies in its capacity to individualize the mass while treating the individual only as a member of the masses. It achieves this as a machinery of *sociological propaganda* which works upon individuals from the bottom up, so to speak, rather than through the imposition of ideologies to influence their minds:

> Such propaganda is essentially diffuse. It is rarely conveyed by catch-word or expressed intentions. Instead it is based on a general climate, an atmosphere that influences people imperceptibly without having the appearance of propaganda; it gets to man through his customs, through his most unconscious habits. It creates new habits in him; it is a sort of persuasion from within. As a result, man adopts new criteria of judgment and choice, adopts them spontaneously, as if he had chosen them himself. But all their criteria are in conformity with the environment and are essentially of a collective nature. Sociological propaganda produces a progressive adaptation to a certain order of things, a certain concept of human relations, which unconsciously molds individuals and makes them conform to society.
>
> (Ellul, 1973)

Sociological propaganda reaches minds through bodies; it works especially upon familied bodies and the tissue of everyday life. Here the specular function of the family soaps may be understood. *Soap operas are essentially defamilizing dramas*, whatever the folklore on them. They are essential to the work of television, occupying as much viewing time as the working week. In soap operas the family is on stage because it is offstage breaking up, falling apart, distrustful, and anomic. Children are largely absent from family soaps because the family is no longer sure of its commitment to reproduce itself. Soap wives either have trouble conceiving by their husbands or else the embryo has even more trouble getting born, as if aware that family life may no longer be the blessing it used to be. Surviving infants turn to a life of illness, accidents, and tragedy, a concern to their helpless parents, whose lives provide no strength because they are always crippled with divorce and infidelity. If the child learns to cope with parents, it learns by coping with their serial marriages. The child's family life is a soap opera. If the soaps remain fun, it is because the props remain reassuringly the same, inhabited by other people's troubles. However, once these troubles turn into our own – as we half suspect they will – the soaps leave us unprepared after all and ready for the professional therapeutic care which is the last resort of the family.

Of course, television resists the bureaucratized therapeutic professions. It is democratic, maverick, and lawless. It favours people without titles, private individuals, common folk, comic children, and ethnics. Thus television is especially concerned to portray the private cop or detective who goes for his man with more passion and concern for speedy justice, more wit and strength than the fat, bureaucratic legal and criminal system. What I have in mind here may be illustrated from certain features of the series *Kojak*. Here we have the law and its pursuit of justice embodied in a fat, bald headed, lollypop sucking Greek. How is this possible? Anyone familiar with the rituals of purity and danger would realize that the symbolism of the law has been seriously polluted by its embodiment in a figure like Kojak, not to mention his equally obese aides and black colleagues. Or are we dealing with a liberal system of justice unfortunately obliged to prey upon an otherwise criminogenic ethnic community? To be brief, the answer is that Anycop's work has been simplified by the technology of crime search, namely, by the bugging devices that permit criminals to tell the police where to look for them. This device raises the efficiency of the search and relieves its parties for the symbolic work of token ethnic representation. As a matter of fact, it even permits policemen to turn into policewomen! My point is that the technology of modern society is indifferent to gender, race, and creed, but may be used to 'refloat' them as though they were now the local, human, and vital elements of modem life. 'Multiculturalism,' which is the Canadian version of this phenomenon, merely floats ethnicity in *an imaginary festival of consensus*. It is an engaging symbolism of liberal consensus, an aesthetic resolution of the endemic conflicts in what remains a stratifying society.

Between them the criminal and the entrepreneurial cop revive the American free enterprise system in settings that celebrate its technology, affluence, and ultimate goodness. By the same token, the lid of authority and professional, bureaucratic power can always be replaced in dealing with the ultimate threats to family and corporate life. Thus crime, illness, disaster, and intrigue are sacrificed on the altar of television in order to reconfirm the justice and goodness of the institutions that defend the family against violence and evil. *But if television defends the family, it does so only in order to redesign it.* Thus in the food commercial, television makes us hungry, teaches us what to eat and how to eat. Television even admonishes us for overeating what it offers us to eat. This is because television is in the business of defamilizing the production and consumption of food. To achieve this, it is necessary to decathect housework, cooking, and cleaning and to install the processed, precooked, and self-cleaning substitutes from television's fantasy world. Food must be reduced to energy; living, too, must be reduced to an energy calculus, fast and efficient. Anything short of this is idiocy and old age. Once the production and consumption of televised food has been defamilized, the symbolism of home, mother, tender and loving care can be refloated as literal ingredients of the substitute foods. It is then ready to be eaten by children without parents, husbands without wives, and working mothers without time. The side effects can be taken care of in the stomach aid and breath conquering advertisements. TV dinners are the totem meal of televisioned living.

The specularization of consumption, coupled with the erasure of production, is marvelously suited to the *materialization of the ideology of equality and happiness*. Television democratizes consumption and is silent upon the stratification of power and privilege generated and reproduced in the system of production. Indeed, the stratifying processes in the production system are resymbolized as levels of taste, desire, and adventure open to advertising. In a world where access to health, education, employment, housing, and food is manifestly unequal, television pictures consumption as a magical school in which we learn to want things for their fetishistic power to alter and improve our lives. Television thereby erases the fact that consumption is part of the system of scarcity/affluence rather than the delivery of abundance. *Television schools us in envy* without the desire to learn anything about the system of deprivation that floats envy, comparison and competition with ourselves, or competition with others. It is for this reason that television feminizes consumption, selling to women the myth of woman, just as it masculinizes consumption, selling to men the myth of man. In this way, human relations are completely relativized, since the logic of capitalism is indifferent to all relationships except as they can be refloated in the system of exchange value.

The specular function of television is therefore to conceal the differentials, comparisons, and exclusions that separate men by surrounding them with the same swarm of images. In other words, it is to broadcast an ideology in which individuals are at the center of things and images, while being absent from the processes that shape these images of their everyday life:

> We can define *the field of consumption*: it is everyday life. The latter is not just the sum of daily events and deeds, the domain of banality and repetition, it is a *system of interpretation*. The everyday consists of the dissociation of a total praxis into a transcendental, autonomous, and abstract and immanent 'private' sphere. Work, leisure, family, friendship are all recognized by the individual in a static mode, outside of the world and history, as a coherent system grounded as the closure of the private, the abstract liberty of the individual....From the objective standpoint of the totality, the everyday life is an impoverished and residual sphere. But it is also triumphant and euphoric in its efforts to achieve a total autonomy and a reinterpretation of the world 'as

an internal usage.' Herein lies the profound and organic symbiosis between the privatized sphere of everyday life and mass communications.

(Baudrillard, 1970: 33; Genosko, 1994)

Mass media culture is *fictional* whether it is delivering information or art, since what it is shaping is not just its images but the kind of public that is organized, that is, privatized through the media. The media do not present the public with information with which to determine their political and economic choices. Rather, the media relay the choices already made in the political economy for *pseudo-ratification* by the viewer-consumer-voter. Thus we can understand, for example, the symbiosis between the self-expanding field of complex information systems and the talk or gossip show. How does the latter thrive in such a world? First of all, the talk show specularizes a dying art. Moreover, it only appears to be an intimate oasis removed from the information system. This is because its gossip revolves around the same values of power, money, and sex as rule the conglomerate world and so convey the same basic message on behalf of the system. The talk show, then, is the intimate end of the machine that never ceases to talk about itself, that is always on because *television is the sun that never sets on the empire of commerce*. Indeed, the whole point is that television is always talking because it never talks *to* us but *at* us. It is a necessary communication in this form since it reproduces the unilateral power structure in which it is embedded. We are all joined in television because we are all separated from knowledge and power in the specularization of information, desire, and intimacy. *Television circulates our isolation*. It does so by embracing us in an imaginary community without local and national boundaries. Television is everybody's sexual partner and the nation's confidante. Your personal computer will confirm this to the very end of your fingertips.

Conclusion: some hypothesis on the specular function of the media

McLuhan notwithstanding, the media do have a message and it is the message that makes the media necessary as instruments of global domination. The basic functions of the media messages are:

1. To float the real worlds of production and consumption in a semiotic system of signs without referents;
2. Within (1) to homologize psychic and social structures;
3. By floating an autonomous semiotic field in life-styles, models, collections, news, information, to hide the system of administrative controls operating on (1–2);
4. To reduce everyday life to a privatized celebration of the benign products of capitalist democracy;
5. To dramatize in individualized morality plays (including psychoanalysis) which save the system the failures, tensions, and reality gaps in the system of administrative controls;

6. To produce political and social amnesia;
7. Not to charge consumers for (1–6). That is why the message, if not the medium, is free. Where else – or why else – can one get something for nothing?

The specular tasks of the media are necessary functions in the legitimation of capitalist democracy. They enable the system to employ sociological propaganda, thereby minimizing more overt political mobilization. To achieve this, the following spectacles are necessary media functions:

1. a. to communicate state or national issues;
    b. to communicate the national 'news';
    c. to televise the national parliamentary or congressional proceedings.

2. a. to continue to portray the market system as though it were the basic legitimating agency of bourgeois values;
    b. to encourage the pursuit of consumerism and leisure.

3. a. expert and technical *administration* processes, and
    b. *public participation.*

4. The requirements of (3) are serviced through the media-mix of

    a. *spectacularizing* the political and economic process, and, at the same time,
    b. raising the level of *civic privatism* and *depoliticizing the public realm.*

5. To the extent that the media can be used to manage the legitimation problem at level (2), that is to say, as a market communication then the state use of the media assumes the form of *sociological propaganda.* In turn, the media generally assume an apparently benign function in fulfilling the leisure time of a highly privatized mass democracy.

6. By and large, what we call mass culture and democracy consists of the mobilization of persons into a structure of self-coercion and domination exercised

    a. *against nature,* as the raw material of industry;
    b. against *human nature* itself, as a primary source of pleasure and gratification;
    c. against the *collective potential for freedom and expression* historically realizable on the basis of the structures of organization and repression in (a) and (b).

7. In short, industrial democracies, as we have known them so far, are the product of *a triple structure of domination over nature, persons, and society,* realized through the instruments of technology, repressive socialization, and the class expropriation of collective political power. This is the matrix of media work.
8. Media work is nevertheless not engaged in a great conspiracy. It gets its job done because in a certain sense *the media are always the media we deserve.* Television puts individuals in communion with themselves while leaving them at their relatively isolated terminals. Together, then, the message

and the medium, the audience and the communications industry are united around TV as their culture's *bard* (Fiske and Hartley, 1978) whose daily task is to compose a series of messages that communicate to the audience a self-confirming vision of themselves and their everyday beliefs and values.

To do so, TV must relay the authority of the community's myths rather than the genius of its producers, an effect it achieves by affirming orality and presence against rationality and absence, or by defending primary institutions in their struggle with secondary institutions.

9. *The bardic functions* of television may be summarized as follows:

   a. To *articulate* the main lines of the established cultural consensus about the nature of reality (and therefore the reality of nature).
   b. To *implicate* the individual members of the culture into its dominant value-systems, by exchanging a status-enhancing message for the endorsement of that message's underlying ideology (as articulated in its mythology).
   c. To *celebrate*, explain, interpret, and justify the doings of the culture's individual representatives in the world out-there; using the mythology of individuality to claw back such individuals from any mere eccentricity to a position of socio-centrality.
   d. To *assure* the culture at large of its practical adequacy in the world by affirming and confirming its ideologies/mythologies in active engagement with the practical and potentially unpredictable world.
   e. To *expose*, conversely, any practical inadequacies in the culture's sense of itself which might result from changed conditions in the world out-there, or from pressure within the culture for a reorientation in favour of a new ideological stance.
   f. To *convince* the audience that their status and identity as individuals is guaranteed by the culture as a whole.
   g. To *transmit* by these means a sense of cultural membership (security and involvement) (Fiske and Hartley, 1978: 88).

10. TV HEALTH WARNING

   a. There is never anything on TV – if there were, the system would break down;
   b. Since all of life is on TV, you can expect to have already seen it;
   c. TV is part of the family – it babysits its mind;
   d. TV is not free – you must give your time to it;
   e. No one knows whether or not TV is real.

References

Aronowitz, Stanley (1973). 'Colonized Leisure, Trivialized Work'. In: *False Promises: The Shaping of American Working Class Consciousness*. New York: McGraw-Hill Book Company, pp. 51–137.

Baudrillard, Jean (1970). *La société de consummation*. Paris: Gallimard.

Baudrillard, Jean (1972). *Pour une critique de l'économie politique du signe*. Paris: Gallimard.

Debord, Guy (1967). *La société du spectacle*. Paris: Buchet/Chastel.

Ellul, Jacuqes (1973). *Propaganda: The Formation of Men's Attitudes*. Konrad Kellen and Jean Lerner (trans). New York: Vintage Books.

Fiske, John and Hartley, John (1978). *Reading Television*. London: Methuen.

Genosko, Gary (1994). 'The Paradoxical Effects of MacLuhanisme?'. *Economy and Society* 23: 407–32.

Goldman, Robert (1992). *Reading Acts Socially*. London: Routledge.

Goldsen, Rose K. (1977). *The Show and Tell Machine: How Television Works and Works You Over*. New York: The Dial Press.

Habermas, Jürgen (1975). *Legitimation Crisis*. Thomas McCarthy (trans.). Boston: Beacon Press.

Lefebvre, Henri (1971). *Everyday Life in the Modern World*. Sacha Rabinovitch (trans.). London: Allen Lane.

O'Neill, John (1978). 'The Productive Body: An Essay on the Work of Consumption'. *Queen's Quarterly* 85 (2): 221–30.

O'Neill, John (2002). 'Language and the Legitimation Problem'. In: *Plato's Cave: Television and its Discontents*. Cresskill, NJ: Hampton Press Inc., pp. 97–101.

Schrank, Jeffrey (1977). *Snap, Crackle and Popular Taste: The Illusion of Free Choice in America*. New York: Delacorte Press.

Shapiro, Jeremy J. (1970). 'One-Dimensionality: The Universal Semiotic of Technological Experience'. In: *Critical Interruptions: New Left Perspectives on Herbert Marcuse*. Paul Breine (ed.). New York: Herder and Herder, pp. 136–86.

8   Empire versus empire*

A post-communist manifesto

Ibelli fata sua habent – the fate of books that announce the end of history, as does Hardt and Negri's *Empire* (2000), is to be swallowed in their own apocalypse. The deployment of American commercial airliners to strike down the World Trade Center on September 11, 2001 also achieved more or less than Osama bin Laden may have entertained. It certainly struck at the heart of American Empire – reversing its own practices of violation whenever its imperial interests are at stake. Just previously, America had been prepared to go it alone in space, embarking on new star wars, and on earth continuing a defiantly self-interested and anti-ecological energy policy. The blow to America's commercial heartland, however, produced a hurried US realignment of international forces and a rebirth of American nationalism and familism in a civilized front against barbarism. The Evil of terrorism now overshadows the domestic politics of class, gender and race, which are reduced to the preoccupations of the morally short-sighted. Into this imperial context – since it is the fate of books, whether philosophical or not, always to arrive late – there steps Hardt and Negri's *Empire* (2000) – of all things, a postmodern, post-imperial communist manifesto. Born out of the Spinozan or schizoid suspension of all previous systems of right and left domination and their limited counter-cultures of emancipation. The choice we are offered is between terrorism and poetry. The terrorist bombards people, who are confined, driving them into the black hole of misery, whereas the poet releases the people to become a multitude with hope, expanding into the cosmos (Deleuze and Guattari, 1987: 345).

Because the American Empire is now allegedly total and universal, it must breed its own transformation towards universal humanitarianism. Thus *Empire* is a postal machine, sending and receiving its own message. Its 'postality' is post-theoretical, post-historical and post-economic. Postality is at once message and medium. Without past or future, postality in effect mediates the fullness of the present. The past and future as present serve only as ballast for the sails of imperial plenitude.

---

* Text of the essay taken from *Theory, Culture & Society*, 19(4) 2002: 195–210. Reproduced with permission.

Hardt and Negri's thesis avoids any foray into the political unconscious of imperialism. Yet, surely it calls for a psychoanalytic supplement on the paranoid-schizoid defences involved in the imperialization of omnipotence. Where Reagan once spoke of the Soviet Union as an 'evil empire', George W. Bush now projects an 'axis of evil'. In both cases, America is split off from its own violence/violation as the world's most aggressive force. Prior to the terrorist attack upon New York, the United States was collectively experiencing depressive anxiety over its ability to preserve its good objects (family, community, jobs) against corporate greed and globalization. Once the collapse of the Soviet Union had removed any real possibility of projecting America's aggression beyond itself, it began to consume itself with domestic but apolitical anxieties, and with an odyssey of virtual wars here on earth and there in the heavens. With the double violation of American soil and symbols in New York and Washington, President Bush was re-elected to suture American civil solidarity to American aggression, refamilialize American security while projecting it once again to the far corners of the American Empire. The only casualty in this has been the sacrifice of the European alliance to America's resolve to go it alone in the recapture of a world where its children will enjoy universal security and peace. Thus Bush's sheriff-like posture reasserts the American myth of defiant individualism while simultaneously mobilizing a huge government subsidy to underwrite its imperial stance as a confirmation of basic American values in contest with the external forces of evil. The result is a double denial of civic anxiety due to the depletion of governance in the name of market anxiety over reduced global competitiveness induced by deficit government. The Republican resolution of this doubled anxiety is to recast government dependency and inefficiency in terms of an omnipotent imperial war machine dedicated to the restoration of American autonomy.

Thus America is re-committed to the very myth which had collapsed with the twin towers of the World Trade Center. This time it will pursue imperialized autonomy in the name of civic solidarity exalted beyond political partisanship. For the rest of the story, stay with CNN. I would refrain, however, from Žižek's thesis (2002) that Americans have already seen September 11 at the movies in the paranoid series from *The Terminator* to *Matrix* which foretells the always (im) possible collapse of any titanic project. Žižek's thesis is part of the movie chain it claims to analyse. Indeed, it advertises Hollywood's faked destruction of its own megalomania coming to a building near you! If we step outside of the movie house, however, the destruction of the World Trade Center is part of the cycle of violence in which the United States is both exporter and importer. For this reason, Baudrillard's thesis (2001) that September 11 merely acts out the spirit of terror in all of us is nothing but low-grade Nietzschean *ressentiment* transferred on to Hollywood's power to dream for US(A). It too relies upon the implosion of the reel/real without any mediation, making the terrorist message the return of singularity to the totalizing system of imperial violence, substituting the ecstasy of communication for the work of political analysis. A similar objection might be made to the Krokers' thesis (2001) on terrorism as a deterritorialized viral power unleashed by the collapse of Cold War nuclearism and stalled Empire. This argument may capture the implosion of post-nuclear violence, intensified by sacrificial versus militarized deaths. But the viral metaphor loses the unequal states of the political systems between which trade and foreign policy interventions operate to simultaneously organize, anarchize, barbarize and terrorize the global world order. Poverty, ignorance, and disease are inextricable effects of globalization, as I have argued with respect to the political cartography of AIDS/HIV (O'Neill, 1990). I still prefer to see these as effects of stratification rather than 'universal contagion', as Hardt and Negri (2000: 136) put it.

How, then, can Hardt and Negri's imperial postality claim any critical function? The answer is that their postality is left-of-left in as much as it releases the left from the millstones of essentialism and totalism. Since postality does not separate the historical narratives of fascism (racism) and communism (utopianism), it thereby inherits the whole endgame by saving everyone from repeating the error and violence of historical orientation. The post-subject of *Empire* is the agent of a deregulated economy, society and ludic identity (Ebert, 1996) surfing upon class, gender and race as flows of virtuality and style (Zavarzadeh, 1995). Imperial postality is the inaugural event of the contemporary ethical moment of in-difference to the historical and political past/future. The task of *Empire* is to recast both capitalism and communism. Neither system is going anywhere – neither by themselves nor in contest with one another. The 'end of history' is a vision held only by those still waiting for the revolution on terms other than those of the new world order. It will be a long wait because global capitalism has shaken off the 'domestic analogy' between national governance and a supranational constitution. Empire is now mandated to guarantee global contracts, to resolve conflicts and to institute perpetual peace, enforced by just wars in the name of humanitarian rights:

> From the beginning, then, Empire sets in motion an ethico-political dynamic that lies at the heart of its juridical concept. This juridical concept involves two fundamental tendencies: first, the notion of a right that is affirmed in the construction of a new order that envelops the entire space of what it considers civilization, a boundless, universal space; and second, a notion of right that encompasses all time within its ethical foundation. Empire exhausts historical time, suspends history, and summons the past and future within its own ethical order. In other words, Empire presents its order as permanent, eternal, and necessary.
>
> (Hardt and Negri, 2000: 11)

Yet the justice of Empire is exercised through a hybrid militarized police function whose task is to quell 'anarchic' elements at home and to conquer once and for all 'evil' elements abroad. In practice, I would argue the distinction between internal and external protest begins to collapse, squeezing democratic protest into 'anarcho-terrorism' and dissolving all protest into 'alienology', as we have seen in the policing of WTO protests. Moreover, the premature imperializing collapse of global spatio-temporal differences produces anomalies of tribal, ethnic and national 'crimes against humanity' abstracted from their own history in order to inaugurate institutions of transnational justice. Because the new world order materializes Kant's categorical imperative by releasing cosmopolitan virtue from domestic vice, so we are told, Empire is the ultimate blend of the virtuous and the virtual – all we have to do is tune in and turn on to watch the trials.

It is a dream of every political order to materialize itself in the willingness of its subjects to rule themselves. The achievement of voluntary servitude (de La Boétie, 1975) aspires to the translation of power into service (Hegel, 1977), sin into salvation and greed into gift (Mauss, 1990). Hardt and Negri tackle the problem of the ratio of repression/emancipation in state power with Foucault's concept of biopower – a mechanism that in my view (O'Neill, 1986) is abstracted from any revolutionary project, let alone the struggle for a welfare state. Yet, left critics have turned Foucault's biopolitics against the managerialism of the welfare state through which we may yet practise a degree of social justice (O'Neill, 1994). What is at stake here is the politico-ethical project elaborated in a civic welfare society whereby we institutionalize the 'moral stranger' (Ignatieff, 1984; Wolfe, 1989), or the practice of our self as one another (Ricoeur, 1992) exercised in the secular gifting of taxation for education, health and social security. Actually, Negri (Hardt and Negri, 1994) once placed considerable weight upon the conservation of welfare practices in the struggle for justice. But in *Empire*, Negri and Hardt concede that the welfare state will be dissolved in the imperial privatization of the commons. I would argue instead that the subject of welfare is a citizen-subject rather than a subjugated subject of a biopolitical regime. We otherwise lose the struggle between civic and productivist regimes of welfare and social policy. The neo-liberal moralization of productive consumerism elides both the autonomy of workers and the dependency of consumers. Worse still, centre-left parties now argue that it is the productive subject who is morally outraged by underclass dependency and vulnerability. In the name of global competitiveness, post-social security sates increasingly subordinate civic autonomy to market dependency (Fitzpatrick, 1999; O'Neill, 1997).

Actually Hardt and Negri (1994) rely less upon Foucault than upon Marx's larger concept of the social reproduction of labour, outlined in the *Grundrisse* (Marx, 1973) and expanded in Deleuze and Guattari (1977, 1987) to project towards communism the capital flows deterritorialized by American republicanism. At first, as the tale goes, America had to conquer itself, its land, its natives, its small farmers and ranchers, its immigrants. Today, 'the planet' itself is America's Promised Land bequeathed to it along with the 21st century, as witnessed by the choral voice of CNN. And, even though the very system of Empire which they project as the vehicle of universal justice continues to exploit 'nearly all of humanity' (Hardt and Negri, 2000: 43), it is still better than all previous systems, they say – in the same way that capitalism is a better productive system than its pre-historical antecedents. For despite the predictions of Marxist-Hegelian dialectics, global Empire washes out socialism's promise to improve on capitalism for the very reason that capitalism is the only social system destined to improve upon itself! Remarkably, Hardt and Negri's revision of the imperial narrative largely overlooks America's cold war freezing of labour history and its fossilizing of Third World colonial movements. Despite Negri's own considerable role in resistance to the violent oppression of labour conflict, emphasis is given to the imperial reproduction of locality stripped of its primitivism and naturalism in the flux of global homogenization and heterogenization. Leftist attempts to localize resistance to Empire are now considered to be like trying to step into the same river twice – a river that is red with the blood of enmity and swollen with the corpse of class and racial politics.

The new vision of imperialism to which we are called is a politics without dialectics and without totalization of the class subject – notions of which *Empire* is *critical* and *deconstructive*. Rather, it embraces a Spinozan Marxism (Negri, 1991) to project the constructive and ethico-political practices of the multitude who will carry old-order imperialism towards the new world order of Empire. What must be jettisoned along the way is any notion of national history, whether proletarian or colonial, because these movements have found their 'response' in the formation of Empire (Hardt and Negri, 2000: 51). Here Negri, especially, appears to have turned his back upon the extraordinary volatile Italian left protest movements around the refusal of work in the 1960s, 1970s and 1980s – *Autonomia Operaia*, *Ya Basta!* and *Tute Bianche*, so active in the Genoa and Prague protests (Callinicos, 2001). Even more paradoxically, Hardt and Negri claim that the age of communication has rendered the great radical struggles of the 20th century 'all but incommunicable' (2000: 54). Yet might one not ask whether the paradox of radical incommunicability which affects WTO protest movements, for example, isn't more the effect of events reported/pictured outside of their narrative frames in response to the postmodern canon of pastiche (Jameson, 1985; O'Neill, 1992). The propaganda effect (witness reportage on Seattle, Ottawa and Genoa) is that the more we get the news the less news there is (O'Neill, 2002a) because its format privileges images without any context other than the self-confirming voice of CNN commentary upon self-indulgent violence and anarchy. But Hardt and Negri invert things, claiming that the media are actually the 'pedagogy of the oppressor' who, so we are told, must learn from the oppressed what to do next to maintain power:

> Imperial power whispers the names of the struggles in order to charm them into passivity, to construct a mystified image of them, but most important to discover which processes of globalization are possible and which are not. In this contradictory and paradoxical way the imperial processes of globalization assume these events, recognizing them as both limits and opportunities to recalibrate Empire's own instruments.
>
> (Hardt and Negri, 2000: 59)

Having deprived emancipatory history of any message or carrier, Hardt and Negri then designate the 'multitude' as the creative and productive force upon which vampire capitalism still battens for want of its own body. To compensate the poor for their 'ontological lack', Empire waits at the gates of human misery offering the bread of peace and order in exchange for the abandonment of revolution born from the outrages of virtual globalization.

Hardt and Negri are postmodernists twice over. As they read it, modernity cut the transcendental cord to give birth to Spinoza's concept of the immanent powers of ontological singularity and self-making humanity (*homo homo*). But it failed to sustain the unleashed enthusiasm of the libidinal multitude and reinstituted the transcendental apparatus of Religion, State, and Reason. Modernity suppressed the programme of emancipatory singularity, running from Spinoza to Deleuze/Guattari and Foucault, in order to reopen the line of modernity that runs from Descartes through Kant and Hegel. The restoration of Transcendental Reason then crossed with the line of the Transcendental Capital State Apparatus running from Hobbes through Rousseau and Adam Smith. With no station for Marx, until the *Grundrisse* (1973) was opened, the roller-coaster ride continues until joined by those melancholic theorists of failed modernity – Weber and Foucault. Moreover, even when Lyotard, Baudrillard, and Derrida come aboard, they are so dependent upon their own construction of the Transcendental State Apparatus that they blind us to the mutation in political sovereignty without boundaries that ends in the new world constitution of Empire. In this respect, postmodernism rubs shoulders with a variety of fundamentalist movements whose postmodernism is as much a contemporary reflection as is postmodernism of the seismic shifts in modernity that have produced Empire. Worse still, I would argue, postmodernism fails to see that its critical concepts of anti-foundationalism, anti-essentialism, and (in)difference are, as the ghost of Marx might have told them, capital practices of a bourgeoisie devoted to shocking rather than being shocked, not to mention Baudelaire (Holland, 1996) and Benjamin (1969) on this effect. Thus the cultural politics of postmodernism (O'Neill, 1995) celebrate what they seek to desecrate because it is impossible to *épater la bourgeoisie!*

As Hardt and Negri read it, the history of the modern sovereign state, whether fascist, communist or Third World republic, is infected with a viral totalitarianism fed by the culture of homogenized populism which sacrifices the multitude to totalitarian democracy (2000: 113). The internal crisis of modernity lies in the inability of the capital state to institute an international realm beyond class and colonial conflict. This has left us the legacy of a populace that, because it lacks the potential virtuosity of the multitude (Hardt and Negri, 2000: 102) is obliged to resort to second-degree nationalist struggles. Prior to their own Manifesto on the Poor (2000: 156–9), all postmodern social theory has abjected the living subject of pure difference – the *multitude of the poor* who from age to age are the figure of poverty and of the power to transcend every regime of poverty. Here, as I mentioned earlier, the reversibility of the subjugated and subject multitude derives not from Foucault but from Deleuze/Guattari's axioms of schizo-analysis (1977: 273–382) which may be summarized as follows:

the collectivity is produced from pressures upon its constituent singularities by welding their molecular desires to molar lack;

(Deleuze and Guattari, 1977: 342–4)

a revolutionary group will remain a *subjugated group* for as long as its pre-conscious desires are identified with the anti-productive forces of repression; a revolutionary group becomes a *subject-group* when it is a group whose libidinal investments are productive of desiring-desire;

(Ibid.: 348)

there are two poles of social libidinal investment –

(a) the paranoiac, reactionary, and fascisizing pole, defined by subjugated groups and
(b) the schizoid, revolutionary pole – defined by subject-groups (1977: 366–7);

the revolutionary schizz is always virtual; though not without capital precon-ditions, it is the death of capitalism.

(Ibid.: 378–9)

Empire is not, of course, a simple translation of the axioms of schizo-analysis. These axioms themselves derive from Deleuze's own complex relation to anti-Hegelianism (see Hardt, 1993), Bergsonism (Deleuze, 1988a), Nietzsche (Deleuze, 1983) and Freud, of course. At the core of these texts is Hegel's master/slave dialectic of the reversal of power/authority into autonomy/civic commu-nity recoded in the micro/macro politics of productive desire (O'Neill, 1996). Deleuze's Spinozanism (1988b, 1990) must be interpreted as an effect of the various (dis)junctures between Marxism and psychoanalysis over the transcend-ence of the pleasure principle (O'Neill, 2002b). 'Deleuzism' is the search for a transcendental empiricism to break out of Hegelianism, along with Derrida and Foucault. But one might say the same of Deleuze's 'misprisions' (Bloom, 1973) of Spinoza, Bergson and Nietzsche. In fact, Deleuze's own practice of philosophical characterization is much closer to Hegel's dramaturgical history of philosophy – indeed, closer to Socrates/Plato. And once Deleuze turns to Marx's *Grundrisse*, are we not full circle to Marx's patient concretization of the Hegelian dialectic in the graft of *social production* and *desiring production* – or the inseparability of capital production/consumption? Is the production of desire theatrical or indus-trial; or cannot the investment of desire and the social move directly and either way? Whereas Freud's oedipalization of the libido stages a familial economy of desire, Luther's subjectivization of faith, combined with Adam Smith's subjec-tivization of labour, represents the institutionalization of productive rather than repressive desire. This is the capital event that Marx grasped as the double text of exploitation and emancipation, whereas Weber could read it only with sadness.

How is the shift/schizz to counter-Empire to be effected upon the terrain of Empire? After all, Empire has no borders from where any attack upon it might be mounted, and no one has a future outside of its suspension of history. The answer is that because Empire is everywhere and nowhere, that is, because it is the *non-place* of global production and exploitation, it produces within itself the multitu-dinous movement of nomads, barbarians, refugees and homeless who swell into a great *anthropological exodus* (2000: 215) from Empire. This multitude passes along its way the ruins of class, race, gender and family, which never brought them anywhere near the non-place of new life forms opened up by contemporary movements of desertion and exodus. Once the industrial working class loses its hegemony, the proletariat becomes the *universal figure of labour* (2000: 256), a Spinozan multitude produced within and by Empire, which will end alienation. For the very reason that imperial capitalism has no outside, there are no aliens with any ground to stand upon, no aliens whom dialectical history has not failed. In short, the end of alienation is a message that imperial capitalism sends itself. The voice of new labour is one of exit. It rejects both statism and populism in the name of preserving what has already been won in the name of welfare and security which are the outline of a virtual republic (despite the earlier comments on this issue). Exodus is not a flight from power because the *general intellect* of new labour overrides the distinction between active and contemplative life – never Marx's idea anyway, despite Arendt (1958) and Habermas (1971), as I have argued elsewhere (O'Neill, 1972). But here, as so often, *Empire* fails to give sufficient space to the very large issue of the struggle for a civic concept of intelligent work, family and community (O'Neill, 1994), although addressed to some extent by Hardt (1998). Instead, we are offered a shockingly revisionist-republican history of Empire!

The revisionist message of *Empire* is that America was destined for imperial sovereignty from the day it decided to market its own multitude. America's Protestantism and pluralism produced and reproduced a mobile frontier of freedom and wealth that absorbed the contradictions of native genocide, black slavery, class struggle and colonialism, which might otherwise have brought American capitalism to a continental standstill, aborting its imperial mission, its emergence from the Cold War and its next act as history's hottest Empire. We are finally at the end of history because there is no place left for American history and politics to breed, no boundary for its viruses of racism and segregation to penetrate and poison. *Empire* is *everywhere and nowhere* (Hardt and Negri, 2000: 190). The factories of the family, school and prison now lie in rust and ruin. All other institutions that homogenize and exclude residual difference are now in permanent crisis in the face of relentless *corruption* (breaking down) that is the driving force of Empire. Today any Marxist critique of capitalism is obsolete because it is predicated upon a cyclical view of history – *plus le capitalisme change, plus c'est la même chose!* What Marxism failed to grasp is that the mode of capital change is not crisis but *corruption*, that is, its capacity for breaking down its internal class conflicts and imperial wars, to deterritorialize itself in global/local production and to recreate the emancipatory multitude that replaces the proletariat as Empire's own other:

> Imperial power is founded on the rupture of every determinate relationship. Corruption is simply the sign of the absence of any ontological relationship. In the ontological vacuum, corruption becomes necessary, objective. Imperial sovereignty thrives on the proliferating contradictions corruption gives rise

to; it is stabilized by its instabilities, by its impurities and admixture; it is calmed by the panic and anxieties it continually engenders.

(Hardt and Negri, 2000: 202)

In place of the missing volumes of *Capital*, which testify to Marx's inability to provide a corrupt genealogy of the shift from European imperialism to American Empire, and despite Negri's attachment to the *Grundrisse* (Negri, 1984), Hardt and Negri fill us in on how it all worked out in the new world. The self-transformation of American capitalism was inaugurated with the New Deal, which refurbished industrial capitalism in time for America's domination of European imperial wars. With time out for the Cold War and the hot wars in Vietnam and Korea, which lit the fires of the 1960s protest movements, the American Empire emerged unscathed by its invention of domestic surveillance, and a militarized police response to protest at home and terrorism abroad. In reality, rather than their own vision, the 1960s were sifting intellectual and manual labour for recruitment into symbolic and service industry providers for computerized capitalism and its new paradigm of subjective production. En route, America had privatized its own commons, including welfare provisions and legislated this policy as a criterion for membership in its new world order. The Soviet Union fell out of the loop because it was unable to switch over from political to industrial surveillance systems with a PlayStation in everyone's home! To achieve its own transition to Empire, American capital had nothing to do but roll over (!) because all the creative moves (anti-war protest, civil rights, women's movement, colonial liberation movements) had already been made for it! Empire hit the jackpot without a system, leaving all its left punters in the dirt and with no idea of how capital accumulation works to this day (Hardt and Negri, 2000: 256–9).

The prospect of Empire is underwritten by the US dollar, trusting in the one-eyed god that watches from the great pyramid overlooking the New Age of Global Order – *Novus Ordo Seculorum*. It is a financial, corporate and military order faced by the G8, GATT, WTO, World Bank, IMF, all towering over the UN, Church, media and NGOs that are charged with representing the interests of the world's people. Yet, as much as Empire strives for constitutional status, it becomes the very site (non-place) of its own contestation abroad as a sovereign political and economic order whose macro-spectacle of consumptive desire is simultaneously shot through with anxiety and fear among its micro-subjects unsure of its centre, as we remarked earlier. The cultural contradiction of global capitalism is that its economy demands an open society bound by the total commitment of its worker/consumers in exchange for pleasure while its political system has donned the mantle of imperialism to control alien threats to the American pleasure at home and abroad. The three faces of the global order are nicely revealed in the transvestite spectacles of its leaders in business suits, in military uniforms and in leisurewear or national costume to suit the occasions of Empire. If we judge Empire from the standpoint of the world's poor, however, the prospect held out for them is world violence, a life that is short, nasty and brutish – theirs because they are on the wrong end of Empire, the always different/same old Leviathan. This

Leviathan delivers immeasurable fear, hunger, poverty, homelessness; it murders and cripples beyond anything imaginable within its own centres of narcissism and greed.

Yet, it is within Empire that Hardt and Negri envision the mustard seed of a universal labouring multitude whose tiny acts of resistance and rebellion are the existential source of the reactive power of imperial nuclearism, monetarism and newsism:

> The ontological fabric of Empire is constructed by the activity beyond measure of the multitude and its virtual powers. These virtual, constituent powers conflict endlessly with the constituted power of Empire. They are completely positive since their 'being against' is a 'being for', in other words, a resistance that becomes love and community. We are situated precisely at that hinge of infinite finitude that links together the virtual and the possible, engaged in the passage from desire to a coming future.
>
> (2000: 361)

The fulfilment of Empire is achieved with the privatization of the post-industrial commons, which includes the welfare state. It is there that we enter the neo-liberal era of the end of big governments, which we abandon like rusty old factories that have lost their orders for the reproduction of modernity and its war machine. The new paradigm of electronic democracy and oligopolistic mechanism (Hardt and Negri, 2000: 299) far exceeds anything that can be held out in the public domain of welfare states. It is the ultimate dispossession of both private and public property – yet, curiously belongs to the multitude who are completely invested in the concepts and practice of commonality:

> Men can desire, I say, nothing more excellent for the preservation of their being than that all should so agree in all things that the Minds and bodies of all should compose, as it were, one mind and one body.
>
> (Spinoza, 1985: IV, 40)

In the end Hardt and Negri's Spinozism transcends the stalled dialectic of left/ right power politics (Thoburn, 2001). The general intelligence and affectivity of post-industrial relations of production exceed the repressive force of late capital production:

> [The worker] steps to the side of the production process instead of being its chief actor. In this transformation, it is neither the direct human labour he himself performs, nor the time during which he works, but rather the appropriation of his own general productive power, his understanding of nature and his mastery over it by virtue of his presence as a social body – it is, in a word, *the development of the social individual which appears as the great foundation-stone of production and wealth.*
>
> (Marx, 1973: 705, my emphasis)

The liberal imagination is obsessed with the double fantasy of monadic individuals and a monadic collectivity, or Leviathan. Totalitarian left politics merely repeated this fantasy in the name of Party/proletarian politics. The Spinozan body politic, however, suspends both socialist state property and the property of the bourgeois self because the multitude of the poor is nothing else than the amplification of like beings in their nature and divinity. What *Empire* promises them is that the prospect of a just peace is at hand in the Spinozan practice of post-prophetic hermeneutics. *Empire* is a Book of Exodus:

> We understand exodus as a fundamental political reality of the present. As the Founding Fathers teach us, an enormous creative energy is accumulated in the Exodus.
>
> (Hardt and Negri, 1994: 269)

On one hand, because the sovereignty of the postmodern state absorbs all politics, domestic protests can only be criminalized. On the other hand, labour protest is now driven by the self-valorization of its cyborg intelligentsia who absolutely reject the disciplinary command of capital management. Spinoza's historicization of religion, philosophy and politics reveals the human capacity for shifting the weight of authority and tutelage to take on the practical yet pious accommodation of reason, freedom, and vulgar society. What is resolved is the long-standing aporia of right/left democratic theory, namely, its *fear of the masses* (Balibar, 1998: 119) and its repression of their possibility/potential for becoming communist:

> According to Foucault and Deleuze, around this final paradigm [control/ communication] there is determined a qualitative leap which allows thinking a new, radically new order of possibility: communism. Historically, the passage which is determined between disciplinary society and the society of communication is the final possible dialectical passage. Afterwards, the ontological constitution cannot but be the product of the multitude of free individuals...
>
> (Negri, 1992: 105)

Thesis, antithesis, synthesis; new labour is a constituent, non-dialectical, non-utopian power of immanent imperial transformation. It is *anarchaeological*: it is neither for itself nor for others a terrorist movement. Nor is it a separatist movement of the weak and powerless. It is the internal power of the People's Republic to reject the virus of imperialism:

> Today's corporeal mutations constitute an *anthropological Exodus* and represent an extraordinarily important, but still quite ambiguous, element of the configuration of republicanism 'against' imperial civilization. The anthropological exodus is important primarily because here is where the positive, constructive face of the mutation begins to appear: an ontological mutation in

action, the concrete of a first *new place in the non-place*...a metamorphosis threat breaks all the naturalistic homologies of modernity.

(Hardt and Negri, 2000: 215–16)

Here Hardt and Negri lapse into Pentecostal and glossolalic implosions of virtuality and reality, reversing the powerful and the meek, planting tents in place of palaces. Once the reproduction of Empire becomes coextensive with the reproduction of intelligent and affective life, it has prepared its own cyborg revolution; it has prepared the wedding of Republican virtuality and post-communist possibility.

Hardt and Negri's Spinozan thesis on the self-transformation of US Empire must be rephrased to recover the dialectical contradictions that structure the interface between its constitutional capitalism (CC) which underwrites the American ideology (AI). In turn, we must factor in the mediating effects of the myth of American exceptionalism (AE) on both its domestic and global fronts, where the Washington consensus operates a largely unilateral internationalism to produce what may be called the global American sublime (GAS). In short, where Hardt and Negri oppose Empire to itself (EvE), I would argue for a more structured and mediated formula of the contradictions of American capitalism:

Constitutional Capitalism (CC) + American Ideology (AI) + American Exceptionalism (AE) = Global American Sublime (GAS).

If we spell out this constellation, its constituent features – so many of which are elided in Empire – are contained in something like the following subsystems of domestic and global capitalism:

US Constitutional Capitalism (CC)

Primacy of corporate business and market forces, weak labour organizations; minimal state, extreme separation of powers, weak political parties, legalist, rights-orientation, residual welfare/workfare state, voluntary associations; maximal military, police and surveillance state.

American Ideology (AI)

Individualism, populism, patriotism; moral inequality, winner takes all, gives back to civic sector institutions (health, education, arts and sciences, social services); Americanism, democratism, racism and prisonism sanction, market success/failure syndrome.

American Exceptionalism (AE)

Only Americans understand America's right to self-invention without either past or future burdens; the next century and next planetary society will be colonized by America, repeating its own national myth of biblical *lebensraum*.

Global American Sublime (GAS)

US capitalism is the norm for global capital development, business and legal standards, dollarization and deregulated financial trade policy as foreign policy exercised through WTO, NAFTA, APEC, IMF, World Bank; the Washington consensus takes precedence over UN and international covenants through unilateralism, opting out, underfunding or use of NGOs to depoliticize development; US military hegemony, nuclearization, arms sales, surveillance and subversion is the violent face of the American sublime abroad, just as its sharp inequality and related culture of violence is the domestic face of US constitutional capitalism.

This constitutional arrangement, rather than the revisionist, republican account of American capitalism offered in *Empire*, is quite unlikely to deliver the world's poor into a post-communist future. We should set aside the exhausted cultural critique of Americanism, which contributes to the depoliticization of both domestic and international politics. We might then recover the constitutional question of the internal and external distortions that hinder a public or civic agenda for sustainable global development (O'Neill, 1994; Kaul et al., 1999; Pieterse, 2001) now at the mercy of Empire.

In the last analysis, *Empire* is a millennial tract. The result is that what affects to be an historical text frequently becomes fabulous, apocryphal, advancing its cause through dream-like condensation and displacement. Events that might be distinguished on the level of historical materialism amalgamate on the level of trans-historical symbolism (Virno, 1996). History is shot through with epiphany and apocalyptic simultaneity. Like the Koran or *Finnegans Wake*, *Empire* moves by abruption and conjunction, ruining its sources, trashing its intellectual past in order to pronounce a new metaphysics of the multitude, resurrecting the dream life of the world's poor. Meanwhile, the old European family, with its awesome powers and gods, hovers in the background, its face pale from the horrors of war and the exhaustion of nihilist realism. Even the relatives who fled to America remain in the shadows of disillusion deepened by the corruptions of choice, privatization, ideological media and the terrorization of protest. Who, then, wears the wedding gown, what are the names of their family? By what migrant routes, what boats, what borders do they arrive? How do they survive the traffic in their own lives? Who goes ahead, who stays, who dies, who is forgotten? When will the long march of the world's poor pass through the gates of the earthly city in 'the irrepressible lightness and joy of being communist' (2000: 413)? When will they reach post-America?

References

Arendt, Hannah (1958). *The Human Condition*. Chicago, IL: University of Chicago Press.
Balibar, Etienne (1998). *Spinoza and Politics*. London: Verso.
Baudrillard, Jean (2001). 'Spirit of Terrorism'. http://www.lemonde.fr/rech_art/0. 5987. 00.htm.

Benjamin, Walter (1969). 'On Some Motifs in Baudelaire'. In: *Illuminations*. Hannah Arendt (ed., intro.). New York: Schocken Books, pp. 155–200.

Bloom, Harold (1973). *The Anxiety of Influence: A Theory of Poetry*. New York: Oxford University Press.

Callinicos, Alex (2001). 'Toni Negri in Perspective'. *International Socialism* 92 (Autumn): 33–61.

de la Boétie, Etienne (1975). *The Politics of Obedience: The Discourse of Voluntary Servitude*. New York: Free Life Editions.

Deleuze, Gilles (1983). *Nietzsche and Philosophy*. New York: Columbia University Press.

Deleuze, Gilles (1988a). *Bergsonism*. New York: Zone Books.

Deleuze, Gilles (1988b). *Spinoza: Practical Philosophy*. San Francisco, CA: City Lights Books.

Deleuze, Gilles (1990). *Expressionism in Philosophy: Spinoza*. New York: Zone Books.

Deleuze, Gilles and Félix Guattari (1977). *Anti-Oedipus: Capitalism and Schizophrenia*. New York: Viking Press.

Deleuze, Gilles and Félix Guattari (1987). *A Thousand Plateaus: Capitalism and Schizophrenia*. Minneapolis: University of Minnesota Press.

Ebert, Teresa L. (1996). *Ludic Feminism and After: Postmodernism, Desire and Labour in Late Capitalism*. Ann Arbor: University of Michigan Press.

Fitzpatrick, Tony (1999). 'Social Policy for Cyborgs'. *Body and Society* 5(1): 93–116.

Habermas, Jürgen (1971). *Knowledge and Human Interests*. London: Heinemann.

Haraway, Donna J. (1985). 'Manifesto for Cyborgs: Science, Technology, and Socialist Feminism in the 1980s'. *Socialist Review* 80: 65–108.

Hardt, Michael (1993). *Gilles Deleuze: An Apprenticeship in Philosophy*. Minneapolis: University of Minnesota Press.

Hardt, Michael (1998). 'The Withering of Civil Society'. In: *Deleuze and Guattari: New Mappings in Politics, Philosophy and Culture*. Eleanor Kaufman and Kevin Jon Heller (eds). Minneapolis: University of Minnesota Press, pp. 23–39.

Hardt, Michael and Negri, Antonio (1994). *Labor of Dionysus: A Critique of the State-Form*. Minneapolis: University of Minnesota Press.

Hardt, Michael and Negri, Antonio (2000). *Empire*. Cambridge, MA: Harvard University Press.

Hegel, G. W. F. (1977). *Phenomenology of Spirit*. A.V. Miller (trans.). Oxford: Oxford University Press.

Holland, Eugene W. (1996). 'Schizoanalysis and Baudelaire: Some Illustrations of Decoding at Work'. In: *Gilles Deleuze: A Critical Reader*. Paul Patton (ed.). Oxford: Blackwell, pp. 240–56.

Ignatieff, Michael (1984). *Needs of Strangers*. London: Hogarth Press.

Jameson, Fredric (1985) 'Baudelaire as Modernist and Postmodernist: The Dissolution of the Referent and the Artificial "Sublime"'. In: *Lyric Poetry: Beyond New Criticism*. Chaviva Hosek and Patricia Parke (eds). Ithaca, NY: Cornell University Press, pp. 247–63.

Kaul, I., Grunberg, I. and Stern, M. A. (eds.) (1999). *Global Public Goods: International Co-operation in the 21st Century*. New York: Oxford University Press.

Kroker, Arthur and Kroker, Marilousie (2001). 'Terrorism of Viral Power'. http://ctheory.net/ctheory_wp/terrorism-of-viral-power/

Marx, Karl (1973). *Grundrisse: Introduction to the Critique of Political Economy* [1857]. Martin Nicolaus (trans.). Harmondsworth: Penguin Books.

Mauss, Marcel (1990). *The Gift: The Form and Reason for Exchange in Archaic Societies*. W. D. Halls (trans.). London: Routledge.

Negri, Antonio (1984). *Marx Beyond Marx: Lessons on the Grundrisse*, Harry Cleaver, Michael Ryan and Maurizio Vianio (trans). Jim Fleming (ed.). South Hadley, MA: Bergin and Garvey Publishers, Inc.

Negri, Antonio (1991). *The Savage Anomaly: The Power of Spinoza's Metaphysics and Politics*, trans. Michael Hardt. Minneapolis: University of Minnesota Press.

Negri, Antonio (1992). 'Interpretation of the Class Situation Today: Methodological Aspects'. In: *Open Marxism: Volume 2, Theory and Practice*. W. Bonefeld, R. Gunn and K. Psychopedis (eds). London: Pluto Press, pp. 69–105.

O'Neill, John (1972). 'On Theory and Criticism in Marx'. *Sociology as a Skin Trade: Essays Towards a Reflexive Sociology*. London: Heinemann, pp. 237–63.

O'Neill, John (1986). 'The Disciplinary Society: From Weber to Foucault'. *British Journal of Sociology* 37 (1): 42–60.

O'Neill, John (1990). 'AIDS as a Globalizing Panic'. *Global Culture: Nationalism, Globalization and Modernity*. London: Sage, pp. 329–42.

O'Neill, John (1992). 'Baudelairizing Postmodernism: A Hyper-Reading'. In: *Critical Conventions: Interpretation in the Literary* Arts and Sciences. Norman: University of Oklahoma Press, pp. 33–52.

O'Neill, John (1994). *The Missing Child in Liberal Theory: Towards a Covenant Theory of Family, Community, Welfare and the Civic State*. Toronto: University of Toronto Press.

O'Neill, John (1995). *The Poverty of Postmodernism*. London: Routledge.

O'Neill, John (ed.) (1996). *Hegel's Dialectic of Desire and Recognition: Texts and Commentary*. Albany: State University of New York Press.

O'Neill, John (1997). 'The Civic Recovery of Nationhood', *Citizenship Studies* 1(1): 19–32.

O'Neill, John (2002a). *Plato's Cave: Television and its Discontents*. Cresskill, NJ: Hampton Press.

O'Neill, John (2002b). 'Marcuse's Maternal Ethic; Myths of Narcissism and Maternalism in Utopian Critical Memory'. *Journal of Classical Sociology* 2(1): 5–24.

Pieterse, Jan Nederveen (2001). *Development Theory: Deconstructions/Reconstructions*. London: Sage.

Ricoeur, Paul (1992). *Oneself as Another*. Chicago, IL: University of Chicago Press.

Spinoza, Baruch (1985). Ethics, Vol. 1 in *The Collected Works of Spinoza*, ed. Edwin Curley. Princeton, NJ: Princeton University Press.

Thoburn, Nicholas (2001). 'Autonomous Production? On Negri's "New Synthesis"'. *Theory, Culture and Society* 18(5): 75–96.

Virno, Paul (1996). 'Virtuosity and Revolution: The Political Theory of Exodus'. In: *Radical Thought in Italy: A Potential Politics*. Paul Virno and Michael Hardt (eds). Minneapolis: University of Minnesota Press, pp. 189–212.

Wolfe, Alan (1989). *Whose Keeper? Social Science and Moral Obligation*. Berkeley: University of California Press.

Zavarzadeh, Mas'ud (1995). 'Post-ality: The (Dis) Simulations of Cybercapitalism'. *Post-ality: Marxism and Postmodernism*. Mas'ud Zavarzadeh, Teresa L. Ebert and Donald Morton (eds). Washington, DC: Maisonneuve Press, pp. 1–75.

Žižek, Slavoj (2002). *Welcome to the Desert of the Real!*. London and New York: Verso.

Part 3
The libidinal body

9 Marcuse's maternal ethic*

Myths of narcissism and maternalism in utopian critical memory

Does the civilizing process merely deepen repression and in collusion with the economic and political forces of oppression make both Right and Left notions of future emancipation an idle daydream? In short, how could Freud possibly be recruited into Marx's utopian project of an end to the double scarcity operative in nature and society? The point of the question, of course, is that such a merger runs the risk of psychologizing history and social structure, or else of watering down general psychology into the sociology of the day (O'Neill, 2001). Yet the vicissitudes of Marxism have brought it to seek a merger with Freudianism to refurbish its historical romance, despite Freud's coldness towards such an embrace:

> If memory moves into the center of psychoanalysis as a decisive mode of *cognition,* this is far more than a therapeutic device; the therapeutic role of memory derives from the *truth value* of memory. Its truth value lies in the specific function of memory to preserve promises and potentialities which are betrayed and even outlawed by the mature, civilized individual, but which had once been fulfilled in his dim past and are never entirely forgotten. The reality principle restrains the cognitive function of memory – its commitment to the past experience of happiness which spurns the desire for its conscious recreation. The psychoanalytic liberation of memory explodes the rationality of the repressed individual. As cognition gives way to re-cognition, the forbidden images and impulses of childhood begin to tell the truth that reason denies. Regression assumes a progressive function. The rediscovered past yields critical standards which are tabooed by the present. Moreover, the restoration of memory is accompanied by the restoration of the cognitive content of phantasy. Psychoanalytic theory removes these mental faculties from the noncommittal sphere of day-dreaming and fiction and recaptures their strict truths. The weight of these discoveries must eventually shatter the framework in which they were made and confined. The liberation of the past does not end in its reconciliation with the present. Against the self-imposed

* Text of the essay taken from *Journal of Classical Sociology*, 1(2) 2002: 5–24. Reproduced with permission.

restraint of the discoverer, the orientation on the past tends toward an orientation on the future. The *recherche du temps perdu* becomes the vehicle of future liberation.

(Marcuse, 1962 [1955]: 18)

The myth of politics

Marcuse's *Eros and Civilization* (1962 [1955]) goes to the heart of utopian theory. It is in the unconscious that we have preserved a time when freedom and happiness were not yet separated by the civilizing demands of repressive sublimation. Thus the future does not erase the past, or else we should have no ground for it. Rather, both our future and our past are structured by our memory, which functions on the two levels of knowledge and morals to provide a critical standard of institutional freedom and happiness. To find theoretical renewal in psychoanalysis, Marcuse had to circumvent Freud's reduction of utopian thought to the dream of a postmortem paradise. In other words, religion undermines political revolt because its impulse is infantile and reinforces authoritarianism. Moreover, religion postpones political hope to the next life. To be successful, Marcuse's return had specifically to revise Freud's essay 'Formulations on the Two Principles of Mental Functioning', where the psychic apparatus is described as follows:

> Just as the pleasure-ego can do nothing but *wish* work for a yield of pleasure, and avoid unpleasure, so the reality-ego need do nothing but strive for what is *useful* and guard itself against damage. Actually the substitution of the reality principle for the pleasure principle implies no deposing of the pleasure principle, but only a safeguarding of it....[T]he endopsychic impression made by this substitution has been so powerful that it is reflected in a special religion myth. The doctrine of reward in the after-life for the – voluntary or enforced – renunciation of early pleasure is nothing other than a mythical projection of this revolution in the mind.
>
> (Freud, 1974 [1911]: 223, my italics)

Whereas Freud had fenced off the imagination from reason, like a 'reservation' or a 'nature reserve' (Freud, 1974 [1916–17]: 372), Marcuse argued that reason's colonization of the imagination is never complete, any more than the ego ever entirely controls the id. The imagination remains a collective, universal force, always opposed to rationalized individuation and 'defamilization'. Freud's reconciliation of Eros and Thanatos in *Beyond the Pleasure Principle* (1920) operates at the mythical interface of philosophy and science. Here Freud momentarily envisaged a non-selfish gene as something akin to an unconscious but mortal drive towards solidarity. Marcuse insists that, *pace* Freud, the imagination is neither a regressive nor an irrational force except from the standpoint of rationalized history, which it resists. Imagination is a progressive mode of knowledge grounded in the refusal of the oppressed to forget a past happiness that may be projected into the future to furnish a critical standard for present institutions: 'In and against the world of the antagonistic *principium individuationis,* imagination sustains the claim of the whole individual, in union with the genus and with the "archaic" past' (Marcuse, 1962 [1955]: 130).

Utopia is neither a 'nobody' enterprise nor a 'nowhere' place, as civilized but repressive reason would have it. Nor is imagination to be set off from the every-day world as the inspiration for merely childish, artistic or mythical stories that distract us from the world but do not change it. To vary Marx, slightly*, phantasy and mythology are good to think and to change the world.* The argument I am introducing has had several previous runs. Martin Jay (1973) has told the story of the Frankfurt School's critical assimilation of psychoanalysis in order to under-stand the failure of revolution in the face of the politics of authoritarianism. In that round, I want to draw attention only to Erich Fromm's focus (1970) upon *mater-nal theory* in Bachofen (1973 [1861]) and Briffault (1927) as a critical alternative to Freud's paternity theory of institutions and failed revolutions. I do so for the reason that it provides the missing institutional background to Marcuse's utopian appeal for a *maternal libidinal morality* (1962 [1955]: 211), as I shall show later. Bachofen's thesis is also at work in the larger debate over the question of cultural decadence that set in at the turn of the 20th century until the aftermath of World War I. The debate involved all the major thinkers and artists of the period, from Nietzsche to Wittgenstein, Baudelaire to Benjamin, Musil, Kraus, Schnitzler, Schoenberg, Adorno and, of course, Freud, Weininger, Groddeck, Fromm, Reich and Fenichel (Buci-Glucksmann, 1994; Le Rider, 1990). Thus Marcuse's lack of anything but a secondary reference to Bachofen is compensated by the larger literature (probably known to Marcuse) in which the question of maternalism, cultural decadence and renewal was debated.

We cannot do more than sketch arguments that were never quite disentangled. The basic thesis in the literature, I believe, is that culture is determined by the psy-chosexual stages of maternalism and paternalism and by their tendency to reversal or regression. The cultural exhaustion of the *fin de siècle* was attributed to male neurasthenia, symptomized in feminization, emasculation and homosexualization. At the same time, there was a celebration of androgyny and of the new (eternal) woman, like Lou Andréas Solomé. More darkly, there were political elements that confounded antifeminism and antisemitism, prefiguring the reversal of Jewish assimilation that had begun in the 18th century. Yet others would attribute the rise of fascism to the return of archaic maternalism, while socialists like Engels and Bebel would embrace maternalism/feminism as a mark of the brightest develop-ment in human relations. Benjamin, skirting between left and right readings of Bachofen, characteristically regarded the figure of the maternal as an historical 'ruin' (rune), an ethical residue resistant to the naturalization of history. Woman is the 'mother of justice' (*Mater der Gerechtigkeit*), combining the two realms of destruction and redemption, as the other face of God (Shekinah). Along these lines, woman is always beneath the law (Schroeder, 1998). Like the parables of the Halakah, hers is the choral voice beneath the scriptural Haggadah of the Torah. In Benjamin, the maternal image is the figure of every just person, incapable of harm-ing anyone, any animal or anything, saving the creation, if not its first genesis story.

The story explodes again in the 1960s with the American debate between Marcuse and Norman O. Brown (1959) over *love's body*, whose character shifts its ground in the 1970s from its embrace of Greek male narcissism to the rejection of corporate America's sponsorship of a narcissistic consumerism ruled by 'momism' and absentee 'popism' (O'Neill, 1972). In the same arena, Lash (1979) held that the politics of narcissism played into the hands of the welfare state to undermine the family, whereas Sennett (1977) held that narcissism results in a *politics of intimacy* that undermines the public realm. Here I would observe that, as Habermas (1975) then argued, the two processes of the decline of the public and the rise of civic privatism work together to underwrite the *political economy of narcissism* (O'Neill, 1991). Finally, the debate shifted into the feminist appropriation of psychoanalysis and Marxism, raising once again the critical functions of female narcissism and maternal bonding/bondage (Cloward, 1983). At first sight, the feminist conjuncture seems as much of a paradox as is the original Marxist move toward psychoanalysis, but it is not entirely so, if we recall Engels' (1956 [1884]) concern with the status of women under the patriarchal property system. Whereas Engels drew upon Bachofen (1973 [1861]), as did Freud more obliquely, there is no direct reference by Marcuse to the history of maternal right (*Mutterrecht*). The result, to anticipate the argument, is that Marcuse completely psychologized the historical location of matriarchal values as the source of critical utopianism, while historicizing Freud's two principles of reality and pleasure. Whereas Freud had repressed the maternal as the always regressive origin, Marcuse invoked the memory of a maternal *temps perdu* and located it in a twice-lost past:

> *Historically,* the reduction of Eros to procreative monogamic sexuality (which completes the subjection of the pleasure principle to the reality principle) is consummated only when the individual has become a subject-object of labor in the apparatus of his society: whereas, *ontogenetically,* the primary suppression of infantile sexuality remains the precondition for this accomplishment.
>
> (Marcuse, 1962 [1955]: 82, my emphasis)

Marcuse argued for an alliance between the superego and the id to underwrite a utopian 'sensuous rationality'. In this connection he makes an indirect reference to Bachofen's primal Mother-Right (1962 [1955]: 209). But the bond between infant primary narcissism and the maternal Eros is rendered 'regressive' from the standpoint of the paternal reality principle. Here Marcuse questions the Freudian schema, asking 'whether the Narcissistic-maternal attitude toward reality cannot "return"' (1962 [1955]: 211) to enlighten the future. Admittedly, Marcuse reworked the myths of Orpheus and Narcissus (adopted from Rilke, Gide, Valéry and Baudelaire) rather than techno-Prometheus to emphasize the world-building character of narcissism, and perhaps play down the misogyny toward Pandora in the Promethean myth (Vernant, 1981). But Marcuse's version of Orphic Marxism (O'Neill, 1995) – as might be learned from Bachofen – needs to be grounded in an historical and sociological theory of family law and religion as well as family psychology.

It turns out, if one reads Détienne (1981), that Marcuse, Valéry, Mallarmé and Freud ignored the *sociological* context of the Orpheus/Narcissus myth, by relying upon the lover's tale given in Ovid's *Metamorphoses* (Book III). But in Virgil's *Georgics* (Book IV), the death of Eurydice occurs in flight from violent pursuit by Aristaeus, the beekeeper. Although Persephone tells Orpheus how to recover his beloved Eurydice, his backward glance lost her forever and he was torn to pieces for his carelessness by the maenads. What is the significance of the beekeeper and why should the maenads be so angry? Plutarch in his *Conjugalia praecepta* (44, 144d) says that the beekeeper must handle the bee (Melissa), itself scrupulously clean and allergic to aromas, with the same care as a faithful husband accords his wife, that is, without any odor of infidelity. Thus Aristaeus was punished with the loss of his bees for attempting to seduce Eurydice, thereby imperiling his own and Orpheus' marriage. But in another myth, it was a nymph, Melissa or Bee-Woman, who discovered honey and prepared the food that brought man out of the wilderness. Now Demeter had entrusted to the daughters of King Melisseus the secret of the ceremonies of lawful marriage (*Thesmophoria*) that effect the shift in status from *nymph* (a young girl ready for marriage) to *thesmophoros* (a lawful wife). But nymphs themselves are not in any wild state. They are females whose age-status lies between that of *koré*, that is, an immature girl, unmarried (*agamos*), and the status of *métér*, that is, a woman who has given birth. Now once a nymph marries, but before she becomes a *thesmophoros* (a ritual Bee), a young bride leads a life of love (*numphion bios*) with its sweet smells, foods and pleasure. It is in this state of 'honeymoon' that Eurydice and Orpheus are destroyed by Aristaeus' attempted seduction while the fury of the nymphs is aroused by the couple's failure to cool the honeymoon and settle into marriage! Now we can explain the rage of the nymphs with both Orpheus and Narcissus, whom they tear apart for *undervaluing* married woman and *overvaluing* (self-) love, thereby collapsing the civilized distance between (wo)man and nature.

Marcuse's reliance upon secondary sources for the myth of Narcissus repeats the element of self-love but loses the sacrifice of the beloved Echo, as well as the punishment demanded by the institution of marriage (Legendre, 1997). To ground the utopian political imagination, Marcuse risked both the reduction of social categories to psychological categories (Elliott, 1992) and his own seduction by the regressive appeal of male narcissism (Alford, 1988). The missing figure in Marcuse's account of Orpheus and Narcissus is *woman*. But, as Bachofen had shown, Eurydice and Echo are the lost bodies of the male imagination, which works in isolation from the function of kinship and state in subordinating sexual reproduction to patriarchal lineage. It is assuredly the Attic race that carried the Zeus-like character of paternity to its highest development:

> Though Athens itself has its roots in the Pelasgian culture, it wholly subordinated the Demetrian to the Appollonian principle in the course of its development. The Athenians revered Theseus as a second woman-hating Heracles; in the person of Athene they set *motherless paternity* in the place of *fatherless maternity*; and even in their legislation they endowed the universal principle

of paternity with a character of inviolability which the old law of the Erinyes imputed only to motherhood. The virgin goddess is well disposed to the masculine, helpful to the heroes of the paternal solar law; in her, the warlike Amazonism of the old day reappears in spiritual form. Her city is hostile to the women who moor their ships on the coasts of Attica in search of help in defending the rights of their sex. Here the opposition between the Apollonian and the Demetrian principle stands out sharply. This city, whose earliest history disclosed traces of matriarchal conditions, carried paternity to its highest development; and in one-sided exaggeration it condemned woman to a status of inferiority particularly surprising in its contrast to the foundations of the Eleusinian mysteries.

(Bachofen, 1973 [1861]: 111, my italics)

We should also consider the story of Heracles rather than the proto-Marxist myth of Prometheus. The Twelve Labours of Heracles make him the very figure of the cultural hero. He was, however, the plaything of his tormenting mother, Hera, who imposed his labours upon him. Heracles' strength was overwhelmed by deadly threats and incredible sufferings that pursued him from his mother's womb, drove him to kill his own children, enslaved and womanized him as the servant of Queen Omphale. Thus Hera and Hera(cles) were locked into a struggle over the boundaries of identity, sexuality, love and hatred. The struggle between Hera and her son (the Glory of Hera) is a struggle between the gods but it is not yet divine, just as the labours of Heracles are a civilizing force but not yet civilized (Slater, 1968). Heracles' narcissism is that of an unstable character, at times bumptious and mostly self-defeating. Yet only he, through suffering and renunciation, became a god. Once again, we need to provide the sociological context that delimits its moral narrative. The story of Heracles belongs to the period between the *heteraic* and matriarchal stages of family formation, reflected in the ambivalent breasts of Hera, which poisoned her son, who in turn wounded Hera's right breast with his arrows (Homer, *Iliad* V, 392–4). Although both practised virgin-birth, Hera's rage was aroused by Zeus' production of Athena from his forehead. Actually, Zeus' reproductive act represents more a *couvade*, that is, an admission that virgin-birth is more likely a solitary female accomplishment than a male possibility. By mimicking female birth in the *couvade,* the male denies parthenogenesis but asserts his *sociological paternity.* Female parthenogenesis is then assigned to the imaginary of the matriarchal period or its ritualization of promiscuous fertility, for example in Hera's own annual rite of 'revirginization' (Devereux, 1982: 178).

For want of a close reading of Bachofen, Marcuse yields to Freud's psycho-sexualization of the conflict between patrilineage and matrilineage and his reduction of Bachofen's historico-structural analysis of the archaic myths to a sexual narrative. The metamorphoses and sexual transgressions characteristic of the heroic myth are only intelligible in terms of its retrospective exaggeration of the heteraic period of sexuality outside of marriage and matriarchy that is in turn remembered wildly once matriarchy has moved under patriarchy (Vidal-Naquet, 1981). Thus

Bachofen (1973 [1861]: 204) located Orphic homosexuality and lesbianism as a reaction to heteraic rather than to matriarchal/patriarchal sexuality. Both are attempts to recombine physical and spiritual love, as in Sappho's poetry. In other words, there is an historical structure of love, kinship, and marriage. This is narrated, at first, in fables of sexual struggle and the transgression of human–animal, human–divine boundaries. But later, these become stories of the violation of religious and property laws. It is, then, the historical vicissitudes of sexuality and law that structure utopian imagination. The imaginary does not arise in any state of nature except as the latter is itself a retrospective fiction of civilized anxiety.

The politics of myth

Rather than follow Marcuse's philosophical appeal to Aristotle, Hegel and Nietzsche in which he seeks to transvalue the return of the past as the fulfillment of the future (*Eros and Civilization*, Chapter 5, 'The Philosophical Interlude'), we should tease out further the matriarchal history that is the institutional basis for the civilizing function of utopian phantasy. I refer the reader to the meticulous account by Jay (1984: 220–40) of the critical issues behind Marcuse's attempt to eroticize Hegel, as well as to Lenhardt (1975) and O'Neill (1977) on the politics of memory. We should then return to the historicist perspective of Bachofen, as well as Marx and Engels on family law, to gain perspective upon the contemporary politics of 'gynesis' (Jardine, 1985). We cannot explore the larger 19th century paradigm of Greek family history and politics at work here (see Patterson, 1998). It should be noted, however, that Bachofen's *Mother Right* (1973 [1861]) and Morgan's *Ancient Society* (1877) were contested by Fustel de Coulanges' *Ancient City* (1901) and by Henry Maine's *Ancient Law* (1917 [1861]), which reversed the historical priority of matriarchy and patriarchy. Engels' *Origin of the Family, Private Property and the State* (1956 [1884]) belonged to the matriarchal school of Bachofen and Morgan, which was taken up in contemporary feminism as a source of woman's 'vision of power' (Webster, 1975: 145) and the end of the 'traffic in women' (Rubin, 1975).

The broad picture of matriarchy may be derived from the comparative analysis of historical and mythological texts that were already puzzling to the patriarchal mind and might be dismissed out of hand as mere myth or legend by modern minds. We have known at least since Vico's *New Science* (1984 [1744]) that we are entirely historical beings whose more contemporary practices are unthinkable except as developments of early forms of language, perception and conduct (O'Neill, 1994b). Thus we cannot start from a radical hiatus between myth and history because the later form of knowledge presupposes the earlier one. Here Vico is a surer guide than Freud's *Totem and Taboo* (1950 [1913]) in lifting the veil of critical theory 'to enter into the fathers (*interpatrari*)' through the creative force of interpretation (*interpretari*):

> The guarding of the institutions began in divine times from jealousy (the jealousy of Juno, the goddess of solemn matrimony) with a view to *the certainty*

of the families as against the nefarious promiscuity of women. Such vigilance is a natural property of the aristocratic commonwealths desirous of keeping family relationships, successions, and consequently wealth and through it power, within the order of the nobles.

(Vico, 1984 [1744]: 985, my emphasis)

What interpretation reveals is the missing marriage of mother and child. Vico's comment is remarkable for its resolution of both the psycho-sexual and the political conflicts that underlie the legal fiction or *fantasia* of patrilineage (*patria potestas*). Patriarchy, we might say, hangs by a genealogical thread (*filo genealogico*), a powerful fiction at the origin of religion and law (Balsamo, 1999) that Freud reduced to an intra-familial phantasy. In *Totem and Taboo* Freud had nothing more in mind than a brief flirtation with anthropology since he had no intention of altering his idea of marriage to his own idea of the place of the mother in psychoanalysis. Freud's investment in the patriarchal origins of culture, albeit in a parricidal politics, erases maternal solidarity in the patriarchal remorse that religiously refounds fraternal society. In this move, Freud rerouted cultural origins away from J.J. Atkinson's thesis in *Primal Law* (1903) to the effect that maternal love constitutes the civilizing break with the endless repetition of expulsion and parricide. To completely expropriate the anthropological alternative, Freud had also to dismiss J.G. Frazer's *Totemism and Exogamy* (1910). Whereas the totem is fatherless, so to speak, because all reproductivity is maternal, Freud shifts consanguinity and commensalism over to the father body as the source of kinship and worship. Freud also reversed the argument in William Robertson Smith's *Lectures on the Religion of the Semites* (1927 [1889]), shifting the totemic feast to a post-parricidal commemoration whose primary function is not the confirmation of (maternal) consanguinity but oedipal conflict (Jones, 1951).

Returning to Bachofen, we find that the Roman patriarchal system presupposed an earlier system of matriarchy that it had usurped but whose seduction it continued to repress, especially its rival values of universality and fraternity. It was the inviolability of the Sabine women and not their ferocious feminism that accounted for their military and political roles. The paradox here is removed once we set aside the patriarchal assumption that strength is physical and male rather than spiritual and female. The religious and civil primacy of pre-Hellenic womanhood was rooted in woman's function as priestess and hierophant, through which she mediated the material and spiritual worlds:

> If we acknowledge the primordial character of mother right and its connection with an older cultural stage, we must say the same of the mystery, for the two phenomena are merely different aspects of the same cultural form; they are inseparable twins. And this is all the more certain when we consider that *the religious aspect of matriarchy is at the root of its social manifestations.* The cultic conceptions are the source, the social forms are their consequence and expression. Kore's bond with Demeter was the source of the primacy of mother over father, of daughter over son, and was not abstracted from

the social relationship. Or, in ancient terms: the cultic-religious meaning of the maternal *kteís* (weaver's shuttle, comb, weaving woman) is primary and dominant; while the social, juridical sense *pudenda* (shame) is derivative. The feminine *sporium* (womb) is seen primarily as a representation of the Demetrian mystery, both in its lower and in its higher transcendent implication, and only by derivation becomes an expression of the social matriarchy, as in the Lycian myth of Sarpedon.

(Bachofen, 1973 [1861]: 88, my italics)

Bachofen does not unearth the lost institution of matriarchy in order to set it beyond the vicissitudes of its own history. He was neither a Romantic nor a left utopian. This would involve mistakenly idealizing the middle or Demetrian period, which had itself overthrown an earlier stage of 'hetaerism' before matriarchy yielded to patriarchy:

Although the struggle of matriarchy against other forms is revealed by diverse phenomena, the underlying principle of development is clear. *Matriarchy is followed by patriarchy and preceded by unregulated hetaerism.* The Demetrian ordered matriarchy thus assumes a middle position, representing the transition of mankind from the lowest stage of existence to the highest. With the former it shares the material-maternal standpoint, with the second, the exclusivity of marriage; it is distinguished from the early stage by the Demetrian regulation of motherhood, through which it rises above hetaerism, and from the later stage by primacy it accords to the generative womb, wherein it proves to be a lower form than the fully developed patriarchal system.

(Bachofen, 1973 [1861]: 93, my italics)

The rituals attending the Thesmophoria and its relative, the Roman festival of Bona Dea (Versnel, 1996), are not entirely intelligible in terms of the fertility/vegetation model of myth. The paradox at the core of the Demeter festival is that the women sleep on beds made of willow – associated with chastity and infertility. There is also the associated puzzle that on the second day of the Thesmophoria the law courts and council meetings were closed. The two are related as instances of exception, of suspension of everyday order in the family (sexuality) and the polis (men's talk). The ritual exclusion of males is combined with the temporary return of the matrons to virgin states (*numphia*) but not virginity. In short, the festival excludes sexuality in favour of the suspension of procreativity. At the same time what is unusual in the ritual detail belongs to what is 'wrong' about the festival and what is 'right' about the ordinary reproduction of legitimate offspring on behalf of the polis. The cult status of women and the exclusion of males serves to remind us of the shift from nature to culture precisely by suspending it!

Matrons did things that were unimaginable in terms of the normal codes of family and society. They usurped man's political roles (dominant functions in the centre of the state), man's cultural privileges (sacrifice, wine), man's language (sexual jokes), and discarded their own specifically female roles (care for the house) and sexual codes (chastity by staying in the house and submission to the phallokratia of their husbands). In sum, during the festivals the ever lurking threat of matrons 'running wild' materialized. This necessarily evoked other stereotyped components of the complex of 'nature' in women's life and behaviour. Female 'wildness' was as inextricably interwoven with – or rather sublimated in – the representation of the *parthenos/ numphe* – including its Amazonian 'masculine' independence – as was incest with parricide or cannibalism as negative signals, and marriage with Olympic sacrifices or agriculture as positive signals of culture. Expose one item in myth or ritual, and others will be automatically attracted.

(Versnel, 1996: 201–2)

To the surprise of later minds, if not our own, the Demetrian institution of marriage upheld an anti-religious restriction upon female sexuality that required a rite to propitiate the god whose law was transgressed by conjugal exclusivity. Thus, the institution of the dowry served to emphasize that families exchanged woman's dignity and chastity rather than her sexuality or commodity value. The dowry removed woman's womb from nature (*iniussa ultronea creatio*) into (agri) culture (*laborata Ceres*). In the 'civilizing process' children are removed from the exclusive power of woman's sexuality, which need not acknowledge fatherhood, into an intermediary stage of motherhood-in-marriage that presupposes an earlier stage of hetaerism just as it is itself determined by a later stage of patriarchy. This development did not occur without struggle. Thus the Dionysian religion mobilized the hetaeric past, rejuvenating women's phallicism, raising Aphrodite over Demeter, putting wine rather than bread on the table! Yet, like Amazonism, Dionysianism also represented a stage in women's history towards the settlement of agriculturally based states organized around the patriarchal system, in which the constitution overrides conception, just as the sky overlooks the earth (*flamma non urens*/flame without fire):

Myth takes this view of the conflict between the old and the new principle in the matricide of Orestes and Alcmaeon, and links the great turning point of existence to the sublimation of religion. These traditions undoubtedly embody a memory of real experiences of the human race. If the historical character of matriarchy cannot be doubted, the events accompanying its downfall must also be more than a poetic fiction. In the adventures of Orestes we find a reflection of the upheavals and struggles leading to the triumph of paternity over the chthonian-maternal principle. Whatever influence we may impute to poetic fancy, there is historical truth in the struggle between the two principles as set forth by Aeschylus and Euripides. The old law is that of the Erinyes, according to which Orestes is guilty and his mother's blood inexpiable; but Apollo and Athene usher in the victory as a new law; that of the higher paternity and of the heavenly light. *This is no dialectical opposition but a historical struggle, and the gods themselves decide its outcome.* The old era dies, and another, the Apollonian age, rises on its ruins. A new ethos is in preparation, diametrically opposed to the old one. The divinity of the mother gives way to that of the father, the night cedes its primacy to the day, the left side to the right, and it is only in their contrast that the character of the two stages stands out sharply.

(Bachofen, 1973 [1861]: 110, my italics)

In the archaic period, the inalienable ancestral lands of the Greek family, based upon ancestor worship and worship of the earth, were assigned a superior position to the vicissitudes of exchanging women and child-bearing. The inalienability of ancestral land set off a retrospective patriarchal anxiety with regard to woman as both grounded and mobile, as a wild card in the genre of property and exchange. The patriarchal principle demanded that consanguinity be both essential and inessential to patronymy. As such, woman is a Pandora figure, hiding all the power of parthenogenetic fertility, releasing all the troubles of heterosexual reproduction:

Earth is thus seen, like the mother and the jar, as self-sufficient, self generating, as giving or withholding; and the contradictory representation of Pandora as secondary, supplementary, fallen, is already an attempt to appropriate to the male the powers of cultivation, reproduction, thesaurization.

(Du Bois, 1988: 57)

In fact, males reversed the fall by assigning autochthony to themselves as gods and by reinterpreting the pains of farming and ploughing woman as punishments due to the race of women (Loraux, 1993). Once the aristocratic male order shifted from a pre-commercial agricultural base to a commercial economy and a relatively democratic polis, the place of women shifted. Citizen women became the reproductive guarantors of male lineages but also submitted to greater controls upon their sexuality. As shown by the Demetrian rituals (or the *Oresteia*), women were rendered archaic, sacral and mythic actors, celebrated by the chorus in tragic conflict with the new political economy of the city launched by Pericles.

The reduction of woman to the status of a male supplement is finally completed in the Platonic doctrine of androgynous love in which woman is supplanted by the man/woman lover. In the *Phaedrus* Socrates' love for his friend does not sow the seeds of family. But the words of philosophy employing the dialectic sew in the friend's mind the true fruits of philosophy. Socrates combines insemination and deliverance of the mind. As a midwife, and like the farmer, he knows what seeds should go into a particular plot of ground or what words will take root in the soul feminized by the loving philosopher. With the aid of Diotima, Socrates completes the journey of *male pregnancy*, ending the archaic struggle over parthenogenesis: 'The male philosopher becomes the site of metaphorical reproduction, the subject of philosophical generation; the female, stripped of her metaphorical otherness becomes a defective male, defined by lack' (Du Bois, 1988: 183).

The marriage of Marx and Freud promises to be a happy one. Yet we cannot separate psychic process from historical social processes. Nor can we start from the modern family structure and its libidinal unconscious (Neumann, 1963: 268–9) as the ground of utopian imagination. In the archaic period sexuality was, so to speak, *beyond* both women and men. It was a mysterious, cosmic force, animal, vegetable and libidinal – not yet bound, not yet tied to kinship and cultivated in marriage. Thus nature preceded both men and women. Woman preceded man once sexuality was brought under matriarchy. It was matriarchy and not patriarchy that first constituted the female unconscious (Briffault, 1927). At this stage woman symbolized the spiritual order of nature and cosmos while man symbolized the instinctive and bestial (like woman before marriage). However, these are contestatory statuses, unsettled because history is still unsettled:

> The succession of male generations is characterized by conflict and death, and yet culture needs a continuity that can survive catastrophe. In order to attain such continuity and demonstrate it, ritual, starting in the Upper Paleolithic, apparently found a special device: *the symbolizing of the feminine.*
>
> (Burkert, 1983: 78, my italics)

The variety of goddess figures (Venus statuettes) that are found throughout Central Europe associated with the hunt, animal sacrifice, war and sexuality do not reflect the historical precedence of matriarchy. Rather, these Goddesses of the Hunt who take and give life, who are at once virgins, lovers and mothers, reflect the male hunter's ambivalence towards the animals that he kills and by which he may be killed. They are the icons of a carnivorous cultural order.

Once patriarchy subordinated matriarchy, the eternal feminine (*ewige Weibe*) migrated into the male/female unconscious as a principle of imagination, creativity and cosmic union. It is from there that Marcuse tried to retrieve it, but without any historical feminist consciousness. For the longest time, the male was at best an ancillary to the reproductive force of the self-birthing mother, recognized only as a baby/son but not as husband/father. It is the institution of property that required woman's subjection to its owner, who cannot stand to be 'raped' through her by another male. Marriage only becomes a 'sexual relation' once it derives from a juridical relation (Briffault, 1927: 95). In the shift from matriarchy to patriarchy, woman shifted shape from being another species, approachable only as the mysterious other, to become the lower being in an hierarchical order of men, (women, children, slaves, animals). Pembroke (1967) argues that what is at issue here is not the historical primacy of matriarchy but its *logical structure* as a topsy-turvy version of the male polis. In other words, the logical structure of patriarchy is that men are the protagonists of a political order from which women and slaves are excluded, whatever their (re)productive force. Thus parthenogenesis does not refer to the self-birthing of female goddesses so much as to those young women (*Parthenai*) who mate outside of marriage, producing offspring *who knew their mothers but not their fathers* (Vidal-Naquet, 1981: 195). Sons who do not know their fathers are marginal to the city; they pervert its political order.

This carnivalesque possibility is preserved in the Saturnalia, where masters served their slaves, and in the Matronalia, where masters served their wives without revolutionizing heterosexual marriage!

What is involved, one might say, is a marital triad whose effect is to mediate gender conflict (Walcott, 1996). On the male side we have:

(a) obsession with personal honour;
(b) need to defend honour against insult/injury to any woman under male protection; and
(c) belief that prevention is better than cure.

On the female side, short of male retaliation for injuries done to them, the integrity of women is better provided by:

(a) arranging daughter's marriage as close as possible to age of puberty;
(b) providing a good dowry as an entitlement to preservation of marriageable prospects; and
(c) domestic confinement, separation of male and female worlds (Cohen, 1996).

Of course, this structure of domestic practices which we distil from both human and divine families – not to mention their metamorphic spill-overs – is underwritten by male reproductive anxiety over female passion and its genealogical disorders (Gardner, 1996). We might say that what the myth mediates is the tension between male cultivation and female promiscuity imagined retrospectively as what *might* have happened, especially when one considers the past behaviours of the gods and goddesses. Pandora, Athena and the Virgin Mary are precipitates of this genealogical anxiety, nicely neither/nor, both/and! It remains undecidable whether males fear more one another or the woman through whom they may be dispossessed. Woman remains the eternal object of seduction, jealousy and poor housekeeping, whatever the strategies of pre- and post-marital control – the sign of economic (*oikos*) and political (*polis*) disorder.

There has never been a state of nature in which matriarchy prevailed, *pace* Pateman (1988), because all institutions are post-natural, including 'nature' itself. Thus, as may be seen from medieval (Bynum, 1982) and Renaissance (Shuger, 1997) patriarchal discourse, the very model of king/subject, husband/wife, parent/child rule could be softened by maternalizing authority in favour of equality and independence or 'voluntary obedience' along parliamentary lines. The evolution of Western family law is the result of a gradual reversal of the material and spiritual orders to produce the cultural inscription of nature and sexuality in the reproductive order of marriage ruled by matriarchy and then by patriarchy. The latter may in turn be expected to shift through further civilizing stages of gender and intergenerational relationships (O'Neill, 1994b), however much it may be resisted. Over a long history (Therborn, 1993), family law has been shaped by the Roman principle of *imperium*, which has lodged the family and the child in the juridical space between public and private life rather than in the primacy of paternal over maternal spirituality. This is not due to any cunning of reason, and far less of providence. It occurs because family law is reshaped by structural changes in the household economy, social democracy and innovations in the bio-technologies of reproduction that are presupposed by current ideologies of sexual identity, maternity, kinship and care.

The discursive revision of gender and kin relationship has once again turned toward the myths and metaphors of ancient cosmology and sexology (Bower, 1991). Current post-Freudian ideologies of gender and family relations often reverse the patriarchal order by opposing it with a vision of heteraic sexuality, forgetting that woman's oppression only became representable (*nachträglich*) as a consequence of the shift into matriarchy and from there to patriarchy. Patriarchy itself is grounded in a mystical act that in turn grounds a class act. The alliance between the artist and maternity, therefore, is not immediately emancipatory for women until both patrician and plebeian women are released from the patrilin-eal myth of legitimacy. Nor is woman's assumption of authorial voice broadly emancipatory if it repeats the patriarchal disavowal of maternity in its espousal of Freud/Lacanian phantasies of self-birth. The myth of parthenogenesis cannot stand both *before* and *after* the Law that we are born of two and not one:

> Fatherhood, in the sense of conscious begetting, is unknown to man. It is a mystical estate, an apostolic succession, from only begetter to only begotten. On mystery and not the madonna which the cunning Italian intellect flung to the mobs of Europe the church is founded and founded irremovably because founded, like the world, macro- and microcosm, upon the void. Upon incer-titude, upon unlikehood *Amor matris,* subjective and objective genitive, may be the only true thing in life. *Paternity may be a legal fiction,* who is the father of any son any son should love him as he any son?
>
> (Joyce, 1971 [1922]: 207)

In the process of reclaiming the imagination from patriarchal culture by re-opening its maternal sources, Marcuse risked locating its critical task in male art-ists open to 'their' femininity but not to imaginative women artist/critics. Thus there is a succession struggle at the heart of utopia that is repeated in later feminist criticism (Ebert, 1996; Hartsock, 1985). The 'gynema effect' (Jardine, 1985: 25) only emerges as an ethic of non-hierarchical male/female relationships in the wider society of citizenship rather than sexuality. Thus, Marcuse's utopian invocation of a *maternal ethic* may be contested because it scrambles its own historical context, as I have tried to show by expanding Bachofen's historical account of maternal values. Had Marcuse derived his maternal ethic from the historicist account in Bachofen – or borrowed it from Engels' version – his revision of the Freudian fam-ily might have survived post-Freudian feminist criticism. As it stands, Marcuse's failure to connect family ethics, law and politics remains an effect of his convic-tion that corporate capitalism sets the family agenda and reduces the welfare state to the warfare state. On this analysis families lose both their private and their public constitution. But any such notion of revising intra-familial relations without addressing the constitution of the family and gender on the level of citizenship weakens the body politic, as I have argued elsewhere (O'Neill, 1994a, 2000).

References

Alford, C. Fred (1988). *Narcissism: Socrates, the Frankfurt School, and Psychoanalytic Theory*. New Haven, CT: Yale University Press.

Atkinson, J.J. (1903). *Primal Law*. London: Longmans, Green, and Co.

Bachofen, J.J. (1973 [1861]). *Myth, Religion and Mother Right: Selected Writings*. Ralph Manheim (trans.). Princeton, NJ: Princeton University Press.

Balsamo, Gian (1999). *Pruning the Genealogical Tree: Procreation and Lineage in Literature, Law, and Religion*. Lewisburg, PA: Bucknell University Press.

Bower, Lisa C. (1991). 'Mother in Law: Conception of Mother and the Maternal in Feminism and Feminist Legal Theory'. *Differences: A Journal of Feminist Cultural Studies* 3(1): 8–37.

Briffault, Robert (1927). *The Mothers: A Study of the Origins of Sentiments and Institutions*. London: George Allen & Unwin Ltd.

Brown, Norman O. (1959). *Life Against Death: The Psychoanalytical Meaning of History*. New York: Vintage.

Buci-Glucksmann, Christine (1994). *Baroque Reason: The Aesthetics of Modernity*. London: Sage.

Burkert, Walter (1983). *Homo Necans: The Anthropology of Ancient Greek Sacrificial Ritual and Myth*. Peter Bing (trans.). Berkeley: University of California Press.

Bynum, Caroline Walker (1982). *Jesus as Mother: Studies in the Spirituality of the High Middle Ages*. Berkeley: University of California Press.

Cloward, Rosalind (1983). *Patriarchal Precedents: Sexuality and Social Relations*. London: Routledge & Kegan Paul.

Cohen, David (1996). 'Seclusion, Separation, and Status of Women in Classical Athens'. In Ian McAuslan and Peter Walcott (eds.). *Women in Antiquity*. Oxford: Oxford University Press. pp. 134–45.

Coulanges, Fustel de (1901). *The Ancient City: A Study of the Religion, Law, and Institutions of Greece and Rome*. Boston: Northrop Lee and Shephard.

Détienne, Marcel (1981). 'The Myth of the Honeyed Orpheus'. In: R.L. Gordon (ed.) *Myth, Religion and Society*. Cambridge: Cambridge University Press, pp. 85–110.

Devereux, Georges (1982). *Femme et mythe*. Paris: Flammarion.

Du Bois, Page (1988). *Sowing the Body: Psychoanalysis and Ancient Representations of Women*. Chicago: University of Chicago Press.

Ebert, Teresa L. (1996). *Ludic Feminism and After: Postmodernism, Desire, and Labor in Late Capitalism*. Ann Arbor: University of Michigan Press.

Elliott, Anthony (1992). *Social Theory and Psychoanalysis in Transition: Self and Society from Freud to Kristeva*. Oxford: Blackwell.

Engels, Frederick (1956 [1884]). *The Origin of the Family, Private Property and the State*. In Karl Marx and Frederick Engels, *Selected Works in Two Volumes*. Moscow: Foreign Languages Publishing House.

Frazer, J. G. (1974 [1910]). *Totemism and Exogamy: A Treatise on Certain Early Forms of Superstition and Society*, 4 vols. London: Macmillan.

Freud, Sigmund (1950 [1913]). *Totem and Taboo: Some Points of Agreement between the Mental Lives of Savages and Neurotics*. London: Routledge and Kegan Paul.

Freud, Sigmund (1974 [1911]) 'Formulations on the Two Principles of Mental Functioning'. In J. Strachey (ed.). *The Standard Edition of the Complete Psychological Works of Sigmund Freud*, Vol. XII. London: Hogarth, pp. 213–16.

Freud, Sigmund (1974 [1916/17]). 'General Theory of the Neuroses'. In: J. Strachey (ed.). *The Standard Edition of the Complete Psychological Works of Sigmund Freud*, Vol. XVI. London: Hogarth, pp. 243–447.

Freud, Sigmund (1974 [1920]). 'Beyond the Pleasure Principle'. In: J. Strachey (ed.). *The Standard Edition of the Complete Psychological Works of Sigmund Freud*, Vol. XVIII. London: Hogarth, pp. 7–64.

Fromm, Erich (1970). 'The Theory of Mother Right and its Relevance for Social Psychology'. In: *The Crisis of Psychoanalysis: Essays on Freud, Marx and Social Psychology*. New York: Henry Holt, pp. 109–36.

Gardner, Jane F. (1996). 'Aristophanes and Male Anxiety: The Defense of the *Oikos*'. In: Ian McAuslan and Peter Walcott (eds.). *Women in Antiquity*. Oxford: Oxford University Press. Pp. 146–57.

Habermas, Jürgen (1975). *Knowledge and Human Interests*. Boston: Beacon Press.

Hartsock, Nancy C. (1985). *Money, Sex, and Power: Toward a Feminist Historical Materialism*. Boston: Northeastern University Press.

Jardine, Alice A. (1985). *Gynesis: Configurations of Woman and Modernity*. Ithaca, NY: Cornell University Press.

Jay, Martin (1973). *The Dialectical Imagination: A History of the Frankfurt School and the Institute of Social Research 1923–1950*. Boston: Little, Brown & Co.

Jay, Martin (1984). *Marxism and Totality: The Adventure of a Concept from Luka'cs to Habermas*. Berkeley: University of California Press.

Jones, Ernest (1951). 'Mother-Right and the Sexual Ignorance of Savages'. In: *Essays in Applied Psycho-Analysis*. London: Hogarth and the Institute of Psycho-Analysis, pp. 145–513.

Joyce, James (1971 [1922]). *Ulysses*. Harmondsworth: Penguin.

Lash, Christopher (1979). *The Culture of Narcissism: American Life in an Age of Diminishing Expectations*. New York: Norton.

Legendre, Pierre (1997). 'Introduction to the Theory of the Image: Narcissus and the Other in the Mirror'. In: Peter Goodrich (ed.). *Law and the Unconscious: A Legendre Reader*. New York: St Martin's Press, pp. 211–54.

Lenhardt, Christian (1975). 'Anamnestic Solidarity: The Proletariat and Its Manes'. *Telos* 25: 133–52.

Le Rider, Jacques (1990). *Modernité viennoise et crises de l'identité*. Paris: Presses Universitaires de France.

Loraux, Nicole (1993). *The Children of Athena: Athenian Ideas About Citizenship and the Division Between the Sexes*. Caroline Levine (trans.). Princeton, NJ: Princeton University Press.

Maine, Henry (1917 [1861]). *Ancient Law: Its Connection with the Early History of Society, and Its Relation to Modern Ideas*. London: Dent.

Marcuse, Herbert (1962 [1955]). *Eros and Civilization: A Philosophical Inquiry into Freud*. New York: Vintage.

Morgan, Lewis H. (1877). *Ancient Society*. New York: Henry Holt.

Neumann, Erich (1963). *The Great Mother: An Analysis of the Archetype*. Princeton, NJ: Princeton University Press.

O'Neill, John (1972). 'Authority, Knowledge, and the Body Politic'. In: *Sociology as a Skin Trade: Essays Toward a Reflexive Sociology*. London: Heinemann, pp. 68–80.

O'Neill, John (1977). 'Critique and Remembrance'. In: John O'Neill (ed.). *On Critical Theory*. New York: Seabury Press, pp. 1–11.

O'Neill, John (1991). 'The Political Economy of Narcissism: Some Issues in the Loss of Family Eros'. In: *Plato's Cave: Desire, Power and the Specular Function of the Media*. Norwood, NJ: Ablex, pp. 59–78.

O'Neill, John (1994a). *The Missing Child in Liberal Theory: Towards a Covenant Theory of Family, Community, Welfare and the Civic State*. Toronto: University of Toronto Press.

O'Neill, John (1994b). 'Vico and Myth'. In: Marcel Danesi and Marcel Nuessel (eds). *The Imaginative Basis of Thought and Culture: Contemporary Perspectives on Giambattista Vico*. Toronto: Canadian Scholar's Press, pp. 99–112.

O'Neill, John (1995). 'Orphic Marxism'. In: *The Poverty of Postmodernism*. London: Routledge, pp. 94–110.

O'Neill, John (2000). 'Cultural Capitalism and Child Formation'. In: Henry Cavanna (ed.). *The New Citizenship of the Family*. Aldershot: Ashgate, pp. 79–98.

O'Neill, John (2001). 'Psychoanalysis and Sociology: From Freudo-Marxism to Freudo-Feminism'. In: George Ritzer and Barry Smart (eds.). *Handbook of Social Theory*. London: Sage, pp. 112–24.

Pateman, Carole (1988). *The Sexual Contract*. Oxford: Blackwell.

Patterson, Cynthia B. (1998). *The Family in Greek History*. Cambridge, MA: Harvard University Press.

Pembroke, Simon G. (1967). 'Women in Charge: The Function of Alternatives in Early Greek tradition and the Ancient Idea of Matriarchy'. *Journal of the Warburg and Courthold Institutes* 30: 1–35.

Rubin, Gayle (1975). 'The Traffic in Women: Notes on the Political Economy of Sex'. In: Rayna F. Reiter (ed.). *Toward an Anthropology of Women*. New York: Monthly Review Press, pp. 157–210.

Schroeder, Jeanne L. (1998). *The Vestal and the Fasces: Hegel, Lacan, Property, and the Feminine*. Berkeley: University of California Press.

Sennett, Richard (1977). *The Fall of Public Man*. New York: Knopf.

Shuger, Deborah Kuller (1997). 'Nursing Fathers: Patriarchy as a Cultural Ideal'. In: *Habits of Thought in the English Renaissance: Religion, Politics, and the Dominant Culture*. Toronto: University of Toronto Press, pp. 218–50.

Slater, Philip E. (1968). *The Glory of Hera: Greek Mythology and the Greek Family*. Boston: Beacon.

Smith, William Robertson (1927 [1889]). *Lectures on the Religion of the Semites*. New York: Macmillan.

Therborn, Go.ran (1993). 'The Rights of Children since the Constitution of Modern Childhood: A Comparative Study of Western Nations'. In: Luis Moreno (ed.). *Social Exchange and Welfare Development*. Madrid: CSIC, pp. 67–121.

Vernant, Jean-Pierre (1981). 'The Myth of Prometheus in Hesiod'. In: R.L. Gordon (ed.). *Myth, Religion and Society*. Cambridge: Cambridge University Press, pp. 43–56.

Versnel, H.S. (1996). 'The Festival of the Bona Dea and the Thesmorphoria'. In: Ian McAuslan and Peter Walcott (eds.). *Women in Antiquity*. Oxford: Oxford University Press, pp. 182–204.

Vico, Giambattista (1984 [1744]). *The New Science of Giambattista Vico*. Thomas Goddard Bergin and Max Harold Fisch (trans.). Ithaca, NY: Cornell University Press. (Orig.)

Vidal-Naquet, Pierre (1981). 'Slavery and the Rule of Women in Tradition, Myth and Utopia'. In: R.L. Gordon (ed.) *Myth, Religion and Society*. Cambridge: Cambridge University Press, pp. 187–200.

Walcott, Peter (1996). 'Greek Attitudes Towards Women: The Mythological Evidence'. In: Ian McAuslan and Peter Walcott (eds.). *Women in Antiquity*. Oxford: Oxford University Press, pp. 91–102.

Webster, Paula (1975) 'Matriarchy: A Vision of Power'. In: Rayna R. Reiter (ed.). *Toward an Anthropology of Women*. New York: Monthly Review Press, pp. 141–56.

10 Structure, flow, and balance in Montaigne's essay 'Of Idleness'*

The use of *exemplum*, an example in the general sense or by extension a fable varying from a few lines to a lengthy essay interspersed with several more *exempla*, as in Montaigne's *Essays*, has had a long history (Vitry, 1890; Welter, 1927; Bynum, 1979). In the Middle Ages, the *exemplum* served to connect the world of the Bible to the daily context of European Christianity, as it still does in the ordinary Sunday homily. In Roman antiquity, exempla served like so many shining memorials to the greatness of the *Urbs Romana*. Similarly, in early and medieval Christianity, the *exempla* drawn from the lives of saints, philosophers, and, above all, the exemplary life of Christ (*exemplum exemplorum*) served to instruct and to guide Christians in their everyday lives as well as in the monastic orders. Gradually, the *exemplum* evolved from the use of starkly contrasted figures of good and evil, of the difference between man and woman, between saint and devil, to figures with a more differentiated psychology, wit and humor, reflecting the more practical values of the late medieval age (Tubach, 1962). By the time the *exemplum* reaches Montaigne, it is open to a further development imposed upon it due to the shifting ratio of *imitatio* and *inventio* reflected in the practice (*exercitio*) of the essay (O'Neill, 1982).

In order to respect the economy of a short conference paper, and in view of other writing (O'Neill, 1985), I shall select for analysis an extremely short essay, 'Of Idleness', since it offers the convenience of full quotation for your scrutiny (see the appendix), even though its condensed form deprives us of the easier access offered by Montaigne's typically more 'rambling' essays. By the same token, we shall see that, despite its title, 'Of Idleness' is concerned with work. Moreover, despite its apparent simplicity as a continuous example, 'Of Idleness' is in fact composed of a set of injunctions regarding the exemplarity of productive work in the triple economy of agriculture, reproduction, and psycho-culture (see Figure 10.1). Within this triple structure, idleness is figured as wilderness, hysteria, and fantasy requiring the farmer, husband, and author to cultivate nature's unruliness.

* Text of the essay taken from *Maps and Mirrors: Topologies of Art and Politics* (2001). Edited by Steve Martinot. Evanston, IL: Northwestern University Press, Pages 28–40. Reproduced with permission.

Thus an apparently simple example requires for its interpretation, that is to say, exemplifies in its own composition, an elaborate cosmology, which it condenses into a single short essay where the preeminent figure is that of the essayist as husband and wife to his own fantasies. Incidentally, the achieved complexity in such an early essay should be enough to set aside commonplaces about the evolution of Montaigne's *Essays*, since the phallocentric imagery (Cottrell, 1981: Chapter 1, 'Conception') in 'Of Idleness' is at once deconstructed in the overall figure of a gendered cosmology (Illich, 1982; O'Neill, 1985) in which nature, society, and the mind are rendered to our service.

The structures and figures that I have identified in Figure 10.1 are offered in the interest of keeping our analysis within some reasonable bounds. However, I am quite aware of the artifactual troubles of such procedures, and I have tried to deal with them elsewhere (O'Neill, 1981; 1986).

Although Montaigne is already at work in the essay 'Of Idleness', he is still unsure of his enterprise. He is, after all, surrounded by examples of potentially more productive activities. He does not set himself above the farmer, the soldier, and the politician, whose work he sees around him. Nor does he set himself above his family or the work of his father managing his estate and the education of his children. Above all, he respects the life-giving birth and nurturance in woman and in nature, where each are husbanded according to their way. By the same token, he believes that nothing is productive, that is, creative and orderly, without human effort guided by the appropriate institutions of the family, farming, religion, and the state. He finds this wisdom in the great literature of the past, which, if itself properly used, also contributes to the fecundity and orderliness of civil life (see Figure 10.1).

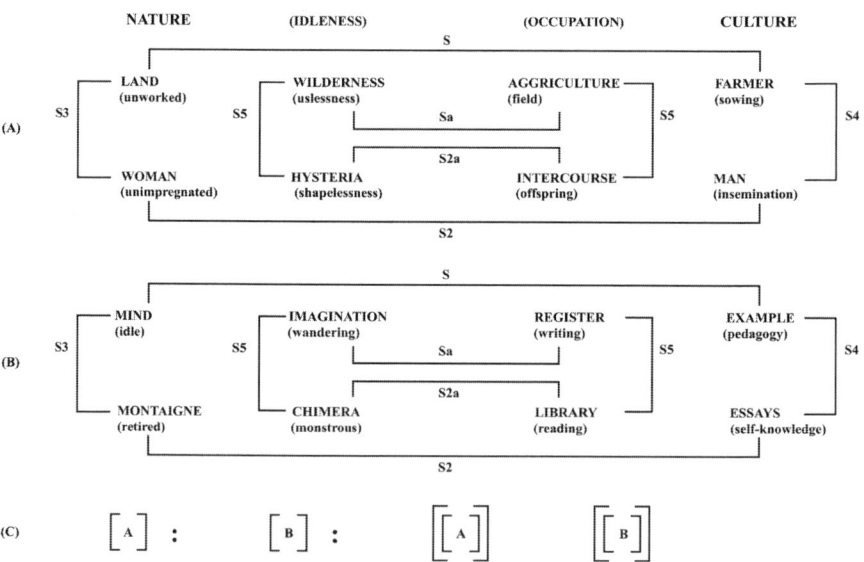

Figure 10.1 Example as similitude(s).

Montaigne, therefore, begins the *Essays* preoccupied with the task of setting them in the right furrow, so to speak. Yet he is simultaneously aware that, inasmuch as he has set to work upon himself, the example of the farmer is overdrawn; his imagination hardly lies before him and is not under his hand like a field of weeds beneath the farmer's plow. Similarly, the figure of the hysterical troubles believed to attend a woman's body until she conceives and gives birth (despite our differences with what it owes to Aristotle's view of reproduction) is applied by Montaigne to himself at the point where he finds himself struggling to conceive the essay form through which his labour as a writer will take hold of his otherwise wandering imagination. Thus no figure is any lower than the other; weeds, hysteria, and chimera all affect Montaigne as a writer in the early stages of his creative task. The writer, therefore, is not above the difference between nature and culture, nor that of man and woman. Rather, he is haunted by the figures of creation, order, and disorder; of procreation, waste, and monstrosity; and of the well-wrought, the felicitous and harmonious expression which composes our arts and crafts.

Montaigne's use of agricultural imagery in the formulation of his ideas on the work of the artist has been given considerable attention by Carol Clark (1978: 5–62, 123–129), in particular, on the question of the respective contributions of nature and nurture to a good outcome. She remarks that Montaigne does not adopt any fierce imagery of uprooting weeds or bad habits. Yet, while she sees the sexual pun carried over from the imagery of seeding the land to seeding women, she can make nothing of Montaigne's borrowing from Plutarch's *Conjugalia Praecepta* the strange idea that without intercourse women produce only shapeless lumps. She assigns it to 'the kind of fascinated disgust inspired in the average uninformed male by the reproductive process' (Clark, 1978: 126). But this will not do, partly because Montaigne is himself a prime commentator on the oddity of man's disparagement of all bodily functions and, for the rest, because what is involved is the historical availability of knowledge about conception, ovulation, and reproduction generally. Here Montaigne could not be ahead of the knowledge of his day, and this is the predicament of both men and women (Lacqueur, 1986).

At this point it may be useful to give the full context of the remark from Plutarch which Montaigne characteristically compresses, but thereby loses the gender balance on which the text turns:

> It is said that no woman ever produced a child without the co-operation of man, yet there are misshapen, fleshlike uterine growths originating in some infection, which develop of themselves and acquire firmness and solidity, and are commonly called 'moles'. Great care must be taken that this sort of thing does not take place in women's minds. For if they do not receive the seed of good doctrines and share with their husbands in intellectual advancement, they, left to themselves, conceive many untoward ideas and low designs and emotions.

> (Plutarch, 1928: 339–40)

Plutarch is advising young husbands that a sexist attitude between men and women reduces the balance of their marriage, which is rather enhanced by the intellectual and moral cultivation of one another. And this is Montaigne's own view, as we know from the *Essays*.

I am trying to avoid – but who does not see that I shall fail? – an effect of tipping the complex structure of the example before us by reading it from any particular bias that can easily be given it, if we extract the writer from the structure to which he has in fact subordinated himself. To this end, I shall insist upon the *grammatological* structure, of text and context, of the essay 'Of Idleness'. I am therefore defending it against a potentially anachronistic reading in terms of its perceived phallocentrism. The latter, I believe, would violate the engenderment of the essay by focusing upon its sexual imagery of impregnation, the reduction of woman to nature and of both to the rule of the plow and the phallus. The current fashionableness of such a reading requires, however, that it be unthought in its composition so that, as in the present example, Montaigne would have unconsciously assimilated himself, as though his imagination were seized by a chimera, to the figure of a 'hysterical woman' in need of the pen as phallus to bring forth a culture child, namely, the essay 'Of Idleness'.

Montaigne is not biblical about weeds and women (Suleiman, 1977) any more than is about hetero- or homosexuality. Rather, he considered sexuality, whether within or without marriage, to be better in friendship, more satisfied in its mirror of give-and-take than in the selfishness of either sex. Montaigne, then, is not the apostle of rigidity. Indeed, it is precisely the rigidity of the exemplary figure that repels him as, for example, with Cato. He rather prefers the chink in the armor – loving Socrates so much the more for the pleasure he took in scratching himself when released from his chains. At other times, Montaigne sets himself up as an anti-example of impotence and irresoluteness, a figure of self-indulgence unworthy of anyone's attention. Yet the *Essays* stand as a monumental resolution of such confessions of inconstancy.

Montaigne speaks of having begun the *Essays* as an act of infidelity, betraying his own otherwise changeable and melancholic nature. For this reason, the essay 'Of Idleness' is particularly challenging. In it we see that Montaigne cannot separate idleness from work. Rather, he wants from the very beginning to bridle himself, to bring his imagination to order, to make his mind ashamed of itself for spawning nothing but shapes that violate their proper form. Yet he did not marry himself to the exemplum. The *Essays* do not record a secondhand morality. They far exceed any such pedagogy and are themselves misunderstood as an anthology to be picked from here and there by beautiful souls. The *Essays* are not a book of hours. They cannot be read idly but demand a productive reader (*un lecteur suffisant*), ready to respond to the intricacies of their composition. For such reasons, then, we think the essay 'Of Idleness' subordinates the restricted economy of its sexual figures to the general economy of love, whose figures are family, marriage, and friendship. Thus, like his father who tended his estate and looked after his children, Montaigne sets about registering his thoughts, to produce a book whose

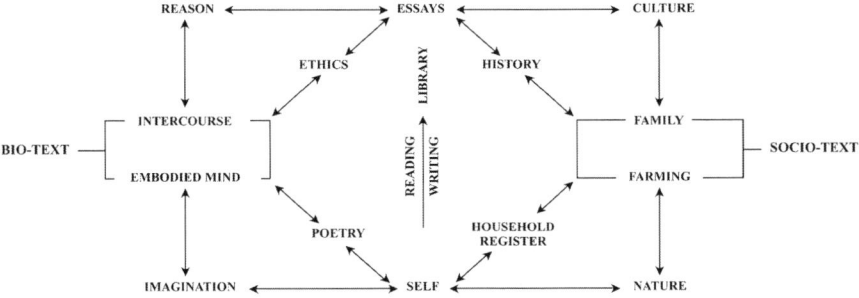

Figure 10.2 Example as grammatology.

pedagogy and politics are contributions to the reproduction of civil society and to the endurance of the body politic. Above all, he sets every relationship within a communicative ethic where nothing is enjoyed without restoration and reciprocity. Here, then, the figures of love, friendship, and the essay itself are inscriptions of the embodied self whose surrounding sociotext is inscribed within marriage, agriculture, politics, and the arts and sciences – in a general economy or grammatology, as represented in Figure 10.2. (I have in mind not so much the Derridean grammatology, as in Gregory Ulmer, 1985, as that of Gilles Deleuze and Félix Guattari, 1977).

I shall conclude with a further schematization of the essay 'Of Idleness' (see Figure 10.3) in order to reveal in it a characteristic movement of wandering and return, which, like the rest of his travels, always brought Montaigne back 'with a fresh love for my family and…a sweeter enjoyment of my home' (Montaigne, 1965: 745, 'Of Vanity'). 'Of Idleness' opens with an eccentric movement surveying the wilderness, the cultivated farm, woman before and after childbirth, the unbridled imagination's monsters and chimeras, Montaigne's busy life and

(A) Just as ...fallow land ...teems with ...useless weeds,...and as we see that women, all alone, produce mere shapeless masses ...so it is with minds

(B)   Virgil, *Aenid*, 8.22-26

(A) And there is no mad or idle fancy that they do not bring forth ...
                                               Horace, *Ars Poetica*, 7

(B) He who dwells everywhere, Maximus, nowhere dwells

                                               Martial, *Epigrams*, 7.73

(A) ...when I retired to my home ...it seemed to me ...my mind ...in full idleness ...|would| stay and settle in itself....
But I find—
                                               Lucan, *Pharsalia*, 4.704

that, on the contrary, like a running horse ...(my mind) gives birth to so many chimeras ...that ...I have begun to put them in writing hoping in time to make my mind ashamed of itself.

Figure 10.3 Example as narrative and deconstruction.

travels before his retirement, and the turmoil of his imagination when idle. As he moves through these spatial and temporal alternations, the quest for an exemplary fixed point becomes more urgent. Just as the land needs to be settled by the farmer and his family, so Montaigne needs to settle on his estate, within his own family and within the *Essays*, marrying himself to himself in the mirror of his own parental love, as well as in the mirror of his friendship with La Boétie (a topic we cannot develop here; O'Neill, 1982: 154–62). The movement from remote and exotic conditions to familiar and local arrangements, repeated in the mind's quest for self-identity, similarly shifting from errant places to the attachment of home, is nicely balanced in Montaigne's choice of Martial's epithet: 'He who dwells everywhere, Maximus, nowhere dwells.'

It turns out, then, that Montaigne's idleness is the product of a lively balance or a dance of thought in which reflection and imagination avoid overtipping the scale upon which Montaigne has set himself.

> We are great fools. 'He has spent his life in idleness,' we say; 'I have done nothing today.' What, have you not lived? This is not only the fundamental but the most illustrious of your occupations.
>
> (Montaigne, 1965: 850, 'Of Experience')

The essayist's retirement is not to be spent hoarding his memories nor in squandering his days in idle fancies. He is resolved to test his own mettle. To do so, Montaigne discovers that he must become a writer, to cultivate a field in which he can manage the family of his thoughts and feelings, not as a figure outside of them, but as father, mother, child of himself in those last days of his life. The *Essays* are Montaigne's 'home'. In them, he is *chez lui*. He had learned as a journeyman never to be very far away from himself, and so, when the time came to compose himself, he needed no extraordinary system of faith nor any practice beyond the daily care of the *Essays*.

Appendix

The English version of Montaigne's 'Of idleness' is reproduced from *The Complete Essays of Montaigne*, trans. Donald M. Frame (Stanford, CA: Stanford University Press, 1965), 20–1; the French version, 'De l'oisiveté', is reproduced from Montaigne, *Essais*, ed. Albert Thibaudet (Paris: Gallimard, 1950), 51–3. Montaigne's spelling has been preserved and Thibaudet's notes are given in square brackets.

Of idleness

Just as we see that fallow land, if rich and fertile, teems with a hundred thousand kinds of wild and useless weeds, and that to set it to work we must subject it and sow it with certain seeds for our service; and as we see that women, all alone, produce mere shapeless masses and lumps of flesh, but that to create a good and natural offspring they must be made fertile with a different kind of seed; so it is with minds. Unless you keep them busy with some definite subject that will bridle and control them, they throw themselves in disorder hither and yon in the vague field of imagination.

> Thus, in a brazen urn, the water's light
> Trembling reflects the sun's and moon's bright rays,
> And, darting here and there in aimless flight,
> Rises aloft, and on the ceiling plays.

VIRGIL

And there is no mad or idle fancy that they do not bring forth in this agitation:

> Like a sick man's dreams
> They form vain visions.

HORACE

The soul that has no fixed goal loses itself; for as they say, to be everywhere is to be nowhere:

> He who dwells everywhere, Maximus, nowhere dwells.

MARTIAL

Lately when I retired to my home, determined so far as possible to bother about nothing except spending the little life I have left in rest and seclusion, it seemed to me I could do my mind no greater favor than to let it entertain itself in full idleness and stay and settle in itself, which I hoped it might do more easily now, having become weightier and riper with time. But I find –

> Ever idle hours breed wandering thoughts

LUCAN

– that, on the contrary, like a runaway horse, it gives itself a hundred times more trouble than it took for others, and gives birth to so many chimeras and fantastic monsters, one after another, without order or purpose, that in order to contemplate their ineptitude and strangeness at my pleasure, I have begun to put them in writing, hoping in time to make my mind ashamed of itself.

De l'oisiveté

Comme nous voyons des terres oysives, si elles sont grasses et fertiles, foisonner en cent milles sortes d'herbes sauvages et inutiles, et que pour les tenir en office, il les faut assubjectir et employer à certaines semences, pour nostre service; et comme nous voyons que les femmes produisent bien toutes seules, des amas et pieces de chair informes, mais que pour faire une generation bonne et naturelle, il les faut emboisoigner d'une autre semence: ainsin est-il des esprits. Si on ne les occupe à certain sujet, qui les bride et contreignes, ils se jettent desreiglez, par-cy par là, dans le vague champ des imaginations.

> *Sicut aquae tremulum labris ubi lumen ahenis*
> *Sole repercussum, aut radiantis imagine Lunae*
> *Omnia pervolitat latè loca, jámque sub auras*
> *Erigitur, summique ferit laqueria tecti.*
>
> > [Comme l'eau qui frémit dans un vaisseau d'airain réfléchit le soleil ou les rayons de la lune, les éclats lumineux voltigent dans les airs et frappent les lambris de reflets incertains. (Virgile, *Énéide,* VIII, 22)]

Et n'est folie ny réverie, qu'ils ne produisent en cette agitation,

> *velut agri somnia, vanae*
> *Fingintur species*
>
> > [Commes des songes de malade, ils se fabriquent des chimères. (Horace, *Art poétique,* 7)]

L'ame qui n'a point de but estably, elle se perd: car, common on dict, c'est n'estre en aucun lieu, que d'estres par tout.

> *Quisquis ubique habitat, Maxime, nusquam habitat.*
>
> > [C'est être nulle part qu'être partout, Maxime …
> > (Martial, VII, LXXIII)]

Dernierement que je me retiray chez moy, deliberé autant que je pourroy, ne me mesler d'autre chose que de passer en repos, et à part, ce peu qui me reste de vie: il me sembloit ne pouvoir faire plus grande faveur à mon esprit, que de le laisser en pleine oysiveté, s'entretenir soy mesmes, et s'arrester et rasseoir en soy: ce que j'esperois qu'il peut meshuy faire plus aisément, devenu avec le temps plus poisant, et plus meur. Mais je trouve,

> *Variam semper dant otia mentem*
>
> > [Oisif, toujours l'esprit diversement foisonne.
> > (Lucian, IV, 704)]

que au rebours, faisant le cheval eschappé, il se donne cent fois plus d'affaire à soy mesmes, qu'il n'en prenoit pour autruy; et m'enfante tant de chimeres et monstres fantasques les uns sur les autres, sans ordre, et sans propos, que pour en contempler à mon aise l'ineptie et l'estrangeté, j'ay commencé de les mettre en rolle [en registre], esperant avec le temps luy en faire honte à luy mesmes.

References

Clark, Carol (1978). *The Web of Metaphor: Studies in the Imagery of Montaigne*'s Essais. Lexington, KY: French Forum.

Cottrell, Robert D. (1981). *Sexuality/Textuality: A Study of the Fabric of Montaigne's Essais*. Columbus: Ohio State University Press.

Deleuze, Gilles and Guattari, Félix (1977). *Anti-Oedipus: Capitalism and Schizophrenia*. Trans. Robert Hurley, Mark Seem, and Helen R. Lane. New York: Viking.

Illich, Ivan (1982). *Gender*. New York: Random House.

Lacqueur, Thomas (1986). 'Orgasm, Generation, and the Politics of Reproductive Biology'. *Representations* 14: 1–41.

Montaigne, Michel de (1950). *Essais*. Ed. Albert Thibaudet. Paris: Gallimard.

Montaigne, Michel de (1965). *The Complete Essays of Montaigne*. Trans. Donald M. Frame Stanford, CA: Stanford University Press.

O'Neill, John (1981). 'The Literary Production of Natural and Social Science Inquiry'. *Canadian Journal of Sociology* 6(2): 105–20.

O'Neill, John (1982). *Essaying Montaigne:A Study of the Renaissance Institution of Writing and Reading*. London: Routledge and Kegan Paul.

O'Neill, John (1985). 'The Essay as a Moral Exercise: Montaigne'. *Renaissance and Reformation* 21(3): 210–18.

O'Neill, John (1986). 'A Realist Model of Knowledge: With a Phenomenological Deconstruction of its Model of Man'. *Philosophy of the Social Sciences* 16(1): 1–19.

Plutarch (1928). Conjugalia praecepta, 145D-E. In: *Plutarch Moralia*, Vol. 2. Engl. Trans. Frank Cole Babbit. London: Heinemann, pp. 339–40.

Suleiman, Susan (1977). 'Le récit exemplaire: Parabole, fable, roman et thèse'. *Poétique* 32: 468–89.

Tubac, Frederic L. (1962). 'Exempla in the Decline'. *Traditio* 18: 407–17.

Ulmer, Gregory (1985). *Applied Grammatology: Post(e)-Pedagogy from Jacques Derrida to Joseph Beuys*. Baltimore: Johns Hopkins University Press.

Vitry, Jacques de (1890). *The Exempla or Illustrative Stories from the Sermones Vulgares of Jacques de Vitry*. ed. T. E Crane. Publications of the Folk-Lore Society, no. 26. London: D. Nutt.

Walker, Caroline, and Bynum, Walker (1979). *Docere Verbo et Exemplo: An Aspect of Twelfth-Century Spirituality*. Missoula, MT: Scholars Press.

Welter, J. Th. (1927). *L'Exemplum dans la littérature religieuse et didactique du moyen age*. Paris: E. H. Guittard.

11 *Mecum meditari**

Descartes demolishing doubt, building a prayer

It now happens that my own thoughts are turned toward the cogito through a chain of events and present circumstances that continue the cultural life of the cogito enriched for me by the gentle and persistent reflections of Merleau-Ponty, to whom I owe much of my philosophical and literary culture (O'Neill, 1989):

> I am thinking of the Cartesian cogito; I want to finish this work; and I can feel the coolness of the paper under my hand and I can see the trees of the boulevard through the window. My life is constantly thrown headlong into transcendent things; it passes wholly outside of me. The cogito is either this thought which took shape three centuries ago in the mind of Descartes, or the meaning of the texts he has left to us, or else it is an external truth which breathes through them; in any case, it is a cultural being to which my own thought reaches out but does not quite embrace, just as my body, in a familiar surrounding, finds its orientation and makes its way among objects without needing to have them expressly in mind.
>
> (Maurice Merleau-Ponty, 1945:
> 423; 1962: 369)

At this very moment, I too write on a cool page across which the winter sunlight falls; the trees outside my window stand dark against the blue sky, and my neighbours' houses seem to nudge closer against the cold. This moment of peace was not there at the start of this work; it has arisen only now, as the shape of what I may have accomplished needs defiant assertion to make itself a beginning. But I must set aside the naughty genius of fiction, of plans and of logic. I have worked on this essay without a study, away from home, with few books, at other times with many. My thoughts have not always been my own, were rarely clear, and, like myself, have had to settle for their present circumstance and predicaments. I have made several journeys and rebuilt my home in the past year, whose time in my life I cannot tell. Rather than separate me from my task, as at times it seemed,

* Text of the essay taken from *Critical Conventions: Interpretation in the Literary Arts and Sciences* (1992). Norman, OK: University of Oklahoma Press. Pages 222–33. Reprinted with permission.

these travels have drawn me to myself; and whereas the task of rebuilding a home might have made this work impossible, it rather revealed to me, as to Descartes, those anxieties that arise with things to be torn down, and it has shown me those hopes from whose roots things may grow up. And just as the peasants I have seen set a tree upon the scaffolding of a new house, for the sake of its life, I set this essay above my present cares for the sake of the prayer I find in the *Meditations*.

Although Chaim Perelman generally treats Descartes as a protagonist of the view that all rhetorical practices must be stripped away from the language of science, he has also a better sense for the inescapable rhetoric of Cartesian discourse itself. Thus he notices Descartes's imagery of the 'chain of ideas', or of 'walking slowly and carefully', 'fearful of falling' (Perelman, 1970). I propose to show how extensive these concerns are in shaping the aims and resolution of the *Meditations*. To the extent I am capable of this exposition, I believe the way is open to further studies of philosophical discourse as a proper object of rhetorical argument (O'Neill, 1982: chapters 6, 7, 8). Thus it is important to pay careful attention to how Descartes conceives the site of philosophical work (for a classical quarrel, see Foucault, 1972 and Derrida, 1978).

What motivates him to want to demolish and to rebuild the world around him? Surely, it is madness to reject the accumulated experience of the senses and of the great articulations of our language in which we think and perceive things, events, and relationships largely as do our fellow beings. Who cannot see that the great edifice and landscape of our senses and common experience is a work that exceeds each one of us; that it has been painstakingly built up by countless generations who have added to it without a single plan, who have made repairs here and there without any thought of tearing everything down to start anew? Who else would entertain the general destruction of our beliefs and opinions in the ordinary business of our lives and institutions, of which they are the common currency, unless he thought himself in possession of some great design for mankind? Such a person, if not mad, would need to be a god, or a philosopher, or else an engineer and architect, if not all of these at once. Above all, to begin such a work of demolition, he would need to be sure that the voice that inspired him was not that of the Devil tempting him with the powers of creation. And yet, if this voice comes rather from God, how can Descartes be sure of the proportion between the divine mind and his own?

'I am quite alone.' Descartes persuades himself that in withdrawing from the world, he has nevertheless a secure place in the world from which to undertake 'this general overview of my opinions'. Descartes, then, means to conduct an assault on himself, to attack the common man in himself with the agile arguments of the philosopher he has become through espousing doubt. Even so, he senses that he has neither the time nor the strength for doubting every one of his beliefs. In other words, it would be unreasonable for an embodied thinker to embark upon a philosophical life that would exceed the limits of ordinary living, which in fact prescribes the uses of certainty and doubt within the framework of 'corporeal nature in general'. So far from being an object in the world of which his senses might be mistaken, or merely an image of itself as in a painting, Descartes acknowledges that his body is rather a mode of perceptual knowledge, reflexively aware of its waking and sleeping states, and as such, the constitutive ground of our being in the world:

> But, although the senses sometimes deceive us, concerning things which are barely perceptible or at a great distance, there are perhaps many other things one cannot reasonably doubt, although we know them through the medium of the senses, for example, that I am here, sitting by the fire, wearing a dressing gown, with this paper in my hands, and other things of this nature. And how could I deny that these hands and this body belong to me, unless perhaps I were to assimilate myself to those insane persons, persons whose minds are so troubled and clouded by the black vapours of the bile that they constantly assert that they are kings, when they are very poor; that they are wearing gold and purple, when they are quite naked; or who imagine that they are pitchers or that they have a body of glass. But these are madmen, and I would not be less extravagant if I were to follow their example.
>
> (Descartes, 1968: 96; 1970: 19–20)

Indeed, to say we exist, or that there is a world, or that we have a body, is to say very much the same thing. Moreover, to say any of these things is ordinarily strange because they articulate the same perceptual faith in much the same way as each of our senses articulates the same body and its world. Questions about the infallibility of our senses, like questions about the purity of our morals, ought never to be abstracted from the ordinary contexts of our living under pain of separating us from our fellow humans – and, worst of all, from ourselves. Whoever seeks absolute certainty, or absolute trust, risks either having to withdraw from the world or being viewed as insane. The grammar of reasonableness in matters of perception and trust is fractured by the lunatic. Wholesale infringements of any local grammar and its institutional practices – rather than minor offenses readily confessed and repaired – will put any of us beyond the pale.

Such exclusion is a sanctioned practice of everyday life and is incurred by children, loved ones, students, workers, and officials as ordinary members of society (O'Neill, 1989: part 2; Michaels, 1980). To invoke and to respond to such sanctions, and not to be ignorant or indifferent to them, is the ordinary mark of one's moral worth, if not of one's rational status. Thus to claim that no one knows anything or sees or hears anything for certain, or that we are asleep when we think we are awake, or hate when we think we love, or that everything might be other than what we ordinarily take it to be, is to exceed even madness – for the lunatic lacks all such distinctions.

Descartes does not consider himself mad. Yet he entertains the project of ridding himself of all beliefs, opinions, judgments, and experiences that are his only in virtue of his commonsense knowledge of things and persons. He means to withdraw from public life and discourse in order to reconstruct the foundations of his knowledge and language. Aware of the huge scope of his project, Descartes tells us that he had to wait until he had achieved a sufficient maturity and leisure in order to begin the general destruction of his previous opinions and to lay fresh foundations, so as to establish something firm and constant in the sciences. Such an ambitious project of demolition might just as well founder upon the corrosive anxiety it engenders rather than lead to a new edifice of confidence and certainty. Indeed, as we shall see later, Descartes could torture himself over his sinful pride in separating himself from the common faith and practices of his fellow men. And in replying to the objections raised against his methodical doubt, he appears more moderate than either the *Discourse* or the *Meditations* give the impression.

Thus he concedes that most of his knowledge has come to him through his senses, or through the senses of others whom he trusted, and especially through language as a thesaurus of things and relationships which are the articulation of our surrounding world. In such a world we may, of course, be mistaken, deceived and misinformed. These experiences, however, do not entirely invalidate our senses. Nor do they cause us to replace trust with wholesale mistrust in our relations to others. Above all, we have no recourse from language, generally speaking. We cannot get rid of words as though they were useless rubble entirely unsuited to the foundations of knowledge and intercourse. Commonsense practice insists rather upon making distinctions. Instead of tearing down the edifice of our senses and society, or withdrawing from the world of discourse, we learn to distinguish occasional errors, deceptions, and misinformation from universal error, deceit, and ignorance. In short, commonsense language, knowledge, and values are that great edifice of our lives which we take them to be precisely because they cannot be toppled over by any single error, or deception, or ignorance.

Such objections were well known to Descartes. We shall argue that they weighed upon him, making him fearful of wandering from the common path and anxious that his work might fall in ruins rather than stand firm in our memory. Not only his critics but he himself could ridicule his solitary pretentions. Thus, anyone who forsakes all fellowship because of a single disappointment must be considered childish – if not infantile, since every child has to learn to accommodate to the lapses of those in whom it trusts. And anyone who abandons reading because he has found one book to correct another must rather be considered foolish than wise, since he who claims to read must in fact be able to evaluate the competing claims in what he reads through what he reads. And so it is with all our senses – their competence with the objects of sight, sound, touch, and taste is never entirely at stake in any single operation. Rather, their corrigibility is proper to their exercise and, so to speak, intrinsic to their practical reflexivity.

Much of the commentary on the cogito, apart from that of Jaakko Hintikka, misses the fact that Descartes does not argue from the *cogito* to the *sum* (Hintikka, 1968; also Caton, 1973: 140–143; Feldman, 1973; Williams, 1978: chapter 3). Had he done so, then the commentary on his arguments for making the copula of thought and existence would be unavoidable. Whatever the challenge offered to philosophers by the Cartesian doubt, none of them any less than Descartes himself hesitates to urge that their own practices of argument, doubt, and validation can render the intelligibility of Descartes's copulation of thought and existence clear to their fellow philosophers. However this is done – and the approaches are quite varied (Doney 1968; Beck, 1965; Kenny, 1968) – what needs to be noticed is that commentators on the *Meditations* treat them as the occasion for a return to analysis without anxiety, that is, as a pretext for showing how any challenge to the certainty that we live knowledgeably cannot exceed the rhetorical practice of philosophy without religion. I think, however, that we can set such commentary aside in favor of trying to understand the *Meditations* in terms of their proper discourse type, that is, as a psychological essay in which Descartes weighs up what it is from his conscious experience he can assert as public knowledge or science (O'Neill, 1982).

In order to carry out such an exploration he needs to imagine himself doubly set apart from the flow of his experience: (a) in the isolation of his study; and (b) in reflective isolation from his senses, perception, and judgment. Thus, Descartes imagines that it might be possible to reconstruct his experience and to rearticulate it without relying on commonsense discourse, thereby laying the foundations of certain knowledge, which others might similarly enjoy, supposing they were to submit themselves to the rigors of philosophical meditation rather than to easy imitation. It is essential to the *Meditations* that the rhetorical effects of social isolation determine the philosophical effect of sensory and perceptual withdrawal by a freely inquiring mind. At the same time, the rhetoric of social withdrawal is transgressed through the philosopher's language, which continues to articulate the public discourse on the difference between waking and dream states, between certainty and uncertainty, between sight and blindness. In this way, the philosopher abrogates to his imagined private experience the authority of public knowledge, as well as its pragmatics of proof and refutation, which he conscripts through the reader's collusion.

It is (only) a rhetorical effect of the philosopher's doubt that appears to separate him from the world of fellow beings and discourse. However much Descartes continues to objectify things in a cognitive space projected from his desk, the philosopher never leaves the greater world within which his meditations make use of his body, the page, the room, the fireside and the desk whose existence presupposes the work of others greater in number and talents than the reader or writer of the *Meditations*. Thus what we witness in the *Meditations* is rather a theater of doubt (Champigny, 1959; Flores, 1983) in which Descartes's struggles with the evil genius (*un certain mauvais génie*) is resolved by calling in a *deus ex machina*, that is, a God who could not possibly allow the philosophical seduction of Descartes by his fantasy of universal doubt. However much Descartes pretends to remove all the props from the stage, he cannot remove the personal/public I, eye (*je vois*) *je*, or *jeu* (play) in the *cogito*, which always leaves the reader on the stage. Even when Descartes appears to have withdrawn body and soul, he remains with the audience all the while as the masked narrator – *larvatus prodeo* (Nancy, 1977) – leading the reader on toward the divine goal of the *Meditations* – *larvatus pro deo*?

The cogito, as Merleau-Ponty observes, is in effect a textual cogito, that is, a verbal effect that absorbs to itself the universality of an anonymous discourse in which language holds us while effacing itself. Just as our body veils the tacit cogito through which we are already worldly creatures before any thematization of subject and object relations:

> The true formula of this *cogito* should be: 'One thinks, therefore one is.' The wonderful thing about language us that it promotes its own oblivion: my eyes follow the lines on the paper, and from the moment I am caught up in their meaning I lose sight of them. The paper, the letters on it, my eyes and body are there only as the minimum setting of some invisible operator. Expression fades out before what is expressed, and this is why its mediating role may pass unnoticed, and why Descartes *nowhere* mentions it. *Descartes, and a fortiori his reader, begin their meditation in what is already a universe of discourse.*
>
> (Merleau-Ponty, 1962: 400–401)

The *Meditations* are surrendered to the ineluctable nature of language, the play within the play written at the philosopher's table by a thinking body whose fantasy of its nonexistence merely reveals the limits of its 'inexistence' distributed as (rhetorical) effects of writing and reading, nowhere else. Thus the *Meditations* cannot reconstruct egological experience elsewhere than within the pragmatics of intersubjective discourse. Language has no outside nature, no origins, but only a structure and history of reciprocity in which you and I amplify each other's discourse and intelligence, enlargening our general culture:

> I should be unable even to read Descartes' book, were I not, before any speech can begin, in contact with my own life and thought, and if the spoken *cogito* did not encounter within me a tacit *cogito*. This silent *cogito* was the one Descartes sought when writing his *Meditations*. He gave life and direction to all those expressive operations which, by definition, always miss their target since, between Descartes' existence and the knowledge of it which he acquires, they interpose the full thickness of cultural acquisition.
>
> (Merleau-Ponty, 1962: 402)

What this means is that it is only the cogito as a performance, and not as a perception, that unites thought and being. It is only by means of my exploration of things, persons, and language that I acquire an inner perception of self; and certainty is built upon these first uncertain relations to our world:

> Certainty derives from the doubt itself as an act, and not from these thoughts, just as the certainty of the thing and of the world precedes any thetic knowledge of their properties....The *cogito* is the recognition of this fundamental fact. In the proposition: 'I think, I am', the two assertions are to be equated with each other, otherwise there would be no *cogito*. Nevertheless we must be clear about the meaning of this equivalence: it is not the 'I am' which is preeminently contained in the 'I think', not my existence which is brought down

to the consciousness which I have of it, but conversely the 'I think', which is reintegrated into the transcending process of the 'I am', and consciousness into existence.

(Merleau-Ponty, 1962: 383)

Despite the rhetorical persuasions of the *Meditations*, the very problematic of the cogito is never wholly Cartesian. Rather, the cogito presupposes a long history of previous philosophical discourse, sustained by others, which will be taken up in future from time to time, as it has in the past which bequeathed to us its question. Viewed in this way, the cogito does not found philosophical discourse, and could not possibly do so, except through a retrospective fiction of the historians of philosophy, whose practices of periodization are themselves only a further convention within the philosophical community. There is, of course, a 'Cartesian' cogito. But it is available only as a particular inflection of the philosopher's question which has its peculiar style because it starts from an obsessive anxiety of grounds that marks Cartesian discourse. Now it may well be that Descartes's anxiety is amplified by his intention to expropriate public discourse in a self-sufficient proclamation of the authorial subject whose voice reechoes the Creator's word/world.

Here we cannot decide on the larger frame of the *Mediations*. All the same, we should not overlook their articulation with Descartes's other works, *The World*, *Dioptrics*, *Geometry*, and the *Discourse on Method*, which in turn raise further questions about the motives of their hidden author (Reiss, 1976, 1977, 1982; Serres, 1982). Perhaps Descartes's anxiety is doubly bound to the expropriation of the *vox populi* and of the *vox dei*. In other words, Descartes's anxiety of method may not be so much the effect of the doubt in the cogito as the undertaking of an equation between the voices of God and of Science proclaimed in the name of Descartes – which thereby becomes fearfully unwritten. This, I believe, is the larger framework for which all Descartes's writings are pretexts. It is against this horizon that we may explore the lesser anxieties and their resolution in the *Meditations*.

Descartes, as we have seen, approaches the cogito without trust in the commonsense world of perception and belief. He is troubled by 'false opinions', 'insecure principles', 'things which are not entirely certain and indubitable', 'things which seem manifestly false'. He is tempted to conclude that because 'I have sometimes found that these senses played me false…it is prudent never to trust entirely those who have once deceived us.' Yet, rather than leave things under the shadow of universal doubt and suspicion, Descartes resolves 'to begin afresh from the foundations', 'to establish something firm and constant in the sciences'. His strategy is then not to exhaust his energies in a critical review of everyone of his opinions, but more like an engineer to demolish the edifice of his beliefs by attacking it at a point whose fall brings down everything else with it: 'Because the destruction of the foundations necessarily brings down with it the rest of the edifice, I shall make an assault first on the principles on which all my former opinions were based.' (Descartes, 1968: 96).

Where did Descartes's anxiety over certainty begin? Was it from childhood disappointments with elders whom he trusted absolutely and whose ordinary fallibility and weakness could not sustain the infantile wish for parental omnipotence (Galston, 1944; Schonberger, 1939)? Are then, Descartes's military and engineering metaphors the sublimated aggression in a long-standing plan to overthrow the parental edifice at its weakest point and to plant just there something as firm and unshakable as the thinking phallus – the thought-self of the *cogito/ sum*? We cannot overlook Descartes's rhetorical expansion of doubt and uncertainty in himself and in others as a particular style of the cogito (Edelman, 1950; Nador, 1962; Romanowski, 1974). Thus, we may contrast the private practice of the *Meditations* with Socrates' public practice of his ignorance in the marketplace, where he found the occasions for those dialogues, which could just as well be enjoyed in a drinking bout like the *Symposium*. Fellowship is essential to the Socratic turn away from nature as a place of truth, justice, and beauty and is not breached even at Socrates' trial.

But Descartes declares no such faith in common practice. He considers his fellow men to be like shifting sand and their company to be avoided in favor of his own thoughts, just as an engineer lays the footings of his buildings according to his own design, rejecting everything he was not inspected for himself. Alternatively, in the *Discourse on Method* Descartes pictures himself as a single-minded traveler, sticking to the main road and not wandering off, turning in circles and going nowhere – which is the way of his fellow men whose opinions always lead them astray. But whether as architect or traveller, Descartes always goes alone, following a path 'so remote from the normal way that I thought it would not be helpful to give a full account of it in a book written in French and designed to be read by all and sundry, in case weaker intellects might believe that they ought to set out on the same path.' (Descartes, 1970: 7:7)

Descartes's solitary vocation, whether as architect or as traveller, merely serves to heighten his anxieties about the security of his foundations and his steps along the right road to certainty. Having questioned the common practice of building roads and houses, everything sinks into the shifting sands of opinion, and the Cartesian cogito becomes the butt of the Jesuit Pierre (rock) Bourdin's parody on its fear of sliding foundations. The *Discourse on Method* and the *Meditations* reveal a profound nausea, an obsession with mud, sand, ruins, falling, straying, and blindness, against which their author pleads for solidity, security, and certainty. It is (no) accident that in one of his dreams on the night of 10 November 1619 Descartes sees himself struggling to walk, holding himself to one side (the left) because he fears falling into a precipice (on the right) (Gouhier, 1958; Smith, 1966). Dragging himself along (under the burden of sin, or shame at the weakness of his limbs or his ambitions) he heads for the safety of the college chapel beckoning to him on the road. But a wind whirls him around on one foot, and when he tries to tum back to greet a man he has passed on the road, it hurls him against the chapel. The chapel image reminds us, in turn, of Descartes's mock rebuttal of Bourdin in which the master builder rebukes the mason who presumed to criticize him for pretending to demolish everything and not make use of a single stone at hand when constructing the foundations of his building:

> Now the very church alone which the Architect has already built proves that all this is the silliest nonsense. For it is quite clear that in it the foundations have been most firmly laid, and that the Architect has destroyed nothing which was not worthy of destruction; and that he has never departed from the precepts of others unless he had some better plan; that the building soars to a great height without threatening to fall; finally that he has constructed not out of nothing, but out of the most durable material, nor nothing but a stable and well-built church to the glory of God. But all this together with other matters in which my critic has suffered from delusions, can be seen clearly enough from the Meditations alone which I published....And certainly all such similes are equally out of place when talking of the Method of inquiring into truth.
>
> (Descartes, 1934: 2:325–44)

Between dream and parody, we discover Descartes's desire for the one true foundations of all belief, the church built upon that rock – Peter/Petrus/Pierre – that was to outlast the sands of time. Thus the *Discourse* and the *Meditations* lay out the road to the site where the foundations can be laid for the philosopher's chapel, in which one of the world's lasting meditations on the one true God is performed *per omnia saecula saeculorum*. Here, with all his senses, passions, loves, hates, errors, and opinions, closed in upon himself, like a little chapel closed in upon itself from the outside world, closed to the sky and its stars, closed to the sights and sounds of the earth, Descartes meditates on the impossibility of thinking and feeling nothingness as the god term of creation. *Ex nihilo nihil*. And since he himself has no idea of himself as either the formal or eminent cause of the world around him, Descartes rests his finitude in the infinite being of God. Thus Descartes, the anxious architect, the anxious traveler, and perhaps the anxious child, discovers in his God that certain paternity with which the craftsman imprints every object of his own making.

> And, in truth, it is not to be thought strange that God, in creating me, should have put in me this idea to serve, as it were, as the mark that the workman imprints on his work; nor is it necessary that his mark should be something different from the work itself. But, from the mere fact that God created me, it is highly credible that he in some way produced me in his own image and likeness, in which the idea of God is contained, by means of the same faculty by which I apprehend myself; that is to say, when I reflect upon myself, not only do I know that I am an imperfect, incomplete and dependent being, and one who tends and aspires unceasingly towards something better and greater than I am, but I also know, at the same time, that he upon whom I depend possesses in himself all the great attributes to which I aspire, and the ideas of

which I find in me, not merely indefinitely and potentially, but actually and infinitely, and that he is thus God.

(Descartes, 1968: 130; 1970: 51–52)

The *Meditations*, then, are nothing else than the road Descartes had to take that would lead to the place where doubt is cut across by faith. Anyone who makes the same pilgrimage, who begins by leaving his everyday surroundings, courting the terrors of the road , will find himself beckoned by a wayside chapel where, if he contemplates his own nature, he will find the certain mark of God upon him – *imago dei*. The *Meditations*, as everyone recognizes, are not ruled by any order of logic. What motivates them is Descartes's life-long quest for a reliable truth, which after all his travels and studies led him back to the chapel of his youth. There, in a profound meditation on the source of his being, Descartes discovered – *pura et attenta mentis inspectio* – in the purity and virginity of his intellect, that he was conceived by God, whose inseparable creature he remained, despite all uncertainty, doubt, and error of his own making. Therefore, we do not read the *Meditations* because they contain a method for their reading – such readings generally disappoint those philosophers who continue nevertheless to insist on such practice. We begin to read the *Meditations* when we are able to face the uncertainty of the boundaries between philosophy and religion. Once this step is taken, we can only comment on the *Meditations* with the same humility that is to be found in them – but without any hope of redeeming ourselves in such greater prayer as rises – *ad majorem dei gloriam* – from them.

Here, then, in my study, at work on the *Meditations*, I am no more alone than were Descartes or Montaigne or Merleau-Ponty. The same shining world surrounds me as it did them once before, while the silence of my study murmurs with their voice in the turning pages of my reading, and their time runs into mine through this hand writing:

> I shall now close my eyes, stop up my ears, turn away all my senses, even efface from my thought all images of corporeal things, or at least, because this can hardly be done, I shall consider them as being vain and false; and thus communing only with myself, and examining my inner self, I shall try to make myself, little by little, better known and more familiar to myself.
>
> (Descartes, 1968: 113)

> Claudam nunc oculos, aures obturabo, avocabo omnes sensus, imagines etiam rerum corporalium omnes vel ex cogitatione mea delebo, vel certe, quia hoc fieri vix potest, illas uc inanas et falsas nihili pendam, meque solum alloquendo et penitius inspiciendo, meipsum paulatim mihi magis notum et familiarem reddere conabor.
>
> (Descartes, 1970: 34)

References

Beck, L. J. (ed.) (1965). *Descartes, A Collection of Critical Essays*. Oxford: At the Clarendon Press.

Caton, Hiram (1973). *The Origins of Subjectivity: An Essay on Descartes*. New Haven, CT: Yale University Press.

Champigny, Robert (1959). 'The Theatrical Aspect of the Cogito'. *Review of Metaphysics* 12: 370–77.

Derrida, Jacques (1978). 'Cogito and the History of Madness'. In: *Writing and Difference*. Geoffrey Hartman (ed.). Chicago: University of Chicago Press, pp. 36–76.

Descartes, René (1934). 'Objections 7, Third Question: Whether a Method Can Be Devised Anew'. In: *The Philosophical Works of Descartes*. Elizabeth S. Haldane and G. R. T. Ross (trans). Cambridge: Cambridge University Press, pp. 2, 325–44.

Descartes, René (1968). *Discourse on Method and The Meditations*. F. E. Sutcliffe (trans.). Harmondsworth, UK: Penguin.

Descartes, René (1970). *Meditatationes de prima philosophia, Méditations métaphysiques*. Duc de Luynes (trans.). Paris: Librairie Philosophique J. Vrin.

Doney, Willis (ed.) (1968). *Descartes: A Collection of Critical Essays*. Notre Dame, IN: University of Notre Dame Press

Edelman, Nathan (1950). 'The Mixed Metaphor in Descartes'. *The Romantic Review* 41: 167–78.

Feldman, F. (1973). 'On the Performatory Interpretation of the *Cogito*'. *Philosophical Review* 1982: 345–63.

Flores, Ralph (1983). 'Cartesian Striptease'. *Substance* 39: 75–88.

Foucault, Michel (1972). 'Mon corps, ce papier, ce feu'. In: *Histoire de la folie à l'age classique*. Paris: Librairie Plon, pp. 583–603.

Galston, Iago (1944). 'Descartes and Modern Psychiatric Thought'. *Isis* 35: 118–28.

Gouhier, Henri (1958). *Les Premières pensées de Descartes: Contribution de l'histoire de l'Anti-Renaissance*. Paris: Librairie Philosophique J. Vrin.

Hintikka, Jaakko (1968). 'Cogito, ergo sum: Influence or Performance?' In: *Descartes: A Collection of Critical Essays*. Willis Doney (ed.). Notre Dame, IN: University of Notre Dame Press, pp. 108–39.

Kenny, Anthony (1968). *Descartes: A Study of his Philosophy*. New York: Random House.

Merleau-Ponty, Maurice (1945). *Phénoménologie de la perception*. Paris: Gallimard.

Merleau-Ponty, Maurice (1962). *Phenomenology of Perception*. Colin Smith (trans.). London: Routledge & Kegan Paul.

Michaels, Walter Benn (1980). 'The Interpreter's Self: Peirce on the Cartesian Subject'. In: *Reader Response Criticism: From Formalism to Post-Structuralism*. Jane P. Tomkins (ed.). Baltimore: Johns Hopkins University Press, pp. 185–200.

Nador, G. (1962). 'Métaphores de chemins et de labyrinths chez Descartes'. *Revue d'histoire de la philosophie* 152: 37–51.

Nancy, Jean-Luc (1977). 'Larvatus pro Deo'. *Glyph* 2: 14–36.

O'Neill, John (1982). *Essaying Montaigne: A Study of the Renaissance Institution of Reading and Writing*. London: Routledge & Kegan Paul.

O'Neill, John (1989). *The Communicative Body: Studies in Communicative Philosophy, Politics, and Sociology*. Evanston, IL: Northwestern University Press.

Perelman, Chaim (1970). 'Analogie et métaphore en science, poésie et philosophie'. In: *Le Champ de l'argumentation*. Bruxelles: Presses Universitaires de Bruxelles, pp. 271–83.

Reiss, Timothy J. (1976). 'Cartesian Discourse and Classical Ideology'. *Diacritics* 6(4): 19–27.

Reiss, Timothy J. (1977). 'The *Concevoir* Motif in Descartes'. In: *La Cohérence intérieure: Études sur la littérature française du XVIIème siècle, présentées en homage à Judd D. Hubert*, J. van Baelen, D. L. Rubin (eds). Paris: Jean-Michele, pp. 203–22.

Reiss, Timonty J. (1982). *The Discourse of Modernism*. Ithaca, NY: Cornell University Press.

Romanowski, Sylvie (1974). *L'Illusion chez Descartes: La structure du discours cartésien*. Paris: Klincksieck.

Schonberger, Stephen (1939). 'A Dream of Descartes: Reflections on the Unconscious Determinations of the Sciences'. *International Journal of Psychology* 20: 43–57.

Serres, Michel (1982). 'Knowledge in the Classical Age: La Fontaine and Descartes'. In: *Hermes: Literature, Science, Philosophy*. Josue V. Harrair and David F. Bell (eds.), J. F. Harari, D. F. Bell (eds). Baltimore, MD: The Johns Hopkins University Press, pp. 15–28.

Smith, Norman Kemp (1966). *New Studies in the Philosophy of Descartes: Descartes as Pioneer*. London: Macmillan.

Williams, Bernard (1978). *Descartes: The Project of Pure Inquiry*. Atlantic Highlands, NJ: Humanities Press.

12 Psychoanalysis and sociology*
From Freudo-Marxism to Freudo-feminism

Reception contexts

Universities continue to organize themselves around the division of faculties. This dictates the division of departments that in turn dictate the division of subjects which constitute their curricula. At the same time, universities are encouraged to espouse multidisciplinary research to which they respond precisely because their faculties and postgraduate students have long recognized the practice of mixed knowledge or blurred genres. The arts and sciences now borrow so freely from each other both on the level of theory and of method that the wall that once separated the two cultures is now more like an overstretched borderline crossed daily by sociologists, philosophers, literary and psychoanalytic theorists. Yet somehow these borderlines still serve to inspire cultural theorists to the celebration of transgression, law-breaking and dis-affiliation (O'Neill, 1995). Here, of course, cultural workers enjoy rights of renunciation, violation and transit not shared by other workers whose transfiguration is blocked or stalled in messianic time.

Our present enlightenment severely tests our previous enlightenment. It therefore strains sociology, which is a child of the Enlightenment. It thereby invites sociologists to turn to psychoanalysis like that elder child in their family whose wounded self-knowledge and painful submission to society may deepen their understanding. The psychoanalysis turn may well appear to involve a retreat from sociology's determination to release us from pre-history, to let us out of the family, to unbind myth and emotion with knowledge and its freedoms. Hence, the wall between sociology and psychoanalysis. But it turns out that in its escape to freedom sociology may well have hurriedly packed its baggage with hasty notions of subjectivity, agency and law, of reason and imagination, of sexuality and of language. The result has been that in the past forty years or so sociologists have been obliged to return to the hermeneutical sciences, in particular to psychoanalysis. There are many shifts within the linguistic turn. In sociology's case, the shifts are through ordinary language philosophy (Wittgenstein, 1958) to hermeneutics

* Text of the essay taken from *Handbook of Social Theory* (2001). Edited by George Ritzer and Barry Smart. London: Sage. Pages 112–25. Reprinted with permission.

(Gadamer, 1975) to critical theory (Habermas, 1971) and to the linguistic return to Freud (Lacan, 1968), shifts that have restored the (un)conscious in reason's project (Ricouer, 1974).

What had to be challenged for Freud's sociological adaptation was his insistence upon universal knowledge of the human species and the primacy of internal over external factors in the determination of eventual behaviour. In 'Totem and Taboo', the struggle between the integrating force of Eros and the destructive force of primary masochism is tipped by the severity of the super-ego against individual desire in favour of the authority of institutions. Human prematurity and helplessness mean that aggression towards objects and others is the latent source of the aggression we form against ourselves in the name of external authorities. Clearly, Freud's position on the structure of the political unconscious is as hard on any Utopian movement as it is upon totalitarian regimes even though it may appear to offer no remedy on either score. The Freudian position is that political ideologies are projections divorced from their unconscious drives and defense mechanisms which prevent their recognition of their internal source of failure. As the creations of a 'purified ego', political ideologies project conflict-free futures guaranteed by the expulsion of the evils located in the father or in the property system. From this perspective, illusion will always have a future but the future will never emerge from illusions.

Psychoanalytic theory entered the social sciences earlier in the United States than the United Kingdom (Bocock, 1976; 1983). It did so prematurely – the effect being realized only in the 1960s and as a carrier of student body-politics, whose failure repeated the earlier failure of prewar Marxism to realize love's body. The second wave of psychoanalytic reception in both the US and the UK had to wait out the rise of 'French Marx' in the 1980s, which was itself a disciplinary response to failed revolution. Meantime, critical attention turned to the analysis of the constitutional bond between knowledge and power, to the madness and oppression in the heart of rationality. In the UK, the works of Laing (1969) and Cooper (1971) developed an existential anti-psychiatry (Sedgwick, 1982), compared to the work of Goffman (1961) and Szasz (1961) in the US and to the work of Foucault (1973) and Deleuze/Guattari (1977) in France. But it is from France that we inherit the 'return to Freud', that is, a return to the classic texts of psychoanalysis, an effect that was then multiplied in literary, philosophical and sociological readings of Freudian psychoanalysis. These studies have inspired the politics of sexual and racial identity, driving the new industry of cultural studies that transgress conventional disciplinary boundaries. They have also contributed to the redefinition of the academic labour force and the larger culture of the university. Thus the 'marriage' between sociology and psychoanalysis which was produced by rethinking the failure of 'the revolution' has contributed to the implosion of 'minoritarian' movements in the past two decades.

Against this rather sweeping characterization of events that far exceeds the contextualization that I have imposed upon them, I shall now follow through 'analytically', as Parsons would say, where sociology took on board what is needed from psychoanalysis to accomplish its own agenda. The Parsonian assumption of

Freud is given here in some detail because it provides a benchmark for many of the assertions and denials in the later, post-oedipal readings developed in particular by feminist theorists. The rubrics I shall have to employ are beholden to the contexts generated by the interaction of sociology and psychoanalysis:

1. Socialization theory
2. Civilization theory
3. Post-oedipal theory

So it must be understood that these organizational rubrics merely gesture towards 'encyclopaedism'. This is because we now live in an age of broken knowledge and fragmented justice whose drive towards integrity and solidarity can take no giant step.

Socialization theory

Parsons' basically Durkheimian theory of culture necessarily sets aside Freud's instinctualism or biologism in order to bring psychoanalysis into the liberal voluntarist paradigm of social interaction. For this reason, he vehemently rejected Wrong's (1961) resurrection of the anti-social instincts and his 'undialectical' construct of the 'oversocialized man'. Parsons' integrative bias overrides Freud's view that ambivalence is the bottom character of our social relations and as such always leaves us open to the possibility of regression. The costs of sublimation and sacrifice on behalf of society are so high that Freud was pessimistic about our ability to sustain them. As we shall see, later theorists (Fromm, Marcuse, Brown) adopt various revisionist strategies on this issue. On the level of psycho-history, Freud's concept of religion as an obsessional neurosis entirely separates him from Parsons' liberal progressive conception of the reinforcements of religion and capitalism in the development of modern individualism. Here, too, Parsons' conception of the liberal professions in the production of health, education and social management places them on a broader stage than Freud's clinic (O'Neill, 1995) – not to mention Goffman (1961) and Foucault's studies of the asylum (1973).

Yet Parsons read Freud very closely for his own analytic purpose. Parsons was especially attracted to Lecture XXXI of the *New Introductory Lecture on Psychoanalysis* (1974 [1933]), where Freud takes up 'The Dissection of the Psychical Personality'. Here Freud re-enters the 'physical underworld' to revisit the forces that result in ego-splitting (the overlapping of self-observation, judgment and punishment) that we attribute to the rule of conscience. Freud's phenomenon, however, is not Durkheim's social concept of conscience but that roller-coaster ride of moral depression and elation experienced by the melancholic. Nor is the super-ego Kant's heavenly lamp. It is a parental image through which the child becomes the severest judge of its fulfillment of the laws of perfection. Moreover, the super-ego cannot be located entirely on the level of ego-consciousness or of unconscious repression. Rather, both the ego and the superego are closer than not to the unconscious, or to the id. What is involved is a permeable psychic system whose subsystems 'translate' each other in the endless task of making more room for ego where there was once almost nothing but id (Freud, 1974 [1923]). Human conduct is structured hierarchically so that inputs are symbolically represented on the levels of the id, ego and super-ego (Figure 12.1).

Parsons appropriates the Freudian psychic apparatus by opening it towards the sociopsychic and psychocultural systems:

> How can the fundamental phenomenon of the internalization of moral norms be analyzed in such a way as to maximize the generality of implications of the formulation, both for the theory of personality and for the theory of the social system?
>
> (Parsons, 1964: 19–20)

In this device Parsons makes several analytical moves:

1. the relocation of the super-ego midway between the ego and the cultural system (with the id located on the level of the organism);

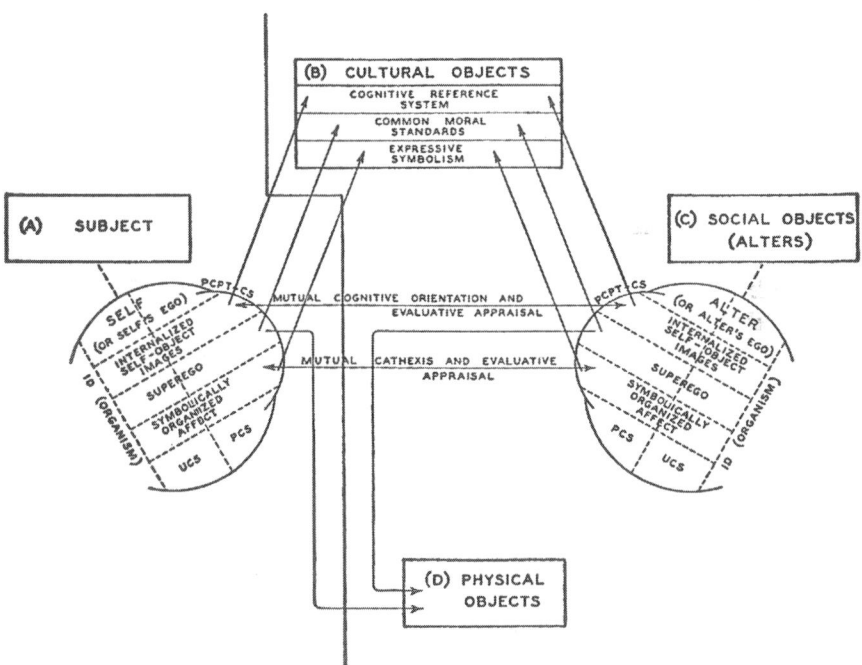

Figure 12.1 Psychic, social, and cultural systems. (From Talcott Parsons, *Social Structure and Personality*. New York: The Free Press, 1964, p. 37, renewed 1992 by Helen W. Parsons. Reproduced with permission of The Free Press, a division of Simon and Schuster, Inc. All rights reserved.)

2. the inclusion of the super-ego in the ego which internalizes three components (cognitive, moral, and expressive) of common culture which may be largely unconscious and subject to repression;
3. the self oriented cognitively and cathectively to a double environment of social and non-social objects within which

   (a) only culture can be internal;
   (b) emotions are symbolically generalized systems;
   (c) only ego-alter relations can be mutual.

Parsons was extremely critical of Freud's alleged separation between the personality system and its cultural environment. Because he neglected their mutual cultural conditioning, Freud was obliged to restrict the ego to a purely cognitive reading of its external environment and to assign all the work of collective identification to the super-ego. The result was to make the super-ego a more remote moral sensor of ego's attachments than need be if their common culture were recognized. Freud's limitation in this respect, Parsons argues, was due to his restricted concept of affective symbolism which he located between the ego and the id. In turn, Freud's parental identification mechanism is too reductive to account for the cultural acquisition of the symbolically generalized system of emotions that integrate the personality system and the social system on the level of the family (Parsons and Bales, 1955).

The socialization process must be seen as a two-way process of the personality system by the social system (here the sociological concept of *role* is the key) and of the social system by the personality system (here the psychoanalytic theory of *identification*, object cathexis, internalization is the other key). Parsons argues that the Freudian key opens the levels of id, ego and super-ego to each other provided what drives the personality system is not the instincts but a social interaction that is already operative at the breast. Here infant and mother learn to interpret one another's reactions and to generalize their pattern. Thus there already occurs an exchange between the endo-psychic and socio-psychic organization of the dyad that prefigures, so to speak, all later socialization on the levels of ego and super-ego. Social reproduction is already at work on the level of metabolism inasmuch as its bare material, physical and instinctual elements of feeding are the site and source of a hermeneutics through which mother and infant inaugurate a level of expectable, sanctionable conduct of care and feeding (O'Neill, 1992).

Parsons' baby is a social actor from the first day it steps onto the family stage. Henceforth, it will live for a love whose conditions it will be taught to win or lose:

> I think it a legitimate interpretation of Freud to say that only when the *need for love* has been established as the paramount goal of the personality can a genuine ego be present.
>
> (Parsons, 1964: 90, emphasis in original)

Parsons nevertheless claims that Freud lost the generalizability in his discovery of infant eroticism by interpreting the identification process in terms of the infant's desire to *be* the mother – with all its oedipal complications. Rather, what a child learns is to interact with the mother in terms of collectively defined roles through which family membership is reproduced. The infant is at first a dependent subject in relation to the mother whose point of view it will come to adopt as its own. Thus the child's investment in the maternal object-choice is the vehicle of its internalization of the collective norms represented to it through the mother's sanctioning of its progressive maturation. Upon this first level of maternal identification, the child can then build identifications with the family as a collective category as well, with its categories of sexual and generational identity. In this process, the mother becomes a lost-object in exchange for membership in the wider family. Once this is achieved, the super-ego is in place:

> The super-ego, then, is primarily the normative pattern governing the behaviour of the different members in their different roles in the family as a system.
> (Parsons, 1964: 96)

Parsons also questioned the restricted symbolic significance of the father in Freud's theory of socialization. The infant has to learn sex-role differentiation as a cultural categorization akin to age and status categorization. At the same time, the child must learn to differentiate instrumental-adaptive and expressive-integrative functions in relation to age and sex categorization. Here, Parsons argues, the incest taboo may be regarded as a cultural mechanism that shifts infant erotic dependency upon intrafamilial models to extrafamilial attachments to peers among whom the child is one of a kind, neither more nor less. By the same token, the parent figures are relativized as competitors among other extrafamilial authority figures just as the family culture yields primacy to school and workplace culture. In this developmental sequence the primacy of the oedipal father yields to authority orientation in the wider society where, of course, it may play a role in attitudes of conformity and rebellion (as we shall see in the following sections).

Civilization theory

It was not until after the Second World War that America again read Freud. This time it was not so much to promote sociology's narrow professional identity, but America itself. The question of America's destiny seriously divided cultural theorists into optimists and pessimists. America had helped to save democracy from fascism as well as to put capitalism in first place and to leave communism/socialism a poor runner-up. In return for Marshall Aid to rebuild Europe, however, the United States imported many European scholars, from rocket scientists to critical Marxists and Freudians. For our story, the irony is that it was the Frankfurt School of critical theory that reintroduced Freud to America. It also imported a sophisticated form of Marxist philosophy of the social sciences and cultural analysis that underwrote the establishment of left academic in Anglo-America (Jay, 1973; Slater, 1977). The Frankfurt School had turned to psychoanalysis to examine the eclipse of the proletarian revolution by fascist and totalitarian state regimes in Europe. With some change, they made the same move to examine why American capitalism subordinated liberal democracy to a corporate agenda masked by an ideology of narcissistic individualism and aggression (Slater, 1970).

Marx and Freud are not, of course, an easy marriage. While it owes as much to the rethinking of psychoanalysis as of Marxism, the birth of 'Freudo-Marxism' introduced an unruly child into the house of theory. The heart of the matter is the temptation to reduce political revolution to sexual revolution (Chasseguet-Smirgel and Grunberger, 1986). This demand requires two other moves, that is, to treat the *economy* as the source of an historically produced *scarcity* and to treat the *family* as the corresponding source of sexual *repression*. One can then reverse Marxist-analysis with psychoanalysis: emancipate sexuality from the (bourgeois) family and the result will be happiness underwritten by an economy of abundance. Only Marx and Freud are left with a frown on their faces! This does not bring them any closer. We are back to the civilization question (Tester, 1992) or the question of the nature of human nature – is it rooted in biology or is its biology *révisable*? Is human nature anti-social and unhappy in civilization or is socialized humanity and its sublimations proof that human nature is only second nature? We should now consider how these arguments took their course in the works of Marcuse (1955), Brown (1959) and Rieff (1959, 1966).

What was needed was the elaboration of an historical materialist psychology to move beyond weak notions of false consciousness among the masses and conspiratorial theories of elite ideology which worked together to 'save' Marxist revolutionary theory from its historical failures. In current terms, it was necessary to spell out the intervening mechanisms through which the economic substructure determines the cultural superstructure in capitalist society. The turn to Freud was a turn from both 'vulgar Hegelian' and 'vulgar Marxist' accounts of the civilization relations between economy, society and personality. This turn was taken in the publication by the Frankfurt Institute of Social Research of *Studies in Authority and Family* (Forschungsberichte, 1936). It was Erich Fromm who made the initial moves, drawing upon Freud's later cultural works (1920 onwards). These drew upon anthropology and social psychology to deal with the central issues of political authority, mass psychology and the role of the super-ego in the allegiance to cultural ideologies. In Freud's essays on 'Totem and Taboo' (1974 [1912–13]), 'The Future of an Illusion' (1974 [1927]), 'Civilization and its Discontents' (1974 [1930]), for example, it is clear that the psyche is socially and historically conditioned, even though Freud seriously overweighs the present and future with the burden of the past. This, of course, is why the very notion of any alliance between Marxism and psychoanalysis has always appeared a retrograde step bound to mire critical theory in Freud's undialectical dualism of Eros and Thanatos (as Reich, 1945, and Marcuse, 1955, were to argue).

Fromm argued that the drives (instincts) are not what determine human history. Indeed, there would be no 'history', that is, no development of humanity without the mediation of institutions which socialize individuals to cathect behaviour that is normative and thereby regular for given constellations of economy, polity and society. The periodization of these institutional contexts is the work of Marxist materialist history. This is not our concern in any detail except to note that historical 'laws' require what J.S. Mill calls 'middle principles' (*Logic*, BK VI) to connect with individual conduct. It is tempting to assign this work to the agency of religion, law and the police. But the analytic issue is how these forces of law and order achieve their purpose through behaviour that is more orderly than not. Why don't individuals withdraw their labour, play truant, abandon themselves to pleasure and perversion? How do they tolerate inequality, racism and genderism? Fromm's answer is that order is not achieved through 'vulgar Freudian' notions of repression and sublimation imposed on the drives by the collusion of the super-ego with the death instinct. Order is achieved through a libidinal adaptation to economic necessity translated through the family's class position, occupation and income. Fromm, following Reich (1945), shifted Freud's emphasis from the intrafamilial dynamics that shape individual fates to the broader structure of economic relations to which families must respond, thereby instituting a largely unconscious environment of possible and impossible conducts (character structure).

The analytic innovation here is the search for a concept of the sociological unconscious which is formed under the pressure of class position and expressed in attitudes towards authority, rebellion and ritualistic conformity in a wider range of cultural and personal behaviour (Richards, 1984). Fromm (1942, 1956, 1984) was concerned with the social contradiction between the ideological sovereignty of the individual and the psychosocial fact of individual impotence and its wide political consequences. The compensatory 'busyness' in everyone from the entrepreneur to the housewife and data-driven researcher – and even the psychoanalyst – is the mark of their alienation from productive humanity. Fromm may even have argued that this impotence underlies critical theory's own inability to connect theory and praxis. Its resolution to live with the 'non-identity thesis', that is, the divorce between empirical and transcendental history, remains the mark of intellectual impotence and its own surrender to repressive tolerance. In this regard, Fromm's early work (1937, 1970) on the administrative techniques of the German state, and school system and penal systems as a disciplinary regime that reinforces petty-bourgeois hegemony and mass submission (O'Brien, 1976), is well ahead of later work by Gramsci and Foucault. Fromm also anticipated the criticism that the Freudian analyst-patient relationship abstains from reflection on the bourgeois character structure of repression and tolerance.

Prior to entering the Marcuse/Brown readings of Freud, it may be useful to insert Rieff's reading of the question to what extent successful psychoanalysis requires adjustment to or rejection of the civilizing process. Unlike Habermas (1971), Rieff separates psychotherapy from any overall emancipatory drive since this only reintroduces an illusion of salvation and community. 'Psychological man' operates on the basis of self-knowledge and world-knowledge, combining the strengths of a scientist and an entrepreneur in acting upon himself. Because he understands his internal dissatisfactions, he can steer through the obstacles set by civilization. For Rieff, Freud is a cultural hero. But not for long; a few years later he found that the psychologization of psychoanalysis had the upper hand:

Where the family and nation once stood, or Church and Party, there will be hospital and theatre too, the normative institutions of the next culture. Trained to be incapable of sustaining sectarian satisfaction, psychological man cannot be susceptible to sectarian control. Religious man was born to be saved; psychological man is born to be pleased. The difference was established long ago when 'I believe', the cry of the ascetic, lost precedence to 'one feels', the caveat of the therapeutic. And if the therapeutic is to win out, then surely the psychotherapist will be his secular spiritual guide.

(Rieff, 1966: 24–5)

The full sense of this observation would involve an extended analysis of arguments regarding the symbiosis between the politics of intimacy, the sexualization of economic life, and the mystification of the bases of social control and power in advanced capitalist society.

In fact this becomes the focus of Christopher Lasch's *The Culture of Narcissism* (1979), whose thesis is his concern with the displacement of the socialization functions of the bourgeois family onto professional, bureaucratic and state agencies. These agencies foster the narcissistic culture generated in the reduced families whose main function is consumption (aided by TV viewing) rather than production. The narcissistic personality is the perfect expression of the weakened family *vis-à-vis* the state and economy which recruit only privatized consumers. Thus Lasch argued that the schools, juvenile courts, health and welfare services, advertising and the media all function to erode the authority of the family. The result is that the family is increasingly a place where narcissistic individuals learn to compete with one another in the consumption of services and goods – emotional, political and economic – but with a diminished capacity for the competence required in their production. Yet, when Lasch himself looked for a counterculture to narcissism, the best he himself could do was to locate it in the hard school of the very rich, realistic about privilege and victimization, busy in the pursuit of studies, music lessons, ballet, tennis and parties 'through which the propertied rich acquire discipline, courage, persistence, and self-possession' (Lasch, 1979: 371).

Whatever Freud's views on utopianism, his reflections on the high cost of 'civilization' permitted a second wave of Marxo-Freudianism in Marcuse's *Eros and Civilization* (1955) and Norman O. Brown's great renunciation of the spirit of Protestantism and capitalism in *Life Against Death* (1959) and *Love's Body* (1966). Both books, despite Marcuse's rejection of Brown's utopianism and Brown's dismissal of Marcuse's inability to get libidinal, became cult texts of the 1960s. The core issue between them – as between Freud and Reich – is over the concept of sublimation or the connection between culture and (infant) sexuality in the sacrifice of pleasure and the realization of society. The 'post-Freudian' solution is to drop the infantile psychic apparatus by historicizing the patriarchal family character to release full genitality, the body without organs (Deleuze and Guattari, 1977), the libidinal economy of *jouissance* (Lyotard, 1993) and (be) coming woman (Jardine, 1985). The danger in these moves is that they fall into the denunciation of institutions and authority in the name of fictionality and desire.

Moreover, the relative autonomy of the cultural sphere guarantees that cultural politics will make headway in academia and the media. Thus particular cultural strategies like (de)constructionism and minoritarianism serve to redistribute symbolic capitals yet not necessarily alter the inequality that governs cultural capitalism (an issue to which we return in the final section of this chapter).

In *Life Against Death* Norman O. Brown attacked capitalism at its very foundations, that is, its excremental vision, its noxious composition of denunciation and denial of the body's gifts unless congealed in the fetishes of property, money and jewelry. Capitalism is therefore a neurosis built out of self-hatred. Its hold upon us deepens once it combines with the anal virtues of orderliness, parsimony and obstinacy prized in the Protestant ethic. Brown pursues the dead body of Protestant capitalism as the proper equivalent of Freud's death instinct which otherwise confounds social progress. He also traces the same life-denying impulses in the domination of science and technology, raising the question of what a life-affirmative or 'non-morbid' science would look like. Brown also looked at archaic economies that were not governed either by overproduction or scarcity. He questioned the Freudian principle of sublimation as a misreading of historical economies of non-enjoyment which conquered the archaic economies of the gift and social solidarity.

The economy of repressive sublimation and anality rests upon the death instinct, Brown argues, because we are *unable to die*. This is rooted in the infant's refusal to be separated from the mother-body and in the prolonged fetalization of human beings. It is the source of our combined morbidity and possessiveness. It is also the origin of our search for self-creation, of our quest for parthenogenesis, hermaphroditism and androgyny and of the current mythology of possessive sexual identities which in effect espouse death-in-life by fleeing from death:

> Science and civilization combine to articulate the core of the human neurosis, man's incapacity to live in the body, which is also his incapacity to die.
>
> (Brown, 1959: 303)

Curiously enough, there is a more profound historical analysis of capitalism in Brown than in Marcuse, to whose historicization of psychoanalysis we now turn. This is because Marcuse was preoccupied with a critique of the conservative consequences of liberalism (rather than fascism) in late capitalism. Mention must also be made of Marcuse's rehabilitation of the *revolutionary* philosophy of Hegel (Marcuse, 1960), if we are to understand his strategy of saving Freud for a revolutionary reading. Marcuse – like Horkheimer and Adorno – was therefore not entirely critical of the bourgeois family inasmuch as it was the site of the struggle between patriarchalism and radical individualism. However, by the time of *One-Dimensional Man* (1964), Marcuse had abandoned the argument that the family was a critical site of emancipation. The corporate agenda now bypasses the family through direct media manipulation of individuals and the individualization of male, female and child labour driven by compulsive desires.

Marcuse adopted two analytical strategies in order to make his argument that psychological concepts are political concepts. The first was to historicize the psychic costs of civilization by placing them wholly on the side of the reality principle, that is, the social organization of an economy of scarcity, rather than on the side of the pleasure principle regarded as an innately anti-social and unsatisfiable drive. This move generated the second argument that repression is always surplus-repression created by the political failure to open up the liberal freedoms that would flow from an economy of abundance. Marcuse rescued the revolutionary principle of the pleasure principle (Freud, 1974 [1920]), not only by arguing for a Utopian future but by grounding it in a cognitive function of preserving the past critical memory of happiness as a standard for political change:

> If memory moves into the centre of psychoanalysis as a decisive mode of *cognition*, this is far more than a therapeutic device; the therapeutic role of memory derives from the *truth value* of memory. Its truth value lies in the specific function of memory to preserve promises and potentialities which are betrayed and even outlawed by the mature, civilized individual, but which had once been fulfilled in his dim past and which are never entirely forgotten. The reality principle restrains the cognitive function of memory – its commitment to the past experience of happiness which spurns the desire for its conscious recreation. The psychoanalytic liberation of memory explodes the rationality of the repressed individual. As cognition gives way to recognition, the forbidden images and impulses of childhood begin to tell the truth that reason denies. Regression assumes a progressive function. The rediscovered past yields critical standards which are tabooed by the present. Moreover, the restoration of memory is accompanied by the restoration of the cognitive content of phantasy. Psychoanalytic theory removes these mental faculties from the noncommittal sphere of daydreaming and fiction and recaptures their strict truths. The weight of these discoveries must eventually shatter the framework in which they were made and confined. The liberation of the past does not end in its reconciliation with the present. Against the self-imposed restraint of the discoverer, the orientation on the past tends toward an orientation on the future. The *recherche du temps perdu* becomes the vehicle of future liberation.
>
> (Marcuse, 1955: 18, emphasis in original)

In this way Marcus released Freud's deadlock between Eros and Thanatos. He denied there is any social organization of the death instinct, although he conceded that aggression is a necessary byproduct of repression. In late capitalism social domination bypasses the patriarchal family. Domination becomes the work of the anonymous corporate administration of individualized desires that supply the content of happiness without the creativity of the pleasure principle.

To resist what he calls 'the corporealization of the super-ego', Marcuse argued that phantasy serves a positive historical task of preserving the collective aspiration for happiness and security, preserved in the cultural myths of Orpheus and

Narcissus rather than the productivist myth of Prometheus, which prolongs the conflict between man and nature. Against Freud, Marcuse reads Narcissus as a figure of subjective and world harmonization and non-repressive sublimation exercised in art, play and contemplation as truly human aspirations, and the basis for an alternative reality principle (see Alford, 1988 for critical discussion). So far from encouraging narcissism in any vulgar sense, Marcuse in fact drew upon the mythological and aesthetic tradition of Narcissus and Orpheus pitted against the tradition of Prometheus:

> The Orphic and Narcissistic experience of the world negates that which sustains the world of the performance principle. The opposition between man and nature, subject and object, is overcome. Being is experienced as gratification, which unites man and nature so that the fulfillment of man is at the same time the fulfillment, without violence, of nature....This liberation is the work of Eros. The song of Orpheus breaks the petrification, moves the forests and the rocks – but moves them to partake in joy.
>
> (Marcuse, 1955: 150–1)

It is in terms of this aesthetic myth that Marcuse then adapted Freud's theory of *primary narcissism*, which he interpreted not as a neurotic symptom but as a constitutive element in the construction of reality and of a mature, creative ego with the potential for transforming the world in accordance with a *new science of nature:*

> The striking paradox that narcissism, usually understood as egotistic withdrawal from reality, here is connected with oneness with the universe, reveals the new depth of the conception: beyond all immature autoeroticism, narcissism denotes a fundamental relatedness to reality which may generate a comprehensive existential order.
>
> (Marcuse, 1955: 27)

In France the Marxist turn to Freud had to get past the official line of the Communist Party on psychoanalysis as a bourgeois subjectifying ideology. It has also to skirt Sartre's (1957) existentialist critique of the positivist bias of psychoanalytic explanation. Yet Sartre, especially through Laing and Cooper in the UK, was also the source of an anti-psychiatric movement, which picked up with Foucault (1973). In the course of events, psychoanalysis provided arguments for the anti-psychiatry movement but then fell foul of it as an establishment ideology of familized order and capitalist repression (Turkle, 1981). The principle work here is *Anti-Oedipus: Capitalism and Schizophrenia* (1977), in which Deleuze and Guattari excoriate oedipalism in the name of the schizoanalytic meltdown of Freudocapitalism.

Desire must be released from the 'Daddy-Mommy-Me' nucleus of capitalist society where desire is constitutionally castrated, where it is always less than itself, always ready to be sacrificed to smaller and more sensible pleasures.

Whereas Freud struggled to re-oedipalize the 'bodies-without-organs' he had discovered in his case histories, especially of Little Hans (1974 [1909]), Wolf Man (1974 [1918]) and Schreber (1974 [1911]), Deleuze and Guattari unleash them as the schizoid exemplars of post-capitalist desire:

> There is no such thing as the social production of reality on the one hand, and a desiring-production that is mere fantasy on the other. The only connections that could be established between these two productions would be secondary ones of introjection and projection, as though all social practices had their precise counterpart in introjected or internal mental practices, or as though mental practices were projected upon social systems, without either of the two sets of practices ever having any real or concrete effect upon the other. As long as we are content to establish a perfect parallel between money, gold, capital, and the capitalist triangle on the one hand, and the libido, the anus, the phallus, and the family triangle on the other, we are engaging in an enjoyable pastime, but the mechanisms of money remain totally unaffected by the anal projections of those who manipulate money. The Marx-Freud parallelism between the two remains utterly sterile and insignificant as long as it is expressed in terms that make them introjections or projections of each other without ceasing to be utterly alien to each other, as in the famous equation money = shit. The truth of the matter is that *social production is purely and simply desiring-production itself under determinate conditions*. We maintain that the social field is immediately invested by desire, that it is the historically determined product of desire, and that libido has no need of any mediation or sublimation, any psychic operation, any transformation, in order to invade and invest the productive forces and the relations of production. *There is only desire and the social, and nothing else.*
>
> (Deleuze and Guattari, 1977: 28–9,
> emphasis in original)

Schizoanalysis merely reiterates the aftereffect of capitalism's desperate attempt to simultaneously dam and to unbind unlimited desire, its invention of non-hierarchical bodies in endless states of agitation, flow, copulation and consumption.

The theoretical *rapprochement* between French Freud and French Marx was the work of Louis Althusser, who developed scientific, that is, structuralist and anti-humanist, accounts of Marx, Freud and Lacan. The common ground was found in the concept of ideology, which Althusser identified with the a-historical unconscious (Žižek, 1989). Thus history has no subject-centre except through 'inter-pellation', or being called up by an ideological apparatus in which any subject (mis)recognizes itself as the subject of social practices and rituals:

> We observe that the structure of all ideology, interpellating individuals as subjects in the name of a Unique and Absolute Subject, is *speculary*, i.e., a mirror-structure, and *doubly* specular: this mirror duplication is constitutive of ideology and ensures its functioning. Which means that all ideology is

centred, that the Absolute Subject occupies the unique place of the Centre, and interpellates around it the infinity of individuals into subjects in a double mirror-connexion such that it *subjects* the subjects to the Subject, while giving them in the Subject in which each subject can contemplate its own image (present and future) the *guarantee* that this really concerns them and Him, and that since everything takes place in the Family (the Holy Family: the Family is in essence Holy), 'God will *recognize* his own in it', i.e., those who have recognized God, and have recognized themselves in Him, will be saved.

Let me summarize what we have discovered about ideology in general.

The duplicate mirror-structure of ideology ensures simultaneously:

1. the interpellation of 'individuals' as subjects;
2. their subjection to the Subject;
3. the mutual recognition of subjects and Subject, the subjects' recognition of each other, and finally the Subject's recognition of himself;
4. the absolute guarantee that everything really is so, and that on condition that the subjects recognize what they are and behave accordingly, everything will be all right: Amen – *'So be it'*.

Result: caught in this quadruple system of interpellation as subjects, of subjection to the Subject, of universal recognition and of absolute guarantee, the subjects 'work', they 'work by themselves' in the vast majority of cases, with the exception of the 'bad subjects' who on occasion provoke the intervention of one of the detachments of the (repressive) State apparatus.

(Althusser, 1971: 168–9)

Althusser's hybridization of Marxism and psychoanalysis brings us full circle. This time the individual is over-socialized through an ideological mirror of subjectivity in which the individual sees subjection as how things are. We have lost the rebelliousness of the unconscious and surrendered transgressive desire to normalcy in the name of the state cultural apparatus. The insight of psychoanalysis is the blindness of sociology.

Post-oedipalism

Here we will treat the main arguments in the reception/rejection of Freudian psychoanalysis that have played a role in the articulation of feminism as a particular strategy within the larger history of women's movements (Lovell, 1996; Mitchell, 1974). It need hardly be said that women experience inferiority, aggression and exploitation. Their sexual lives prior to and within marriage are largely controlled by patriarchal ideologies which in turn have dominated their economic and political lives (Ortner, 1974; Rubin, 1975). The specific exploitation of women has been a blind spot even in Marxist thought and has again necessitated a turn to Freud in order to rethink woman's sexuality, the socio-psychic costs of reproduction and the need to redefine heterosexual relations. It was necessary to historicize the second-sex ideology of woman's otherness (de Beauvoir, 1961; Rich, 1978; Wittig, 1973), the feminine mystique (Friedman, 1963) that confined women to Victorian hysteria, to patriarchalism (Eistenstein, 1981; Figes, 1970) and, above all, to psychic and social castration (Greer, 1971). Feminist scholarship (Greene and Kahn, 1985) is now so vast and so well-received that it is impossible to summarize without losing the nuances of early Anglo-American feminism and of Franco-feminism fuelled by Lacanian psychoanalysis, deconstruction and semiotics (Marks and de Courtivron, 1980). The result has been to reconstruct patriarchal ideas of the feminine (Pateman, 1988), of mothering, household and childcare in ways that encourage women to assume social and political agency in their own right/write.

The feminist fascination with Lacan has to be one of the most difficult relationships to understand – it is perhaps *the* enigma of the woman's movement (Benjamin, 1988; Cixous and Clement, 1986; Flax, 1990; Gallop, 1982; Irigaray, 1985; Kofman, 1985; Ragland-Sullivan, 1987). Since all the versions cannot be satisfactorily explored, we must try to set out an analytic core in Lacan. Taken with the earlier accounts of Parsons and Althusser, this excursus may help the reader to estimate the balance of the feminist 'return to Freud'. Lacan re-read Freud and was in turn read into philosophy, psychoanalysis, anti-psychiatry, women's studies and so on, only to be rejected by critics of his own residual Freudianism! Lacan's departure was to revise Freudian psychologism just as Althusser rejected Marx's humanism and once again reconnected Marxism and psychoanalysis. Analytically, then, Lacan's contribution to sociology was to reject the search for influences or determinisms between individual behaviour and social institutions. Society is never beyond the individual because it dwells in the language each of us speaks and thereby appropriates subjectivity/objectivity, masculine/feminine etc. Society does not erase a state of nature with its imposition of Law. The categories of kinship and patriarchy are invoked in the oedipal family to shift the pre-oedipal infant from the imaginary order of maternal fusion to the symbolic order of social difference. For Lacan individualism is an illusion that originates in the (maternal) mirror and thereafter constitutes the subject as an endless question for its own return. This is the modus operandi of the subject of slavery and seduction, of the patient and student subject, of the consumer and political subject, in short of innumerable capital bodies that are the objects of psychoanalytically based culture criticism.

While the tension between psychoanalysis and feminism has been enormously creative, its source should not be overlooked. The feminist appropriation of psychoanalysis involved a political *volte face*. Jacqueline Rose puts the nub of the issue:

> The difficulty is to pull psychoanalysis...towards a recognition of the faulty social constitution of identity and norms, and then back again to that point of tension between ego and unconscious where they are endlessly re-modeled and endlessly break.
>
> (Rose, 1986: 7)

To the extent that post-oedipal feminism abandons the pre-oedipal matrix, its anti-patriarchal politics of women's sexuality overlooks the pre-oedipal limits set by the unconscious to identity and plurality claims around sexual difference, patriarchal ideology and aggression as purely social constructs. Thus feminist legal theorists (Bower, 1991) have taken conflicting positions on the question of motherhood and the maternal in public life. In turn, the challenges of combining working and mothering, reproductive control, especially abortion practice, and affirmative action directed by women's identity politics has also led to considerable theoretical work by legal feminists (Cornell, 1991; Mackinnon, 1983), and even to a maternal jurisprudence (West, 1988).

It may be useful here to insert Kristeva's attempt to move beyond the alternatives represented by *liberal* feminism (equal access to symbolic capital) and *radical* feminism (deconstruction of symbolic capital) in the name of difference. Kristeva opens up a *metaphysical* deconstruction of the masculine/feminine dichotomy (Kristeva, 1981). In positive terms, Kristeva embraces marginality, subversion and dissidence grounded in the pre-oedipal mother-body and its semiotic transcendence of gender division. However, other feminists have not aligned with this position since, like Chodorow (1978), they start from the position that motherhood merely reproduces patriarchalism and commits daughters to an ideology of care and rearing from which they must be emancipated to become women. They have been even more reluctant to take on Kristeva's re-appropriation of religion and the trinitarian semiotics of maternal divinity (Crownfield, 1992).

Any remarks on the range of women's theorizing have to be qualified by conceding the problem of generalizing upon specific grounds and strategies of advancement that women have adopted in government, social policy, health, childcare, education and the workplace. Obviously, women have made major gains in redefining the institutions that affect their lives. Here the task is to estimate what has been the role of women's appropriation of psychoanalysis in their expanded socioeconomic and political lives. In the first place, women have broadened the distinction between 'pure knowledge' and 'political knowledge' (Haraway, 1991; Jardine, 1985) inasmuch as the realities they challenge prove to have been gendered constructions that privilege male interest. They have also broadened the male narrative that governed modernity, either to soften it with its own female side (Silverman, 1992) or to set out an open-ended female socio-narrative of becoming-woman (gynesis). More recently, Judith Butler (1993) has suggested that gays/lesbians adopt the strategy of appropriating the designation of 'queer', to extricate it from its normative stigma as pathological practice and to reassign its performative power through self-naming. A similar strategy has appealed to gays, lesbians, blacks and those with disabilities seeking to deconstruct and re-assign their place in a democratic society. Yet it cannot be presumed that there is no remainder of self-assigned difference within these groups. It remains a difficult matter to gauge the effectiveness of political theatre based upon 'acting up' underprivileged identities. The political tolerance (which includes funding) of its margins is at least as much a sign of the power of a social system as of its potential transformation.

In fairness, it must be noted that the work of deconstructing male/female dichotomies has engaged male theorists as much as female theorists. In the US the work of Stoller (1968) and of Money and Ehrhardt (1972) on the biological and cultural factors in sexual differentiation was path breaking. Once the door to social constructionism (Berger and Luckmann, 1967; Goffman, 1961) opened, a great deal of the programme was set for later gender and race studies. Women have demystified their self-concept, empowered themselves in the field of symbolic capital and implemented organizational forms of practical action whose development will be in their own hands. What is at stake are new formulations of politics, ethics and aesthetics, at one level, and new relations of authority, care and democracy in the lifeworld that will shift the intergenerational burdens of women.

The shift from early capitalist gendered economies (contemporaneous with traditional economies) to late capitalist economic sexism (Illich, 1982) has not altered the contradiction between increased exploitation of women and their new freedom in the market place (O'Neill, 1991). Here the current reconfiguration of the welfare state is of enormous consequence for women and children in single parent households, for working women and elder women (O'Neill, 1994). It is important to remember that it is easier for academic women to make inroads on the canon, figurability and the erotic imagination, in short, to re-write and re-read 'woman', than it is for women outside of academia to achieve such voice.

Conclusion

Sociology cannot ignore its basic assumptions about human nature. All the same, sociologists do not wish to trade upon religious, philosophical and psychological conceptions of human nature. This is because sociologists suspect that any theory of human nature is a covert theory of social and political order. It turns out that all social thinkers have to make some fundamental decision on what we may call the *Hobbesian problem of order* (Carveth, 1984; O'Neill, 1972), that is, how far is human nature sociable, or other-regarding? We are divided between egoists and altruists; we are split between the parties of order and dis(order), between Eros and Thanatos. No theory is adequate that ignores the complexity of the relations between reason and the passions, or the costs of socialization and sublimation. No social theory can entirely separate history and structure without inviting deconstruction and revision. Thus sociology and psychoanalysis remain uneasy yet necessary partners.

References

Alford, C. Fred (1988). *Narcissism: Socrates, the Frankfurt School, and Psychoanalytic Theory*. New Haven, CT: Yale University Press.

Althusser, Louis (1971). *Lenin and Philosophy and Other Essays*. London: New Left Books.

de Beauvoir, Simone (1961). *The Second Sex*. New York: Bantam.

Benjamin, Jessica (1988). *The Bonds of Love*. New York: Pantheon Books.

Berger, Peter, and Luckmann, Thomas (1967). *The Social Construction of Reality*. New York: Doubleday.

Bocock, Robert (1976). *Freud and Modern Society: An Outline and Analysis of Freud's Sociology*. New York: Holmes and Meier.

Bocock, Robert (1983). *Sigmund Freud*. Chichester: Ellis Horwood Ltd.

Bower, Lisa C. (1991). 'Mother in Law: Conceptions of Mother and the Maternal in Feminisms and Feminist Legal Theory'. *Differences: A Journal of Feminist Cultural Studies* 3(1): 8–37.

Brown, Norman O. (1959). *Life Against Death: The Psychoanalytical Meaning of History*. New York: Vintage Books.

Brown, Norman O. (1966). *Love's Body*. New York: Random House.

Butler, Judith (1993). *Bodies That Matter: On the Discursive Limits of 'Sex'*. New York: Routledge.

Carveth, Donald L. (1984). 'Psychoanalysis and Social Theory: The Hobbesian Problem Revisited'. *Psychoanalysis and Contemporary Thought* 7(1): 43–98.

Chasseguet-Smirgel, Janine, and Grunberger, Bêla (1986). *Freud or Reich? Psychoanalysis and Illusion*. Trans. Claire Pajaczkowska. London: Free Association Books.

Chodorow, Nancy (1978). *The Reproduction of Mothering: Psychoanalysis and the Sociology of Gender*. Berkeley, CA: University of California Press.

Cixous, Hélène, and Clement, Catherine (1986). *The Newly Born Woman*. Minneapolis: University of Minnesota Press.

Cooper, David (1971). *Psychiatry and Anti-Psychiatry*. New York: Ballantine Books.

Cornell, Drucilla P. (1991). *Beyond Accommodation: Ethical Feminism, Deconstruction, and the Law*. New York: Routledge.

Crownfield, David R. (ed.) (1992). *Body/Text in Julia Kristeva: Religion, Women, and Psychoanalysis*. Albany, NY: State University of New York Press.

Deleuze, Gilles, and Guattari, Félix (1977). *Anti-Oedipus: Capitalism and Schizophrenia*. New York: The Viking Press.

Eisenstein, Zillah R. (1981). *The Radical Future of Liberal Feminism*. Boston, MA: Northeastern University Press.

Figes, Eva (1970). *Patriarchal Attitudes*. London: Faber and Faber.

Flax, Jane (1990). *Thinking Fragments: Psychoanalysis, Feminism, and Postmodernism in the Contemporary West*. Berkeley, CA: University of California Press.

Forschungsberichte aus dem Institut fur Sozialforschung (1936). *Studien über Autoritat und Familie*. Paris: Alcan.

Foucault, Michel (1973). *Madness and Civilization: A History of Insanity in the Age of Reason*. New York: Vintage Books.

Freud, Sigmund [1974 (1909]. 'Analysis of a Phobia in a Five-Year-Old Boy'. *Standard Edition of the Complete Psychological Works*. Vol. X. London: Hogarth Press.

Freud, Sigmund (1974 [1911]). 'Psycho-Analytical Notes on an Autobiographical Account of a Case of Paranoia (Dementia Paranoides'. *Standard Edition of the Complete Psychological Works*. Vol. XII. London: Hogarth Press.

Freud, Sigmund (1974 [1912–13]). 'Totem and Taboo'. *Standard Edition of the Complete Psychological Works*. Vol. XIII. London: Hogarth Press.

Freud, Sigmund (1974 [1918].'From the History of an Infantile Neurosis'. *Standard Edition of the Complete Psychological Works*. Vol. XVII. London: Hogarth Press.

Freud, Sigmund (1974 [1920]). 'Beyond the Pleasure Principle'. *Standard Edition of the Complete Psychological Works*. Vol. XVIII. London: Hogarth Press.

Freud, Sigmund (1974 [1923]). 'The Ego and the Id'. *Standard Edition of the Complete Psychological Works*. Vol. XIX. London: Hogarth Press.

Freud, Sigmund (1974 [1927]). 'The Future of an Illusion'. *Standard Edition of the Complete Psychological Works*. Vol. XXI. London: Hogarth Press.

Freud, Sigmund (1974 [1930]). 'Civilization and its Discontents', *Standard Edition of the Complete Psychological Works*. Vol. XXI. London: Hogarth Press.

Freud, Sigmund (1974 [1933]). 'New Introductory Lectures on Psychoanalysis'. *Standard Edition of the Complete Psychological Works*. Vol. XXI. London: Hogarth Press.

Friedman, Betty (1963). *The Feminine Mystique*. New York: Dell Publishing.

Fromm, Erich (1937). 'Zum Gefühl der Ohnmacht'. *Zeitschift für Sozialfurschung* 6: 95–119.

Fromm, Erich (1942). *Escape from Freedom*. London: Routledge.

Fromm, Erich (1956). *The Sane Society*. London: Routledge.

Fromm, Erich (1970). *The Crisis of Psychoanalysis: Essays on Freud, Marx and Social Psychology*. New York: Henry Holt and Company.

Fromm, Erich (1984). *The Working Class in Weimar Germany: A Psychological and Sociological Study*. Trans. Barbara Weinberger. Leamington Spa: Berg.

Gadamer, Hans-Georg (1975). *Truth and Method*. New York: The Seabury Press.

Gallop, Jane (1982). *The Daughter's Seduction: Feminism and Psychoanalysis*. Ithaca, NY: Cornell University Press.

Greene, Gayle, and Kahn, Coppelia (1985). *Making a Difference: Feminist Literary Criticism*. London: Methuen.

Greer, Germaine (1971). *The Female Eunuch*. New York: McGraw-Hill.

Goffman, Irving (1961). *Asylums: Essays on the Social Situation of Mental Patients and Other Inmates*. New York: Doubleday, Anchor Books.

Habermas, Jürgen (1971). *Knowledge and Human Interests*. Boston, MA: Beacon Press.

Haraway, Donna J. (1991). *Simians, Cyborgs, and Women: The Reinvention of Nature*. New York: Routledge.

Illich, Ivan (1982). *Gender*. New York: Pantheon Books.

Irigaray, Luce (1985). *This Sex Which Is Not One*. Ithaca, NY: Cornell University Press.

Jardine, Alice A. (1985). *Gynesis: Configurations of Woman and Modernity*. Ithaca, NY: Cornell University Press.

Jay, Martin (1973). *The Dialectical Imagination: A History of the Frankfurt School and the Institute of Social Research, 1923–1950*. Boston, MA: Little, Brown and Company.

Kofman, Sarah (1985). *The Enigma of Woman: Woman in Freud's Writings*. Ithaca, NY: Cornell University Press.

Kristeva, Julia (1981). 'Women's Time'. *Signs* 7(1): 13–35.

Lacan, Jacques (1968). *The Language of the Self: The Function of Language in Psychoanalysis*. New York: Dell Publishing.

Laing, R. D. (1969). *Politics of Experience*. Harmondsworth: Penguin.

Lasch, Christopher (1979). *The Culture of Narcissism: American Life in an Age of Diminishing Expectations*. New York: W.W. Norton.

Lovell, Terry (1996). 'Feminist Social Theory'. In: *The Blackwell Companion to Social Theory*. ed. Bryan S. Turner. Oxford: Blackwell, pp. 307–39.

Lyotard, Jean-François (1993). *Libidinal Economy*. London: The Athlone Press.

Mackinnon, Catherine (1983). 'Feminism, Marxism, Method and the State: Toward Feminist Jurisprudence'. *Signs* 8 (4): 635–58.

Marcuse, Herbert (1955). *Eros and Civilization: A Philosophical Inquiry into Freud*. Boston, MA: Beacon Press.

Marcuse, Herbert (1960). *Reason and Revolution: Hegel and the Rise of Social Theory*. Boston, MA: Beacon Press.

Marcuse, Herbert (1964). *One-Dimensional Man*. Boston, MA: Beacon Press.

Marks, Elaine, and de Courtivron, Isabelle (1980). *New French Feminisms*. Amherst, MA: University of Massachusetts Press.

Mitchell, Juliet (1974). *Psychoanalysis and Feminism*. London: Penguin Books.

Money, John, and Ehrhardt, Anke M. (1972). *Man and Woman Boy and Girl: The Differentiation and Dimorphism of Gender Identity from Conception to Maturity*. Baltimore, MD: The Johns Hopkins University Press.

O'Brien, Ken (1976). 'Death and Revolution: An Appraisal of Identity Theory'. In: *On Critical Theory*. ed. John O'Neill. New York: The Seabury Press, pp. 104–28.

O'Neill, John (1972). *Sociology as a Skin Trade: Essays Towards a Reflexive Sociology*. London: Heinemann.

O'Neill, John (1991). 'Women as a Medium of Exchange: Defamilization and the Feminization of Law in Early and Late Capitalism'. In: *Plato's Cave: Desire, Power and the Specular Functions of the Media*. Norwood, NJ: Ablex Publishing Corporation, pp. 79–80.

O'Neill, John (1992). 'The Mother Tongue: Semiosis and Infant Transcription'. In: *Critical Conventions: Interpretation in the Literary Arts and Sciences*. Norman, OK: University of Oklahoma Press, pp. 249–63.

O'Neill, John (1994). *The Missing Child in Liberal Theory: Towards a Covenant Theory of Family, Community, Welfare, and the Civic State*. Toronto: University of Toronto Press.

O'Neill, John (1995). *The Poverty of Postmodernism*. London: Routledge.

Ortner, Sherry B. (1974). 'Is Female to Male as Nature is to Culture?' In: *Women, Culture and Society*. ed. Michelle Rosaldo and Louise Lamphere. Stanford, CA: Stanford University Press.

Parsons, Talcott (1964). *Social Structure and Personality*. New York: The Free Press.

Parsons, Talcott and Bales, Robert (1955). *Family, Socialization and Interaction Process*. New York: The Free Press.

Pateman, Carol (1988). *The Sexual Contract*. Oxford: Basil Blackwell.

Ragland-Sullivan, Ellie (1987). *Jacques Lacan and the Philosophy of Psychoanalysis*. Urbana, IL: University of Illinois Press.

Reich, Wilhelm (1945). *Character Analysis*. New York: Farrar, Straus and Giroux.

Rich, Adrienne (1978). *The Dream of a Common Language*. New York: Norton.

Richards, Barry, ed. (1984). *Capitalism and Infancy: Essays on Psychoanalysis and Politics*. London: Free Association Books.

Ricouer, Paul (1974). *The Conflict of Interpretations*. Evanston, IL: Northwestern University Press.

Rieff, Philip (1959). *Freud: The Mind of the Moralist*. New York: Viking Press.

Rieff, Philip (1966). *The Triumph of the Therapeutic: Uses of Faith After Freud*. London: Chatto and Windus.

Rose, Jacqueline (1986). *Sexuality in the Field of Vision*. London: Verso.

Rubin, Gayle (1975). 'The Traffic in Women: Notes on the Political Economy of Sex'. In: *Toward an Anthropology of Women*. ed. Rayna Rapp Reiter. New York: Monthly Review Press. pp. 157–210.

Sedgwick, Peter (1982). *Psychopolitics: Laing, Foucault, Goffman, Szasz and the Future of Mass Psychiatry*. New York: Harper and Row.

Silverman, Kaja (1992). *Male Subjectivity at the Margins*. New York: Routledge.

Slater, Philip (1970). *The Pursuit of Loneliness: American Culture at the Breaking Point*. Boston, MA: Beacon Press.

Slater, Philip (1977). *Origin and Significance of the Frankfurt School: A Marxist Perspective*. London: Routledge, Kegan Paul.

Stoller, Richard J. (1968). *Sex and Gender: On the Development of Masculinity and Femininity*. New York: Science House.

Szasz, Thomas (1961). *The Myth of Mental Illness: Foundations of a Theory of Personal Conduct*. New York: Hoeber-Harper.

Tester, Keith (1992). *Civil Society*. London: Routledge.

Turkle, Sherry (1981). *Psychoanalytic Politics: Freud's French Revolution*. Cambridge, MA: The MIT Press.

West, Robin (1988). 'Jurisprudence and Gender'. *University of Chicago Law Review* 55(1): 1–72.

Wittgenstein, Ludwig (1958). *Philosophical Investigations*. Oxford: Clarendon Press.

Wittig, Monique (1973). *The Lesbian Body*. New York: Avon.

Wrong, Dennis (1961). 'The Oversocialized Conception of Man in Modern Sociology'. *The American Sociological Review* 26(2): 183–93.

Žižek, Slavoj (1989). *The Sublime Object of Ideology*. London: Verso.

Part 4
The civic body

13 Vico's arborescence*

There was a time when mankind clothed itself with such protective images as the Tree of Life. Of course, its more problematic offshoot – The Tree of Knowledge – put a price upon our hope of making the human world more civilized. Today the current state of the manufactured world surely defeats any great generalization about the historical prevalence of order over chaos, tempting us to abandon the grand narrative of reason and liberty as intertwined effects of each other. The modern world no longer has any mirror or cognitive frame in which to behold a steady identity. Cosmos is out; chaos is in. Or else, between cosmos and chaos we may at best entertain fleeting episodes of continuity, short stories, and local knowledge but never again any grand universal (O'Neill 1994; 1987). This is the conclusion that many now draw from our political life even though it seems to be contradicted by the current strain toward globalization and common markets in our economic life. However the ruling forces of political economy settle themselves, we must expect that our cultural life, our arts and sciences will adjust their paradigms and base metaphors to the new relativity of cosmos and chaos:

> The science of chaos draws Western assumptions about chaos into question by revealing the possibilities that were suppressed when chaos was considered merely as order's opposite. It marks the validation within the Western tradition of a view of chaos that constructs it as not-order. In chaos theory chaos may lead to order, as it does with self-organizing systems, or in yin/ yang fashion it may have deep structures of order encoded within it. In any case, its relation to order is more complex than traditional Western oppositions have allowed.
>
> (Hayles 1991: 3)

Without claiming Vico's *New Science* for chaos theory, it may nevertheless be argued that his rejection of the Cartesian project in favor of the complexity of the

* Text of the essay taken from *Comparative Political Theory and Cross-Cultural Philosophy: Essays in Honour of Hwa Yol Jung* (2009). Edited by Jin Y. Park. New York: Lexington Books. Pages 345–55. Reprinted with permission.

philological arts and sciences places him in the genealogical line of the explorers of the deep structures of non-linear cognition. Thus Vico's central metaphor of the Tree of Knowledge, I shall argue, represents a heroic attempt to relativize order and chaos by building into the structure of the human mind a capacity for unpredictability and new knowledge that nevertheless returns through itself through the recursive symmetry of the *New Science* itself. By the same token, it might be argued that Vico's imaginative universals with which the human mind improves itself represent self-organizing responses to cultural entropy, keeping civilization alive long after their own star may have been extinguished. Such an imaginative universal is Lucretius's concept of the *clinamen* – the swerve in the physical order that relativizes fate and chance as well as the physics of war and the poetry of love. Thus as Serres (1982) shows, Lucretius's new physics prefigures a new science in which Mars succumbs to Venus.

The first vortices. *Turbantibus aequora ventis*: pockets of turbulence scattered in flowing fluid, be it air or salt water, breaking up the parallelism of its repetitive waves. The sweet vortices of the physics of Venus. How can your heart not rejoice as the flood waters abate (*décliner*) and the primordial waters begin to form, since in the same lofty position you escape from Mars and from his armies that are readied in perfect battle formation? In these lofty heights that have been strengthened by the wisdom of the sages, one must choose between these two sorts of physics. The physics of the military troops in their rank and file formation of parallel lines, chains, and sequences. Here are the federated ones bound to fate, sheets of atoms bearing arms, exactly arranged, *instructa*, in a well-ordered fashion, in columns. This is the learned science of the teachers, the structure of divisions, the Heraclitean physics of war, rivalry, power, competition, which miserably repeats to death the blind shadows of its redundant law. Arrange yourselves in ranks; you will learn about order, about the structure of order, about the chain of reasons, the knowledge of ranks, of blood. Or else the physics of vortices, of sweetness and of smiling voluptuousness. On the high seas, people work among these vortices: they are tossed about in the roll that, until recently, was called 'turbination'. They are perturbed. The *uexari*, however, is only cruel to a few landlubbers who have never been at sea. The sea-swept movement of intertwined lovers, or the voluptuous movements of the roll of the high seas. Listen to the line that swirls its spirals: *suaue, uentis, uexari, uoluptas*. It's the revolution of voluptuousness, the physics of Venus chosen over that of Mars (Serres, 1982: 100–101).

In view of this, it may be that we shall have to concede that the metaphor of the Tree of Knowledge is cut off from its own dynamics as soon as it is rendered as a spatialized, abstracted yet specifically European logic-tree. The artifactual troubles of bifurcation in the tree-diagram therefore require continuous rhetorical repair to keep it alive at its roots, so to speak. And this is what we propose in exposing the Vichian tree to the rhizomatic critique of the Western tree-model in order to relativize its bias toward globalization – a limitation that applies also to labyrinth theories (Weissert, 1991). In each case, what we now seek is some reflexive device that permits us to switch frames between a local and a universal perspective without privileging either one – except as we make a deliberate choice of epistemic orientation (Rossi, 2000). Thus it is not a question of opposing minoritarian knowledge and values to hegemonic knowledge, nor of rejecting universalism in favor of the particularisms of the day, as is currently the vogue in university discourse. What is needed is the ability to make transformations at points in a field of inquiry where the problem-object repeats itself on another level so that reorientation can be achieved only through a change – rather than reduction – in paradigm, model, or episteme. Such is the operation of what Vico called the *heroic mind*:

> All the while that you are under instruction, concentrate solely on collating everything you learn so that the whole may hang together and all be in accord with any one discipline. For this task your guide will be the very nature of the human mind which rejoices in the highest degree in that which forms a unity, comes together, falls into its proper place; as witness to the Latin, which seems to have derived *scientiae* – that pregnant noun – from the same root that *scitus* comes from, meaning the same thing as 'beautiful'. It follows that just as beauty is the due proportion of the members, first each to each and secondly as a whole, in any outstandingly lovely body, so knowledge should be considered as neither more nor less than the beauty of the human mind, and once men have been captivated by this, they assuredly do not need bodily forms, how radiant so ever. So far are they from being disturbed by such things!
>
> (Vico, 1976: 239)

The unity of knowledge derives its vitality from its representation as *arbor scientiae*, as 'tree' of knowledge, rather than from the positivist program of the methodological 'unification' of the sciences extracted by abandoning large areas of knowledge that are resistant to their language model. Nothing withers on the Vichian Tree of Knowledge:

> because the origins of all things must by nature have been crude...we must trace the beginnings of poetic wisdom to crude metaphysics (*metaphysica rozzo*). From this, as from a trunk, there branch out from one limb logic, morals, economics, and politics, all poetic; and from another, physics, the mother of cosmography and astronomy, the latter of which gives their certainty to its two daughters, chronology and geography – all likewise poetic.
>
> (Vico, 1970: para. 367)

Everything roots and branches, saps and grows at a different pace, according to its circumstances, yet all modes of knowledge retain the stamp of the arborescent mind. Moreover, because the human mind is not regarded as a modernist machine whose logical operations require that it render obsolete (because it cannot – 'process') large functions of human perception, language and experience, Vico's Tree of Knowledge is more akin to the Tree of Life both in its wholeness and its cultural continuity. Indeed as we may see from the passage above, Vico's Tree of Knowledge is a family tree. Its constituent arts and sciences branch out and flourish according to their time while never losing a certain 'family resemblance', as Wittgenstein would say, to one another because of their crude poetic origins.

Vichians, however, must avoid resting with the lazy gardener content to contemplate Vico's Tree of Knowledge without any effort to prune and pare its branches so that they may bear the full weight of new sciences with roots in the soil of different historical periods – 'divine', 'heroic', and 'human' – and with further sub-branchings to keep pace with the mind's own self-discovery. Understood this way, Vico's 'tree' offers a more resilient model of unity of knowledge than Bacon's 'pyramid' of the sciences, or Descartes' tree with metaphysics for its roots and physics as its trunk from which branch out all other knowledges. Similarly other 'encyclopaedic' models of the unity of knowledge in Leibniz, Kant, Comte and Cassirer, Tagliacozzo (1969: 599–613) points out, all suffer from an inability to weave together the synchronic and diachronic dimensions of the integrity and the particularity of human knowledge captured in Vico's 'tree':

> The radical novelty of Vico's Tree becomes apparent immediately in a study of its key features: (a) three main branches issuing from the trunk (instead of the trunk being merely extended), the result of Vico's discovery of two aspects of 'wisdom' which had been overlooked by philosophers up to this time – 'religious wisdom' and 'poetic wisdom'; (b) identical names and an identical number and organization of the key sciences in three co-existing branches, which indicate the 'religious' and 'poetic' origins of each science and, more generally, that any science (as well as any of its 'daughters', 'granddaughters', and so on) traverses an unlimited series of changes; (c) the fact that, once born, the older stages of any science (known today as 'outdated theories') survive infinitely beside the newer ones…. Or, to put it more straightforwardly, the Vichian 'Tree of Knowledge' is revolutionary precisely because it is historical-genetic-semantic.
>
> (Tagliacozzo, 1969: 604–605)

'As Paci' (1969: 497–515) formulates it, the weakness of the positivist programme from a Vichian perspective is that it represents a regression on both the metaphysical and the historical fronts. It reinvents a barbarism of abstraction, an ideology that erases the founding subject of civil knowledge. The *logic of the learned*, because of its forgetfulness of the lifeworld knowledge, arts and technologies, constitutes a barbarian culture *(metaphysica rozzo)* equally ignorant of its debts to the human past and its obligation toward the continuing humanization of the future. The uncharitable sciences of the modern world lose their bond with humanity, taking pride in their abstracted critique of the lifeworld whose grounded reflexivity they ruin in their own favour, even while proclaiming the abstract universal good of science-based democracies. In its most general terms, then, the positivist 'encyclopaedia' cannot sustain its proclaimed futurism because it cuts itself off from the generativity of the past. By the same token, positivist culture constricts its own present, choking on a barbarous contemporaneity, now celebrated in the dead time of postmodernism and the repetition of its places (O'Neill, 1995).

By contrast, it is especially Vico whom Joyce understood to have provided us with a great humanist license for finding ourselves where we have first put ourselves – expanding the realm of art by delimiting the world of Providence through the litter of our own mind (O'Neill, 1989). In Joyce, as Lorraine Weir (1989) has shown, the Vichian Tree of Knowledge must be internalized by his reader as the performance of an artful memory, recreating the tree, wood, paper, cut, and bark of the book:

> Is it in the now woodwordings of our sweet plantation where the branchings then will singingsing tomorrows gone and yesters outcome as Satadays afternoon lex leap smiles on the twelvemonthsminding?
>
> (Joyce, 1976: 280)

Thus the Joycean corpus reworks, reknits, nets, and weaves its reader's body, connecting it to itself like food, water, blood, and semen, all river-run into the world's history of each and anyone. And so every reader of the *Wake* is read by Finnegans' fall into writing love letters, curried notes, once current puns and quashed quotatoes.

All models of thought come to ruin inasmuch as the human capacity for differentiation exceeds the models of the 'tree', the 'encyclopedia', the 'labyrinth', the 'frame' and the 'text'. As Eco (1984) has shown with the Porphyrian tree, eventually the tree of logic breaks under its own branching process. Thus Tagliacozzo's rendering of the Vichian tree is itself overwrought by trying to marry what Hwa Yol Jung (1982) calls its 'graphic reading', or spatial mode, and its 'epi-reading', or orphic-mode. Tagliacozzo's Tree of Knowledge fattens under its own weight while struggling tantra-like to hold up the sciences on its myriad fingers reaching toward the sky. Above all, his sense of the 'historical-genetic-semantic' unity of the arts and sciences obliges him to provide us with an extensive legend (Tagliocozzo, 1960: 1969) for what I suggest must become a rhizomatic reading of the temporality that exceeds the spatial artifact despite the wild overarching beauty of its arborescent reach in Tagliocozzo's design (see Figure 13.1).

With the previous observations in mind, I think it may be useful to consider the rhizomatic or genealogical model of knowledge and power espoused by Deleuze and Guattari (1987) inasmuch as it starts from assumptions that otherwise are treated as subordinate propositions introduced to 'save' the Tree of Knowledge. The multi-dimensionality of the rhizome is anti-genealogical and anti-panoptical. It is the model of the mixture of blindness and insight – of the *myopic algorithm* – now celebrated in the postmodern diaspora of thought and feeling where interpretivity, like life itself, loses all hope of unification. Between two conflicting myths of time – of time closed and of open time, the serpent in the Tree of Knowledge (and Life) guards the ultimate temporal mystery – that of death and resurrection. Here Christ on the cross offers us perhaps our only hope (*spes unica*) of a

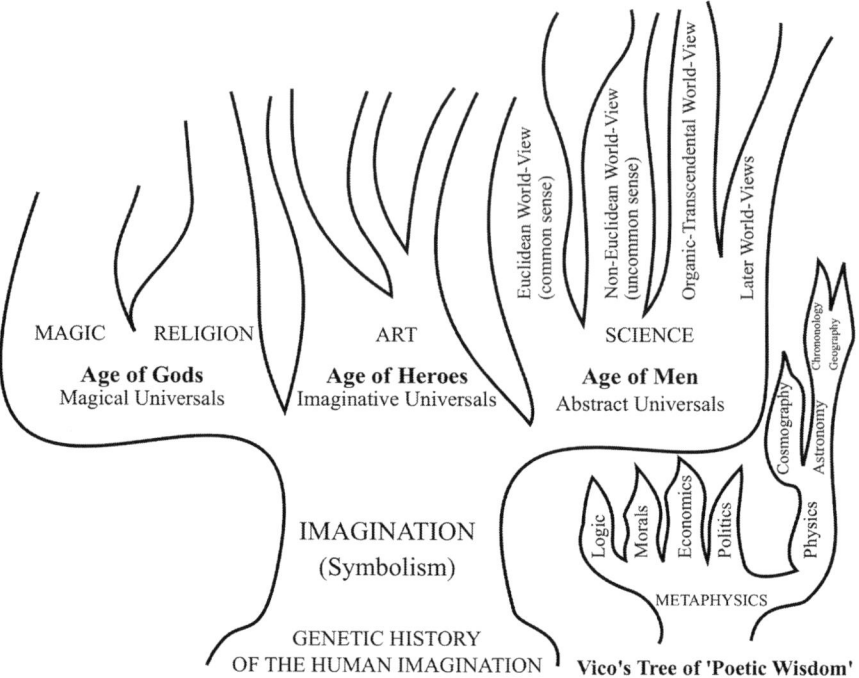

Figure 13.1 Tree of Knowledge. (Based on Tagliacozzo, 1960; Tagliacozzo, 1993; and Vico, 1968 [1744], Book II, para. 367, page 112.)

victory over time and mortality. Or, as Durand (1984) argues, if *Khristos* is close to *Krishna*, which means 'essence, perfume, oil', and both derive from *Khrio* (to rub, or to anoint), then it is the Tree of Life that must bear the graft of the Tree of Knowledge – so that neither can ever be fully separated from the other any more than the fruitful seasons of love, music, song, and dance in which the human heart takes flight and home:

> This place of endearment! How it is clear! And how they cast their spells upon, the fronds that thereup float, the bookstaff branchings! The drugged stems, the leaves incut on trees! Do you can their tantrist spellings? I can lese, skill mistress aiding. Elm, bay, this way, cull dare, take a message, tawny runes ilex sallow, meet me at the pine.
>
> (Joyce, 1976: 571)

Deleuze and Guattari (1987) have also commented on the instability of the nature/culture split introduced by the 'law of the Book' whose own figure cannot avoid the multiplicity at the heart of nature. The classical book was a 'root-book' developed according to a binary logic of division and dialectic that still rules in linguistics, psychoanalysis, structuralism, and even the information sciences. In the radical-system, or 'fascicular root' book, the principal root is subject to multiple grafts, as in Joyce's work, or Nietzsche's aphoristic text. But even so, these texts of modernity are haunted by their yearning for a transcendental unity of thought-word-and-language, which is absolutely foreign to the rhizomatic processes of the brain, memory, and sexuality upon which we have hitherto imposed the tree model at such great civilization cost:

> It is odd how the tree has dominated Western reality and all of Western thought, from botany to biology and anatomy, but also gnosiology, theology, ontology, all of philosophy…the root-foundation, *Grund, racine, fondement*. The West has a special relation to the forest, and deforestation; the fields carved from the forest are populated with seed plants produced by cultivation based on species lineages of the arborescent type; animal raising, carried out on fallow fields, selects lineages forming an entire animal arborescence…. Transcendence, a specifically European disease. Neither is music the same, the music of the earth is different, as is sexuality: seed plants, even those with the two sexes in the same plant, subjugate sexuality to the reproductive model: the rhizome, on the other hand, is a liberation of sexuality not only from reproduction but also from genitality. Here in the West, the tree has implanted itself in our bodies, rigidifying and stratifying even the sexes. We have lost the rhizome, or the grass.
>
> (Deleuze and Guattari, 1987: 18)

Deleuze and Guattari challenge the cultural order in which the Vichian Tree of Knowledge flourishes. They propose a new stratigraphy of knowledge that offers a revolutionary model for the de-hierarchization of institutions built upon binary code systems whose ultimate order is paternalistic. *Rhizomatic knowledge* is an essentially emancipatory force of the body-politic:

(1) A rhizome ceaselessly establishes *connections* between semiotic chains, organizations of power, and circumstances relative to the arts, sciences, and social struggles. (Deleuze and Guattari, 1987: 7)
(2) There are no points or positions in a rhizome, such as those found in a structure, tree or root. There are only lines. (Ibid.: 8)
(3) *Transversal communications* between different lines scramble the genealogical trees. Always look for the molecular, or even the submolecular particle with which we are allied….The rhizome is an anti-genealogy. (Ibid.: 11)
(4) A rhizome is not amenable to any structural or generative model. It is stranger to any idea of genetic axis or deep structure…(which) are above all infinitely reproducible principals of *tracing*…on the basis of an overcoding structure or supporting axis, something that comes ready-made. (Ibid.: 12)
(5) Unlike the tree, the rhizome is not the object of reproduction as image-tree nor internal reproduction as tree-structure. The *rhizome is an anti-genealogy*. It is a short-term memory, or *anti-memory*. (Ibid.: 21)

(6) In contrast to centered (even polycentric) systems with hierarchical modes of communication and preestablished paths, the *rhizome is an acentered, non-hierarchical, nonsignifying system* without a General and without an organizing memory or central automation, defined solely by a circulation of states. (Ibid.: 21)

(7) What is at question in the rhizome is a relation to sexuality – but also to the animal, the vegetal, the world, politics, the book, things natural and artificial – that is totally different from the arborescent relation: all manner of 'becomings'. (Ibid.: 21)

This rhizomatic manifesto clearly offers the most serious challenge to the Vichian concept of cultural arborescence. Its postmodern cartography inverts the mirror-relation between the world and the image, disestablishing the categories and grids through which we have hitherto domesticated nature. Nature is no longer outside of society and society is extra-natural: each is the product of the other, as Marx observed. The exchanges between nature and society occur at a pace that has thrown our ability to capture it into what Baudrillard (1988) calls an 'ecstasy of communication', to capture the discursive strategies that characterize the hyper-modern economy of global capitalism. Here, then, is a new challenge to Vico's poetic economics, which, as I have tried to show elsewhere, may well be capable of furnishing a critique of the postmodern economy (O'Neill, 1983). But we shall have to turn our minds to this task with great determination if we are not to be overwhelmed by the postmodern celebration of electronic capitalism. For I must confess that I espouse a central place for the Tree of Knowledge in what I think of as the garden of culture set in the heart of the city to be enjoyed and worked upon by contemporaries who thereby celebrate their bond with the long history of human culture that has cost us such extraordinary suffering while remaining the chief source of our delight (Frye 1971).

As a Marxist, one's intelligence is marked by a double awareness of the pain of production that underlines all consumption but – at its worst – excludes the greater part of humanity from even a modicum of comfort. Thus it is necessary to reject the postmodern celebration of the over-production of consumerized culture because it ignores the abandonment of the polis and the civic body that is resistant to the sensate culture of mass society and its docile politics. Here, too, the postmodern celebration of 'denarrativization' represents the latest treason of the intellectuals and their feigned alliance with the sub-culture of everyday life under 'late' or global capitalism, which now intensifies its grip on world culture.

Today, as for the world's forests, the question is whether the Tree of Knowledge will be allowed to stand or not. I take it that as Vichians we are all enlightened canonists, that we are republicans rather than democrats because we are concerned with the wholeness and civic integrity of the institutions within which we educate future generations (O'Neill, 2004). For this reason, while we do not believe that local knowledge should be barbarized by abstract learning, we nevertheless hold that minoritarian knowledge and values must be so conceived that they save for us the delight of wandering in Vico's groves, along the mountain tops and into the great forum of civic intelligence and beauty opened to us in the *New Science* and in that long history of the history of everyone's humanity.

References

Baudrillard, Jean (1988). *The Ecstasy of Communication*. Brooklyn, NY: Autonomedia.

Deleuze, Gilles, and Félix Guattari (1987). *A Thousand Plateaus: Capitalism and Schizophrenia*. Brian Massumi (trans.). Minneapolis: University of Minnesota Press.

Durand, Gilbert (1984). *Les Structures anthropologiques de l'imaginaire*. Paris: Dunod.

Eco, Umberto (1984). *Semiotics and the Philosophy of Language*. Bloomington: Indiana University Press.

Frye, Northrop (1971). *The Bush and the Garden: Essays on the Canadian Imagination*. Toronto: Anansi.

Hayles, Katherine N. (ed.) (1991). *Chaos and Order: Complex Dynamics in Literature and Science*. Chicago: University of Chicago Press.

Joyce, James (1976). *Finnegans Wake*. New York: The Viking Press.

Jung, Hwa Yol (1982). 'Vico's Rhetoric: A Note on Verene's *Vico's Science of Imagination*'. *Philosophy of Rhetoric* 15(3): 187–202.

O'Neill, John (1983). 'Naturalism in Vico and Marx: A Theory of the Body Politic'. In: *Vico and Marx: Affinities and Contrasts*. Giorgio Tagliacozzo (ed.). Atlantic Highlands, NJ: Humanities Press, pp. 277–89.

O'Neill, John (1987). 'Vico *mit Freude* Re-Joyced'. In: *Vico and Joyce*. Donald Phillip Verene (ed.). Albany: State University of New York Press, pp. 160–174.

O'Neill, John (1989). *The Communicative Body: Studies in Philosophy, Politics and Sociology*. Evanston: Northwestern University Press.

O'Neill, John (1994). *The Missing Child in Liberal Theory: Towards a Covenant Theory of Community, Welfare and the Civic State*. Toronto: University of Toronto Press.

O'Neill, John (1995). *The Poverty of Postmodernism*. London: Routledge.

O'Neill, John (2004). *Civic Capitalism: The State of Childhood*. Toronto: University of Toronto Press.

Paci, Enzo (1969). 'Vico, Structuralism and the Phenomenological Encyclopedia of the Sciences'. In: *Giambattista Vico: An International Symposium*. Giorgio Tagliacozzo and Hayden V. White (eds.). Baltimore: Johns Hopkins University Press, pp. 497–515.

Rossi, Paulo (2000). *Logic and the Art of Memory: The Quest for a Universal Language*. Chicago: University of Chicago Press.

Serres, Michel (1982). *Hermes: Literature, Science and Philosophy*. Josue V. Harari and David F. Bell (eds.). Baltimore: Johns Hopkins University Press.

Tagliacozzo, Giorgio (1960). 'The Tree of Knowledge'. *The American Behavioral Scientist* IV(2): 6–12.

Tagliacozzo, Giorgio (1969). 'Epilogue'. In: *Giambattista Vico: An International Symposium*. Giorgio Tagliacozzo and Hayden V. White (eds.). Baltimore: Johns Hopkins University Press, pp. 599–613.

Tagliacozzo, Giorgio (1993). *The Arbor Scientiae Reconceived and the History of Vico's Resurrection*. Atlantic Highlands, NJ: Humanities Press International; New York: Institute for Vico Studies.

Vico, Giambattista (1970). *The New Science of Giambattista Vico*. Abridged Translation of the Third Edition (1744). Thomas Goddard Bergin, Max Harold Fisch (trans). Ithaca: Cornell University Press.

Vico, Giambattista (1976). 'On the Heroic Mind'. In: *Vico and Contemporary Thought*. Giorgio Tagliacozzo, Michael Mooney, and Donald Phillip Verene (eds.). Atlantic Highlands, NJ: Humanities Press, pp. 228–45.

Weir, Lorraine (1989). *Writing Joyce: A Semiotics of the Joyce System*. Bloomington: Indiana University Press.

Weissert, Thomas P. (1991). 'Representation and Bifurcation: Burges's Garden of Chaos Dynamics'. In: *Chaos and Order: Complex Dynamics in Literature and Science*. N. Katherine Hayles (ed.). Chicago: University of Chicago Press, pp. 223–63.

14 Oh, my others, there is no other!*

Capital culture, class, and Hegelian other-wiseness

There are signs that our current political discourse has settled into a stalemate between what Scott Lash nicely calls the two idioms of *community* and *difference* (Lash and Featherstone, 2002). Identity politics (race, sexuality, multiculturalism) now represents the main thrust in the politics of recognition. Yet I will argue there is a danger that cultural politics so strains towards the idiom of absolute otherness and non-identity as to lose what I call the *civic idiom of inter-subjectivity and community*. If this happens, the baby thrown out with the bathwater will be the unfinished project of a civic welfare state (O'Neill, 1994). Because I am concerned with the question of whether capital society has any civic limit or moral commons (O'Neill, 1994), I think it necessary to restate the case for a Hegelian politics of recognition. I am not unaware of the French case against Hegel (O'Neill, 1992, 1995), yet I think it can be questioned by showing what is at stake in the politics of welfare which I think must be defended against the current remoralization of a-civic autonomy. I shall argue, therefore, that a civic politics of recognition must be grounded in a proper grasp of the Hegelian fourfold structure of the intra- inter-subjective doubling of self/other relations (O'Neill, 1996). This structure of recognition or *other-wiseness* delimits both the absolute otherness of the other and the absolute selfness of the self. From an Hegelian standpoint the two idioms of otherness and selfness belong to the (im)possibility of the state of nature, i.e. they are subcultures of a regressive politics of arbitrariness and unknowability from which 'we' have already exited. Despite Derrida and Levinas, there is neither an absolute subject nor an absolute otherness of the other except as filial phantasies of post-Hegelian deconstruction. Since I have argued this at length elsewhere (O'Neill, 1989, 1996, 1998, 1999) I will now restate the Hegelian position that is central to a *politics of civic recognition*.

Identity politics tempts us to turn away from the more historically grounded project of revising capitalism's civic self-correction in the welfare state (O'Neill, 1997). The result will be to reduce further the welfare state both by *neo-right* arguments that employ the very multicultural relativism of identity politics to dissipate the project of social justice and by *left–liberal* (Derrida, 1992) arguments

* Text of the essay taken from *Theory, Culture & Society*, 18(2–3) 2001: 77–90. Reprinted with permission.

against the immorality of the subject/other gift which aggravates left/right discontent with the welfare state (O'Neill, 1999). The challenge to contemporary society is to sustain its secular gifting, which includes all forms of conventional charity and public transfers of income, education, health, and civic infrastructures. The secular rationale for these gift practices need not pit independence against dependence or locate rationality in the market instead of the state. All society is post-individual (Durkheim, 1933: 277–80). Difference is a civilizational process. In archaic society (Mauss, 1990) alliances ruled the economy of difference whose excess could be destroyed in a festival of gifts beyond the everyday effort to bind exchange to solidarity. The challenge today is to raise the minimalist liberal political contract to a civic level of recognition under a rule of political tolerance extended to universal strangers as civic others (Rawls, 1971, 1993; O'Neill, 1994; Habermas, 1996, 1998). That is the ideal of the welfare state (Marshall, 1964; Titmuss, 1970). We are currently engaged in revising our political vision of one another. We do not need to ask who deserves citizenship because this perversely moralizes scarcity. But we should ask what is a socially just distribution of the goods (health, education, housing, employment) that underwrite civic cohesion. This is an exercise that presupposes we share some common institutions and that we understand and feel things in much the same way. A civic democracy is hardly imaginable without such assumptions. We should not shed the long history of moral and political struggles through which we have created institutions that have softened the inequality of income, health and education that mark all of our lives. Rather, we share a common political will to alter our institutions in the direction of social justice and with a civic regard for the inclusion of the most disadvantaged and vulnerable members of society (Walzer, 1983). These arrangements constitute a social covenant that, despite their political differences, parties on the right and on the left have honoured without monopoly by either one and without any belief that this covenant should be broken.

As I see it, liberal democracies are risking a return to a 'state of nature' whose cruelty was considerably if not willingly counteracted in the civic practices of 19th-century capitalism. Even in the context of class struggle, or precisely because of the will-to-class struggle, the welfare state was the civilized peak of liberal capitalism, an achievement that we owe as much to the right as to the left (Wiener, 1981). What is abhorrent about the New Right is its ignorant will-to-destroy the civic covenant, thereby aggravating the fundamentalism and neo-ethnicism it so fears. If we do abandon the will-to-civic covenant, we shall lose what I call its *other-wiseness*. We shall lose our civic understanding that rich and poor, male and female, young and old, past and present, present and future are not entirely alien to one another but overlap and modify each other's claim upon our civic potential.

Capital culture

The modern state owes its distinctive form to the ways in which it answers to the articulation of an industrial society. In short, the polity, economy and socio-cultural institutions of modern society have assumed particular constellations at given stages of mercantile, industrial and post-industrial capitalism. Whenever these constellations of capitalism begin to shift, we are driven to examine their history or genealogy in order to estimate their probable path. To delimit the contesting political discourses that emerge in a period of paradigm global shift, we are obliged to take a stand on the base grammar of capitalism. The globalized imperatives of the current stage of capitalism code the celebrated features of postmodernism (subjectivity, decentering, pluralism, deconstructed racism and genderism) more for its symbolic elites than its production and service workers. What must be asked is whether these cultural dispensations are rather the ideological effects through which individuals misrecognize the evacuation of capital power from sites the techno-political centre once thought it needed to hold. Where nothing is contested by capitalist interests, nothing is gained by identification with the fallout from the erasure and realignment of institutional relations demanded periodically by capitalist elites. Every shift in the institutional forces of capitalism offers us an opportunity to deepen our ignorance of those forces. Indeed, our contemporary ignorance is guaranteed if we proliferate difference and drift, despite the overwhelming global practice of mergers that narrow the rest of our civic practices. In fact, by allowing its loyal opposition to attack its presumed notions of authority, art, sexuality and politics, late capitalism achieves a benign solidity and tolerance. Neither mastery nor victimage can be espoused in a cultural system that can recycle all of its class, sexual, artistic and political symbols to re-embody a-temporal and a-spatial identities whose social contexts no longer delimit the space-time of late capitalism.

The global division of labour and the exodus of transnational corporations that employ the state apparatus to offset the nation-state have produced a new configuration of the forces of integration and fragmentation within and between regional economies. Yet global capitalism is still corporate capitalism whose global consistency generates ubiquitous contradictions, foreclosures, and marginalization. Meanwhile, the new division of globalized wealth and poverty is now declaring its own hard line on the ethics of survival and obsolescence. Today, we are told by the New Right that our civic covenant is an immoral and profligate exercise that can only be indulged by the nation-state through the blindness of its politicians to the morality of the new world order. In an explosion of Darwinistic fervour, we are called to believe that a sudden shift in our economic environment has left every one of our social institutions obsolete – except for the market. Only by downsizing our moral and political baggage can we enjoy the proper release of that lean and mean individual energy that is demanded and rewarded by the market (Gordon, 1996). In short, global capitalism proposes to remoralize us by returning us to a *state of nature* from which it would then draw us in accordance with the absolute law that our industry be ruled by a capital information elite. To understand what institutional re-orientation is involved here, we need to remind ourselves of the social compact that is now under reconstruction if not dismantlement. The primary social fact is that production relations generate class relations and state/economy relations. Production is primary in the material sense but not necessarily politically. In modern times this is because the liberal state is operative in the dominance of industrial over mercantile and agrarian capitalism. The liberal state may also operate as an imperial nation-state on behalf of the mass production phase of capitalism, with domestic class relations harmonized through a national pact between business, labour and government:

> A certain kind of political culture is, indeed, a condition for tripartism, one in which the state is regarded both as the instrument of civil society and at the same time as the agency for harmonizing civil society's divergent interests. Government is thought of both as the channel for procuring satisfaction for separate interests and as a force constraining these interests toward reconciliation.
>
> (Cox, 1987: 77–8)

Tripartism has, of course, never achieved perfect political balance; any partner to the pact may be seen to dominate it. With the globalization of production relations, we are experiencing the collapse of tripartism – the erosion of unionism, the hegemony of the global market, and the subordination of the redistributive welfare state(s) that we have known for the last 50 years. We can now see that the neoliberal state was committed to growth as much as redistribution and to inflation as the price of tripartism. Inflation, however, when combined with the stagnation of the mid-1970s, began to erode the national income policies of tripartism. At the same time, the informal cooperation between the central agencies of government and the globalizing corporations was strengthened. Finally, the conflict between the interests of international capital accumulation and the national welfare of vulnerable groups has come to a head. National governments are now subordinate to international finance and trade institutions that enforce the new world order of production:

> The state disengages from civil society – it reverses the trend toward interpenetration and blurring of the edges between state and society that corporatism promoted – in order to force more radically the adjustment of national economies to the world economy.
>
> (Cox, 1987: 289)

The result is that the civic capital expenditures of nation states have been severely discounted, resulting in lower credit ratings, i.e. higher interest rates that further aggravated the national deficit. Yet, it is the welfare component of the deficit that is blamed for the overall drag upon national economies.

Currently, there is a considerable withdrawal of the legitimacy accorded to the neoliberal welfare state, expressed in anti-state movements, tax revolts and new elite ideologies of self-interest and zero-altruism. These events, coupled with the severe polarization of incomes since the 1980s, have put considerable strain upon civic society, which is caught between the anomic violence of marginalized groups and a generalized fear of new scarcities and insecurities. Global capitalism imperils our political potential for civic 'other-wiseness', grounded in the welfare state.

By rejecting the corporatist contract between business, government, and labour that has softened class differences in the last half century, global capitalism now subjects everyone to the dominion of monetarism and the market, downsizing organizations and breaking unions. All this weakens the welfare state as a brake upon capitalism. Worse still, the fragmentation of social citizenship is now accelerated by the New Right's curious adoption of left cultural relativism, especially in media coverage of such events as the demonstrations against the World Trade Organization (WTO) in Seattle, Quebec City and Genoa, to claim that there are no objective moral principles to guide the pursuit of social justice:

> Ideas of social justice and of basic needs, which form the threadbare clothing of contemporary social democratic movements, are of minimal help here. Criteria of desert and merit, such as enter into popular conceptions of social justice, are not objective or publicly corrigible, but rather express private judgments grounded in varying moral traditions. Conceptions of merit are not shared as a common moral inheritance, neutrally available to the inner city Moslem population of Birmingham and the secularized professional classes of Hampstead, but instead reflect radically different cultural traditions and styles of life.... The objectivity of basic needs is equally delusive. Needs can be given no plausible cross-cultural content, but instead are seen to vary across different moral traditions.
>
> (Gray, 1983: 181–2)

The ideology of the New Right rejects any notion of the political manipulation of the allocative efficiency of the market that might redistribute income within or between nations. Just as the New Right rejects neo-Keynesian policies on the state level, so it rejects the last 50 years of state-driven development in the Third World. We are all asked to believe that there is no dual economy of labour, no comparative disadvantage or non-market mentality. Economics is a general science of human behaviour unless prohibited or violated by politics and morals. The only accountability is what is imposed by the market, namely, a rule against inefficiency but not any rule against inequality. Rather, markets encode inequalities as competitive differences that optimize social efficiency. According to the New Right, there can be no equation between inequality and injustice. The blindness of the market rather than the blindness of justice is the ultimate guarantee of merit and reward. Social inequality is natural and moral whereas the policies of equality are unnatural and immoral.

Capital class

It is too early to abandon the welfare society. The abstractive power of capitalism lies in its power to absorb labour, race and gender subject to the maintenance of its own persistence as a system of class inequality invariant across all industrialized societies (Shavit and Blossfeld, 1993; Marshall, 1997). Poverty, racism, and genderism are structural effects of a class society not of its sub-cultures. What cultural and value relativists overlook is that the differences that flourish *within* classes do not challenge but even confirm the difference *between* classes. Poverty is colourless and genderless however much it marks women and racial minorities. Likewise, although it has discriminated against women and ethnic groups (Williams, 1995), the welfare state remains a strategic resource for the reduction of inequality and the expansion of civic citizenship. I am therefore coming down on the side of the *class idiom* in the gender/race/class paradigm rather than on the side of the identity idiom in the paradigm (Brenkman, 1999). This is not because I think equality overrides identity but because I propose that the figure of *civic citizenship* draws together its constituent figures of *person* and *public* in our political tradition. The politics of race and gender must attach to this civic tradition, or else win cultural battles but lose the class war.

The structural agency of class cuts across race and gender and is analytically prior to them precisely because its referent is the abstract(ive) system of power that reproduces capitalist society. Class does not reside *in* a class but *between* social classes, i.e., in their relative wealth/poverty which hardly varies in the industrial world. This system has no borderlines or hybrids that can make any difference to it that is not a difference enjoyed by some group or other within the class system. Class is everywhere and nowhere – a feature described but not analysed in postmodern deconstructions of essence and appearance, race and gender, space and time:

> A culturalist politics, though it glances worriedly at the phenomenon of class, has in practice never devised a politics that would arise from a class 'identity.' For while it is easy enough to conceive of a self-affirmative racial or sexual identity, it makes very little sense to posit an affirmative lower-class identity, as such an identity would have to be grounded in the experience of deprivation per se. Acknowledging the existence of admirable and even heroic elements of working-class culture, the affirmation of lower-class identity is hardly compatible with a program for the abolition of want. The incommensurability of the category of class with that of race or gender (class cannot be constructed as a social identity in the *same way* as race or gender because it is not, in the current affirmative sense, a 'social identity' at all) does not, on the other hand, dis-enable a description of the relation between these social modalities. This was after all the problem sociology once addressed by means of the distinction between class and *status*. The current equation of gender, race, and class as commensurable minority identities effaces just this structural distinction.
>
> (Guillory, 1993: 13)

It is therefore debatable whether multiculturalism constitutes an adequate basis for 'the politics of recognition' (Taylor, 1992) to eliminate racism and sexism. One could easily dismiss this move on the ground that it is a belated response to the hidden (ethnic) injuries of class (Sennett and Cobb, 1972) and civic deprivation (Hamacher, 1997). Once late capitalism has hollowed out all other identities than market position, one can expect a return of the cultural repressed (family, roots, ethnicity), played out in multicultural curricula, films, art, dress and food and furniture. In short, *capitalism has no Other* once it reaches its full development in global capitalism.

Because global capitalism is now its own Other – due to the transnational displacement of its major corporations – its domestic politics soon display a paranoid combination of elite distance and populist presence that undermines citizenship and civic politics. This is fertile ground for the return to a new liberal state of nature and its nasty narrative of fear, hunger, and brute power. It is now clear that the New Right intends to remoralize political life by starving it to a bare minimum. The New Right wants class politics out of the state, out of business, out of work, out of the family. It wants to abandon the civic covenant like an old factory. The New Right proclamation of the end of class politics is only the beginning of its new politics of the market-place, of the dominion of international finance and the self-reporting corporate media endlessly discovering its own dictates in the quasi-natural movements of the global economy.

Hegelian otherwise-ness not post-political alienation

As I see it, the postmodern dismissal of the Hegelian-Marxist grand narrative of the complementarity of reason and freedom (O'Neill, 1996) could not have been more ill-timed, let alone ill-advised. It is Hegel who explores the illusory idiom of the sovereign subject commanding nature and alien others in the name of its independent desire and purpose. Hence Hegel's experiment with the minimal conditions of the state of nature to show that, even at the level of animality, life presupposes certain general categories, e.g. edible/inedible, if it is to achieve its barest aims. The heart of the matter is reached when the predatory self realizes that, by projecting every other thing as its thing, it is condemned to a fate that is always potentially its own death or enslavement. Strictly speaking, this moment of reflection is not available in the state of nature. It involves a complex inter- and intra-subjective splitting and recognition of the desire for society. Human independence lies not in its origins but in its ends which we come to realize in society and history. Human nature, therefore, is second nature (*Bildung*). Any question about human origins or ends presupposes a cultural narrative that, in our case, is populated with the figures of Stoicism, Scepticism, the Covenant and the Social Contract. This is the narrative through which we understand ourselves on the way to the romance of individualism (O'Neill, 1998).

Hegel mercilessly deconstructs the anthropological assumptions of foundationalist epistemology while simultaneously reconstructing it in terms of the historical transformation of the community of belief that it figurates (*Gestalt der Bildung*). There is neither justice nor injustice in the state of nature, no rights, no contracts and no law (Peperzak, 1995). In fact, there is no identity. This is because everybody is a *nobody*, i.e. merely the object of another's fear, appetite or desire. Bodies cannot exercise natural rights by recognizing common bodily states of desire, hunger and fear. To the contrary, so far from underwriting political society, natural rights derive from a moral community whose members recognize in one another those rights that become second nature to them in a given historical period. Hegel certainly understood how the subjective shape of modernity is reinforced by its political economy. What he opposed was the pathological individualism in modernity's appropriation of desire, knowledge and labour (Žižek, 1989). The reified self-concept of individuals systematically misrecognizes the collective reality (*die Sache selbst*) of their 'we-like' (*wirhaftige*) relations (Marcuse, 1987: 254). Lacking mutuality, the physical and sexual conquests of the natural self neither relieve loneliness nor shorten the shadow of death that it drags along with it. The critical task of the *Phenomenology*, therefore, lies in the restoration of the middle principle of the intersubjectivity of subjectivity (O'Neill, 1989). Short of this, the idealist and empiricist philosophies of individualism are tied to a state of nature and animality where desire is endlessly mortified for want of an encounter with an 'other' by whom its 'self' is neither aggrandized nor enslaved.

In the *Phenomenology*, Hegel historicizes consciousness as a structure *within* difference, as a living entity with subject (Ego) and object (Other) polarities that continually cancels any exclusivity in either object-awareness or self-awareness. In Figure 14.1, the desiring Ego (1) can never be satisfied on the level of appetite because the living body is a complex structure of differentiation and integration, involving higher levels of endo-/exo-structuring. Hence, in stages (2) and (3) Ego's senses are subject to fading and exhaustion in the wake of the embodied subject even before the Ego encounters the higher level of intersubjectivity. The projection of subject- and object-consciousness appears to break down in the experience of desire since, in cancelling its object, the desiring consciousness merely reproduces its object as the essence of desire. Consciousness is therefore obliged to treat the object of its desire as something living, as an Other endowed with an opposing consciousness. Having achieved primacy over the

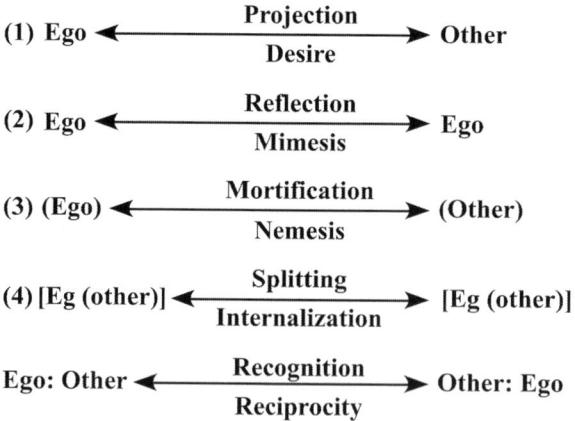

Figure 14.1 Dialectic of desire and recognition.

object, self-consciousness has still to press on with the articulation of its own self-determination. To achieve this, in stage (4) self-consciousness must both split and integrate its awareness of its self qua 'self' and its awareness of objects as other than its self. Thereafter, consciousness exists in a *double entente* of mutual recognition, i.e. as an intra-subjectivity that is an intersubjectivity. Each consciousness achieves a social identity accorded to one another rather than the project of a possessive self excluding all others except as objects of appropriation and domination. Self-consciousness must seek reason and freedom as higher goods than its own independence since in the worst possible scenario only one self might survive the struggle for life and death. But this negative freedom would return us to the very impossibility of self-possession that the *Phenomenology* recounts.

We should not abandon the Hegelian-Marxist narrative unless we wish to trash the narrative of the civic transformation of society, mind and personality that figurates Western history of philosophy, political economy and sociology. The antagonism between the idioms of conformity and individuation, between lordship and bondage, between subjectivity and intersubjectivity demands their sublimation (*Aufhebung*) but not the suppression of one or the other side. Sublimation is not repression. The desire to overcome repression without 'working through' (*durcharbeiten*) the necessity of sublimation results in the oppression of opposites in an 'I' that merely declares itself a 'We' or a 'We' that is nothing but an 'I', says Hegel (1910: 227). Individual and cultural maturity (*Mundigkeit*) is achieved through compromise and reconciliation (*Versöhnung*), i.e. through dialectical communication.

In Hegel the nature/culture relation does not involve an idealist repetition of the material aspect of life. The subjective cohesiveness and individuality achieved on the level of the economy is not identical with the ethic-political achievement of community and reciprocity (Dickey, 1987). A civic state exceeds the formal universalization of bourgeois private life and property – but it does so without any metaphysical leap. Put another way, Hegel's critique of political economy locates it at the first level of a collective servitude to the quasi-natural laws of the market. The economy operates to atomize individuals and the effect is to divide political and economic life, excluding the propertyless, women, and children. But there is a second level of the dialectic of recognition where the project of citizenship can only be achieved by responding to a political vocation on behalf of civic life (*Sittlichkeit*). Hegel is nevertheless determined not to speak of civic life in purely idealist terms. Civic life is impossible apart from the historical acquisition of the technical and socio-practical intelligence operative in the economy. Actually, Hegel locates the major shift in our cultural intelligence in the political articulation of the difference between economic morality (*subjective Sittlichkeit*) and civic intelligence (*objective Sittlichkeit*). The ethic of the market remains limited in its concept of human need even on its own level due to property restriction. But on the civic level, defined by the need for mutual recognition, the material ethic of political economy involves an even more restricted economy and is not at all the general economy it proclaims to be. Bourgeois prestige chokes upon itself like a lord whose honour prevents him from according any recognition to his slave.

The lord's contempt for his slave starves himself as well as the slave, just as the sadist is bound to the empty fetish that enslaves the masochist. In each there is no recognition and no jouissance because neither party can internalize a relationship that is constituted entirely through abjection and projection.

Post-script: Hegel in a bottle

Let us reconsider the postmodern politics of identity and minority values. Can there be public discourse, evidence, and argument on the nature of personal and social identity that rejects civic authority in the name of the contingency of values? What can be the appeal of an idiom of the subject that is limited by the contingency of every other subjectivity with whom it can presume no commonality of knowledge and values? Such a theory would require an epistemic loan while simultaneously renouncing the trust which underwrites it (Cole, 1994). Since even anti-social behaviour can only achieve its purpose through the social recognition it disclaims, what can be the objection to the advances of a civic idiom of social cohesion? We cannot achieve the aims of any personal behaviour, opinion or values without bringing them to a public forum for validation (O'Neill, 1994). We need a civic forum for the expression and evaluation of individual opinion precisely so that *one's* opinion can be given some common weight rather than remain on the level of personal taste. For here, too, one's public and private interests are not wholly different kinds of interests, as though a citizen differs entirely from a worker or consumer. To imagine that we have no way of translating and revising our interests as citizens and our interests insofar as class, race and gender weigh upon us, is to surrender politics to cultural fragmentation.

Today, we experience great difficulty in reconciling the idioms of civic community and ethical identity. Indeed, the rejection of 'we' formulations as authoritarian, essentialist, and colonizing practices is taken for granted in enabling or empowering political identity. Yet, even on the level of ethical identity, we need translations between desire and value if we are to avoid the current endorsement of the idiom's impulse and anger as moral insight. The need for such translation or mediation in the constitution of ethical identity returns 'us' to the very civic reflexivity we reject but need if we are to avoid the reduction of intersubjective recognition to minoritarianism. In short, the welcome pluralization of ethical identity cannot be fulfilled without recognition of an implicit mediation process on the level of civic citizenship. The practice of minoritarian politics presupposes the civic recognition of ethical identity claims. Unless this is cancelled, one's life, reasons and desires only achieve currency in a public world and a public discourse that they presuppose for their identification, evaluation and acknowledgement. The self, in other words, is a communicative self, endlessly invoking another similarly communicative self to sustain its projects (O'Neill, 1989). This is a message that is lost once we put Hegel in a bottle and toss it out to sea – or into the Seine! The 'missing subject' at the heart of modernity is that the self-identity we have come to cherish involves misrecognition of the historical, social structures of mind, self, and society:

A certain mental breathing space seems indispensable to modern man, one in which his independence not only of any master but also of any god is affirmed, a space for his irreducible autonomy as individual, as individual existence. Here there is indeed something that merits a point-by-point comparison with a delusional discourse. It's one itself. It plays a part in the modern individual's presence in the world and in his relations with his counterparts. Surely, if I asked you to put this autonomy into words, to calculate the exact indefeasible freedom in the current state of affairs, and even should you answer, the *rights of man*, or *the right to happiness*, or a thousand things, we wouldn't get very far before realizing that for each of us this is an intimate, personal discourse which is a long way from coinciding with the discourse of one's neighbour whatsoever.

(Lacan, 1993: 133)

Once again we are seducing ourselves with a delusional idiom of individualism. To accommodate global capital we are drawn to capital bodies, intelligence, sexuality, and possessions. Once again, we are tempted to reject the unemployed, the welfare poor, immigrants, and refugees as moral aliens whose fates lay no claim upon our own. We fancy that we can set up new walls between the rich and the poor, between personal and civic life, between today's enjoyment and tomorrow's misery that will fall upon children and youth who are not our own. In the name of an absent capital god we are being asked to break the civic covenant, to fragment our communities, to exit from the city in order to reconnect in an abstractive, vertical union with our global other in the world's finance, film, and fashion houses. Meanwhile, the sweatshops, the refugee camps, and the prisons do not close; exploitation and violation do not cease; hunger does not abate. We are asked to close our minds, to harden our hearts, and not to cry out.

References

Brenkman, John (1999). 'Extreme Criticism'. *Critical Inquiry* 26 (Autumn): 109–27.

Cole, Stephen E. (1994). 'Evading the Subject: The Poverty of Contingency Theory'. In: Herbert W. Simons and Michael Billig (eds.). *After Postmodernism: Reconstructing Ideology, Critique*. London: Sage, pp. 38–45.

Cox, Robert (1987). *Production, Power and World Order: Social Forces in the Making of History*. New York: Columbia University Press.

Derrida, Jacques (1992). *Given Time: 1. Counterfeit Money*. Peggy Kamuf (trans.). Chicago, IL: University of Chicago Press.

Dickey, Lawrence (1987). *Hegel: Religion, Economics and the Politics of Spirit* 1770–1807. Cambridge: Cambridge University Press.

Durkheim, Emile (1933). *The Division of Labor In Society*. London: Macmillan.

Gordon, David M. (1996). *Fat and Mean: The Corporate Squeeze of Working America and the Myth of Managerial 'Downsizing'*. New York: Free Press.

Gray, John (1983). 'Classical Liberalisms, Positional Goods, and the Politicization of Poverty'. In: Adrian Ellis and Kristian Kumar (eds.). *Dilemmas of Liberal Democracies: Studies in Fred Hirsch's Social Limits to Growth*. London: Tavistock, pp. 174–85.

Guillory, John (1993). *Cultural Capital: The Problem of Literary Canon Formation.* Chicago, IL: University of Chicago Press.

Habermas, Jürgen (1996). *Between Facts and Norms: Contributions to a Discourse Theory of Law and Democracy.* William Rehg (trans.). Cambridge, MA: MIT Press.

Habermas, Jürgen (1998). *The Inclusion of the Other: Studies in Political Theory.* C. Cronin and P. de Grieff (eds.). Cambridge: Polity Press.

Hamacher, Werner (1997). 'One 2 Many Multiculturalisms'. In: Hent de Vries and Samuel Weber (eds.). *Violence, Identity, and Self-Determination.* Stanford, CA: Stanford University Press, pp. 284–325.

Hegel, G.W.F. (1910). *The Phenomenology of Mind* [1807]. J.B. Baillie (trans.). London: George Allen and Unwin.

Lacan, Jacques (1993). *The Seminar of Jacques Lacan, Book III: The Psychoses 1955–1956.* Jacques-Alain Miller and Russel Grigg (eds.). New York: Norton.

Lash, Scott, and Featherstone, Mike (eds.) (2002). *Recognition and Difference: Politics, Identity, Multiculture.* London: Sage.

Marcuse, Herbert (1987). *Hegel's Ontology and the Theory of Historicity.* Seyla Benhabib (trans.). Cambridge, MA: MIT Press.

Marshall, Gordon (1997). *Repositioning Class: Social Inequality in Industrial Societies.* London: Sage.

Marshall, T.H. (1964). *Class, Citizenship and Social Development.* New York: Doubleday.

Mauss, M. (1990). *The Gift: The Form and Reason for Exchange in Archaic Societies.* W. D. Hall (trans.). London: Routledge.

O'Neill, John (1989). *The Communicative Body: Studies in Communicative Philosophy, Psychology and Politics.* Evanston, IL: Northwestern University Press.

O'Neill, John (1992). *Critical Conventions: Interpretation in the Literary Arts and Sciences.* Norman: University of Oklahoma Press.

O'Neill, John (1994). *The Missing Child in Liberal Theory: Towards A Covenant Theory of Family, Community, Welfare and the Civic State.* Toronto: University of Toronto Press.

O'Neill, John (1995). *The Poverty of Postmodernism.* London: Routledge.

O'Neill, John (ed.) (1996). *Hegel's Dialectic of Desire and Recognition: Texts and Commentary.* Albany: State University of New York Press.

O'Neill, John (1997). 'The Civic Recovery of Nationhood'. *Citizenship Studies* 1(1): 19–32.

O'Neill, John (1998). 'Lost in the Post: (Post) Modernity Explained to Children'. In: Chris Rojeck and Bryan S. Turner (eds.). *The Politics of Jean-François Lyotard: Justice and Political Theory.* London: Sage, pp. 128–38.

O'Neill, John (1999). 'What Gives (with Derrida)?' *European Journal of Social Theory* 2(2): 131–46.

Peperzak, Adriaan (1995). 'Hegel and Hobbes Revised'. In: Ardis B. Collins (ed.). *Hegel on the Modern World.* Albany: State University of New York Press, pp. 199–218.

Rawls, John (1971). *A Theory of Justice.* Cambridge, MA: Harvard University Press.

Rawls, John (1993). *Political Liberalism.* New York: Columbia University Press.

Sennett, Richard and Jonathan Cobb (1972). *The Hidden Injuries of Clan.* New York: Knopf.

Shavit, Yoshi and Hans-Peter Blossfeld (1993). *Persistent Inequality: Changing Education Attainment in Thirteen Countries.* Boulder, CO: Westview Press.

Taylor, Charles (1992). *Multiculturalism and the Politics of Recognition.* Princeton, NJ: Princeton University Press.

Titmuss, Richard M. (1970). *The Gift Relationship: From Human Blood to Social Policy.* London: Allen and Unwin.

Walzer, Michael (1983). *Spheres of Justice: A Defense of Pluralism and Equality.* New York: Basic Books.

Wiener, Martin J. (1981). *English Culture and the Decline of the Industrial Spirit, 1850–1980.* Cambridge: Cambridge University Press.

Williams, Fiona (1995). 'Race/Ethnicity, Gender and Laws in Welfare States: A Framework for Comparative Analysis'. *Social Politics: International Studies on Gender, State and Society* 2(2): 127–59.

Žižek, Slavoj (1989). *The Sublime Object of Ideology.* London: Verso.

15 *Ecce homo**

The political theology of good and evil

Our public life owes much to our expectation that we will prefer good to evil in our everyday exchanges with one another. Admittedly, this expectation is as much disturbed by exceptional acts of goodness as of evil. In either case, we are forced to examine our commonplace assumptions invested in the injunction to do more good than harm towards others whose vulnerability we share. This is that law of the Gospel:

> Whatever you require that others should do to you, that do ye to them. And that law of all men, *quod tibi fieri non vis, alteri ne feceris*.... Do not that to another, which thou wouldst not have done to thyself.
>
> (Hobbes, Leviathan,
Ch. XIV: 85; Ch. XV: 103)

I am aware, of course, that the global scale of the two-sided misadventures in contemporary political life threatens to overwhelm any notion of sympathy – if not the very idea of suffering altogether. It may also overwhelm our very own capacity for thinking at all upon events that reach us only as the dark side of entertainment, news and weather. At the very heart of things lies the problem of the conjunction of good and evil that is the scandal in our theology, politics and ethics. Our responses to it range unevenly from hope and resistance to despair and defeatism, depending on where we locate exemplary cases of the pursuit of goodness or of incorrigible evil. Here we propose to explore Hannah Arendt's notorious solecism on 'the banality of evil' appended to her *Eichmann in Jerusalem* (1963).

> Out of the unwillingness or inability to choose one's examples and one's company, and out of the unwillingness or inability to relate to others through judgment, arise the real *skandala*, the real stumbling blocks which human powers cannot remove because they were not caused by human and humanly understandable motives. Therein lies the horror and, at the same time, the banality of evil.
>
> (Arendt, 1982: 113)

---

* Text of the essay taken from *Roots, Rites and Sites of Resistance: The Banality of Good* (2010). Edited by Leonidas Cheliotis. Basingstoke: Palgrave. Pages 80–95. Reprinted with permission.

Arendt's extended *Report on the Banality of Evil* (1963) is resolutely anti-sociological. It is not directed to a study of the 'Eichmann effect' as the work of everyone and no one. Rather, it asks, 'Who was he to judge?' It is essential to her case against Eichmann that she dismisses any naturalization of the history and causes of evil. This would exempt us from individual responsibility, allowing us to wash our hands of events that exceed one's moral imagination. Instead, her report on the Jerusalem trial seizes upon Eichmann's bad faith and his clownish, idiotic surrender of our commonplace capacity for thoughtful conduct. Eichmann is charged with acting upon the poor man's reduction of Kant's Categorical Imperative to not daring to *think otherwise than others*, but rather to adopt their faceless choices as if they were his own 'semblance' (Arendt, 1977: 38). Her final verdict is that the 'inability to think' is the bedrock of the collective evil that swamped Eichmann and his times in the triumph of evil over Reason.

> The banality of evil makes its appearance in many forms, but always fueled by the delirium of blind loyalty that substitutes for thinking. In this sense, and in this sense only, Arendt saw Eichmann as Everyman pointing to the need to understand what we mean when we say in our commonsense language, that we are capable of thinking.
>
> (Bergen, 1998: 34–35)

I propose to treat Arendt's reflections on the 'banality' of evil and the very possibility of moral resistance in terms of the identity (or 'who') question as it is posed in the context of the biblical trial of Jesus (*Ecce Homo*) at Jerusalem (John 18:27–19:22; see also Figure 15.1). Here it is Pontius Pilate who sought to judge otherwise than the parties to the murder of an innocent man (*homo sacer*). Although the harshness of Arendt's judgment of Eichmann as a moral 'idiot' blindly loyal to a genocidal regime – if not as an exemplary figure of modernity's sociological 'thoughtlessness' (Arendt, 1958) – is only the preface to her exposition of a Kantian concept of self-knowledge and answerability (Arendt, 1977), both her moves are excessive expressions of critical irony. In the first place, Arendt's turn to the Kantian reformulation of the Golden Rule (Luke, 6:31) as the Categorical Imperative to capture Eichmann's stalled ethical will ignores the biblical narrative of 'answerability' located in the Godhead's own change of heart (*metanoia/conversio*) from acting as the Lord of Violence to becoming the Lord of Love. I would argue, rather, that Kant's Categorical Imperative must be read in terms of the political theology of The Sermon on the Mount. The latter underwrites resistance to ourselves as the source of a reified alterity (hardness of heart/hearing/seeing) that projects itself in an 'alienology' of evil. It is important to recall that Arendt's identity-question – *Who* did Eichmann even imagine he was to judge? – was first put to Jesus by Pontius Pilate: 'Who of us has the power to forgive?' Here Pilate asks, how are the two kingdoms of power and love to be ordered? This question is put to one who preached the 'scandal' of our loving one another on the model of forgiveness prefigured in the biblical narrative of God's relation with Israel and Israel's relations with the Gentiles. To be fair, in *The Human*

Figure 15.1 Ecce homo (or *Christ before the people*) by Albrecht Dürer (c. 1497–1500). Reprinted with permission from the Michigan Museum of Art.

Condition Arendt (1958: 212–23) had earlier turned to the Gospel texts on forgiveness and promise in a last effort to reverse the unhappy split between freedom and sovereignty that has disappointed both right and left parties in the history of political modernity (O'Neill, 1972a: 20–37; O'Neill, 1972b: 57–67). But, as we shall see, she grounds the ultimate source of forgiveness – at dispute between Pontius Pilate, the Sanhedrin and Jesus – in the *human* capacity for forgiveness as enabling God's very own forgiveness. Yet, at the same time, Arendt excludes the labouring majority of mankind from the revisionary human speech acts of promise and forgiveness which renew history and politics on the ground that the banality (*banausia*) of their work condemns them to the repetition and homogenization that constitute mass society and totalitarian politics (Featherstone, 2008).

Ecce homo: behold the man!

'Who are we?' as opposed to 'what are we?', that is the revelation whose inherent tension enlivens Arendt's philosophical work.

(Kristeva, 2001: 172)

We must now turn to the more specific, if not scandalous, Biblical formulations of the Golden Rule or Commandments that forbid killing and prescribe love and forgiveness rather than the tit-for-tat (*lex talionis*) in our intemperate relations with one another. These prescriptions are, of course, embedded in the political theology of Israel (Baudler, 1992) and the narrative transition from the Law's law to Love's law achieved through God's own change of mind or heart (*metanoia/conversio*) revealed in the teachings of Jesus. The Law's law is its sovereign power over bare life exercised in death and exile (Agamben, 1998). This is the model of kingdom that Pontius Pilate represents; the power to take or to release a life, as he reminds Jesus and the crowd who press for his execution:

Pilate, therefore went forth again, and saith unto them, Behold, I bring him forth to you that ye may know that I find no fault in him.

Then came Jesus forth, wearing the crown of thorns and the purple robe. And Pilate saith unto them, Behold the man!

When the chief priests, therefore, and officers saw him, they cried out, saying, Crucify him, crucify him! Pilate saith unto them, Take ye him, and crucify him; for I find no fault in him.

The Jews answered him, We have a law, and by our law he ought to die, because he made himself the Son of God.

When Pilate, therefore, heard that saying, he was the more afraid;

And went again into the judgment hall, and saith unto Jesus, From where art thou? But Jesus gave him no answer.

Then saith Pilate unto him, Speakest thou not unto me? Knowest thou not that I have power to crucify thee, and have power to release thee?

Jesus answered, Thou couldest have no power at all against me, except it were given thee from above; therefore, he that delivered me unto thee hath the greater sin.

And from then on Pilate sought to release him; but the Jews cried out, saying, If thou let this man go, thou art not Caesar's friend; whosoever maketh himself a king speaketh against Caesar.

(John 19:4–12, *Holy Bible* 1967)

Thus what the Passion narrative (Marin, 1980) preserves is the *collective* rather than individual pragmatics of confession, avowal and disavowal. The irony in Pilate's question is twofold. Is this the man (*this wretch*) whom you think threatens my kingdom with his talk of salvation when all that can save him from common crucifixion is the law's pleasure? And do you refuse him that forgiveness? The confrontation of the two kingdoms of life and death is inscribed in the figure of the Man of Sorrows, the King of the Jews, presented to the Roman governor Pilate. What unfolds in the gospel trial narrative is a catastrophe foretold and yet to be taken up as the gift of life that ransoms death from the dereliction of the Cross, to which the Roman centurion is witness: 'Truly, this was the Son of God...a righteous man' (Mark, 15:39, Luke, 23:47).

When Arendt shifts her own foundation myth of political action (promise and forgiveness) from Greece back to Rome and Jerusalem, she reverses the ground of what I shall call the *theological novelty* in the Old and New Testament narratives of *promise and forgiveness*. Although she notes that Jesus's teaching on forgiveness has its precedent in the Roman Law's provision for sparing the life of a prisoner (*parcere subjectis*), she reduces it to a political demand on the part of a small dissident community within Israel. At the same time, however, she argues that the religious context of the doctrine of forgiveness should not prevent its appropriation in a 'strictly secular sense', that is, provided that it be understood to have reversed the biblical priority of divine and human forgiveness:

> It is decisive in our context that Jesus maintains against the 'scribes and pharisees', first, that it is not true that only God has the power to forgive, and second, that this power does not derive from God – as though God, not men, would forgive through the medium of human beings – but on the contrary must be mobilized by men toward each other before they can hope to be forgiven by God also. Jesus' formulation is even more radical. Man in the gospel is not supposed to forgive because God forgives and he must do 'likewise', but 'if ye from your hearts forgive', God shall do 'likewise'. The reason for the insistence on a duty to forgive is clearly 'for they know not what they do' and it does not apply to the extremity of crime and willed evil, for then it would not have been necessary to teach: 'And if he trespass against thee seven times a day, and seven times in a day turn again to thee, saying, I repent; thou shalt forgive him'. Crime and willed evil are rare, even rarer perhaps than good deeds; according to Jesus, they will be taken care of by God in the Last Judgment, which plays no role whatsoever in life on earth, and the Last Judgment is not characterized by forgiveness but by just retribution (*apodounai*).
>
> (Arendt, 1958: 215–16)

Thus, Arendt insists upon Jehovah's creation-power of beginning the made-world (*factum*) shifting to the birth (*genitum*) of one who is a beginner himself – (*Initium*) *ergo ut esset, creatus est homo, ante quem nullus fuit* / 'that there be a beginning, man was created before whom there was nobody' (Augustine, 1952, *De Civitate Dei*, XII: 20). But because she separates work from speech, consigning labour to banausic repetition whilst assigning innovation to speech, Arendt abandons any notion of an emancipatory political voice of labour and social justice:

> What in each of these instances saves man – man *qua animal laborans, qua homo faber, qua* thinker – is something altogether different; it comes from the outside – not, to be sure, outside of man, but outside of each of the respective activities. From the viewpoint of the *animal laborans*, it is like a miracle that it is also a being which knows of and inhabits a world; *from the viewpoint of* homo faber, *it is like a miracle, like the revelation of divinity, that meaning should have a place in this world.*
>
> (Arendt, 1958: 212, my emphasis)

Thus, to reverse our secular historical and political evils, Arendt turns to a 'miraculous' trinitarian formula of the faculties of speech, forgiving and promising:

> The case of action and action's predicaments is altogether different. Here, the remedy against the irreversibility and unpredictability of the process started by acting does not arise out of another and possibly higher faculty, but is one of the potentialities of action itself. The possible redemption from the predicament of irreversibility – of being unable to undo what one has done though one did not, and could not, have known what he was doing – is the faculty of forgiving. The remedy for unpredictability, for the chaotic uncertainty of the future, is contained in the faculty to make and keep promises. The two faculties belong together in so far as one of them, forgiving, serves to undo the deeds of the past, whose 'sins' hang like Damocles' sword over every new generation; and the other, binding oneself through promises, serves to set up in the ocean of uncertainty, which the future is by definition, islands of security without which not even continuity, let alone durability of any kind, would be possible in the relationships between men.
>
> (Arendt, 1958: 212–13)

Here, surely, Arendt's quest for an *ethics of natality* has embraced its own extraordinary sacrificial logic. In effect, her counter-intuitive notion of the 'banality' of evil only arises from her figure of speechless labour outside or beyond the domain in which we forge our humanity, our deeds and misdeeds (Morris, 1990). The separation of work and speech excludes a large part of humanity from the politics and poetics of suffering and resistance that are more enduring than its ideological misadventures. Above all, Arendt's insistence upon the speechlessness of labour cuts off the critique of the sacrificial logic underlying religion, politics and society that runs from the Bible, through the Gospels to Hobbes (1651/1946), Kant (1790/1951), Marx (1844/1959), Rawls (1972) and Ricoeur (1995), which we must now explore.

Otherwise than the law

To elaborate the anti-sacrificial logic that is the underlying norm of civic charity and social justice, I shall argue that it is the God of violence who 'repents' (*metanoia/conversio*). His first history to become the God of Love. The moment God withdraws the monotheistic privilege of the chosen people, He has cancelled the law of genocide as its sanction. In effect, the God of Love suspends the patriarchal family in favour of a non-sacrificial fraternity. We may then envisage an ethical covenant in which the Law of Love proscribes the exclusion of the least one amongst us. By commuting the violence of ethnic, class and gender difference into the violence of unjustifiable difference, we inaugurate a double covenant of social justice and personal inviolability for which we assume civic responsibility (O'Neill, 1994, 2004).

Consider the parable of the labourers in the vineyard (Matthew 20: 1–16) who were paid the same wage at the end of the day, despite being hired for a longer or shorter period, but who complained of the 'injustice' in the master's policy. How are 'we' to hear this story? We might take the viewpoint of any of the individual labourers whose ordinary sense of justice (equal pay for equal work) is violated by the master. In turn, the master might well consider his dealings with the labourers to be given solely by his right of ownership. His rejection of the labourers' inegalitarianism would then be a Derridaean exercise of the autonomy of the gift (Derrida, 1991; O'Neill, 1999). Rather, what the master challenges is the labourers' weak capacity for fraternity. What they are ready to risk in the name of justice is demanding that the master treat them equally but as exploited day labour! Here, then, is the old sacrificial logic of collectively (mis)recognized violence. But the master's act exemplifies God's mercy and grace in forgiving difference. What 'we' (moderns) do is to subsume the Two Kingdoms in the Categorical Imperative, suppressing Love's lexical ordering (firstness/secondness) of them in favour of a Benthamite minimax rule of majority happiness that accepts the daily misery of a disadvantaged remainder. But it is the incalculability of the turn (*metanoia/conversio*) from the law of everyday difference and inequality towards love's indifference to our capital accounting that funds Christian fellowship.

Metanoia/Conversio (a change of heart) is not achieved in a single moment of epiphany. The old law of violence is not simply melted down by the new law of Love. It requires a double reorientation (a) with respect to one's knowledge of the everyday world, and (b) with respect to one's ethical orientation to events in (a) so that in the process our grasp of the law is deepened yet turned towards love whose behaviour is otherwise than the law. Christian love is enabled by the prior gift of God's grace towards us which universalizes individual worth, even though we cannot consciously draw upon its credit without turning the contingency of love into a ritual account. Our hearts are opened up (*metanoia/conversio*) by the narrative of God's incarnation and assumption of human suffering. The incarnate God of the New Testament no longer inflicts violence upon us because He is not the 'wholly other' whom our sacrifices never appease – anymore than Matthew, the former tax collector, is the same man who relativizes the two kingdoms of God and Caesar. By the same token (Incarnation), we cannot spin-off the forgiveness of sins into a 'celestial economy' (Caputo, 1997: 223) to float charity upon a Derridaean 'aneconomy' of the gift – or a 'religion without religion'. By substituting for the God-term the polarity of an absolute alterity with whom we experience only 'a fraternity existing in extreme separation' (Levinas, 1989: 84), these gestures still strain towards autonomy apart from reciprocity.

I am not arguing that there is no God of Love in the Old Testament, nor that the God of Neighbourly Love dwells only in the New Testament. It is the lexical order of the two love-imperatives that is the question:

> Thou shalt love the Lord thy God
> With all thy heart and with all thy soul,
> And with all thy mind;
> And thy neighbour as thyself.
>
> (Luke, 10:27, *Holy Bible* 1967)

The message is the same in Mark (12:29–31). In each case, Jesus is questioned about the law. The Sadducees ask, 'Will the Levirate rule in the Kingdom of Heaven?' The answer is that there is no family in the after-life. In the same text, the Pharisees ask Jesus, 'Which is the first commandment?' They are told that there are two commandments of equal weight. In Luke, it is a lawyer who asks, 'What must be done to get eternal life?' When told, the lawyer puts the supplementary question: '*And who is my neighbour?*' (Luke, 10:29, *Holy Bible* 1967).

The answer is that the love we owe to God and to our neighbour cannot be particular; it is no longer tribal, nor familial; not sexual, nor even meritocratic. It is beyond calculation even of sin:

> Ye hath heard that it hath been said,
> An eye for eye, and a tooth for a tooth;
> But I say unto you that ye shall not resist evil,
> But whoever shall smite thee on thy right cheek,
> Turn to him the other also.
>
> (Matthew, 5:38–39, *Holy Bible* 1967)

The divine economy of love and forgiveness

To render what is outrageous in Matthew's economy of forgiveness, I propose to schematize the relation between the Two Kingdoms of religion and politics in the Judaeo-Christian narrative as follows:

1) *Love thy neighbour* (as thyself) but not as

    (a)   God exclusively loved Israel, nor

    (b)   under God's threat of exclusion and punishment (*lex talionis*);

2) Love thy neighbour *as God loves us*, that is, by giving His Son

    (a)   to change our heart (*metanoia/conversio*), as He did Himself;

    (b)   to suspend the law of difference and violence, and to subordinate tribalism, familism, racism and sexism to fellowship; therefore

3) *Love thine enemies*, that is, with the same love you have for your neighbours as fellow beings in accordance with 2 (a, b, c).

The lexical order (Rawls, 1972: 42–43) of the Two Commandments – Love thy God and Love thy Neighbour (enemies) – cannot depend upon a first-order *self-love* as the guarantee of ethical autonomy. The love of fellowship must be modeled upon God's renewed love (*metanoia/conversio*) and not by the universalization of our *self-love* (as in Kant's translation of the Golden Rule into the Categorical Imperative). Thus, the order of the First and Second Commandments must be:

(i) God's love
(ii) Neighbourly love
(iii) Love for God who loves us (through His incarnate Son)
(iv) Self-love.

(Nygren, 1969: 219; modified)

I have underscored (i) and (iv) as versions of God and Self that cannot drive the commandment to love thy neighbour as thyself until (iii) *God's incarnate love for us* provides the model for neighbourly love (ii) and fellowship.

A Kantian, I believe, would argue that the change of heart (*metanoia/conversio*) that I have moved from the exclusionary Hebrew God (i) to the inclusive Christ/God (iii) can occur on the level of (iv) self-love grounded in the autonomy of rational will to secure (ii) fellowship and freedom (Adams, 1996). However, I am arguing that Christian love transcends family and thereby the 'murder in the family' that may be traced to God's first violent affection for Israel and its colonization of the land of Canaan (Cross, 1973; Assman, 1996; Dozeman, 1996). To achieve this, God redeemed the Covenant through the death of His Son so that all of humanity is called into brother/sisterhood, displacing tribalism and familism, friendship/enmity as determinants of neighbourliness and self-love. In the redeemed economy of love (*Agape*), however, the specifically ethical principle of fellowship is funded by the 'forgift' (*par-don*) of God's mercy (*grace*) which is the model for what I shall call the *declaration of forgiveness* in the Lord's Prayer.

PATER NOSTER
Our father, who art in heaven,
T(i)   Hallowed be thy name.
T(ii)   Thy kingdom come.
         Thy will be done in earth, as it is in heaven.
W(a)   Give us this day our daily bread.
W(b)   And forgive us our debts, as we forgive our debtors.
W(c)   And lead us not into temptation, but deliver us from evil.
T(iii)   For thine is the kingdom, and the power, and the glory, forever, Amen.

(Matthew, 6:9–13, Holy Bible 1967; emphasis added
to show embedding of Thou/We petitions)

The *Pater Noster* may be read to show a further deficiency in the Derrida/Caputo (1997: 226–229) attribution of an 'aneconomy' of prayer in Matthew. Consider the doubling of the 'Thou-petitions' (T) and 'We-petitions' (W), as they are called (Jeremiàs, 1967: 98–103; Vögtle, 1978). I shall call the T-petitions (i–iii) *Promise-Petitions* and the W-petitions (a–c) I shall call *Forgiveness-Petitions*. Once again, there is a lexical order ruling the two petition-clusters so that they are not to be read so as to *polarize* into the power of the Kingdom of Heaven and the passivity of the community on earth. Nor are Promise-petitions to be read only *eschatologically*, that is, without any transformation by the Forgiveness-petitions. Thus W(a) 'Give us this day our daily bread' invokes the 'hallowing of life' depicted in Christian commensalism. The latter also practices at table the fraternal suspension of difference through the efficacy achieved in W(b) 'And forgive us our debts, as we forgive our debtors', which expresses our resolve to forgive others the harms we do ourselves. However, the principle of Forgiveness (Pardon, Atonement) in W(b) cannot, *pace* Derrida/Caputo, come in *equal* amounts from us and from God – anymore than, *pace* Arendt, can it be a lazy reliance upon God's munificence. That is why in the total economy of the Lord's Prayer, the We-petitions are lexically ordered to follow the Thou-petitions through which we seek to resist evil.

Civic theology

The Kingdom of Heaven is not a 'kingdom' at all. For the same reason, it does not have a celestial economy providing for its members to live like improvident birds or the bare-naked lilies of the fields. Love's indifference does not ask us to close our eyes to social difference nor does it hypnotize us into believing the poor are the other side of heaven. The two kingdoms cross over in this world, that is, in the mundane practices of fellowship mediated by the civic state (O'Neill, 2004), which clothes bare need in the goods of welfare administered in our name, but not as an individual gift (Titmuss, 1970; Ignatieff, 1990). Today, the two kingdoms overlap through tax transfers that transform another's needs into civic rights to our duties of support and care. What is difficult is to weigh the practices of equality which cancel exclusion with the practice of respect for what in each of us is a remainder of character and circumstance that tests our fellow love. In effect, Christian love operates through a 'veil of ignorance', setting aside social inequality in favour of moral equality. Christian love preaches equality in the midst of inequality because of its indifference to difference, or its embrace of Rawls's blind choice of justice principles that favour the 'least advantaged' amongst us, the poor who may thereby hope in citizenship (Rawls, 1972).

Ethical reason without enabling civic institutions grounded in a *non-sacrificial logic* is soon starved of any goodness in this world. Whilst Kant's rejection of 'particular duties' cuts us off from natural determinism, it does so at the price of lifting our anchor in the life-world. It also risks putting us beyond the absolutely non-sacrificial blessing of the life-world loved *unknowingly* in-the-name-of-God:

For I was hungry, and ye gave me food;
I was thirsty, and ye gave me drink;
I was a stranger, and ye took me in;

Naked, and ye clothed me;
I was sick, and ye visited me;
I was in prison, and ye came unto me

Then shall the righteous answer him,
saying, Lord, when saw we thee hungry,
and fed thee; or thirsty, and gave thee drink?

When saw we thee a stranger, and took thee in, naked, and clothed thee?

Or when saw we thee sick,
or in prison, and came unto thee?

And the King shall answer and say unto them.
Verily I say unto you, Inasmuch as ye have
done it unto one of the least of these my brethren,
ye have done it unto me.

(Matthew, 25:35–40, *Holy Bible* 1967)

Christ's reference to what we may call an *ethical unconscious* is puzzling because it appears to divorce moral achievement from ethical insight. But I think what is involved is the reminder that the ethical subject cannot stand apart from the everyday involvements, interests and preoccupations occasioned by the needs one encounters anywhere, anytime, and to which one responds without elaborate reflection upon self-or-other-regarding principles (O'Neill, 1975). This is a matter of a *Divine surd* in moral habit rather than those random acts of love or beauty called for on bumper stickers. The love we owe to one another is the expression of our moral capacity for civic love which we cannot neglect without injury to our own personality. What is revolutionary in the *gift* of civic love is its prescription for the integration of the whole individual into a whole society – working against its own practices of exclusion and exploitation on the basis of religion, race, class, gender and disability (Marshall, 1950). What remains difficult is to discover those social policies and charitable practices which exemplify that kingdom of ends in which none of us is fated to be sacrificed to power and efficiency or to cruelty and greed.

In my view, Arendt overburdens the innovations of promise and forgiveness as singular acts that lift us out of the repetitive, dead-end temporality of work and mass society which she holds to be the root of the politics of evil. If we are to conceive history and politics as *otherwise than they have been*, we must regard ourselves as those others upon whom the violence of history continues to fall. Thus it is the *mutual vulnerability of anyone of us as another* that is invoked in the Golden Rule (Ricoeur, 1991, 1992, 1995, 2004). This is the gospel story we are to *re-member*; it is the lesson of radical compassion (*Agnus Dei*) that is the gift in-and-of the biblical narrative itself as a civic theology whose ethical norm is the practice of public generosity. Here, perhaps, we are beyond Arendt's question 'Who am I?' We set aside heroic deeds for prosaic acts of kindness whose promise and forgiveness respond to our vulnerability and to our recognition of one another's (mis)deeds as one's own possibility. Here, too, once we concede that established religions must resist their own temptation to power, we may still hope to find civic poets and compassionate communities which struggle to bring Love's word to justice, resisting our own evils.

References

Adams, R. M. (1996). 'The Concept of a Divine Command'. In: D. Z. Phillips (ed.) *Religion and Morality*. New York: St. Martin's Press, pp. 59–80.

Agamben, Georgio (1998). *Homo Sacer: Sovereign Power and Bare Life*. Stanford, CA: Stanford University Press.

Arendt, Hannah (1958). *The Human Condition: A Study of the Central Dilemmas Facing Modern Man*. New York: Doubleday Anchor Books.

Arendt, Hannah (1963). *Eichmann in Jerusalem: A Report on the Banality of Evil*. New York: Viking Press.

Arendt, Hannah (1977). *The Life of the Mind I: Thinking*. New York: Harcourt Brace.

Arendt, Hannah (1982). *Lectures on Kant's Political Philosophy*. R. Beiner (ed.). Chicago, IL: The University of Chicago Press.

Assman, J. (1996). 'The Mosaic Distinction: Israel, Egypt, and the Invention of Paganism'. *Representations* 56(Fall): 48–67.

Augustine of Hippo (1952). *City of God (De Civitate Dei)*. G. G. Walsh and G. Monahan (trans). Washington, DC: The Catholic University Press.

Baudler, G. (1992). *God and Violence: The Christian Experience of God in Dialogue with Myths and Other Religions*. Springfield, IL: Templegate Publishers.

Bergen, B. J. (1998). *The Banality of Evil: Hannah Arendt and 'The Final Solution'*. Lanham, MD: Rowman and Littlefield Publishers.

Caputo, J. D. (1997). *The Prayers and Tears of Jacques Derrida: Religion Without Religion*. Bloomington, IN: Indiana University Press.

Cross, F. M. (1973). *Cannanite Myth and Hebrew Epic: Essays on the History of the Religion of Israel*. Cambridge: Cambridge University Press.

Derrida, Jacques (1991). *Given Time, 1: Counterfeit Money*. Chicago, IL: University of Chicago Press.

Dozeman, T. B. (1996). *God at War: Power in the Exodus Tradition*. New York: Oxford University Press.

Featherstone, Mark (2008). *Tocqueville's Virus: Utopia and Dystopia in Western Social and Political Thought*. New York: Routledge.

Hobbes, Thomas (1946). *Leviathan, or the Forme and Power of a Commonwealth Ecclesiastical and Civil*. M. Oakeshott (ed.). Oxford: Oxford University Press.

Holy Bible (1967). New York: Oxford University Press.

Ignatieff, Micheal (1990). *The Needs of Strangers*. London: The Hogarth Press.

Jeremiàs, J. (1967). 'The Lord's Prayer in the Light of Recent Research'. In: *The Prayers of Jesus*. London: SCM Press, pp. 82–107.

Kant, Immanuel (1951). *Critique of Judgment*. J. H. Bernard (trans.). New York: Hafner.

Kristiva, Julia (2001). *Hannah Arendt*. New York: Columbia University Press.

Levinas, E. (1989). 'Ethics as First Philosophy'. In: *The Levinas Reader*. S. Hand (ed.). Cambridge, MA: Basil Blackwell, pp. 75–87.

Marin (1980). *The Semiotics of the Passion Narrative: Topics and Figures*. Pittsburgh, PA: Pickwick Press.

Marshall, T. H. (1950). *Citizenship and Social Class and Other Essays*. London: Heinemann.

Marx, Karl (1959). *The Economic and Philosophical Manuscripts of 1844*. Martin Milligan, Dirk J. Struik (trans). Lawrence & Wishart.

Morris, M. (1990). 'Banality in Cultural Studies'. In: *Logics of Television: Essays in Cultural Criticism*. P. Mellenkamp (ed.). Bloomington, IN: Indiana University Press, pp. 14–43.

Nygren, A. (1969). *Agape and Eros*. New York: Harper & Row.

O'Neill, John (1972a). 'Public and Private Space'. In: *Sociology as a Skin Trade: Essays towards a Reflexive Sociology*. London: Heinemann, pp. 20–37.

O'Neill, John (1972b). 'Violence, Language and the Body Politic'. In: *Sociology as a Skin Trade: Essays towards a Reflexive Sociology*. London: Heinemann, pp. 56–67.

O'Neill, John (1975). *Making Sense Together: An Introduction to Wild Sociology*. London: Heinemann.

O'Neill, John (1994). *The Missing Child in Liberal Theory: Towards a Covenant Theory of Family, Community, and the Civic State*. Toronto: University of Toronto Press.

O'Neill, John (1999). 'What Gives (with Derrida)?' *European Journal of Social Theory* 2(2): 131–145.

O'Neill, John (2004). *Civic Capitalism: The State of Childhood*. Toronto: University of Toronto Press.

Rawls, John (1972). *A Theory of Justice*. Cambridge, MA: Harvard University Press.

Ricoeur, P. (1991). *From Text to Action: Essays in Hermeneutics, II*. Evanston, IL: Northwestern University Press.

Ricoeur, P. (1992). *Oneself as Another*. Chicago, IL: University of Chicago Press.

Ricoeur, P. (1995). 'Ethical and Theological Considerations on the Golden Rule'. In: *Figuring the Sacred: Religion, Narrative and Imagination*. Minneapolis, MN: Fortress Press, pp. 293–302.

Ricoeur, P. (2004). 'The Difficulty to Forgive'. In: *Memory, Narrativity, Self, and the Challenge to Think God*. M. Junker-Kenny, P. Kenny (eds). Muenster: LIT, p. 616.

Titmuss, R. M. (1970). *The Gift Relationship: From Human Blood to Social Policy*. London: George Allen and Unwin.

Vögtle, A. (1978). 'The Lord's Prayer: A Prayer for Jews and Christians?' In: *The Lord's Prayer and Jewish Liturgy*. J. J. Petuchowski and M. Brocke (eds). London: Burns and Oates, pp. 93–118.

16 The circle and the line*

Kinship, vanishment, and globalization narratives in a rich/poor world

We are asked to consider an impossibility – the horror of the missing child, the anxiety of the lost youth, a life unlived, a death unmarked. 'Vanishment' arouses in us the fear that our cultural narrative is collapsing around us and with it the stories of our lives, our families and communities. Of course, we do play peek-a-boo with ourselves but we expect to be found – just as we collectively expected to survive the last millennium played out on our TV. Even so, our survival narratives contain a test imposed by a devouring god or monster, a parent, a sibling who may be oneself. The Sphinx's riddle – what goes on four legs in the morning, on two legs at noon and on three legs in the evening – is not a question about man's *life-cycle* from baby, to man, to old man on a cane: nor woman's passage from mother, to wife, to widow. It asks *who is subject to the law of intergenerationality?* The Sphinx's riddle asked Oedipus, who has scrambled the space which we owe to one another within families and between generations? In other words, do we have any right to shorten, abuse or erase the stages of human life that are the gift of intergenerationality that must be exchanged and not hoarded from jealousy or greed? The life-cycle is therefore more than a figure of biology; it is the figure of *moral kinship* and *civic intergenerationality* – it is the very mirror of self and society:

> Look in thy glass, and tell the face thou viewest
> Now is the time that face should form another,
> Whose fresh repair if now thou not renewest,
> Thou dost beguile the world, unbless some mother.
> For where is she so fair whose uneared womb
> Disdains the tillage of thy husbandry?
> Or who is he so fond will be the tomb
> Of his self-love to stop posterity?
> Thou art thy mother's glass, and she in thee
> Calls back the lovely April of her prime;
> So thou through windows of thine age shalt see,

* Text of essay taken from *Vanishing Youth? Solidarity with Children and Young People in an Age of Turbulence* (2006). Edited by Mary Ann Glendon and Pierpaolo Donati. Pontifical Academy of Social Sciences. Vatican City, pages 55–74. Reprinted with permission.

Despite of wrinkles, this thy golden time.
But if thou live rememb'red not to be,
Die single, and thine image dies with thee.

(Shakespeare, Sonnet 3).

In his magisterial survey of the shifts in world family patterns, Goran Therborn (2004) concludes that the overall effect of the demographic shifts in the past century is that rich countries no longer replace themselves but have displaced this burden upon poor countries. What raises our fear of vanishment, then, is that families in rich countries have refigured themselves in a complex struggle over the good(s) life at home and abroad. Yet the will-to-marriage has accommodated premarital sex, cohabitation, divorce, single parenting, same-sex unions, adoption and surrogacy. In rich countries the life-cycle has lengthened for elders while the periodization of childhood and youth has been extended through schooling, contraception and personal autonomy. The result is that love and marriage, marriage and family are more deliberative arrangements (education → employment → family) than the traditional marriage of horse and carriage that nevertheless survives in more expensively staged wedding rituals. On both the national and global stage, it is state and UN contraceptive policies that have acted as our parent of last resort! Yet, there remains a considerable cultural conflict between our global *will-to-family* and our globalizing *will-to-inequality* and genocidal violations of humanitarian kinship. Thus we may imagine life's journey as a *line* – some are in front, others at the back, many in the middle, uncertain where the line is moving. These are the queue lines for food, water and rescue. They are lines of death and despair. But if we imagine life as a *circle,* we remember since childhood wanting to be in, holding hands, singing, dancing and the circle widening so that no one is left outside. The circle is made from a line but the line must become a circle if we are not to scramble the world's family.

Let us consider for a moment the cover page of our conference proceedings (Figure 16.1). What we see is Picasso's *Family of Saltimbanques* which captures the eternal pathos of the wandering family, caught together and apart, at home wherever it is, juggling its sorrows and dreams – like and unlike ourselves; inside and outside the city, the church, the marketplace, together and alone they wander somewhere between Bethlehem, Paris…anywhere along the gypsy roads of Europe, from circus to circus, season to season, from childhood to death. Within this family we are drawn to the figures of the little girl, Raymonde, looking away from the half-turned but empty-armed woman, Fernande Olivier.

Sometimes, in half-pauses, a tenderness tries
to steal out over your face to your seldomly
tender mother.

(Rilke, 1963 'The Fifth Elegy')

How close is a child to itself or its elders, or they to themselves in life's tumble and turn? After adopting Raymonde, Picasso and Fernande who was his mistress asked the poet Max Jacob to return the little girl to the orphanage. The story goes

VANISHING YOUTH?
Solidarity with Children
and Young People
in an Age of Turbulence

Edited by
MARY ANN GLENDON
PIERPAOLO DONATI

*The Proceedings of the Twelfth Plenary Session
of the Pontifical Academy of Social Sciences*

28 April-2 May 2006

Figure 16.1 Cover for 'Vanishing Youth?' conference proceedings. (From *Vanishing Youth? Solidarity with Children and Young People in an Age of Turbulence.* Edited by Mary Ann Glendon and Pierpaolo Donati. Pontifical Academy of Social Sciences. Vatican City, 2006. Reprinted with permission.)

that the poet could not bring himself to do it but neither could he keep her and they too parted – each in their way 'a lost child' (Crespelle, 1967).

It is a curiosity of late modernity that it endlessly celebrates its overpowering command of nature and itself. And yet it remains haunted by images of self-destruction and disappearance. The very societies that claim to live longer and better, to extend their love of themselves and others towards nature, to its oceans and forests, to its fauna and wild creatures are equally obsessed with images of extinction, exhaustion and vanishment. Whereas earlier societies embedded themselves in the repeating cycle of nature's living and dying, we are embarked upon making the gift of life our own unique gift (O'Neill, 2004a). None of this is reversible; none of it unnatural. What is noble in our species, as Sophocles put it in his Ode to Mankind, is that we are determined to cross the seas, unmatched by any greater terror than ourselves, overcoming all odds – except Death, the divine price of Life. We are by nature unnatural. Nor are such reflections resolved by turning from poetry or existential philosophy to the sobriety of the social sciences that are at the engine of modern self-knowledge and reproduction. Here, too, media images and statistical data are interwoven in narratives of development and despair, of cooperation and conflict, where at times the rule of law shines through lawlessness and at other times love seems overshadowed by evil, inequity and disease. Yet our kinship with ourselves and nature is the mark of the changes we experience in one or the other (Strathern, 1992).

What may be said is that we are currently subject to excesses of culture that vanish nature which is then reworked in the name of fundamental norms or benchmarks in a world of ephemeral cultural fashions. It is unavoidable that 'the' family and its life-cycle – infancy, childhood, youth, adulthood, old age are also caught in our revisions of nature, society and self or of our divinity, humanity and sacrament (Wagner, 1975; 1986). As well, our concept of ourselves and relations to one another are enormously expanded in a global narrative of development that simultaneously puts all relations to nature and society at risk. But we are not helplessly stalled between the claims of culture and our own agency because their corrigibility is the very story of our lives:

> There is a life-long dialectic between objectivity and subjectivity because circumstances can change (necessarily or contingently) and so can we again necessarily, as we move through the life cycle, and contingently because we can re-assess our concerns.
>
> (Archer, 1996: 141)

I propose, then, to treat Western capitalism as a *corrigible narrative* in which the claims of polity, economy, society and personality, despite internal conflicts, have developed an overall bias toward *civic capitalism* (O'Neill, 2004b). This is also a contested concept in terms of its own history of left and right politics, as well as from the standpoint of global capitalism (Dasgupta and Serageldin, 2000). It might be said that early-modern industrial society had to learn to repair the natural risks incurred by its technological apparatus as well as devise welfare regimes to reduce the civic risks endemic to its class/property apparatus (Esping-Anderson, 1990). However, while we are still concerned to tinker with the industrial and social risks engendered by a wealth-driven political economy, we now have to learn how to repair the huge risks to sustainable civic institutions that are incurred by the global economy.

> For what we do when we declare this or that good to be a *needed good* is to block or constrain its free exchange. We also block any other distributive

procedure that doesn't attend to need – popular election, meritocratic competition, personal or familial preference, and so on. But the market is...the
chief rival of the sphere of security and welfare; and it is most importantly the
market that is preempted by the welfare state. Needed goods cannot be left
to the whim, or distributed in the interests of some powerful group of owners
or practitioners.

(Walzer, 1983: 89)

This means that we must extend – rather than reduce – welfare state practices
to include the reduction of ill-health generated not only by the self-contaminating
products and hazards of global industrialism but also by its dereliction of civic
well-being. This is the broader framework of any adequate concept of well-being
in respect of the world's children and their families (Sen,1985; Nussbaum and
Sen, 1993). It is possible that this global framework of risk may induce a certain
solidarity between adults, children, and youth. For whereas in class terms *some*
are never afflicted by the risks of poverty, *no one* escapes the afflictions of globalized risks to our air, water, food chain, forests, and heavens. Having said this,
we have still to rework our cognitive and moral maps to rethink civic sustainabil-
ity rather than continue to rely upon scarcity-thinking to ration out the unequal
risks of the emerging global economy of industrialized hazards.

We are obliged to *globalize our moral map* since it is increasingly impossible
to set up national and class walls to protect privileged moral environments. It
follows that the moral environment of children can no longer be isolated. We
can no longer imagine childhood as a pre-political or pre-economic realm safe
from the hazards of the adult world without indulging a fantasy of child-immunity
that is constantly violated through the intrusions of generation, class, race, and
nation (Glendon, 1987; Donati, 2000). Nor can we reasonably treat the middle
levels of privilege in industrial societies as the normative environment for every
other underprivileged group either within industrial democracies or outside of
them (Nieuwenhuys, 1994). It is a basic concept of civic capital theory that the
cognitive and moral formation of the child cannot be understood apart from the
child's location in a more or less intelligent and ethical society. Thus, the ecological exchanges between the family, school, economy, and the state that work to
capitalize child and youth development may be represented in the accompanying
schema (Figure 16.2).

We may read the diagram to trace inputs to social (left side) and individual
(right side) capital formation that foster a life-cycle of child, youth, and adult
well-being that in turn feeds back into economic growth. Assuming globalized
market effects and state policies, the redistributive functions of a civic state produce health, social cohesion and competence that contribute to economic innovation and growth. State, community, and family capital transfers underwrite health,
education, and individual agency. Disinvestment in any of these areas weakens
both the polity and the economy, contributing to social and personal destitution
(Dasgupta, 1993). All children should be able to see in their families, schools,
and communities the prospect of their own turn to adulthood and family with

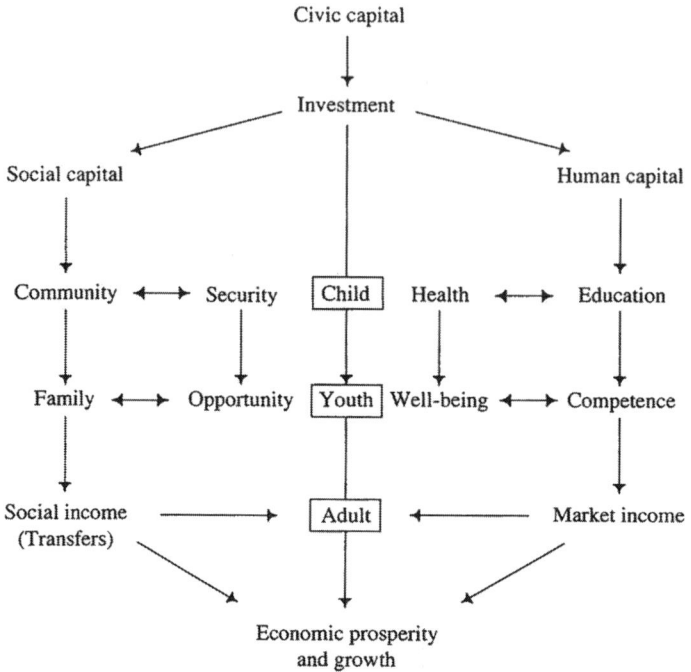

Figure 16.2 Civic capital exchanges in child development and economic growth (O'Neill, 2004b: 22). Reprinted with permission from University of Toronto Press.

reasonable security for their elders. *The fragmentation of intergenerationality must be regarded as one of the severest injuries of poverty.*

In the civic state the child is both a moral and political subject whose voice is heard only when adults subordinate their present selves to their future selves. This sacrifice is an exercise in civic citizenship and *continuity of care* (Alstoff, 2004) – not a confirmation of backward ideologies of familism and privatism. We seek rather to offer to any child a number of basic civic assurances grounded in the best child research (Bronfenbrenner and Neville, 1994), which we cast as follows:

1. A child's development is more secure (cognitively and ethically) the more complex and intensive are its interactions with its primary caretakers – that is, a child benefits from those conditions that sustain a *narrative of parental love.*
2. A child's development is more secure the more its home culture overlaps with its civic environment (physical, cultural, and emotional) – that is, a child benefits from those conditions that sustain a *narrative of social competence.*

3. A child's development is more assured the more its parental, sibling, school, and neighbourhood cultures are congruent – that is, a child benefits from those institutional conditions that sustain a *narrative of civic transitions.*

4. A child's development is more assured the more its home, its care institutions, its school, and its parental workplace(s) are in communication to balance their competing demands upon the child – that is, a child benefits from the communicative practices that sustain a *civic narrative of the child's worth.*

5. A child's development is more assured the more the state adopts child-focused family support policies – that is, a child benefits from national policy that sustains a *narrative of the civic value of children.*

6. A child's development is more sane wherever nation states enforce the United Nations Convention of the Rights of Children as an index of national achievement – that is, the child benefits from those international laws that enforce the *narrative that children are the world's treasure.*

Re-shaping the world narrative

Today we are experiencing an extraordinary strain between our narrative of kinship and our narratives of globalization and development. We are dividing into rich and poor countries, rich elders and poor youth, families that choose whether or not to replace themselves and families that are powerless against infant mortality, disease, unemployment and war. The challenge is to recast our national practices of kinship and kindness on a global level in order to sustain both economies rather than starve one in favour of the other. It is intolerable that '*we*' should deny that the world is round and reduce it to a line-up of first, second and third world children waiting for food, shelter and justice. By the same token, a '*round world*' is not the '*flat world*' evoked recently by Thomas Friedman whose best-selling global scenario of digitized knowledge and communication culminates in a children's war:

> Girls, when I was growing up my parents used to say to me, 'Tom, finish your dinner – people in China and India are starving'. My advice to you is: Girls, finish your home work – people in China and India are starving for your jobs.
>
> (Friedman, 2005: 237)

Coupled with this homely advice to his daughters, Friedman's message of *compassionate flatism* to the rest of America envisages the most extraordinary reversal of fates to counter globalized competition between the world's advantaged and disadvantaged youth:

> The way I like to think about this for our society as a whole is that every person should figure out how to make himself or herself into an *untouchable*. That's right. When the world goes flat, the caste system gets turned upside down.... Untouchables, in my lexicon, are *people whose jobs cannot be outsourced.*
>
> (Friedman, 2005: 237–38)

Friedman's wake-up call to American parents destroys their children in the very name of Americans' national myth of themselves as innocents at home and abroad (Dorfman, 1983). Yet it is a remarkable expression of the credo of neo-liberal familism which may be summed up as follows:

1. children should *not be visibly predictable* winners/losers in the inequality game;
2. children must be *procedurally equal* in any process of talent discrimination;
3. no child should be a predictable *winner* or *loser* as a result of the cumulative class effects of competition;
4. because children are even more condemned by competition than their parents – whose individualizing ideologies they have not yet acquired, they must be *lovingly schooled to develop a competitive edge.*

Friedman's *Flat World* anxieties are better addressed in Branko Milanovic's *Worlds Apart…* (2005) where the plutocratic divide between wealth and poverty is subject to extremely sophisticated statistical measurements of income inequality in individual and cross-national households. While there are no 'laws of motion' of world income distribution, nevertheless:

1. inequality between incomes in rich and poor countries is widening rather than converging;
2. the middle-class is shrinking along with middle-income countries;
3. the richest one per cent of world households enjoy as much income as fifty-seven per cent of the poorest;
4. the wealth of the richest countries grows at the expense of the poorest countries.

We live in a global plutocracy coded through international treaties and organizations (World Bank, IMF) that are not properly speaking organs of democratic governance, as Joseph Stiglitz has revealed with such moral energy in his *Globalization and Its Discontents* (2002). This is the backdrop for the endless flow of data and imagery concerned with the two billion or more people living on less than two dollars a day, of children who live in hunger, who die daily in the thousands from lack of shelter and sanitation. Here too is the real ground for Friedman's *child war*, namely, in the extraordinary capacity of the few to command the labour of the many (Homer-Dixon, 2005). Once we turn to more sober scenarios of global trends in wealth and poverty, the tide seems well set against the world's children. We read that the birth of 50 million infants are never registered at all – not to mention millions of aborted females; a hundred million children have lost a parent, work in dangerous factory, mining, farming jobs; a quarter of a million are conscripted as child soldiers (Shepler, 2005).

Overall, even if the United Nations Millennium Goals for 2015 were met, we can still expect child deaths on the order of 3.8 million, down from 8.7 million. Similar facts can be found in country by country annual reports on child and family poverty, ill-health and under-education. *A child dies every three seconds as a result of extreme poverty* (www.makepovertyhistory.ca). Yet so often these reports seek to mobilize change by pointing out how little it would cost to *save the children* – for, say, half of what we spend yearly on cigarettes in Europe or less than we spend on beer in the USA. In Bob Geldof's *Live 8 Campaign* we were witness to a curious marriage of overdeveloped youth culture and the hard core issues of debt relief, trade justice and AID/S to produce an impatient charity whose last line of rational appeal is that in helping others we help ourselves... 'We are the world, we are the children' (https://en.wikipedia.org/wiki/We_Are_the_World), we chant! The difficulty with such events is that they too are at risk as self-consuming artifacts that are folded with the cameras and the tents, leaving to others the long march through the institutions on the ground. Here organization and sustainable local practices in health, education, gender equality and employment are the daily bread of global justice. They are also the necessary staples that must be conveyed in high-school and university curricula to increase the *civic literacy* (Milner, 2002) of today's youth who are so deeply divided between political alienation and global protest. Here, of course, the digital divide is not only a matter of global *winners* and *losers*. This division is aggravated by the lack of *civic education* which strengthens democratic participation and debate from the side of youth so largely consumerized and demoralized by forces beyond them. Here, too, youth suffer very much from media representations of their lawlessness which is both reviled and celebrated throughout our culture (O'Neill, 2002).

Bono introduces Jeffrey Sachs' *The End of Poverty* (2005) – as if to arrange a marriage of expertise and enthusiasm that will produce the very first generation to eradicate 'bad trade, bad debt, and bad luck' (Sachs, 2005: XVII). Sachs' work in *clinical economics,* as he calls it, also produces a *global family portrait.* The result, however, is to make it clear that the world's population is set upon the Sisyphean labour of climbing the *ladder of economic development.* At the foot of the ladder, there struggle one-sixth of the world's population – *the poorest of the poor,* for whom the very life-cycle has imploded, where grandmothers raise orphaned children condemned to labour, illiteracy and diseases that decimate already stunted lives. At the top of the ladder, are the one-sixth of the world for whom the pace of global development has set apart the distance between the top and bottom steps of the ladder more than twenty-fold (Sachs, 2005: 30). Whereas Friedman's flat earth thesis is obsessed with China and India reaching the middle rungs of the ladder, Sachs' clinical economics *familizes* the development process – each case must be treated on its own terms and yet within the concerns of a world community, as expressed in the UN Millennium Development Goals, 2005/2015. Yet once again, we run into our own scrambled culture of hope and cynicism to which Sachs' alliance with Bono attests. In an appeal for the viability of the narrative of *Enlightened Globalization* (Sachs, 2005: 358–359), separating himself from the anti-globalization movement, anti-corporatism and American imperialism, Sachs pleads for an *end of poverty* among the poorest of the poor to meet the 2015 Millennium Development Goal of cutting world poverty by half:

The truth is that the cost now is likely to be small compared to any relevant measure – income, taxes, the costs of further delay, and the benefits from acting. Most important, the task can be achieved within the limits that the rich world has already committed: 0.7 percent of the gross national product of the high-income world, *a mere 7 cents out of every $10 in income*. All of the incessant debate about development assistance, and whether the rich are doing enough to help the poor, actually concerns *less than 1 percent of rich-world income*. The effort required of the rich is indeed so slight that to do less is to announce brazenly to a large part of the world, 'You count for nothing'. We should not be surprised, then, if in later years the rich reap the whirl-wind of that heartless response.

(Sachs, 2005: 288, my emphasis)

Sachs' warning is, I think, representative of the crossed rationality and irrationality, hope and despair – even seriousness and frivolity – in Western concepts of aid, charity and development.

Civic futures

The current intensification of risks to families, children, and youth that derives from the globalization of market forces should not stampede us into stripping our civic institutions into lean and mean instruments of competition where self and community become ever-thinner concepts wasted by irresponsible greed and the privatization of the commons:

What a community requires, as the word itself suggests, is a common culture, because, without it, it is not a community at all.... But a common culture cannot be created merely by desiring it. It rests upon economic foundations. It is incompatible with the existence of too violent a contrast between the economic standards and educational opportunities of different classes, for such a contrast has as its result, not a common culture, but servility or resentment, on the one hand, and patronage or arrogance, on the other. It involves, in short, a large measure of economic equality – not necessarily, indeed, in respect of the pecuniary incomes of individuals, but of the environment, habits of life, of access to education and the means of civilization, of security and independence, and of the social consideration which equality in these matters usually carries with it.

(Tawney, 1931: 28–39)

Civic institutions are not created for any single purpose nor can they be exhausted in any single use. They do not belong to us except as an endowment that obligates us towards past and future generations, to whom we believe our present care of the *civic commons* to be owed. But today our commitment to civic futures is made despite an alternative scenario that puts in question the very future of the future. *We are experiencing a massive shift in our conception of where and how people are produced.* A few decades ago, such a statement would have raised the horrible vision of Orwell's *Animal Farm* (1946), a state-medical hatchery in which family is a lost memory, a dream punishable by the guardians. In the distance created by our future biotechnologies, we may one day erase our maternal memory and with it the world's great model of love. Yet beneath the fantasy of the new genetics, we may sense old-order questions. Who am I? Why am I? What am I to do? My parents are not my parents – they are DNA shoppers; my mother was not my mother – her mother was to help her out; my sex is not my sex – it is the sex picked by those who bought me. I am the child of the end of the family. Henceforth I shall be ruled by conjugal convenience rather than any family romance. Henceforth I shall not need to think for myself but rather to keep up with the fashions in the bio-market, in the market schools, and in the marketplace. Henceforth I am both omnipotent child and the impotent offspring. The genetic nativity scene requires no self-discovery beyond a bare look into the microscope. No life stories emerge beyond the history of one's bio-repairs. *The end of childhood.*

We have set forth a *civic genealogy* of the family foundation because it is fast becoming a shibboleth of social reporting that 'the family' no longer exists. What is actually contested is that a secular variant of the family, i.e., a married couple with two or more children and a single wage, should any longer be the political norm. But nobody enters the world except by means of another body whose bond with yet another body is the basic social cell of intercorporeality presupposed in the birth of any individual. It is only a romantic fiction that marks birth as the appearance of an *individual* rather than as the reappearance of *family*. What is involved here are two time-frames within the life-world. *Birth* marks both an *intra*generational event within a marriage and an *inter*generational event between families. Or we might say that the advent of birth marks the inaugural moment of the *parents,* in the first case, and of the *grandparents,* in the second. No family is *the family*, since the idea of family as an institution founded upon the absolute value of intergenerationality can only be honoured in principle (Barry, 1978; Dasgupta, 1994; Heyd, 1992). At the same time, the *intergenerational family* may serve as a regulative notion in the derivation of social policies whose task is to sustain families in difficulties of one kind or another but for which we need some benchmark of viability (Silverstein, 2006). It is only on an extremely narrow understanding of *procreation* that the implicit institutional concerns inscribed in the term *pro*-(on behalf of) *creation* can be ignored in favour of its biological sense as sexual reproduction, any more than we should ignore the institutional trace contained in the word *re*-(again) *production.* If we undermine the distinction between the responsibility for life and the reproduction of life, we lose the civic assurance that goes with childhood and youth as intergenerational passages.

Concluding sociological prayer

The zero point of civilization looms once nature and culture no longer produce *the good gift* or when civilization is ruled by incontinence and indifference, where nothing is sacrificed to limit, exchange and the double legacy of present and future generation. Despite the contemporary celebration of endless exchange value, we cannot abandon the idea of *use value*. But *use* must mean *good enough* to serve its purpose and thereby to earn a similarly well-produced return. The gifts of milk and blood are not good because they are exchanged, but are exchanged because they are good, for society and for posterity. Life is doubled from the standpoint of collective and intergenerational circulation. All gifts are *eco-gifts* – that is *eco* from *oikos*, as *source of sustainable life*. Or better, they are *civic goods* to which we have right of production as well as a duty of consumption (Titmuss, 1970). Hence milk and blood – and water, air, 'green' – are garnishes of the sacred. *Sacred* means not appropriable (in mimetic rivalry) because life ought not to be opposed to itself – but repeated here and there –parochially, *per omnia saecula saeculorum*. Therefore, what is secular is not opposed to what is sacred. Rather the *secular* is what is given to be continued, to be repeated and be reproduced within the fold of the sacred. The *sacred* marks off the clearing, the lightning space, in which there arises a civic domain from which all other human institutions arise. The sacred is not a vision of things beyond what lies before us; it is the vision that discerns the very realm of thought, an appropriation of reality according to a language whose own history will differentiate the realms of law, science, economy, art and literature – but from an original matrix of poetry and fable, as Vico demonstrated in *The New Science* ([1744] 1970).

Here my argument may be found in Talcott Parsons' extraordinary *tableau religieux* (Figure 16.3) where the sociological figures of structure and agency – invoked at the outset of my essay – are translated into the core symbolism of *reciprocal gifts* that bind family to our divinity and our humanity. In the *inner* rectangle of Figure 16.3, the social categories of sex (masculinity/femininity) and age (birth, life, and death) are translated into the symbolic exchanges of Mary's gift of birth to Jesus and the gift of social recognition by Joseph, which mediate God's gift of His only begotten son, Jesus, who will in turn give (sacrifice) his body and blood (Eucharistic bread and wine) to redeem all generations through the church's gift of grace (church as Christ's Bride and our Holy Mother):

1. God's gift of Christ to Humanity;
2. Mary's gift of life to Jesus;
3. Christ's gift of his death to redeem life for humanity; and
4. the death of the individual, especially in the fullness of a complete life, as itself the gift which constitutes a full reciprocation of the original gift of life. (Parsons, 1978: 267).

The *outer* rectangle represents the relativization of the categories of the divine and human, mortality and immortality, past (covenant) and future (redeemed) generations, once again mediated through Christ's reciprocation of the gift of life with His death which funds the Divine gift of eternal life.

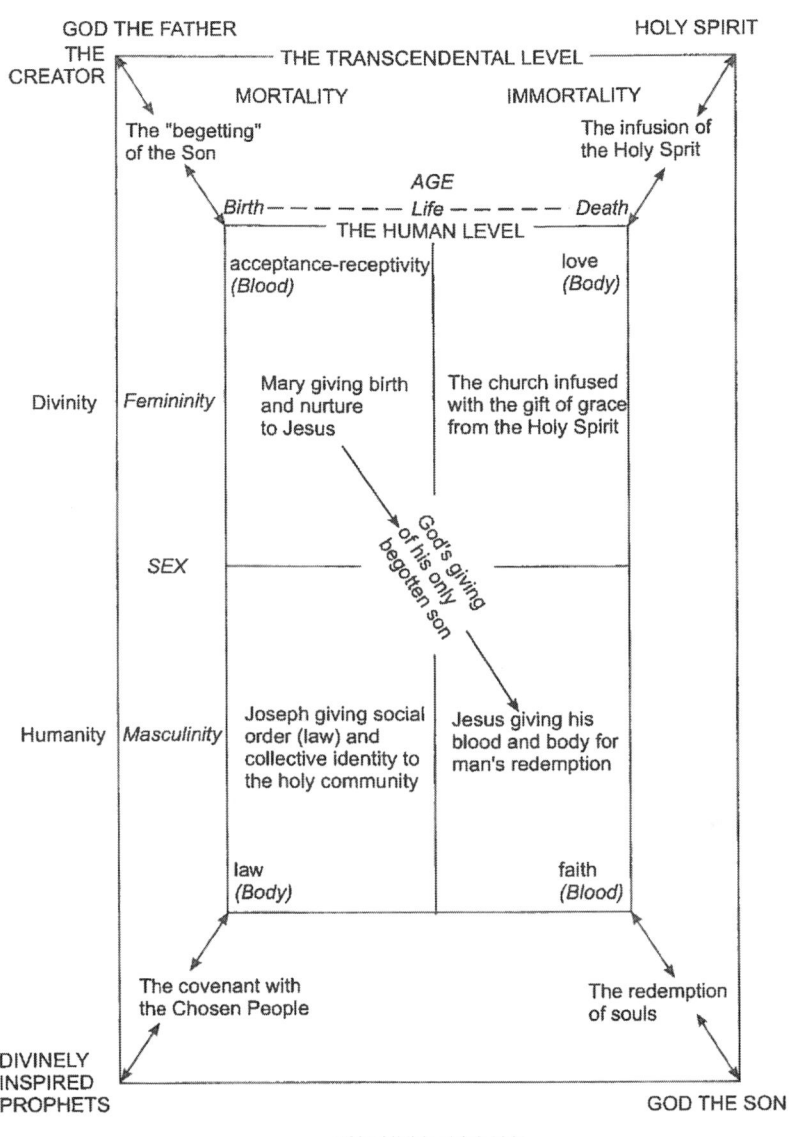

Figure 16.3 Christian syndrome as gift complex: The human as symbolically organized about age and sex. (From Talcott Parsons. 'Religion in Postindustrial Society: The Problem of Secularization'. *Social Research*, 41(1) 1974: 194, © The New School. Reprinted with permission of Johns Hopkins University Press.)

Parson's God is a sociologist! The core symbolism of high mediaeval Christianity reveals God as an action theorist, a secularist, ordaining an institutionalized individualism whose 'transcendental activism' is mediated by the Christian Church:

> ...If the conception of 'agency' is meaningful, to be 'ultimate' in the currently relevant sense, the agent cannot be either a 'human' or a 'natural' entity but must have, in accord with our whole line of argument 'transcendental' credentials.
>
> (Parsons, 1978: 391)

Post script

I have constructed a narrative of kinship, of kindness crossed by unkindness. This narrative is itself embedded in a liturgical year that has taken me through the birth, life and death of a holy child and its family. Whatever is sacred in this narrative is repeated in the everyday events that deepen disease, destroy families and impoverish children, while simultaneously seeking to foster and save them. I have set this terrible alternation in the contrastive imagery of the *circle* and the *line* – the lines of starving, homeless families, and the circle or round world that embraces difference, celebrated in our choirs and concerts loved by youth and elders alike.

The Mother Church, in whose vicinity we are gathered for our conference, may also be read as the setting of our narrative (Kitao, 1974; Napier, 1992). If we now look at Figure 16.4, we can see that we enter the Square of Saint Peter through Bernini's *Piazza Obliqua*, an oval form flanked by colonnades which embrace and release all who come to practice their faith and curiosity. In doing so, we cross the threshold where the bread of life repeats the cycle of death/life through which our divinity and our humanity are repeated *per omnia saecula saeculorum.* Thus the Petrine Church – the rock of our faith – is approached through the womb of the world – *petra genetrix* – leading up to the great altar upon which we lay our prayers for safe pregnancy, birth and infancy.

Would it strain things, then, if we were to locate the Vatican circle in that moment of vanishment caught in Piero della Francesca's *Annunciation* (circa 1470)? There divinity becomes a *born* thing (*genitum non factum*) turning from the *made* world into a fleshed world that will have been the human family? Yet the Angel Gabriel's tactful interruption of Mary's reading (which must contain her own story of conception, birth and family) introduces the male conceit of virgin birth and nomination....*Ave*/Eve! Nevertheless, I believe we are challenged to re-find the lost girl (*Kora – puela sacra*) in this tale and to set this task as a model of research (*heuresis*) and pedagogy in the human sciences. Let us pray that the Petrine Church will open itself to incorporate its women, our mothers, our sisters and daughters without whose intelligence and love – we walk on one leg.

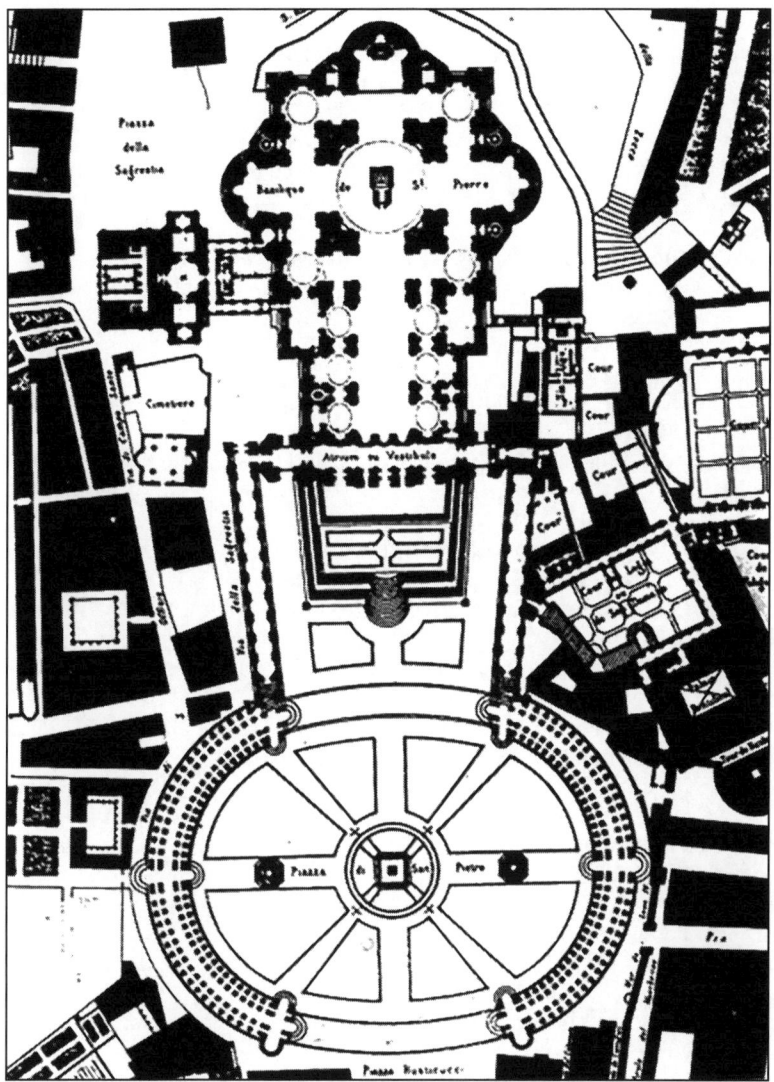

Figure 16.4 Square of Saint Peter, Bernini's *Piazza Obliqua*. (From *Vanishing Youth? Solidarity with Children and Young People in an Age of Turbulence*. Edited by Mary Ann Glendon and Pierpaolo Donati. Pontifical Academy of Social Sciences. Vatican City, 2006, pp. 55–74. Reprinted with permission.)

References

Alstoff, Anne L. (2004). 'What Does A Fair Society Owe To Children—And Their parents?'. *Fordham Law Review* LXXII (5): 1941–79.

Archer, Margaret (1996). *Culture and Agency: The Place of Culture in Social Theory*. Cambridge: Cambridge University Press.

Barry, Brian (1978). 'Circumstances of Justice and Future Generations'. In: *Obligations to Future Generations*. R.I. Sikora and Brian Barry (eds.). Philadelphia: Temple, pp. 204–48.

Bronfenbrenner, Urie and Peter R. Neville (1994). 'America's Children and Families: An International Perspective'. In: *Putting Families First: America's Family Support Movement and the Challenge of Change*. San Francisco: Jossy-Bass Publishers, pp. 2–27.

Crespelle, J. P. (1967) *Picasso: Les femmes, les amis*, l'oeuvre. Paris: CLF.

Dasgupta, Partha (1993). *An Inquiry into Well-Being and Destitution*. Oxford: Clarendon Press.

Dasgupta, Partha (1994). 'Savings and Fertility: Ethical Issues'. *Philosophy and Public Affairs* 23(Spring): 99–127.

Dasgupta, Partha and Ismail Serageldin (eds.) (2000). *Social Capital: A Multi-Faceted Perspective*. Washington, DC: The World Bank.

Donati, Pierpaolo (2000). 'The New Citizenship of the Family: Concepts and Strategies for a New Social Policy'. In: *The New Citizenship of the Family: Comparative Perspectives*. Henry Cavanna (ed.). Aldershot: Ashgate, pp. 146–73.

Dorfman, Ariel (1983). *The Empire's Old Clothes: What the Lone Ranger, Babar, Reader's Digest and Other False Friends do to our Minds*. London: Pluto Press.

Esping-Anderson, Gosta (1990). *The Three Worlds of Welfare Capitalism*. Oxford: Blackwell Publishers.

Friedman, Thomas L. (2005). *The World Is Flat: A Brief History of the Twenty-First Century*. New York: Farrar, Strauss and Giroux.

Glendon, Mary Ann (1987). *The Transformation of Family Law: State, Law and Family in the United States and Western Europe*. Chicago: University of Chicago Press.

Heyd, David (1992). *Genethics: Moral Issues in the Creation of People*. Berkeley: University of California Press.

Homer-Dixon, Thomas (2005). 'The Rich Get Richer, the Poor Get Squat'. *The Globe and Mail*. Sunday, July 30, D3–4.

Kitao, Timothy K. (1974). *Circle and Oval in the Square of Saint Peter's: Bernini's Art of Planning*. New York: New York University Press.

Milanovic, Branko (2005). *World's Apart: Recovering International and Global Inequality*. Princeton, NJ: Princeton University Press.

Milner, Henry (2002). *Civic Literacy: How Informed Citizens Make Democracy Work*. Hanover, NH: University Press of New England.

Napier, A. David (1992). 'Bernini's Anthropology: A Key to the Piazza San Pietro'. In: *Foreign Bodies: Performance, Art and Symbolic Anthropology*. Berkeley: University of California Press, pp. 112–38.

Nieuwenhuys, Olga (1994). *Children's Lifeworlds: Gender, Welfare and Labour in the Developing World*. London: Routledge.

Nussbaum, Martha and Amartya Sen (eds.) (1993). *The Quality of Life*. Oxford: Clarendon Press.

O'Neill, John (2002). *Plato's Cave: Television and its Discontents*. Cresskill, NJ: Hampton Press, Inc.

O'Neill, John (2004a). *Five Bodies: Re-Figuring Relationships*. London: Sage.

O'Neill, John (2004b). *Civic Capitalism: The State of Childhood*. Toronto: University of Toronto Press.

Orwell, George (1946). *Animal Farm: A Fairy Tale*. New York: Harcourt Brace.

Parsons, Talcott (1974). 'Religion in Postindustrial Society: The Problem of Secularization'. *Social Research* 41(2): 193–225.

Parsons, Talcott (1978). *Action Theory and the Human Condition*. New York: Free Press.

Rilke, Rainer Maria (1963). *Duino Elegies*, the German Text, With An English Translation, Introduction, and Commentary by J.B. Leishman and Stephen Spender. New York: Norton Library.

Sachs, Jeffrey D. (2005). *The End of Poverty: Economic Possibilities for Our Time*. New York: Penguin Press.

Sen, A.K. (1985). *Commodities and Capabilities*. New Delhi: Oxford University Press.

Shakespeare, William (1986). *The Sonnets and A Lover's Complaint*. John Kerrigan (ed.). New York: Viking Penguin.

Shepler, Susan (2005). 'Globalizing Child Soldiers in Sierra Leone'. In: *Youthscapes: The Popular, the National, the Global*. Sunaina Maira and Elisabeth Soep (eds.). Philadelphia: University of Pennsylvania Press, pp. 119–36.

Silverstein, Merrill (2006). 'Intergenerational Family Transfers in Social Context'. In: *Handbook of Aging and Social Sciences*. Robert H. Binstock and Linda K. George (eds). Burlington, MA: Academic Press, pp. 165–80.

Stiglitz, Joseph (2002). *Globalization and Its Discontents*. New York: W.W. Norton & Company.

Strathern, Marilyn (1992). *After Nature: English Kinship in the late Twentieth Century*. Cambridge: Cambridge University Press.

Suarez, Marcelo M. and Desirée Baolian Quin-Hilliard (eds.) (2004). *Globalization: Culture and Education in the New Millennium*. Berkely: University of California Press.

Tawney, R.H. (1931). *Equality*. New York: Harcourt Brace and Co. Therborn, Goran (2004). *Between Sex and Power: Family in the World*, 1900–2004. London: Routledge.

Therborn, Goran (2004) *Between Sex and Power: Family in the World*, 1900-2004. London: Routledge.

Titmuss, R.M. (1970). *The Gift Relationship: From Human Blood to Social Policy*. London: Allen and Unwin.

Vico, Giambattista (1970). *The New Science of Giambattista Vico*. Thomas Goddard Bergin and Max Harold Frisch (trans). Ithaca, NY: Cornell University Press.

Wagner, Roy (1975). *The Invention of Culture*. Englewood Cliffs: Prentice-Hall.

Wagner, Roy (1986). *Symbols That Stand for Themselves*. Chicago: University of Chicago Press.

Walzer, Michael (1983). *Spheres of Justice: A Defence of Pluralism and Equality*. New York: Basic Books.

Appendix A

Body politics, civic schooling, and alien-nation: An interview with John O'Neill

This television interview with John O'Neill aired on the Knowledge Network in 1998 as part of the series 'Conflicting Publics: Social Philosophy, Social Contract, Civics'. The programme was hosted by Ian Angus, then Associate Professor of Sociology and Humanities, Simon Fraser University, Vancouver, and a graduate of the Programme in Social and Political Thought at York University, which John O'Neill co-founded in 1972. From the cover of the VCR recording:

> Conflicting Publics focuses on the role of public debate in contemporary democracies. It is not about political institutions or established practices – such as voting – but about social movements and the energy of popular participation. Movements force institutions to be responsive to the public. They propose new forms of participation that can prevent democracies from stagnating. Through a series of six interviews with widely-known contemporary social and political thinkers who have been chosen for their insights into the difficulties and prospects of democracy today, Conflicting Publics explores the preconditions for democracy and the possibilities for its contemporary renewal.

The other scholars interviewed for the series were Jean Elshtain, Arne Naess, George McRobie, Axel Honneth, Chantal Mouffe and Ernesto Laclau. O'Neill's discussion with Angus touches on a wide range of themes that concerned O'Neill at the height of his career, including the promise of sociology, the meaning of socialism, the legacy of phenomenology, and the challenge of social movements, increasing inequalities, child welfare, and the civic commons. The transcript of the interview has been edited for clarity, and the title has been provided by the editors. Copyright © 1998 by the Institute for the Humanities, Simon Fraser University. Transcribed and published with permission.

Ian Angus: Perhaps we can begin if I ask you about your formative intellectual and political experiences. How did you get started being a sociologist and social philosopher?

John O'Neill: Well, at the risk of seeming to have always known, a large part of the answer is that I've never quite known why I was doing anything at any particular point. But there are things that when you think about it were defining moments. So I would like to say that one of the things that got me going was not knowing anything at all, but knowing that I didn't know anything at all. I'm the first person educated in my family and I could see that my father's way of figuring out the world derived largely from newspapers, and overall was a view that we would think of as conspiratorial: 'everything happened because they wanted us to do this, that and the other'. I don't know what the source is but I remember I read an article about the nature of economic rent, and I could suddenly see how the collective efforts of people were appropriated by some other group of people. And I knew then that that was called economics, so you needed to learn whatever the rest of that discipline was from which that comes. I think that's a very important starting place for my sense of socialism. It matched up with the experience of my family.

IA: So would you say you experienced education and reading and social theory as a kind of a liberation, as a way of understanding the culture and the class from which your people came?

JO: Always opening up the world. The other place would be as a Catholic in England, and when I grew up to say you were Catholic was sort of like shutting the lid down on your whole life. But I was not a defined Catholic, I was a dumb Catholic (*laughter*). What was decent about being a dumb Catholic was I would go to mass and the point that attracted me was always the homilies. The homilies and the church itself were another way of situating what I'll call our kitchen. I have a notion of the primal scene of theorizing not being sexual at all but familial. So in the kitchen where I grew up my father was doing the football pools, my mother was making the meals, my sister was washing her hair, and I was trying to study (*IA laughs*). And so I think that I've always learned to work under those conditions and the things I've learned have never alienated me from that. These experiences have kind of taken that little world and brought down upon it these larger worlds, but not as alien worlds.

IA: Well, you seemed to have learned quite well. (*JO laughs*). Your early work was characterized by a synthesis of phenomenology and Marxism. What was it that attracted you to these intellectual traditions as a way of broadening your horizons?

JO: Well that came much later on. As I say, being working class doesn't make you necessarily a Labour type socialist, and being socialist doesn't make you a Marxist. These are all levels of life, but I think the underlying impulse was to know how society works. And whenever it happens to you that you come across a page of Marx, it seems to be telling you that. It seems to be telling you that in such strong ways, and that is the enlightenment. It's not just that historical period but it's the conviction that 'yes, if I'm going to understand what has been happening to us I'll need to be able to think, speak, write that way'. There's another story within the story about how I actually come to read Marx. After I was an undergraduate at the London School of Economics I read Marx in America at the University of Notre Dame

(*French pronunciation*), or Notre Dame (*American pronunciation*) as I learned to call it, in the mid-Fifties when there was no Marxism in North America and certainly no critical theory. Phenomenology was similarly a late activity for me after graduate school in the Fifties, which was ruled by ordinary language philosophy. On coming to Canada, and in particular to York in Toronto, there was time to read in one's office (*laugher*).

IA: Which there isn't much of these days!

JO: No, no. It's only an illusion that Canada was bilingual, so I thought I better read something. I read Sartre for a while and then in the back of my mind was a word, I'm not sure how it got there, but it was Merleau-Ponty. And that was phenomenology, a phenomenology that grounded reason very deeply in the kind of being that an embodied being is. And that seemed to link up my whole life. One thinks one's supposed to do something with philosophy, and that Wittgenstein was always saying that the point about ordinary language philosophy was that it would release you from the pain and knots of philosophy. I didn't find that ordinary language philosophy did that to me; its triviality, in fact, seemed to knot me up worse than anything (*laughter*). But phenomenology seemed to do that for me. Once I'd read Merleau-Ponty I felt that I had gotten things together.

IA: Perhaps it would be fair to describe your work as working the border between sociology and philosophy. It's been very philosophically informed but at the same time in many cases quite concrete social analysis. How do you understand the task of sociology as an intellectual discipline?

JO: Well I think the task really has had beautiful formulations, for example, by C. Wright Mills when he says it's to fit private troubles to public issues. It very much suits the current organization of our political lives to have what are very important public issues discussed as though they were only private troubles because there's a way in which private troubles are incalculable, they're implosive, they're never ending, and they're all absorbing. At the level of public issues, there's a possibility that you may call for a paradigm change, that there's a certain amount of energy at your disposal, and there's a sense of time and that 'this must happen rather than that'. Whereas on the level of the private, it's all so terribly important to each one; it fragments and is divisive. So I would say I think of the sociologist as always trying to link the point where one finds one's self with a larger public or even cosmological level of inclusion. That's always been the challenge to any scientist though, to enter some very tiny pond of water and show that in fact there are universal structures, law-like structures of happenings going on there. And in human behaviour, since we can't experiment with one another, we take a piece of given behaviour and try to look at it in such a way that it relates to a number of other pieces of behaviour.

IA: And so when it comes into the public realm, we tend to see movements oriented towards addressing certain social problems. How do you see the relationship of social movements to the perception of public problems?

JO: I'm weak on social movements. I'm not sure social movements go anywhere.

IA: Why would that be?

JO: (*pauses*) Because I think the structural arrangements of power in our society are more served by the idea that things could change at the rate at which social movements need to have things changed because they're composed of individuals whose own sense of time has been radically destroyed through personalization. The sense of a movement must be made up of those persons, and it tends to want and hope to be understood as bringing about this or that when in fact I think it's just mopping up energy. Almost from the time it comes into being, a movement is subject to a sort of negentropic commentary, that having started it will live so long and it will die. I think the personal is on that level: our passions and our interests flare up and they're gorgeous to have, and then they go down. So what comes in between is this awful, long, abstract, boring stuff. I think that only a few people have a calling for that, and if those people don't have heart, if they don't have the public heart and the historical sense to go with it...well, to put it the other way, they must have that; otherwise they fall between these two cracks.

IA: (*interjecting*) Yes. How do you see societies as changing then, or do you? Do you see macroscopic, large-scale forces as being more important than or more effective than movements?

JO: (*sighs*) Well...it's a sad thing....I think the way human affairs have turned out is that we have rendered them so unequal that those few people that have most of the resources are always situated so as to set the terms, broadly speaking, of the next move. It's not that they absolutely know what it's going to be, but – through the very resources they command – they're going to be able to second guess it better than anybody else. And so when things do shift, for example, it may not be that the elites understood the information society through and through, but they can certainly get the best advice about where it's going. And then two things happen. One is that they're situated to take the first run of profits out of a paradigm shift; in fact they can claim that they own it although in some sense they don't own really own it because we're not that far-sighted. The second thing is that they can behave genocidally towards those who are not suited to the paradigm shift or the next stage of the society shift; they can decide: 'well, we don't need you anymore.'

IA: So there's a panic now [1998] over being computer literate, because if you aren't, you don't know what's going to happen to you.

JO: Computer literate: the dark night of exclusion. Now I'm not against computer literacy. The computer age should come, but what we need is some way of not treating that as a quasi-natural change, and we need voices that will say: 'look, it's here, but despite Bill Gates being this, and so-and-so being the whiz kid of that, this is a collective change. And since we're all going to have to go through it, you guys should not be able to appropriate all there is to be made. Nor should you be setting up a discourse that we already have in place around IQs and symbolic elites and computer illiterates in order to treat the persons on the outs of that as though they were dinosaurs.'

IA: Yes.

JO: So…I would say society goes through these massive changes.…They're not real, *real* changes; they're recoding the ground rule of inequality.

IA: So if I understand you rightly, you're saying that because of the large scale and deeply entrenched social inequality, you're sceptical about the ability of social movements to really address this or to really be able to change it.

JO: Yes, I am sceptical, but I would say that to get their business done, they have to know enough about how the elite works. Now so far the elite hasn't been so solidary that once it's got its paradigm in place it can't be made to soften it. So I would say in the shift from feudalism to capitalism that paradigm shift was at first very severe and cruel. It seemed even to the factory owners themselves that they wouldn't be able to get enough money unless they had kids and workers in factories for a 16-hour day, and then when it changed to 14 they thought that would be the end of the world, and so on down to 8 and so on. It seemed that although they knew the paradigm, they misread it as requiring greater levels of exploitation than it did, and so they came to live with that. Now, there had to be members of their similar class who could say 'look, we can soften this'. And indeed industrial capitalism was softened through Christian reform movements, following that sense of movements.

IA: From your description of these social conditions, I hear a tension between, on the one hand, an emphasis on vast inequality of wealth and power, and on the other hand, your argument that there has to be some form of commonality, that there has to be some sense that we're all in this together, that the computer world of the future, for example, is something that we're all going to inhabit. In this world of inequality, how does the possibility of commonality emerge?

JO: We can bring it back to that body we were talking about. The paradox of the way in which human beings behave so differently towards one another is that they can only do that on the basis of a first body that is roughly the same in every one of us. Now when that body is new, as in a child, we all feel 'well now we'll be restarting this'. It's very hard to say that anyone's child is less lovely than another, should live any longer than anyone else's, or worse still, *less* longer than anyone else's. So we have that first experience of a body politic; it's a body that if anyone has, everyone has. It's a body which, when we think of it that way, is not a positional good, one whose very enjoyment turns off somebody not having that to enjoy. Now I don't think it's part of one's health that someone else is sick, or that it's part of one's parenthood that you know that there are other parents who can't feed their children. In fact, *qua* parents we want exactly the same things for one another.

IA: Is that true John? I mean, it seems to me that inequality and class does play into this. One can have a kind of sympathy for somebody else and their child, but if we're in a competitive world where there's only so many university places, if this child doesn't get in then my child has a better chance of getting in, no?

JO: Yes. I'm saying that one has to be able to say that the way we treat each other unequally turns off us the paradox that we need first of all to be equal in order to be become unequal. We need the same body in order for somebody to have a bigger appetite than we do or a right to eat more than others, because of the nature of the 'we'. Now we try to break that 'we'; for example, I might say you're white and I'm black, and therefore you don't need this or that. But I cannot: when I say that you're black and I am white, I still need you to be a human being. You're not a black robot and I am a white human being. I may try to 'thinkify you' as much as possible, but I cannot and nor can you. You might serve me up some of that stuff, but there'll be a double talk, there'll be a double life. And very often it's religion that cuts into that and says 'well okay, they're playing that game with us but it'll be reversed'. So the paradox of inequality is it's a game that only can be played by people of the same species. It's very weird thing – Montaigne says that the thing about human beings is that there's more difference between them than there is between humans and animals.

IA: There is this continual interplay between identity or commonality and difference in human social life, and we can speak here about the history of socialism as well as the history of sociology. There has been this attempt which is key to the project of socialism to find some basis for commonality. I've always been struck by how in the history of socialist rhetoric the terms brothers and sisters always comes up. It is a familial metaphor, and it seems to me you're doing a very interesting thing by using familial metaphor but shifting it to the child, to the next generation.

JO: And the body, because I may seem not to have picked up on that commonality enough. As Marxists we may not have done that because Marx put a great deal of emphasis on how the system lives off surplus value. It takes from its workers more than it gives to them. But what is the more that it takes? It's that commonality. When you try to exploit a worker, he or she has to be smart enough to know they're being exploited (*laughing*).

IA: Yes.

JO: And they *are*. So depending on what their circumstances are, most workers will know how to cheat or work to rule, quite apart from union provisions for that. They will know that this is an unjust situation. They will know that their deafness, or their intelligence, or their honesty is being exploited. So I think capitalism lives off *moral* capital, and that moral capital is the communal capital. Because we all live off that sameness: I can't raise my children unless you raise yours; I can't breathe unless you can breathe. Now we know that the system renders some of that capital scarce but there's a sense in which part of its enjoyment can never be so scarce. On another level, if persons don't have it at all then they're dead, and then it's committing a kind of murder.

IA: You've said recently that there is no place for the child in liberal theory. What do you mean by that?

JO: (*pauses*) In terms of this paradox of the promise we hold out for one another, and the way in which that promise is rendered scarce and unavailable to many people, I was looking for a strong place to formulate that promise in a society that's going off class, that's going off gender, that's going off race. I mean it may talk a lot about all that but those discourses are also wearing out. Now, I think that surely people ought to be able to see that the way we harden up intra-generationally becomes a little less bearable when thought of as an inter-generational practice. Whatever you might feel once you're an adult about what we deserve for good and bad, because we are hard enough on one other by then, in the name of children we might soften the game. So what I wanted to find was a strong contrastive notion to the contract society where children and women are read out. I came up with the notion of a covenant society, and there again I dug back to something I remembered reading in the university, Fustel de Coulanges. I seemed to remember that he said that the ancient family was, as I'd now put it, a machine for worshipping previous and future families. In other words, the family didn't own itself. It wasn't grounded in sexuality; it wasn't grounded in any ownership notion of the body; it was grounded in piety. You are a family because someone else was a family…your grandparents…

IA: Yes.

JO: …and because your children would become a family. So this modifies a very possessive sense of family. See, when the family becomes possessive, funnily enough (and I suppose that's what Marx teaches us) then you can have dispossessed families. In what we insultingly call primitive or wormlike segmental societies in sociology (*laughs*) no one owns the family. It's quite the other way around; everyone is owned by it.

IA: So you're looking at the child as the core of the family, and trying to use this to resuscitate an ethic of solidarity or of caring in our society?

JO: Well, would it be a new standard for an ethic? I think we have come some way. I think the welfare state did something about modifying class relations. I think since the Sixties, our uses of Freud and Freudo-Marxism have done something to modify the relations between the sexes, the idea that woman is not simply what it is that man thinks she is or ought to be or has to be. And indeed that man isn't properly himself unless he has a concept of woman as properly herself. There's not just a simple reversal of male-female positions but a fourfold structure of man-woman, woman-man interacting. So to make that work would be very complex. It's a complex grammar of the redefinition of male-female relationships. We've tried to do that in terms of ethnicities and so on. But it looks as though the child is the last place – it's an unworked place. And you could see that just by simple little details: why must it be very hard for us to do something for children, precisely when it costs so little? When UNICEF can point out to you that if, for about 20 percent of the price of the coffee we had before we were doing this, you could give a child eyesight, or you might be able to give it a day's schooling? And no one does. So you have to think, 'Well, God almighty what is that about?' In other words, the sentimentalization of the problem and the appeal only works so much.

IA: You've been emphasizing for us, John, how every new child is a new opportunity. And yet once we have new children we tend to put them into schools and institutions which are very much like the old schools and institutions. What do you see going on now as a trend in schooling?

JO: Some very, very distressing things. I do believe that the school should be regarded as an absolute sanctuary. Not an unreal place, not a play-place, but the holiest of holies. It means our teachers ought to be accorded great honour. I still think of the university as a school – tying back to what we said earlier – because of this idea that it's a place where your world can keep opening up. Now the concept of school in this sense is what I'd call a civic concept. It's the idea that we should bring children to school as a reaffirmation of their commonality. It's not their averageness, and has nothing to do with averaging them. It should reaffirm their commonality. It should not be what it now is in danger of becoming more and more, namely, a race that they're being made to toe a line for, a race that in many cases is over even before it starts. We have currently the new bell curve controversy. It's a curious restoration of the idea that we're divided 80/20: that 20 percent of us have brains, 80 percent don't, and when you combine that with managerialist discourses you get the argument that it's a waste of social resources to educate the 80 percent, that you really only need to pass them through the schools so that they're disciplined. And the other 20 percent are the obvious carriers of the culture, and so the resources should go to them. Now that will be destructive of schools and universities. It destroys the entire romance of education, and it will destroy the university. Now of course it will never be completely put into place. What it will do is take the already rich places in the school system and the already rich – I mean culturally rich – places in the school and university system and privatize them.

IA: So there's a sense of time wasting in schools; that you're being prepared for something that in fact you'll never see.

JO: It's not time wasting, it's your capacity to deal with the dead time that you are. The message is that you don't have enough brains. So your life is not going to be very much. Other people do have a lot of brains and their life is going to be very rich, and the best you can do is live with that.

IA: Where does this trend in schooling come from then? I don't know what your experience is, but most of the people I've met who are teachers are generally a very dedicated group of people.

JO: Yes they are, and it's being imposed on them, since school is split between teachers and administrators, while administrators and politicians are at the levels at which this managerialist and quasi-biological discourse about brains and no-brains can be injected. It couldn't be injected so easily if it were not part the current crisis of the welfare state. I think we have to understand that the schools are a part of the welfare state.

IA: What's the current crisis of the welfare state?

JO: The current crisis of the welfare state is that when the global elite go into globalizing themselves they're in about the same state of panic as the nineteenth century factory capitalists were over whether or not they could afford more than the little they were willing to give. Just as they stripped down the kind of feudal poor law system and charity system and put in its place the poor house and criminalized poverty, in this present stage the greedy globalists think they can't afford a liberal democratic and civic society, they can't afford opera, they can't afford ballet. In a sense they have a terrible anal complex. You could say that they're not sure now that they can afford any of the civic productions of sport on every level except the professional level of music that comes out of anywhere and everywhere. They think that they can have it all in one efficient, relatively costless place upon which they will make huge profits, and they think that's how the world should go. Now we have to hope that will break down; we have to just hope and push wherever there's a chance to make it break down. Schools are part of that process; the schools are not outside the problem of health, education, and employment. We really do need to realize that the schools are a central part of that. We've got a debate going about post-secondary education. Now again that's a debate because in some sense life is over when you're adult, and people will actually listen to discourses about whether they're expendable or not. So 'do we have too much?' or 'is it too costly to have the university system?' – these all have to be seen as part of this discussion. I mean the universities come out of the schools, and the schools come out the nursery school; all must be seen as one complex, as what the welfare state is about, not just what it costs.

IA: So on the one hand, we have no money for culture in the sense of teaching people to appreciate culture and for schools and for art and for things that might allow people to understand their world better. That's all just spending as it's called. On the other hand, there are terrific global culture industries – television, films and so forth – that are making terrific amounts of money out of culture. And here, of course, the worldview, the agenda of the corporate global economy is pervasive. So we don't get many alternative ideas, is that what you're suggesting?

JO: Yes. But what I want to try to say underneath that is that even capitalists sometimes know and sometimes don't know that money is a fiction. Money is a fiction; that means it can be a political fiction. That is to say, when Britain, Canada, and then the US decided that they couldn't have millions of people unemployed and so on, they went in for the welfare state and the New Deal, and they made the money that made those institutions work that made the money work. In the early days all sorts of pieces of the information age were available, but they didn't become institutionalized, and instead they looked like pure fictions: 'Well that won't work, we won't make enough money on that, it's crazy to say that one day everybody will own a computer'. But once that fiction becomes a corporately backed fiction, it's a reality. What will happen I think is that capital theory already has a version of itself called *human* capital theory, which is the recognition that, after all, capitalism isn't driven so much by the machines as by the brains that go into them and the brains that use them. So labour is actually quite intelligent, and quite a very good thing to have. So then there will be reinvestments in schools and education and so on. That's in fact to some extent already going on, but we don't control yet the discourse of saying how that reinvestment should go.

IA: You would suggest that any kind of capitalism as a social system requires some degree of agreement to proceed and that the task then is to pressure people to recognize their civic duty. This recognition, how might it happen? Do you see, for example, the public service strikes in Ontario now as a means of pressuring for the recognition of a civic duty?

JO: Yes, I think they are. They are saying, as the Canadian people say when polled, 'We want the welfare state, we also don't want certain things, we have reached a limit of tolerance.' I think that the trouble for strikes generally in the twentieth century is that the semiotics are wrong. They happen outdoors and the gross vulgarity of bodies angrily making their point, which they properly should be making, doesn't fit with the facelessness and the rational grammars of the rest of the society. In a way they look like they are throwbacks, when the problem is that they have a real central moral point that I think they'd be better off making inside the hotels. Or maybe not in hotels, but somehow the settings are wrong. When the unions strike and so on, why don't they have their own media? That amazes me, because the way they are presented in the media is always to their disadvantage.

IA: Yes. I mean, organized labour to some extent walks the very same difficult line that teachers walk. On the one hand, there are some repressive aspects of signing agreements with the system and agreeing to go along and so forth: self-policing you might call it. On the other hand, it does open up a space for more humane pay rates, for better working conditions, for better teaching conditions. It's a difficult trade-off, that one.

JO: Yes. I think nothing looks worse than teachers outside their own schools carrying badly written signs, sometimes misspelt (*laughs*), and coffee cups, than, say, bringing the people they're bargaining with into the school to bargain, where the kids are.

IA: Well, for example, in the university we are also workers in the sense we have a right to defend our working conditions and so forth, just as telephone operators or any other group of people have that right. But the moral purpose of preserving education is somewhat distinct from that right. I think we have that purpose too.

JO: In the university, in the school system, in the medical system, there's that sacred thing at the bottom of every one of those things. Professionals perhaps have not been the best guardians of that flame. I think in a way that would be their ultimate thing. In the language of strikes, you put out the flame, you don't teach that day, you don't operate that day, you let some poor bugger hang instead of not hang. But that's not it: you should operate that day, teach that day, and then they really are up against something. So that whole world of rational utilitarian things suddenly meets a limit. Now it's not a Martian limit. We and the capitalists, we're not different beings. Otherwise all the talks are totally dark and we might as well get out the ray guns. You can't be talking unless on the other end of it there's one like yourself. However, whatever the distance is it's not the absolute distance.

IA: And this perhaps brings us full circle to where we started, where I started asking you about the task of sociology. Do you see this larger picture of trying to bring into being a form of speaking that addresses the other as another as part of the task of sociology?

JO: Yes, and it's in danger nowadays because of what I would call the implosion of 'alien-nation'. We're in danger of talking as though a businessman and a politician and a layman were totally different kinds of people. That men are totally different kinds of people from women. That kids are totally different from adults. And each of the professions is totally different. And then we try to pull it all back into the abstract language of persons who are sort of anonymous things making claims, when if we accept that we overlap then it's within that overlap that we can be characters and then sold. We need another language of relatedness and difference than the one we're mounting now, which often runs the risk of what I'd call race, gender, and class alienism. We're celebrating the ways in which we don't and cannot understand and overlap. But really that can only be viable if we imagine that we're all addressing some super-transcendental thing, usually what's left of the state, to legalise and bind it together.

Appendix B

Biographical notes on John O'Neill, with an autobiographical postscript

John O'Neill is Distinguished Research Professor Emeritus of Sociology at York University in Toronto, Canada. He has authored dozens of books, edited collections, and translations, as well as hundreds of conference papers and lectures delivered all over the world. Beginning with his writings on and translations of the philosopher Maurice Merleau-Ponty and his breakthrough book, *Sociology as a Skin Trade: Essays Towards a Reflexive Sociology* (1972), O'Neill went on to develop an original approach to the sociology of the body and the critical theory of the body politic that has inspired generations of scholars and students in the humanities and social sciences.

At York O'Neill participated in shaping the scholarly direction of the Department of Sociology and co-founding the Programme in Social and Political Thought in 1972, teaching and serving as chair in both units. He was a member of the Centre for Comparative Literature at the University of Toronto; Senior Scholar at the Laidlaw Foundation, where he was part of the Children at Risk Programme; and founder of the Communications and Culture Joint Programme at York and Ryerson Universities. He became a Fellow of the Royal Society of Canada in 1985. O'Neill has served on the editorial boards of numerous journals, including *Body & Society*, *Theory, Culture & Society*, and *Phenomenology and the Human Sciences*, and was co-editor for many years of the *Philosophy of the Social Sciences*, *International Studies Quarterly*, and the *Journal of Classical Sociology*. He has been a visiting professor at universities in the US, the UK, and Europe, and a teaching award at York University is named in his honour. Over the years, he has engaged in memorable encounters and exchanges with many other prominent scholars in the humanities and social sciences, including Harold Garfinkel, Marshall McLuhan, Hannah Arendt, Anthony Giddens, Jürgen Habermas, Gayatri Spivak, Mary Douglas, Paul de Man, and Jacques Derrida.

John O'Neill was born 17 July 1933 in Hendon in northwest London, where he grew up in a council house with his Irish Catholic parents and younger sister Joan. O'Neill would later dedicate his book *Five Bodies* to his sister and commemorate the hard work of his parents in the closing lines of *Sociology as a Skin Trade*: 'I am a Marxist without a revolution, though my mother and father still work. My mother's hands. My father's hands. How shall I separate what is cruel from what is beautiful in the story of their lives?'

O'Neill was granted scholarships to attend grammar school, Hendon Technical College (now Middlesex University), and the London School of Economics, where he read classic texts in social and political theory from Plato to L.T. Hobhouse, graduating with a BA in sociology in 1955. O'Neill received a Fulbright scholarship and completed his masters in political science at Notre Dame in Indiana in 1957. After graduation, he studied for a semester at Harvard. In Boston, O'Neill was introduced to Paul Sweezy, the famous American Marxist who had given up his teaching position at Harvard in order to focus on editing the *Monthly Review*. Since O'Neill was looking for a doctoral advisor in an interdisciplinary programme with expertise in Marxist political economy, Sweezy suggested he pursue a PhD at the History of Social Thought Research Center at Stanford with his friend Paul Baran, one of the few Marxists able to remain in American academia at the time, and whose *The Political Economy of Growth* had just been published in 1957. O'Neill followed Baran's work in political economy while developing his own approach to Marxist social theory and Hegelian philosophy for his doctoral dissertation, *Marxism and Scientism: An Essay in the Philosophy of Social Science*, which he defended in 1962. During his time in California, O'Neill supported himself by teaching French, Greek, and Latin at a Jesuit college in addition to working as Baran's research assistant. At that time Baran and Sweezy were co-authoring their seminal text, *Monopoly Capital*. Baran died suddenly in 1964, leaving Sweezy to complete the book, which was published in 1966. O'Neill would later edit Baran's papers on the critique of political economy in a volume titled *The Longer View*, and he acknowledges his incalculable debt to 'the two Pauls' in *For Marx Against Althusser*.

Although O'Neill hoped to remain in California after graduation, as a Fulbright scholar he was required to settle in a Commonwealth country or return to England. Before his death, Baran and his academic friends had suggested that O'Neill seek advice from the political theorist C.B. Macpherson at the University of Toronto. Murray Ross, a sociologist and founding president of York University (from 1959–1970), was hiring professors for this new Sixties-style university. O'Neill began his career at Glendon College in Toronto in 1964, at that time the main campus of York University. Shortly afterwards, he moved to Founders College, the first to be built on donated farmland, on the large campus in Downsview north of the city.

O'Neill married Maria Doerig in 1963, settling the following year in Toronto, where they raised their children Daniela (b. 1965), Gregory (b. 1967), and Brendan (b. 1971) in the Lawrence Park neighbourhood. As O'Neill writes in the acknowledgements to *Civic Capitalism*, 'like any child, a book starts life beholden to its immediate family'. This sentiment is expressed in the dedications to many of his books, including *Making Sense Together* (Maria); *Essaying Montaigne* (Brendan, Daniela, Gregory); *Critical Conventions* (Daniela); *The Poverty of Postmodernism* (Gregory); and *Plato's Cave* (Brendan).

At some point during these early years, O'Neill began to make a serious study of Maurice Merleau-Ponty (1908–1961), whose major works were then being translated into English. Among O'Neill's first publications in the 1960s are his translations with introductions of Merleau-Ponty's *Humanism and Terror, The Prose of the World, Themes from the Lectures at the Collège de France*, a collection of translated essays titled *Phenomenology, Language, and Society*, and O'Neill's first book, *Perception, Expression and History: A Study of Merleau-Ponty's Social Phenomenology* (1970). Inspired by Merleau-Ponty's focus on the communicative body as a medium of the history, culture, and political economy of the world, and by the emerging counter-culture of student and worker opposition to war and the corporate agenda, O'Neill went on to develop his own distinctive sociology of the body and critical theory of the body politic.

O'Neill was introduced to H.T. (Tom) Wilson in the fall of 1967, initiating a friendship and conversation that have continued ever since, often touching on their shared interests in Marx, Weber, social phenomenology, and the Frankfurt School of critical social theory. At the time, Wilson was in the Faculty of Administrative Studies, later joining Osgoode Law School and the Programme in Social and Political Thought and publishing books and articles in a wide range of theoretical and practical fields. When O'Neill was writing his essay on 'The Hobbesian Problem in Marx and Parsons' (included in *Sociology as a Skin Trade*), Wilson discussed his experiences in an advanced undergraduate class of Talcott Parsons at Harvard in 1960, where he also heard Parsons' student Harold Garfinkel present a paper later included in his *Studies in Ethnomethodology* (1967). O'Neill dedicated his edited collection *Hegel's Dialectic of Desire and Recognition: Texts and Commentary* to Wilson.

In 1985 O'Neill and Susan Hallam moved to the St. Clair and Oakwood area of Toronto. With Tom Wilson as their best man they were married on Bloomsday 1990, the date James Joyce (one of O'Neill's literary passions) met Molly, and a month later a Catholic Church blessing was held at Sandhurst with friends and relatives. Susan and John hosted his Monday night graduate classes in contemporary social theory and his Tuesday afternoon seminars on the theory of the text in the dining room of their home, where they lived for 32 years. Often these seminars were so full that students and visitors had to line the staircase in the hall. Since John wrote all his books and essays by hand, Susan typed many of his manuscripts from yellow pads and over multiple drafts, each time incorporating corrections, addressing minute details of punctuation, and meticulously moving paragraphs in and out. In the acknowledgements to *The Domestic Economy of the Soul*, he thanks Susan for 'graciously bringing typescript home to book', and he dedicated both that book and *The Communicative Body* to her.

O'Neill traces his interest in Michel de Montaigne (1533–1592) to Merleau-Ponty's essay 'Reading Montaigne', which inspired him to undertake close readings of the *Essays* in his graduate seminars in 1976 and 1977 winter terms. *Essaying Montaigne: A Study of the Renaissance Institution of Writing and Reading* inaugurated his studies in literary interpretation, semiotics, and post-structuralist theory. *The New Science* by Giambattista Vico (1668–1744), which historian Hayden White had recommended to him, became a pivotal reference point in several books and essay collections and for his alternative genealogy of the human sciences. Long familiar with key features of psychoanalytic theory through Herbert Marcuse's *Eros and Civilization* (1955/1962), Norman O. Brown's *Life Against Death* (1959), Paul Baran's *Marxism and Psychoanalysis* (1960), and Talcott Parsons' *Social Structure and Personality* (1964), O'Neill began a focused study of Sigmund Freud's works in the early 1980s, teaching graduate seminars on 'French Freud French Marx' (1981–1982), 'Scientific Discourse and the Therapeutic State' (1981–1984), and 'Theory of the Text' (1985–2010). The latter was devoted to close readings of key texts in Freudian psychoanalysis, including the five case histories, *Beyond the Pleasure Principle*, and the study of Leonardo Da Vinci. *The Domestic Economy of the Soul: Freud's Five Case Studies* weaves together insights generated from these seminars, which have launched the careers of many graduate students in a variety of academic and professional fields. Two short books on the theory of the welfare state, *The Missing Child in Liberal Theory* and *Civic Capitalism,* extend O'Neill's phenomenological and psychoanalytic studies of childhood into a political economic critique of neoliberal capitalism and a moral defense of intergenerational justice and the civic commons.

Autobiographical postscript

In the early 2000s, John O'Neill wrote the following self-portrait which he occasionally distributed at lectures and later posted on his website:

> My research and teaching is devoted to the acquisition of frontier knowledge in the humanities and the social sciences. In the 1960s the unifying thrust for my studies came from research in the philosophy of the social sciences. Here there were two directions, namely, Frankfurt critical theory and Continental phenomenology, and in particular their focus upon the problem of the complementarity between causal and hermeneutical explanations in an emancipatory social science. In this period, I became a specialist in phenomenological sociology, developing the work of Maurice Merleau-Ponty on politics, history, language, and art in several volumes of translation, as well as my book, *Perception, Expression and History* (1970). At the same time, I was involved in the critical rethinking of sociology which contributed to the radicalism of the sixties in Canada, the United States, and Western Europe. Numerous articles on critical social theory, political economy, and mass culture, along with two further books, *Sociology as a Skin Trade* (1972) and *Making Sense Together* (1974), were concerned to bring about interdisciplinary studies in sociology, phenomenology and ethnomethodology. Within the same period, I became a co-founder of York University's Graduate Programme in Social and Political Thought which continues to attract brilliant students who pursue a wide range of research topics in European social theory. In 1971, I became a co-editor of *Philosophy of the Social Sciences*, an international quarterly now in its thirtieth year as a leading journal in a field of research to which its

title gave official recognition. In 2001, I became co-editor of *The Journal of Classical Sociology*, fostering advanced research in this area by international scholars.

In the 1980s, my research continued to explore various problems in the political economy and semiology of embodiment. For years I introduced to undergraduates a variety of research issues in the sociology of the body which anticipated basic problems in current women's, race, and colonial studies. I published this work in *Five Bodies,* which treats such topics as medical bodies, consumer bodies, and the industrialization of women's bodies. Over the years, materials from my research in this area (in *The Communicative Body*, 1989; *Plato's Cave: Television and Its Discontents*, 2001), have been useful to a number of media researchers as well as to other colleagues in the social sciences.

Most recently, my research has turned to studies in the theory of textuality and discourse production. Here I attempt to treat the body as a text, as both bio-text and socio-text and to treat the text itself as a body. Thus I investigated a particular corpus, Montaigne's *Essays*, to develop a theory of writing and reading as corporeal conduct and I argued for this interpretation against the conventional scholarship in my book *Essaying Montaigne: A Study of the Renaissance Institution of Writing and Reading* (1982/2001). I broadened this argument into a psychoanalytic theory of homotextuality in which I analyze Freud's famous five case histories in order to construct a meta-psychoanalysis of the Freudian text (*Incorporating Cultural Theory: Maternity at the Millenium*, 2002). I have also developed methods of analyzing the literary production of scientific writing in several specific disciplinary formats in my book *Critical Conventions*: *Interpretation in the Arts and Sciences* (1992) and *The Poverty of Postmodernism* (1995). Most recently, I have been working on issues of childhood and family in the context of liberal-communitarianism to formulate a concept of civic capitalism, first sketched in my book *The Missing Child in Liberal Theory* (1994).

Despite the apparent diversity of my studies, I consider them steadily devoted to research in the wake of the linguistic turn initiated by Wittgensteinian speech act theory and amplified in phenomenological, structuralist, and deconstructionist theories of discourse production and inter-textuality. Research within this perspective requires considerable knowledge of the conventional and unconventional wisdom in literary, philosophical, and psychoanalytic disciplines. As such, it is in the best tradition of scientific innovations achieved through the 'blurring of genres', or through paradigm breaks of the sort that Kuhn has identified as the engine of 'revolutionary' science. In either case, frontier knowledge in the arts and sciences requires similar energy. In part, this energy is narcissistic; for the rest, it must be fostered by the university. From day to day, it owes much to our graduate students and their resolve to think otherwise then we do.

Appendix C
Selected works by John O'Neill

Books

1970. *Perception, Expression and History: The Social Phenomenology of Merleau-Ponty.* Evanston: Northwestern University Press (revised and reprinted in 1989 above).

1972. *Sociology as a Skin Trade: Essays Towards a Reflexive Sociology.* London, Heinemann, and New York: Harper & Row.

1974. *Making Sense Together: An Introduction to Wild Sociology.* London: Heinemann, and New York: Harper & Rowe (revised and reprinted in 1989 above).

1982. *For Marx Against Althusser, and Other Essays.* Washington, DC: Center for Advanced Research in Phenomenology and University Press of America.

1989. *The Communicative Body: Studies in Communicative Philosophy, Politics and Sociology.* Evanston: Northwestern University Press (French translation 1995; Japanese translation 1992).

1992. *Critical Conventions: Interpretation in the Literary Arts and Sciences.* Norman: University of Oklahoma Press.

1994. *The Missing Child in Liberal Theory: Towards a Covenant Theory of Family, Community, Welfare and the Civic State.* Toronto: University of Toronto Press.

1995. *The Poverty of Postmodernism.* London: Routledge.

2001. *Essaying Montaigne: A Study of the Renaissance Institution of Writing and Reading.* Liverpool: The University of Liverpool Press (revised from 1982 edition with Routlege & Kegan Paul).

2002a. *Incorporating Cultural Theory: Maternity at the Millennium.* Albany: State University Press of New York.

2002b. *Plato's Cave: Television and Its Discontents.* Cresskill, NJ: Hampton Press Inc. (revised from 1991 edition with Ablex Publishing Corporation).

2004a. *Civic Capitalism: The State of Childhood.* Toronto: University of Toronto Press.

2004b. *Five Bodies: Re-figuring Relationships.* London: Sage Publications (revised from 1985 edition with Cornell University Press; Chinese translation 1996; German translation 1989).

2011. *The Domestic Economy of the Soul: Freud's Five Case Histories.* London: Sage Publications (Chinese translation 2016).

2020. *Writing the Body Politic: A John O'Neill Reader.* Mark Featherstone and Thomas Kemple (eds.). London: Routledge.

Journal articles, book chapters, and edited collections

Works marked with an asterisk (*) are from books edited or translated by John O'Neill. Unless otherwise noted, earlier versions of revised or reprinted essays and chapters in the books listed above (including those in this *O'Neill Reader*) have not been included here. The following selection is taken from hundreds of published articles and book chapters.

1963. 'Alienation, Class Struggle and Marxian Anti-Politics'. *The Review of Metaphysics*, XVII 3): 462–71.

1964. 'The Concept of Estrangement in the Early and Later Writings of Karl Marx'. *Philosophy and Phenomenological Research*, XXV (1): 64–84 (revised and reprinted in 1972a and 1982).

*1969a. 'Translator's Note'. In: Maurice Merleau-Ponty, *Humanism and Terror: An Essay on the Communist Problem*. John O'Neill (trans.) Boston: Beacon Press, pp. vii–xi.

*1969b. 'Introduction: Marxism and the Sociological Imagination'. In: Paul Baran, The Longer *View: Essays Toward a Critique of Political Economy*. John O'Neill (ed.). New York: Monthly Review Press, pp. xiii–xvii.

*1970a. 'Preface' and 'Introduction: Perception, Expression and History'. In: *Phenomenology, Language, and Society: Essays from Maurice Merleau-Ponty*. John O'Neill (ed.). London: Heinemann, pp. v–lxii (revised and reprinted in 1989).

*1970b. 'Translator's Preface'. In: Maurice Merleau-Ponty, *Themes from the Lectures at the Collège de France 1952–1960*. John O'Neill (trans., ed.). Evanston: Northwestern University Press, pp. xi–xvii.

*1972. 'Scientism, Historicism, and the Problem of Rationality'. In: *Modes of Individualism and Collectivism*. John O'Neill (ed.). London: Heinemann, pp. 3–26.

*1973a. 'Hegel and Marx on History as Human History'. In: Jean Hyppolite, *Studies on Marx and Hegel*. John O'Neill (ed., trans.). New York: Harper Torchbooks, pp. xi–xx (earlier version in 1972; revised and reprinted in 1982).

1973b. 'On Simmel's Sociological Apriorities'. In: *Phenomenological Sociology: Issues and Applications*. George Psathas (ed.). New York: Wiley, pp. 91–106 (earlier version in 1972).

*1973c. 'Translator's Introduction: Language and the Voice of Philosophy'. In: Maurice Merleau-Ponty, *The Prose of the World*. John O'Neill (trans.). Evanston: Northwestern University Press, pp. xxv–xlvi (revised and reprinted in 1989).

1974a. 'Philosophy and Revolution: A Review.' *Telos*, 22: 163–71.

1974b. 'Philosophical Speech and the Poetry of Review.' *Semiotica*, X (3): 288–91.

1975a. 'Gay Technology and the Body Politic', pp. 291–302. In: *The Body as a Medium of Expression*. Jonathan Benthall and Ted Polhemus (eds.). London: Allen Lane.

1975b. 'Facts, Myths, and the Nationalist Platitude'. *Canadian Journal of Sociology*, 1: 107–24.

1975c. 'Lecture Visuelle de l'Espace Urbain'. In: *Colloque d'Esthétique Appliquée á la Création du Paysage Urbain*. Paris: Copedith, pp. 235–44.

1976a. 'Time's Body'. In: *Giambattista Vico's Science of Humanity*. Giorgio Tagliacozzo, Donald Phillip Verene (eds.). Baltimore and London: The Johns Hopkins University Press, pp. 333–39 (earlier version in 1974a).

*1976b. 'Critique and Remembrance'. In: *On Critical Theory*. John O'Neill (ed.). New York: Seabury Press; London: Heinemann, pp. 1–14.

1977. 'When is Sociology Phenomenological?' *The Annals of Phenomenological Sociology*, II: 1–40.

1978a. 'Socratic Essay'. In: *What it Means to be Human*. Ross Fitzgerald (ed.). Oxford: Pergamon Press, pp. 25–43.

1978b. 'Mind and Institution'. In: *Interdisciplinary Phenomenology*. Don Ihde, Richard M. Zaner (eds.). The Hague: Martinus Nijhoff, pp. 99–108.

1980. 'From Phenomenology to Ethnomethodology: Some Radical Misreadings'. *Current Perspectives in Sociological Theory*, 1: 7–20.

1981a. 'A Preface to Frame Analysis'. *Human Studies*, 4: 359–64.

1981b. 'McLuhan's Loss of Innis-Sense'. *Canadian Forum*, LXI/709: 13–15.

1983a. 'Vico on the Natural Workings of the Mind'. *Phenomenology and the Human Sciences*, Supplement to Philosophical Topics, 12: 117–25.

1983b. 'Naturalism in Vico and Marx: A Theory of the Body Politic'. In: *Vico and Marx: Affinities and Contrasts*. Giorgio Tagliacozzo (ed.). Atlantic Highlands, NJ: Humanities Press, pp. 277–89 (earlier version in 1982).

1983c. 'Reflection and Radical Finitude'. *Journal of the British Society for Phenomenology*, 14: 17–22.

1985a. 'Phenomenological Sociology'. *The Canadian Review of Sociology and Anthropology*, 22 (5): 748–70.

1985. 'The Essay as a Moral Exercise: Montaigne'. *Renaissance and Reformation*, 21 (3): 210–18.

1986a. 'Decolonization and the Ideal Speech Community: Some Issues in the Theory and Practice of Communicative Competence'. In: *Critical Theory and Public Life*. John Forester (ed.). Cambridge: MIT Press, pp. 57–76.

1986b. 'To Kill the Future?' In: *Environmental Ethics: Philosophical and Policy Perspectives*. Philip P. Hanson (ed.). Burnaby: Simon Fraser University Press, pp. 163–73.

1993. 'McTopia: Eating Time'. In: *Utopias and The Millenium*. Krishan Kumar and Stephen Baum (eds.). London: Reaktion Books, pp. 129–37.

1994b. 'Two Body Criticism: A Genealogy of the Postmodern Anti-Aesthetic'. *History and Theory*, 33 (1): 61–78.

1994c. 'Vico and Myth'. In: *The Imaginative Basis of Thought and Culture: Contemporary Perspectives on Giambattista Vico*. Marcel Danesi and Frank Nuessel (eds.). Toronto: Canadian Scholars Press, pp. 99–111.

*1996a. 'Introduction: A Dialectical Genealogy of Self, Society, and Culture in and After Hegel'. In: *Hegel's Dialectic of Desire and Recognition: Texts and Commentary*. John O'Neill (ed.). Albany: State University of New York Press, pp. 25–40.

*1996b. 'The Question of an Introduction: Understanding and the Passion of Ignorance'. In: *Freud and the Passions*. John O'Neill (ed.). University Park: Penn State Press, pp. 1–11.

1997. 'Is The Child A Political Subject?' *Childhood: A Global Journal of Child Research*, 4 (2): 241–50.

1998a. 'Endless Knowledge'. *Social Epistemology*, 12 (1): 79–84.

1998b. 'Civic Capital: Education and the National Economy'. In: *The New Higher Education: Issues and Directions for the Post-Dearing University*. David Jary and Martin Parker (eds.). Stoke-on-Trent: Staffordshire University Press, pp. 303–18.

1999a. 'Children and the Civic State: A Covenant Model of Welfare'. In: *Counseling and the Therapeutic State*. James J. Chriss (ed.). New York: Aldine De Gruyter, pp. 33–54.

1999b. 'Have You Had Your Theory Today?' In: *Resisting McDonaldization*. Barry Smart (ed.). London: Sage Publications, pp. 41–56.

2001. 'Horror Autotoxicus: The Dual Economy of Aids'. In: *Contested Bodies*. Ruth Holliday and John Hassard (eds.). London: Routledge, pp. 179–85.

Index